D1345506

Brainwashing

Brainwashing

THE SCIENCE OF THOUGHT CONTROL

Kathleen Taylor

OXFORD
UNIVERSITY PRESS

OXFORD

UNIVERSITY PRESS

Great Clarendon Street, Oxford OX2 6DP

Oxford University Press is a department of the University of Oxford.
It furthers the University's objective of excellence in research, scholarship,
and education by publishing worldwide in

Oxford New York

Auckland Bangkok Buenos Aires Cape Town Chennai
Dar es Salaam Delhi Hong Kong Istanbul Karachi Kolkata
Kuala Lumpur Madrid Melbourne Mexico City Mumbai Nairobi
São Paulo Shanghai Taipei Tokyo Toronto

Oxford is a registered trade mark of Oxford University Press
in the UK and in certain other countries

British Library Cataloguing in Publication Data
Data available

ISBN 0192804960

Typeset in Dante by
Footnote Graphics Limited, Warminster, Wilts
Printed in Great Britain by
Clays Ltd, St Ives plc

Contents

Figures

Preface

While I was writing this book it became apparent that people's reactions to the idea of a book about brainwashing almost always fell into one of two categories. The first, much larger, group said 'How fascinating!' and asked lots of questions. The second reacted derisively. 'Brainwashing? You do know it's all hogwash, don't you?'

Obviously I don't think so or I wouldn't have written this book, but it is certainly fair to say that brainwashing has some dubious, even seedy, associations. Like consciousness and emotion, until recently it has been considered unworthy of scientific attention, the product of deranged conspiracy theorists or, at best, peculiar political circumstances. But brainwashing is much, much more than that. At its heart is a malignant idea, the dream of totally controlling a human mind, which affects all of us one way or another. Brainwashing is the ultimate invasion of privacy: it seeks to control not only how people act but what they think. It arouses our deepest fears, threatening the loss of freedom and even identity. Yet we know remarkably little about it. Given the advances in our scientific understanding of brains and their behaviours since the heyday of brainwashing studies in the 1950s, it is more than time we took another look at this mysterious and terrifying phenomenon.

The book is divided into three parts. **Part I: Torture and seduction** (Chapters 1–6) focuses on the history and social psychology of brainwashing. The term itself originally referred to political programmes in Communist China and Korea, but the concept was too good to waste, and before long allegations of brainwashing were being hurled at any activity which involved changing minds. Are such claims justified? *Brainwashing* investigates a number of domains: religion, politics, advertising and the media, education, mental health, the military, the criminal justice system, domestic violence, and torture. We discover that brainwashing is an extreme form of social influence which uses mechanisms increasingly studied and understood by social psychologists, and that such influence can vary hugely in its intensity. And we explore a range of situations involving individuals, small groups, and entire societies, in all of which the types of influence we call 'brain-washing' are characterized by the use of force or deceit or both.

We also see that the terror of brainwashing, the fear of one's mind being broken down and then reshaped to someone else's specification, draws its power from our preferred view of ourselves as free, rational, decisive individuals. We like to think our minds are strong and solid, pure and unchanging entities which bear a close resemblance to the religious concept of an immortal soul. We prefer to think that, like diamonds, they keep their shape as the pressure on them rises, until at last (under the force of brainwashing) they shatter into pieces. We tend to believe that mental power derives from reason, so we view emotions as weak-nesses. And we think of ourselves as having free will, choosing whether or not to be influenced by other people. To understand whether our fears about brain-washing are appropriate, we need to look at the accuracy of these beliefs.

That means understanding more about human brains, so **Part II: The traitor in your skull** (Chapters 7–11) considers the neurosciences. Be warned: this is the most difficult part of the book. There is just no way to talk neural without going into detail; brains refuse to be reduced to soundbites. I have included a beginner's guide (Neuroscience in a nutshell, p. 106), diagrams, and as few technicalities as possible. But I have used a lot of examples, not all of which may seem to have much to do with brainwashing. Bear with me; there are reasons for this. For one thing, direct modern scientific evidence of what happens to brains during brain-washing is non-existent: ethical objections forbid such research from taking place. For another, we need to understand how brains normally work before we can make sense of the abnormal processes in brainwashing. The themes of **Part II**—brain change, beliefs, emotions, how brains generate actions, self-control, and free will—are each so complex that they require considerable explaining. I have therefore risked chasing tangents in pursuit of clarification.

Part II shows that the picture of minds as solid and static is misleading. Minds are more like malleable clay than diamonds. We humans are not the resolutely independent individuals on whose unbending rationality so much of conse-quence is predicated (like the doctrine of criminal responsibility, which expects those it judges to have been acting freely and choosing rationally). Rather, human beings are born and then made; self-fashioned, of course, but also hugely shaped by social circumstances—especially the ideas we take from our societies and the emotions with which we take them. We underestimate the extent to which even mild forms of influence can change the way we think and act.

Part III: Freedom and control takes this new conception and investigates its implications for brainwashing. Chapter 12 considers individuals, asking what makes some people victims and some predators, vulnerable to brainwashing or attracted by its malevolent potential. Chapter 13 asks the same question about societies. The concept of brainwashing, linked from the very beginning to totalitarian states, is deeply political, so what are the social agents of thought control? Chapter 14 moves from present to future to ask what impact scientific developments may have on brainwashing techniques. Finally, I consider perhaps the most important question of all: can we resist brainwashing? Arguing that the best form of defence is to take advance precautions, I discuss ways in which each of us can boost our personal protection against unwanted influence attempts.

But individuals by themselves can only do so much. Brainwashing is not a magic bullet, a short cut to thought control. Rather, it is a complex phenomenon which uses increasingly well-understood psychological processes to wreak its havoc. While this may seem reassuring, the consequence is that no magic bullet exists for 'anti-brainwashers' either. Brainwashing is above all a social and political phenomenon, and our best defences will also be at the level of society: only politics can maximize protection. To defend ourselves we need to favour certain kinds of political approaches—those which emphasize the importance of personal freedoms—and avoid belief systems which value cultures, organizations, or societies more highly than individual human beings. *Brainwashing* therefore culminates, perhaps surprisingly, in a discussion of politics. Throughout the book I have tried to answer some of the questions of the many people who reacted positively when they heard the proposed book's title: what happens during brainwashing? Is it real? How does it work? Is it still going on? How can we stop it?

I should add three technical notes. Firstly, I have used [*sic*] to confirm peculiar spellings only for modern quotations. John Milton, for example, wrote in an age before English spelling had been standardized, so I have left his words as his editors have rendered them. Secondly, italics in quotations are original unless stated otherwise. Thirdly, English poses a problem for those attempting to write gender-neutral prose: 'he or she' is clunky, 's/he' abominable. I have used 'he or she' at times, but where that is painfully clumsy I have resorted to the male pronoun in most cases. This is partly for convenience, but mostly for historical reasons: brainwashing first emerged as a weapon of war, and most of the people involved—as perpetrators, victims, or researchers—were men.

Now to acknowledgements. I would like to thank everyone who has contributed, however indirectly, to this book—including the scholars cited in the text whose mighty resources I have plundered, I hope to good purpose. Faults which remain are mine alone, but they are fewer than they were thanks to all the help I have had. Particular thanks are due to Professor Quentin Skinner and Dr Helen Sutherland for their kindness and patience in reading and advising on sections of the text and in supplying source material. Dr Peter Hansen also commented on some chapters. Dr Xuguang Liu provided the ideograms in Chapter 1, Mr Alan Taylor an image in Chapter 10, Andy Bennett a picture of mountains used in Fig. 10.3, and the Council of Europe assistance with a query. Dr Kathy Wilkes

Preface

gave generously of both time and advice; her untimely death in 2003 was a great loss to me as to many others. Heartfelt thanks are also due to Dr Tim Littlewood and his colleagues, without whom this book would never have been written.

Oxford University Press has given me a great opportunity, and my especial thanks go to Michael Rodgers and Marsha Filion for unstintingly generous encouragement and inspiration, support (when needed), and criticism (likewise). Abbie Headon, Debbie Sutcliffe, and Michael Tiernan were also very helpful. The three reviewers of the original book proposal, Professor Elliot Aronson, Professor Miles Hewstone, and 'Reviewer B', provided careful and constructive reports which were extremely useful in shaping the book; their input was much appreciated. Professor Hewstone also read the first full draft; his comments were invaluable. Professor John Stein deserves thanks for helping me to study neuroscience in the first place, and I should also acknowledge the role of Oxford University, an institution which has taught me a great deal (not just about neuroscience) and which provided much of the motivation for writing this book.

Finally, I owe a debt beyond words to Alison Taylor, David Taylor, and Gillian Wright for their unfailing help and patience in shaping *Brainwashing*—and its author's mind—for the better. To these, my three great influences, this book is dedicated.

At this point authors often say that 'writing this book has been a voyage of discovery'. I can't help hoping that my voyage is only beginning; but writing *Brainwashing* has certainly taught me a lot. I hope you enjoy the journey, as I have done.

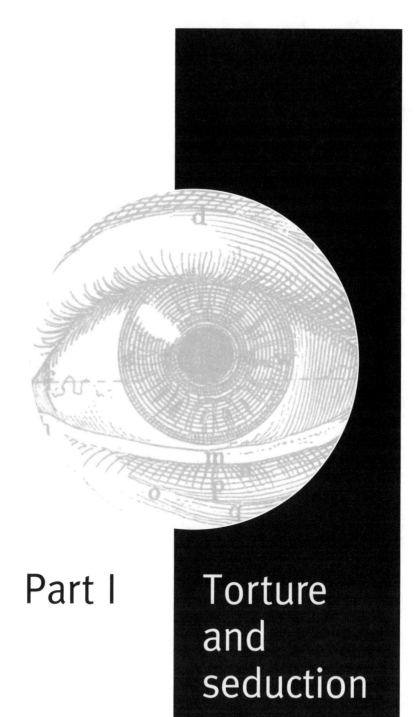

Part I   Torture and seduction

Chapter 1: The birth of a word

The systematic and often forcible elimination from a person's mind of more established ideas, especially political ones, so that another set of ideas may take their place; this process regarded as the kind of coercive conversion practised by certain totalitarian states on political dissidents

Definition of 'brainwashing' in the *Oxford English Dictionary*

The intent is to change a mind radically so that its owner becomes a living puppet—a human robot—without the atrocity being visible from the outside. The aim is to create a mechanism in flesh and blood, with new beliefs and new thought processes inserted into a captive body. What that amounts to is the search for a slave race that, unlike the slaves of olden times, can be trusted never to revolt, always to be amenable to orders, like an insect to its instincts

Edward Hunter, *Brainwashing*

The term 'brainwashing' was born in the crucible of war. Not, as one might expect, the Second World War—though it was retrospectively applied to Nazi techniques—but the Korean War. This conflict broke out in 1950 when North Korea, supported by China's Communist regime, invaded South Korea, to which the young United Nations then sent a multinational force. The United States, the major participant in this joint effort, soon noticed that something strange was happening to US troops taken captive by the enemy. Some emerged from prisoner of war camps as, apparently, converted Communists, ready to denounce their country of birth and sing the praises of the Maoist way of life. Of course, the phenomenon of prisoners forced to laud their captors was not a new one. But some of these soldiers continued their bizarre—and passionate—disloyalty even after they were free of the Communists' grip. Unnerved by their behaviour, and concerned about potential effects on morale, the US began to investigate what their CIA operative Edward Hunter had in 1950 publicly christened 'brainwashing'.

Hunter himself expresses his negative reactions very clearly in describing a victim of the strange new phenomenon.

Those who interviewed him were bewildered and horrified not only by what he said [...] but by the unnatural way in which he said it. His speech seemed impressed on a disc that had to be played from start to finish, without modification or halt. He appeared to be under a weird, unnatural compulsion to go on with a whole train of thought, from beginning to end, even when it had been rendered silly. For example, he spoke of no force being applied to him even after someone already had pointed out that he had been seen in shackles. He was [...] no longer capable of using free will or adapting himself to a situation for which he had been uninstructed; he had to go on as if manipulated by instincts alone. This was Party discipline extended to the mind; a trance element was in it. It gave me a creepy feeling.

Hunter, *Brainwashing*, pp. 14–15

That war, like other extreme situations, could do strange things to human beings had been known for centuries. William Shakespeare refers to the madness of war; so does the Bible. More recently, William Sargant's 1957 book *Battle for the Mind* recounts his work as a doctor and psychiatrist with veterans in the Second World War. Many of these men were suffering from what used to be called shell shock or combat stress and is now known as post-traumatic stress disorder. Sargant notes extraordinary changes in personality, wild fluctuations in mood and behaviour, alarming increases in suggestibility, and loss of self-control shown by both soldiers and civilians affected by traumatic experiences. Clearly the stresses of war could have a catastrophic impact on human brains.

But brainwashing is more than neurosis or psychosis. Such states may be induced as part of the brainwashing process, but they are only a step on the way to the goal of forcing the victim to succumb to the propaganda of the brainwashers. Edward Hunter's books, *Brain-washing in Red China* and *Brainwashing*, themselves fine pieces of propaganda, emphasize the deliberate, mechanistic malice of the Communist enemy. Brainwashing is characterized in wholly negative terms as a kind of mental rape: it is forced upon the victim by an attacker whose intention is to destroy the victim's faith in former beliefs, to wipe the slate clean so that new beliefs may be adopted.

Origins and cognates

The word itself, according to Hunter, is a translation of the Chinese concept of *xi-nao* or *hsi-nao* (the Chinese ideograms are shown in Fig. 1.1). This term was used as a colloquial rendering of *szu-hsiang-kai-tsao* ('thought reform'; see Fig. 1.2), the Chinese Communists' formal term for their procedures. However, the concept of *hsi-nao*, 'heart washing' or 'cleansing the mind' using meditation,

洗 脑

Figure 1.1 The Chinese ideograms which represent the concept of *xi-nao*, translated as 'brainwashing'.

思 想 改 造

Figure 1.2 The Chinese ideograms which represent the concept of *szu-hsiang-kai-tsao*, translated as 'thought reform'.

is much older than Communism. Hunter claims that it dates to the time of Meng K'o (known as Mencius in the West), a fourth-century BC Confucian thinker. If so, it is an early example of the long tradition of applying metaphors of washing and cleaning to human minds, spirits, or souls. In English, this tradition is well illustrated by the seventeenth-century poet Lucy Hutchinson, writing long after Mencius but nearly three centuries before Edward Hunter. This devoutly Christian woman, having translated the work of the philosopher Lucretius and found it 'blasphemously against God', writes that she 'found it necessary to have recourse to the fountain of Truth, to wash out all ugly wild impressions, and fortify my mind with a strong antidote against all the poison of human wit and wisdom that I had been dabbling withal'.[1]

Not quite the word 'brainwashing' but very close. Hutchinson, however, is using her concept in a positive sense—the fountain of (Christian) Truth washing her brain clean of the corruption caused by translating pagan Lucretius. Many followers of Chairman Mao viewed their techniques of 're-education' or 'thought reform' in a similarly positive light, their aim being to scrub out the poison of imperialist and reactionary thoughts. As the psychiatrist Robert Jay Lifton says in his seminal work on the subject, 'it is most important to realize that *what we see as a set of coercive maneuvers, the Chinese Communists view as a morally uplifting, harmonizing, and scientifically therapeutic experience*'.[2] The pejorative sense we now associate with re-education, thought reform, and brainwashing came from Mao's opponents at the time, the USA, and distorted the original meaning.

5

The birth of the term 'brainwashing' reflected a need to label what were seen as terrifying new dangers. This need had become increasingly pressing with the Soviet show trials of the 1930s, in which discredited former leaders of the Communist Party stood up and publicly denounced their entire careers, policies, and belief systems with apparently inexplicable sincerity. When Americans in China and Korea started showing similar behaviour the need to explain how this could happen became urgent. Edward Hunter's label was able to paper over, if not actually fill, the conceptual gap: the very fact that there was now a word for whatever mysteries had gone on in Chinese prison camps calmed the American public's fear of the unknown. It has also been argued that the concept of brainwashing allowed Americans to avoid confronting the idea, implicit in the Christian doctrine of original sin (and the fallout from Hiroshima and Nagasaki), that they themselves were capable of great evil. As Scheflin and Opton note in *The Mind Manipulators*, brainwashing '*sounds like* an explanation', apparently shifting responsibility elsewhere and obviating the need to look at ourselves too closely; this capacity to reassure makes it 'a strangely attractive idea'.

As initially conceived, brainwashing was a State-controlled process, administered by a totalitarian regime against dissidents, whether citizens or foreigners. Such a term, however, was far too useful to remain in its original political territory, and 'brainwashing' as a term of abuse was soon being applied to smaller groups and even to individuals. The highly political nature of the term 'brainwashing' reflects one of the central questions about brainwashing. Does it actually exist, or is it a totalitarian fantasy, dreamt up by an American journalist to describe the menace of an alien culture? Certainly the term is often used today in casual denigration to mean any attempt to influence the minds of others. Advertising and the media, education, religion, and the mental health professions have all, as we shall see, been accused of brainwashing, broadening and devaluing the term from Hunter's usage. Robert Lifton bemoans 'irresponsible usages by anti-fluoridation, anti-mental health legislation, or anti-almost anything groups leveled against their real or fancied opponents'.[3] His book was first published in 1961, a mere eleven years after 'brainwashing' entered the language. Today, brainwashing is often little more than a casual term of abuse, often used ironically.[4]

In the febrile anti-Communist paranoia of 1950s America, however, brainwashing was anything but a casual concept. Rather, it was a terror—a fear of losing control, free will, even identity.[5] Reviled as another lethal aspect of the Red Menace, it was quickly taken up to fuel the fires of popular outrage. In this, it is similar to the concept of evil—still popular as an easy explanation—and the older concepts of witchcraft and demonic possession which have haunted America since the Salem witch trials and earlier.[6] Although the idea of possession has lost ground as society has become more secularized, it is arguable that brainwashing is in fact a secular equivalent, possession being brainwashing by a super-natural agent rather than a human one. Certainly, the concept of brainwashing has re-emerged into public consciousness at intervals ever since its birth, usually in response to particular high-profile events which seem to admit of no other explanation: a last-resort concept, a veil drawn over one of the many gaps in our understanding of ourselves.

As already noted, Hunter's concept did not appear out of nowhere. Human beings have been trying to change each other's minds since they first discovered they had them. Often with the best of intentions: the Greek εὐαγγέλιον (euangelion)—good message—gave us 'evangelism', while from the Latin *propago*—to extend, to plant—came the *congregatio de propaganda fide*, a com-mittee of cardinals set up by the Roman Catholic Church to oversee foreign mis-sions. 'Education' is from *educere*—literally, to draw out; 're-education' is simply a second attempt. Similarly, 'thought reform' brings with it positive overtones of cognitive improvement. 'Indoctrination', which has acquired increasingly negative connotations since its introduction into English in the seventeenth century, comes from the Latin *doctrina*, a body of knowledge or learning. And 'conditioning', made famous by Ivan Pavlov's work training dogs to salivate at the sound of a bell,[7] derives from *condicere*: to appoint, settle, or arrange. Spreading good news, bringing out the best in people, learning, making arrange-ments. What could be more harmless? Only 'coercive persuasion', the approxi-mate synonym for thought reform used by the psychiatrist Edgar Schein in his book of the same name, hints at the darker side of influence techniques.[8]

If someone disagrees with you, you can of course kill him, but that is risky. Alternative methods were already being developed by the earliest human groups. Lifton identifies four such methods: coercion, exhortation, therapy, and realiza-tion. Coercion says: 'You must change in the way we tell you, or else …'; it may involve death as an extreme penalty. Exhortation invokes a higher moral authority to argue: 'You should change, in the way we suggest, to become a better person.' Therapy says: 'You can change, with our guidance, to become healthy and free of suffering.' Finally, realization says: 'You can change, and come to express your full potential, if you are willing to confront new ideas and approaches.' Like many methods of persuasion, thought reform as practised by the Chinese Communists uses elements of all four classes. However, what Lifton calls 'ideological totalism'—a tendency towards extreme, all-or-nothing modes of thought characteristic of totalitarian regimes—'leans most heavily upon the first two', coercion and exhortation.

By the time tribes had started to conquer other tribes, persuasive arts of all types were already esteemed. The Old Testament Book of Exodus (Chapter 4, verses 10–16) records Moses, when confronted with God's plans for him, plead-ing to be excused on the basis that 'I am slow of speech, and of a slow tongue.'

The Lord replies: 'Is not Aaron the Levite thy brother? I know that he can speak well ... he shall be thy spokesman unto the people.' Even earlier in Biblical history is Abraham, greatest of the Jewish patriarchs, who at one point bargains with the Lord over the fate of the city of Sodom and succeeds in extracting a promise that if even ten virtuous men can be found there the place will be spared. This argumentative attitude goes unpunished, although unfortunately for Sodom only one good man—Lot, Abraham's nephew—can be found. Still, 'it came to pass, when God destroyed the cities of the plain, that God remembered Abraham, and sent Lot out of the midst of the overthrow' (Genesis, 19:29). Persuading the Almighty to change his mind is an achievement modern spin-doctors can only dream of. (It is noticeable that, as in the case of thought reform, examples of coercion and exhortation are far easier to find in the Old Testament than instances of therapy and self-realization.)

As empires and their administrative burdens grew the need to control subject peoples became ever greater. The violence of armies was the ultimate threat; but armies could not be everywhere. And, as the Roman Empire found when it came up against the Jews, creating too many martyrs could be counter-productive. Some systems, like the Persian Empire (*c.*550–330 BC), adopted a pragmatically liberal approach: pay your taxes, keep the peace, your gods and customs are your own. Others were more dictatorial. Each culture developed its own forms of increasingly sophisticated control: networks of spies, management hierarchies to keep the revenues flowing, the coercion or bribery of local leaders, and legal and social institutions. Many of these relied heavily on methods of compulsion such as torture, which might be brutally physical or more subtly psychological. From this rich heritage of coercion come many of the techniques associated with brainwashing: indeed, the line between brainwashing and psychological torture may be so fine as not to be worth drawing. I will explore this topic further in Chapter 5.

Aspects of brainwashing

Clearly there are several points to be made about the term 'brainwashing'. Firstly, if we want to think about brainwashing we cannot avoid discussing politics: the two are intertwined. Brainwashing, like God or love or freedom, means different things to different people depending on their background and agenda. This by itself does not discredit the term. If we could explain all the different mechanisms by which people change each other's minds, would we still need Hunter's word? I think so. There may be atheists out there able to avoid the word 'God', determinists convinced that free will is an illusion who never say 'I chose', and physiologists who replace declarations of passion with, 'Darling, I'm having a hormone-surge', but most of us still use the language of love, choice, and (however attenuated) religion. Similarly, there is more to the usage of brainwashing than the processes which may or may not explain it.

Secondly, brainwashing has a variety of aspects which can be teased apart. As well as its political function as a term of abuse, it can also be used as a functional description of a scientific process or processes for achieving such control. Those sceptics who argue that 'it's all hogwash' are arguing against the idea that such scientific processes exist: that minds have ever been totally dominated in the way suggested by *The Manchurian Candidate*, whose brainwashed protagonist murders when ordered to do so, even when the target is the girl he adores.[9] I will return to the sceptics later. For now, it is worth noting that such objections neglect all but the most mechanical aspects of brainwashing. But brainwashing is not just a set of techniques. It is also a dream, a vision of ultimate control over not only behaviour but thought as well, of having the secret skills possessed by Matthew Arnold's gipsies:

… arts to rule as they desired
The workings of men's brains,
And they can bind them to what thoughts they will.
Arnold, The Scholar-Gipsy, lines 45–7

Brainwashing is more ambitious, and more coercive, than simple persuasion, and unlike older cognates such as indoctrination, it has become closely associated with modern, mechanistic technology.[10] It is a systematic processing of non-compliant human beings which, if successful, refashions their very identities. This association of mass technology with the obliteration, psychological or physical, of human beings is one of the nastiest legacies of the twentieth century—Auschwitz and Hiroshima cast long shadows across the post-war years. Dreams of control can be potent determinants of action; they should not lightly be ignored.

Finally, brainwashing has a guise as a concept of last resort, a screen pulled across to hide the abyss of our ignorance. We invoke it when we have no other explanation, or are not motivated to look for one.[11] When faced with something extraordinary, such as apparent mass voluntary suicide, or the sympathy of some kidnap victims for their captors, our first instinct is to describe the dead of Jonestown, or Patty Hearst, as brainwashed; we have to call it something, and we do not know what else to call it. I will return to Jonestown in the next chapter. For now, however, the story of Patty Hearst provides the first of five case studies, illustrating some of the ways in which the concept of brainwashing has been used in the half-century since its birth.[12]

Case study: Patty Hearst

On 4 February 1974, Patricia Hearst, heiress and granddaughter of the powerful US media magnate William Randolph Hearst, was kidnapped by an organization calling itself the Symbionese Liberation Army (SLA). She was kept bound and blindfolded in a closet for several weeks, physically assaulted, forced to have sex with SLA members, and threatened with death. Meanwhile the SLA demanded a ransom from the Hearst Corporation, including not only requests for money but for a food give-away worth millions of dollars and the release of two SLA members jailed for murder.

On 14 April of the same year Patty Hearst caused a sensation by participating in the SLA robbery of a bank in San Francisco, after which she publicly denounced her family and expressed her commitment to the SLA. Finally arrested in September 1975, after at least one other armed robbery and a gun battle with police in which six SLA members were killed, she described her occupation as 'urban guerrilla' and proclaimed her revolutionary beliefs. At her trial, the central issue was whether she was acting voluntarily at the time of the robbery. The defence's two-pronged argument—that she was coerced, and that she was brainwashed—put brainwashing centre stage. The prosecution argued strongly that if she was acting under duress at the time of the bank robbery, she was not brainwashed; if she had been brainwashed, duress would not have been necessary. The prosecution also concentrated on observable facts: that Patty had been living for months separately from any SLA members; that she had had a number of chances to escape—and a gun; that on the videotape of the San Francisco bank robbery she appeared to know exactly what she was doing; and that she took the Fifth Amendment (the right not to answer a question when the answer could be incriminating or dangerous) forty-two times. The jury sided with the prosecution and sent Patty Hearst to prison.[13]

Was Patty Hearst brainwashed? Her case illustrates four important aspects of the concept of brainwashing: its purposeful nature, the 'cognitive difference' between the beliefs held by a victim before and after the alleged brainwashing, the timescale over which belief change occurs, and the use, already remarked upon, of brainwashing as a 'concept of last resort'.

Purpose
Brainwashing is a deliberate act; that is, intentional behaviour on the part of the brainwasher is part of the essence of brainwashing. This purpose may not be malicious—the brainwasher may sincerely believe that the victim will benefit from 're-education'—but judging an act as malicious depends heavily on perspective, so hostility is not the essential point. What matters is that the action is intended and carried out in order to change the victim.

However, purposeful attempts to change someone's mind do not in themselves constitute brainwashing, or the 1950s US authorities would have arrested every lawyer in the country (in an adversarial justice system such as America's or Britain's, changing the minds of jurors and judges plays a key role). What else is needed? We can distinguish three other important components of the concept of brainwashing.

Cognitive difference

The first is the strangeness of the new beliefs compared to the old. Imagine a fanatical football fan who claimed to have been brainwashed into believing that his team's captain was in fact the best footballer in the world. He probably wouldn't get much sympathy or interest. But a young American heiress who is kidnapped and then caught committing armed robbery is a different story. The discrepancy between Patty Hearst's luxurious upbringing and the ideals of the Symbionese Liberation Army seemed so huge that brainwashing became a popular explanation at the time of her trial.

It is also worth noting that the newly acquired beliefs of a brainwashing victim may or may not be 'sensible' beliefs to hold in their current environment. For prisoners in Chinese thought-reform camps, adopting the prevalent (Communist) belief system was the only way out of extreme deprivation and torture. Yet some continued publicly to maintain these 'enemy' beliefs even once they were back in the United States. Given the strength of feeling about anything Communist-related at the time, this was not a prudent way to behave. Beliefs acquired through brainwashing, like beliefs acquired by more routine methods, may not actually benefit the holder. In some cases they may be positively harmful.

Timescale

Beliefs and personalities change continually as people grow. My belief about the existence of Santa Claus is now diametrically opposed to the belief I had when I was young. Was I brainwashed by the adult world? No. I simply grew up, gradually accepting along the way that there was no such person as Santa Claus. But consider my friend Keith's extremely strong belief in Christianity. If Keith were to vanish for a month and then reappear a fervent atheist I would suspect that someone had been exerting undue influence, whereas if I hadn't seen Keith for ten years I would be much more likely to attribute the lapse to natural causes. In other words, the shorter the time of transition—between old and new beliefs— the more likely that some form of brainwashing has occurred.

Last resort

Finally, as noted earlier, brainwashing (when it is not being used as a casual insult) is often a 'concept of last resort', typically invoked only when no other explanation is apparent. In Patty Hearst's case, for example, the argument that she was brainwashed was a way of bridging the gap between her upbringing as a scion of an exemplary capitalist dynasty and her apparently voluntary participation in a radical and violent left-wing group.

Two other aspects of brainwashing also need to be taken into consideration. The first is the strength of the beliefs involved, and their association with emotion, both during the brainwashing itself and later, in the victim's response to attacks on their new beliefs. People who work with victims of cults, for example, often observe that the new beliefs are associated with extremely emotional states. Challenging such a belief rationally is difficult if not impossible. The victim not only perceives any such challenge as hostile but refuses to engage in rational debate; the new beliefs are considered 'sacred' and beyond the reach of reason. This is something we all do to some extent, but the hostile resistance of an alleged brainwashing victim can be extreme. The content of the new beliefs can also strike outsiders as bizarre—though again, this is a matter of perspective.

It is often assumed that brainwashing involves a change from one set of strong beliefs to another. However, this may not necessarily be the case. The Americans shocked by their brainwashed compatriots assumed that initial belief in the American way of life was as strong as the belief in Communism which these men later adopted. This may or may not have been so. The Americans had been the champions of the Second World War; their way of life was beginning to dominate. Beliefs held in a relatively free society which has just won a war, and in which freedom and individualism are important ideals, do not need to be held with such conviction as beliefs held in an authoritarian society which sees itself as under threat from the outside world, as the Chinese Communists did. It should also be noted that even for the minority who returned to the US as Communist converts, their strongly held opinions tended to fade with time, often accompanied by increasing confusion and in some cases mental illness.

The second aspect is the use of force and terror: the coercion in coercive persuasion. In brainwashing of the type allegedly carried out on the US prisoners in Korea, force was very much of the essence. The guards were trying to break their captives down; both mental and physical tortures were employed to achieve this. However, although force is often used, it is not essential. Many cults woo their victims with love, rather than brutality. It is also extremely difficult to define what is force and what isn't, as the Patty Hearst case shows. The most disconcerting thing about some victims of alleged brainwashing is the vehemence with which they claim to have free will, to have chosen their destiny rather than to have been coerced into it.

My next case clearly illustrates these two aspects of brainwashing. It also demonstrates that many of the techniques associated with Edward Hunter's term draw on much older methods, particularly those used in torture. It is a case of imperfect brainwashing which dates from almost four centuries before the birth of the word. Its victim was the English Protestant Archbishop and theologian Thomas Cranmer.[14]

Case study: Thomas Cranmer

Archbishop Cranmer was a leading scholar and Protestant reformer under King Henry VIII. Following the accession to the English throne of Henry's fiercely Catholic daughter Mary, Cranmer was sent to the Tower of London on 14 September 1553. Born in 1489, he was in his sixties, an old man by the standards of the time. His trial for treason, held without defence counsel on 13 November, condemned him to death. But his symbolic importance to Protestants, and the fragility of Mary's hold on power, prevented immediate execution. Instead Cranmer became the target of systematic attempts to make him publicly renounce his views and endorse Catholicism.

In March 1554 Cranmer and his fellow prisoners, Bishops Latimer and Ridley, were moved to Oxford. Between then and his death two years later, Cranmer suffered uncertainties about his future and considerable, unpredictable variation in his quality of life. He was in the power of other people who deprived him not only of liberty but of treasured privileges like books. His close circle of friends, on whom he had always relied, was removed. Lonely, humiliated, and afraid, he was subjected to intense psychological pressure, including public accusations, private attempts at persuasion, and debates on theology which attacked his intellectual and spiritual self-confidence.

At times, this pressure erupted into blatant terrorism, as when Cranmer was forced to watch the agonizing death by burning of Latimer and Ridley. The sight appalled him; wavering, he began to sign the necessary documents. Then he learned that his conciliatory move was to go unrewarded and that his expectation of clemency from the Queen was a hollow one. Convinced that Mary's harshness reflected the inadequacy of his attempt to appease her, he collapsed and recanted fully. The result was acceptance and a warm welcome into the Catholic Church. From being persecutors, the priests surrounding Cranmer began to show him affection as a sinner saved. Although he was still to die, his soul had been rescued.

But it was not enough. Not only had Cranmer been given no way to escape his impending death (still a frighteningly painful prospect, however strong one's belief in one's immortal soul), but his gaolers also appear to have made two fatal mistakes. The first was allowing him contact with his vigorously Protestant sister. What she said to him is not known, but it is unlikely to have bolstered his self-respect in his new faith.

The second error was a harsh reaction from one of the priests when Cranmer wept at the thought of his son. A 'Father' sneering at a father's grief; did Cranmer see the irony even through his pain? The warm welcome which had greeted his conversion, so meaningful for a desperately lonely old man, must have suddenly seemed so false. A little compassion might have won him, but this brutal contempt for his grief undermined all the previous coercion. Cranmer's own unease at his psychological contortions must have been augmented—and because there was no clemency on offer he had nothing to lose. To his captors' horror, he made a pre-execution speech denouncing his recantation, and died with great courage, unrepentant.

Cranmer underwent months of what we might well call psychological torture. Deprived of privileges, friends, and eventually hope, his intellectual foundations—and his very identity as a Protestant—attacked, he saw his colleagues meet the same hideous death with which he was threatened. Fear, grief, loneliness—the central roles of emotion and coercion are clear. The intellectual attacks on Cranmer's beliefs seem to have shaken him, but they were not solely responsible for his decision to comply with his captors. That compliance was brought about by the terrible pressures he suffered: ongoing uncertainty as to his fate, the loss of the books and friends he loved, the fear and horror of seeing colleagues burned alive. Positive emotion also played a part, as Cranmer still hoped that by giving in he could appease Mary and so avoid death by fire. Overwhelmed and exhausted by all these strong feelings, he took the only available escape route out of the maelstrom: obedience. Similarly, later on, it appears to have been two highly emotional stimuli—the meeting with his sister, and the priest's contempt when Cranmer wept for his son—which contributed most to the failure of his forced conversion.

Cranmer's example shows that brainwashing techniques did not suddenly spring into existence in the Korean War. They are part of a long lineage of forcible persuasion, often including physical and mental torture. As we shall see in Chapter 5, many of the methods used in brainwashing have been refined over centuries and were already well developed by Cranmer's time. The use of uncertainty as a psychological weapon; exposure to a group of people with the beliefs to which the victim is to be converted; removing the victim from his or her former environment and from any chance to reinforce old beliefs by, for example, talking to friends; the threat of death, severe physical pain, or both; loneliness, lack of privacy, and the sense of being unable to control one's fate—all these were used quite deliberately by the priests in charge of Thomas Cranmer.

The situation in Chinese reform camps, half a world away and four centuries later, was very similar. Prisoners were cut off from their homes and friends, sometimes isolated even from other prisoners, sometimes threatened with death or physical ill-treatment. Often their fate was unclear to them, as Cranmer's was to him for most of his time in prison. Individuals were typically put into small groups of 'believers' and subjected to prolonged discussion meetings, in which intensely detailed self-criticism, and criticism by other group members, was required. The aim of this criticism, which was used on Chinese citizens as well as on prisoners of war, was to 'bring out political and ideological viewpoints' and 'to overcome erroneous thoughts, to correct various ideological errors, to elevate the Party consciousness of the Party members, and to assist the comrades'.[15] Diaries, if kept, were public documents, inspected at meetings to assess ideological progress; the cramped living conditions made privacy impossible. Finally, as many researchers have emphasized, the sheer amount of repetition experienced by those undergoing thought reform was mind-numbing. For hours every day and sometimes for months or even years, the Party apparatus reinforced, with lectures, posters, broadcasts, or discussion meetings, its ideological messages. Sheer exhaustion undoubtedly contributed to the victims' psychological surrender. Cranmer, in his long and wearisome verbal duels with the Catholic theologians, must have felt a similar fatigue.

Victims and environments

Man is not a solitary animal

Bertrand Russell, *History of Western Philosophy*

One obvious conclusion which we can draw from the literature on brainwashing is that in its alleged status as a process—an evil and terrifying magic which turns free citizens into zombies—it is essentially a social process, requiring at least two participants. Brains are changed by signals from the world around them all the time, but we do not call noticing birdsong, the smell of fresh bread, or the sound of a passing car 'brainwashing'. For that term we require a coercive agent or agents, and whatever occurs in brainwashing, as in any form of persuasion, involves a social interaction between brainwasher and victim.

Since to date we humans have been unable to change brains directly (except by crude methods like knives, bullets, drugs, and the odd lobotomy),[16] we have had to rely on indirect methods: changing the signals which the brain receives. This can only be done by manipulating the physical or social environment of the victim. Of course, changing other people's environments is something we all do: we are all influence technicians—but there are degrees. Brainwashing is extreme: the brainwasher aims for total control over his victim's world, in order that he may eventually control his victim's mind.

People who follow their dreams of control are more likely to resort to extreme, non-consensual methods of persuasion. The same is true of governments. We describe the former as psychopathic, the latter as totalitarian, but they have many features in common. Both prefer absolutes and tend to see the world in black and white terms, both espouse the doctrine that the end justifies the

means, and both can show a lethal disregard for their victims. It was from a totalitarian government that the term 'brainwashing' first emerged, and it has been
totalist individuals, as we shall see when we come to discuss cults in Chapter 2,
who have provided the word with most of its employment.

So how do totalitarian States, or individuals, try to implement their dreams of
control? For governments, Robert Lifton[17] identifies eight psychological themes
characteristic of thought reform and, he argues, of totalitarian ideologies in
general (see Table 1).[18] Milieu control is the attempt to dominate 'not only the
individual's communication with the outside (all that he sees and hears, reads
and writes, experiences, and expresses), but also—in its penetration of his inner
life—over what we may speak of as his communication with himself'. Mystical
manipulation involves manipulating a person in order 'to provoke specific patterns of behavior and emotion in such a way that these will appear to have arisen
spontaneously from within the environment'. Mystical manipulation often refers
to higher purposes or supernatural authorities such as fate, the hand of history, or
God, or to being chosen, or to the divine or semi-divine status of the controlling
organization as representative of a supernatural authority. Then there is the
demand for purity which follows from the binary oppositions inherent in totalist
thought: Party/non-Party; Communist/imperialist; person/non-person; good/
evil. Just as in George Orwell's *Animal Farm* the slogan of 'four legs good, two legs
bad' becomes the animals' guiding 'essential principle', so in other ideologies the
stereotypical dualism of good and evil leads to the poisonous (and unrealistic)
demand that elements outside the chosen realm should be eliminated lest they
contaminate the saved.

Lifton's fourth theme is the cult of confession, which rejects individual privacy
and glorifies confession as an end in itself, used to exploit and control rather than
to console. He also lists sacred science, which like mystical manipulation involves
a moral/spiritual mystique, in this case applied to the ideology's basic tenets. As
sacred science, these are regarded as morally unchallengeable—the very act
of challenge can render the challenger a 'non-person'—and scientifically exact;
'thus the ultimate moral vision becomes an ultimate science'. Loading the
language is the mind-numbing process by which 'the most far-reaching and complex of human problems are compressed into brief, highly reductive, definitive-
sounding phrases, easily memorized and easily expressed', whose aim is to shut
down independent thinking. These 'thought-terminating clichés' imply group
unity, and the Party's control over language and, ultimately, thought.

Finally, Lifton lists as characteristic of totalist regimes the primacy of doctrine
over person—the idea that the doctrine is more true and more real than anything
experienced by an individual human being—and the dispensing of existence:
the right granted to the Party, it believes, to determine the fates not only of its
adherents but also of the non-people beyond its sphere. This right follows from

Table 1 Robert Lifton's eight totalist themes

1	Milieu control	Control of an individual's communication with the external world, hence of his or her perceptions of reality
2	Mystical manipulation	Evoking certain patterns of behaviour and emotion in such a way that they seem to be spontaneous
3	The demand for purity	The belief that elements outside the chosen group should be eliminated to prevent them contaminating the minds of group members
4	The cult of confession	The use of and insistence on confession to minimize individual privacy
5	Sacred science	Viewing the ideology's basic dogmas as both morally unchallengeable and scientifically exact, thus increasing their apparent authority
6	Loading the language	Compressing complex ideas into brief, definitive-sounding phrases, 'thought-terminating clichés'
7	The primacy of doctrine over person	The idea that a dogma is more true and more real than anything experienced by an individual human being
8	The dispensing of existence	The right to control the quality of life and eventual fate of both group members and non-members

the Party's belief that there is only one path to truth—'I am the way, the truth, and the life; no man cometh unto the Father, but by me' (John, 14:6)—that it alone knows that path, and that false paths must be eliminated. Like most varieties of Christianity (Calvinism, which believes in predestination, is an exception), thought reform believed that the non-person can be converted into a person. Thus it did not in principle make the further assumption that not only false paths but also those who followed them must be destroyed. In this it differed from some other ideologies, most notoriously Nazism: as the historian Daniel Goldhagen has argued,[19] one of the most toxic elements in Nazi ideology was the belief that the Jews' biology rendered them irredeemable.

Case study: Father Luca

Lifton's eight themes are clearly illustrated by his discussion of Father Francis Luca, an Italian priest who had lived in China for several years when he was arrested and underwent thought reform. Luca found himself in a world whose every aspect was controlled, where Communist doctrine was unchallengeably good and Western imperialism stereotypically bad. His fate was in the hands of people who demanded that he purify himself of every undesirable thought. Lifton describes his case in detail; I will summarize the main points here.

Father Luca was alert to the possibility of arrest—because of his friendship with another priest, Father C, who had been involved in anti-Communist activities—

and had already planned his defence. In the initial interrogation he was defiant and critical of his captors. Their response was to use sleeplessness and pain, subjecting Luca to night-time interrogations in which his legs were chained with twenty-pound weights and his arms handcuffed. He was forced to sit on the ground with his legs stretched out; when he could no longer maintain this position, 'he would lean backwards; his weight would then fall on his wrists, which were shackled behind his back. Finding the pain of the handcuffs digging into his skin and the general discomfort of his position to be unbearable, thoughts of surrender and compromise came to him for the first time.'

When he was not being interrogated, Luca was placed in a small bare cell with other prisoners, chosen for their compliance and told that assisting in Luca's thought reform would further their own release. Their duty, which they carried out enthusiastically for hours at a time, was to 'struggle' him with a torrent of questions and accusations about his activities and beliefs, demanding that he confess and severely criticizing anything he said. He was forced to stay standing until his legs swelled with fluid and became infected, and was kept awake almost continuously (on one occasion he was allowed to sleep after he fainted). He endured this treatment for a month, during which he made several completely false confessions and became so confused that he had great difficulty in remembering what he had confessed. By that stage, as he later reported to Robert Lifton, 'I would say almost anything they wanted me to say.'

After a month, the judge ordered Luca's chains removed and told him to sleep for two days, expressing the hope that this would help him come up with a better confession. When he failed to do so he was beaten so severely on his back that he was left physically helpless. A doctor who examined him told him that his spine had been broken, but would heal in time. His cellmates were, to say the least, unsympathetic, and although he eventually received some medical treatment for his bed sores, it was over a year before he could walk any distance. During this time the 'struggle' and physical abuse, which had abated immediately following his injury, resumed, and his original confessions were rejected. Finally, he took the only way out he could think of: presenting real events as more incriminating than they actually had been.

The resulting exaggerations were greeted with approval by his captors, who encouraged Luca to write down more and more about himself. His cellmates were replaced with new ones, and the old regime of physical abuse gave way to the psychological pressure to confess any 'bad thoughts' and, especially, to condemn the Catholic Church, which Luca had so far refused to do. He began to invent 'bad thoughts', claiming, for instance, a fondness for the American President, Harry Truman, which he had never actually had. This produced a friendlier attitude in his interrogators, alternating with continued criticism of Church behaviour. It caused Luca mental agony, but 'increasingly he stifled whatever inner protest he felt, and began to express himself cautiously, in a manner consistent with the Communist point of view wherever possible'. He also continued to revise his confession. He was rewarded with a more liberal regime and the hope of release, but he was also expected to write a letter denouncing his former activities, and to help new prisoners confess, which he did. Eventually, after being photographed and recorded reading his confession aloud, he was released and expelled from China, three and a half years after his imprisonment. He was left feeling weak, ashamed, and struggling to understand his ordeal, more critical than before of the Catholic Church's mission in China, regretful of his lost life there, and aware that he had undergone an important personal transformation.

Father Luca found his horizons broadened by his experience of thought reform. He was able, though not without profound discomfort, to accept and integrate much of the Communist criticism of his beloved Catholic Church—for example, that priests had lived in comparative luxury and in some cases taken up arms against the Communists. He achieved this largely by sharpening the distinction between his basic religious principles, which survived thought reform, and the behaviour of the Church and its priests, which did not emerge unscathed. His tolerance of new ideas allowed his mind to change, but not to break, under the shock of thought reform, so he was able to emerge comparatively intact. As our next case study shows, not all victims of thought reform were so fortunate.

Case study: Father Simon

Father Simon was a Catholic priest who had spent twenty years in China teaching science before he was arrested and underwent thought reform.[20] He had openly criticized Communism, and was initially extremely defiant under interrogation. But he loved China deeply and dreaded the thought of having to leave. He also had a strong conscience, which led him to feel guilty about events that others would have seen as trivial, such as an occasion when he had talked to an intelligence officer from the American army. And the prison environment allowed him to live among Chinese people in a way he had never felt able to do before. The combination of powerful positive and negative emotions was overwhelming—and effective. Finding that he could resolve his guilt, and in some sense get closer to the China he adored, by confessing his sins against the Communists and then adopting their beliefs, he became compliant.

Unlike Father Luca, however, Father Simon's compliance was far from superficial. When interviewed by Robert Lifton after his release, he was fiercely critical of Catholic colleagues for their anti-Communist 'distortions'. He also denied that he had experienced brutality in prison (despite reports to the contrary from other prisoners), and he praised Communism with fervent enthusiasm. Like Father

Luca, Father Simon retained his deepest religious principles. Unlike Father Luca, he was saddened by the Communists' conviction that a person could not be both a Communist and a Catholic. He also believed that Catholicism could learn much from Communist techniques. Needless to say, his former colleagues were appalled by his ideas. Nevertheless they took him back, hoping that over time he would gradually return to his previous convictions. This hope appears to have been optimistic—the interview with Lifton occurred three and a half years after Father Simon's experience of thought reform, at which time his adherence to Communism showed no signs of abating.

Comparing the stories of Father Luca and Father Simon shows the differences personality can make to a person's susceptibility to brainwashing. Both were deeply religious, fond of China and the Chinese, and well educated. But Father Simon's personality was less flexible and more emotional than Father Luca's: Robert Lifton paints a picture of a tense, angry man, prone to strong feelings and to all-or-nothing thinking. These were the weaknesses on which thought reform played to such great effect.

The final example I have chosen to illustrate brainwashing is fictional. It is taken from a book written in 1948, two years before the word officially entered the English language. Nevertheless, it has become known throughout the English-speaking world as a brilliant novel and a terrifying warning of the dangers of totalitarianism. Told in the third person, it avoids the problems of unreliable narration arising when brainwashing was described either by its victims or by the US propagandists who observed them. It is as good a description of the concept as you will find anywhere.

Case study: *Nineteen Eighty-Four*

George Orwell's lonely protagonist, Winston Smith, lives in a world dominated by three warring superpowers, Oceania, Eurasia, and Eastasia. His home, once London, is in Oceania, and he works for the lower levels of the totalitarian ruling Party. His job is to falsify records of the past so that Party policies, even when they directly contradict previous policies, appear to have been consistent throughout. He is part of a gigantic effort to control history itself, required because the Party presents itself as infallible: 'no change in doctrine or in political alignment can ever be admitted. For to change one's mind, or even one's policy, is a confession of weakness'.[21]

But the Party does not restrict itself to the manipulation of history. Lifton's eight themes (see Table 1, p. 17) are clearly relevant; this organization is a potent example of ideological totalism. Milieu control ensures that Party members are subjected to a rigid discipline of thought control in every waking moment. Every home has a telescreen which provides the Party-controlled channel for all information about the external world. And the channel is two-way, a potential spy portal for the authorities. The Thought Police may be watching anyone's telescreen at any time. Regular outbreaks of mass emotion ('The Two Minutes Hate') are encouraged, in which a whipped-up frenzy of hate and fear is directed against the enemies of the Party. 'A Party member is expected to have no private emotions and no respites from enthusiasm. He is supposed to live in a continuous frenzy of hatred of foreign enemies and internal traitors, triumph over victories, and self-abasement before the power and wisdom of the Party. The discontents produced by his bare, unsatisfying life are deliberately turned outwards and dissipated by such devices as the Two Minutes Hate, and the speculations which might possibly induce a sceptical or rebellious attitude are killed in advance by his early acquired inner discipline.'

Staged events like the Two Minutes Hate show the planned 'spontaneity' characteristic of mystical manipulation and the frenzied self-flagellation of the cult of confession. The demand for purity, meanwhile, resonates throughout *Nineteen Eighty-Four*: Winston's job is to purify history. The Party glorifies its leader, Big Brother, and its sacred science cannot be challenged. Even when the doctrines contradict themselves from one day to the next, they still take precedence over personal experience. Winston's job, for example, requires him to accept, even reinforce, the doctrine that Oceania is at war with Eurasia and has always been at war with Eurasia, even though he remembers a time when Eastasia was the enemy. In addition, the Party undoubtedly dispenses the right to live or die.

Winston is a rebel tormented by memory. From his rebellious perspective he relates the processes by which the Party exerts its thought control. One such process is the modification of language. The Party is gradually implementing Newspeak, a pared-down version of English in which 'dangerous' words like 'freedom' no longer exist. The idea is that without the words to express certain concepts, the concepts themselves will fade and die: 'Newspeak was designed not to extend but to *diminish* the range of thought.' Those words which remain are ideologically loaded, clear examples of Lifton's thought-terminating clichés.

But the real strength and terror of the Party lies in uncertainty. Winston never knows who is on his side—everyone is a potential informer. Worse, there are no laws, so nothing is, strictly speaking, criminal; yet any unorthodoxy may be punished and punishment is by removal—people simply disappear. No one knows what is and is not dangerous, who the Thought Police are, or even how to defend themselves against false allegations, so they live in constant fear and, since information is under Party control, in extreme ignorance. Winston, who has vague memories that things used to be different, longs for a friend, someone he can talk to, someone understanding. This in itself is thoughtcrime, and knowing it drives him to increasingly reckless behaviour. In due course the authorities pounce. Winston is tortured, broken, and 're-educated'. From hating and fearing Big Brother, he becomes converted to love.

> But it was all right, everything was all right, the struggle was finished. He had won the victory over himself. He loved Big Brother.
>
> Orwell, *Nineteen Eighty-Four*, p. 240

Brainwashing as process

Orwell's spartan prose takes us into the worlds of both victims and administrators of coercion techniques. He illustrates the purposeful nature of the Party's methods of control, the cognitive difference between the beliefs held by Winston before and after his conversion, and the relatively short timescale over which that conversion occurs. Force, powerful emotions, repetition, and psychological and physical torture are clearly used against Winston, as they were against Cranmer, Patty Hearst, and Fathers Luca and Simon. Winston's torment culminates in 'the worst thing in the world', when he is taken to the now-legendary Room 101 and threatened with his ultimate fear. It is this—for Winston, the thought of a rat eating its way through his face—which achieves his total submission.

Communist thought reform also involved considerable emotional pressure. Chinese students sent to universities for re-education found themselves immersed in a group where dissident thoughts were always under attack. Every aspect of behaviour was constantly open to criticism by other students, and self-criticism, one of the key aspects of thought reform, was insistently encouraged. Privacy was non-existent; lectures often went on for hours; and in long training days consisting largely of lectures and self-criticism meetings, emotions could become intensely heated. One ex-student interviewed by Hunter noted the high rate of suicide at thought reform academies. Lifton, who interviewed forty Chinese and Western people who had been through thought reform, details the frequent use of threat and physical torture to break down their resistance in terms very similar to those described by Orwell, as the case study of Father Luca showed.

Nineteen Eighty-Four also illustrates some of the features which lead people to allege brainwashing, rather than just persuasion. The first is the type of beliefs adopted by the alleged victim. Not only are these typically very different from beliefs held previously, but they may be unrelated to reality or to majority beliefs, or even disadvantageous for the victim (as when religious believers are persecuted). The Party creates its own reality, which may have little or nothing to do with what is actually happening in the world. This is made clear throughout *Nineteen Eighty-Four* by descriptions of meaningless quotas, victories that lead nowhere, and an endless war against arbitrarily changing opponents.

A second characteristic of victims of alleged brainwashing is their emotionality. They may appear disconnected when dealing with relatives or outsiders, or they may react with strong hostility to any challenge to the new beliefs. At the end of the book, Winston recalls his earlier attitudes as 'cruel, needless misunderstanding!' and his earlier self as 'stubborn' and 'self-willed'. Edward Hunter quotes from a Communist propaganda play in which a student angrily declares that 'I could not see the murderous blade lying behind the masks of the American teachers and professors; I could not hear the guns and bombs behind their musical films. Now I thoroughly know and understand the entire situation.'[22] The change in behaviour may appear so extreme that relatives of cult members, for example, often complain that their loved one 'just isn't the same person any more'. Winston at the end of *Nineteen Eighty-Four* certainly seems a very different person from the restless protagonist of earlier in the book. The fire which sustained him in opposition days has gone out; his concerns have narrowed to the immediacies of everyday life. Out go truth, memory, history; in come the endless telescreen and the size of his drinks bill.

Brainwashing as idea

. . . has man always inhabited a world like the present [...] where the love of order is confounded with a taste for oppression?

De Tocqueville, *Democracy in America*

'Brainwashing' is often used as a concept of last resort. However, new explanations can erode the requirement for such concepts, rendering this use of 'brainwashing' increasingly superfluous. In the rest of this book we will look at a number of alternative explanations of various situations once labelled 'brainwashing' which have emerged since the term was coined. We will see that psychology—in particular social psychology—and neuroscience can provide huge insight into how people influence each other, ranging from the casual, short-term effects of everyday conversation through to the life-changing consequences of torture and coercion. The case studies have provided no evidence for a 'magic' process called 'brainwashing', though many (including the US government) have spent time and money looking for such a process. Rather, the studies suggest that brainwashing, in its aspect as process, is best regarded as a collective noun for various, increasingly well-understood techniques of non-consensual mind change.

However, there is another aspect of brainwashing for which such explanations are irrelevant—its conceptual nature as a potential totalitarian threat. Once again we turn to Orwell. During Winston's agonizing conversion, his torturer O'Brien gives a definitive and distinctly evangelical statement of the link between brainwashing and totalitarianism:

When finally you surrender to us, it must be of your own free will. We do not destroy the heretic because he resists us: so long as he resists us we never destroy him. We convert him, we capture his inner mind, we reshape him. We burn all evil and all illusion out of him; we bring him over to our side, not in appearance, but genuinely, heart and soul. We make him one of ourselves before we kill him. It is intolerable to us that an erroneous thought should exist anywhere in the world, however secret and powerless it may be.

Orwell, *Nineteen Eighty-Four*, p. 205

This statement, chillingly reminiscent of what happened to Thomas Cranmer, is the ultimate totalitarian fantasy: not only behaviour, but every single thought in every single brain in all the world conforming to a single ideological format. It is the hunger to be truly superhuman, not to be the loving God worshipped by Christians nor the merciful Allah praised by Muslims, but a mad dictator God. It is a demand for perfection, stifling any possibility of freedom, deviance, or change. Other than complete destruction, it is difficult to imagine a more horrifying conception; and there is a skin-crawling quality to this conception which mere destruction does not possess.

Summary and conclusions

Demystifying brainwashing, the ultimate change process, can perhaps serve to highlight much about the workings of the ordinary human mind. For the factors that can be combined to force such sudden change are perhaps equally responsible, in their various combinations and unconsciously over time, for the formation of our characters in the first place. It may make us question the foundations instead of the façade

Denise Winn, *The Manipulated Mind*

This chapter has introduced the concept of brainwashing and explored its history as insult, concept of last resort, description of one or more processes, and dangerous idea. In later chapters we will ask whether this ultimate totalitarian fantasy has ever been realized. We will ask if it ever could be realized. And we will consider the *idea* of brainwashing, the dream of total control. What does it say about us and our free will? And how do we minimize the appalling consequences which occur when people try to chase the dream?

Chapter 2: God or the group?

If God be for us, who can be against us?

Romans 8:31

Since 1950, when it was first enunciated, the concept of brainwashing has spent much of its life in the seedy undergrowth of popular culture. Lurking in movies and thrillers, increasingly despised by academia, it has surfaced into public awareness typically as a response to certain extreme traumas, a last resort for commentators trying to explain the apparently inexplicable. Such traumas are not accidental; they are inflicted by a person or persons, usually driven by political or religious motives. In this chapter, I will ask what it is about such motives, and the social and psychological contexts in which they flourish, which makes them so dangerous.

The accursed power

For the West, the worst such recent trauma occurred in the United States of America, erupting on the morning of 11 September 2001 when a jet aeroplane loaded with passengers hit one of the twin towers of the World Trade Center in New York. For the first few minutes the world assumed a dreadful accident, until a second plane crashed into the other tower. A third hit the Pentagon; a fourth was brought down in Pennsylvania when passengers, hearing of the earlier attacks by mobile phone, tried to overpower their hijackers. Both the World Trade Center towers collapsed and the final death toll ran into thousands. Those who, like me, happened across the story and watched it unfold live on television, will not easily forget the trembling disbelief in the reporters' voices as they struggled to grasp what they were seeing. For those involved, and for the American people, 9/11 has left appalling scars.

In the first days after the tragedy, alongside the hunt for bodies and people to blame, some voices described 9/11 as a uniquely evil act. But of course, as others quickly pointed out, it was not. Not only had there been an earlier attempt to destroy the World Trade Center (linked to Al-Qaeda, the same radical Islamic group which would be blamed for 9/11), but America had previously suffered terrorism on its own soil and from its own citizens. Timothy McVeigh's politically motivated bombing of a government building in Oklahoma on 19 April 1995 killed 168 government employees and civilians and injured over 500. And McVeigh's attack was itself only the latest in a genealogy of terrorism driven by political and/or religious motives, a worldwide genealogy stretching back far beyond 1950. Elements of that dark lineage have triggered renewed discussion of brainwashing ever since the term became available; 9/11 was no exception.

Religion and politics

What redeems it is the idea only [...] and an unselfish belief in the idea—
something you can set up, and bow down before, and offer a sacrifice to
Joseph Conrad, Heart of Darkness

In the post-Reformation West, religion and politics have tended to become increasingly separate (at least in principle) as enshrined, for example, in the US Constitution and the French policy of separating Church and State.[1] But, as Al-Qaeda shows, this is not the case in many countries. This disparate organization, headed by the wealthy Saudi dissident Osama bin Laden, is described as 'radical Islamic', but as well as the goal of spreading its version of Islam it also professes political aims to do with the limiting of Western, particularly US, hegemony. For example, bin Laden's stated aim of removing American troops from Saudi Arabia is a political goal, motivated at least in part by religious reasons since the Americans are regarded as profaning holy soil. Politics and religion are so closely intertwined in this and many other conflicts that it becomes impossible to separate them.

Secular commentators in Britain, used to a form of religion largely defanged, often remark on the peculiar viciousness of religious conflicts. Yet it is a matter of debate as to whether religion is uniquely to blame here. Even distinguishing religious from other motives can be difficult. For example, in Northern Ireland, still frequently cited as an archetypal religious conflict, the two main communities are driven apart by a complex collection of motivating forces which includes concerns about status, human rights, and democratic obligations, as well as more atavistic fears of being oppressed, swamped, or even eliminated.

It seems undeniable, however, that there are certain motives, including religious and political ideals, which can drive human beings to commit appalling atrocities against one another. These motives, though superficially very different—contrast fighting for *liberté* in the French Revolution with Basque nationalism or Al-Qaeda fighting for Allah—seem to have certain features in common. They use abstract, ambiguous, and value-laden ideas, link them to strong emotions, and use the resulting synthesis to justify the denigration of people who don't agree with them.

The ideas

Both politics and religion call on certain core ideas (freedom, a State, God) which are so highly abstract that I will refer to them as 'ethereal'. Ethereal ideas are so ambiguous that they are often interpreted very differently by different individuals (political theorists describe political ethereal ideas, such as liberty and equality, as 'essentially contested').[2] This ambiguity makes them hard to challenge with rational debate; participants in such a debate may, in effect, be talking at cross-purposes. Speakers often use such 'glittering generalities'[3] to mask impracticalities, hidden catches or other devils in the detail of their aims and objectives, or in the hope of evoking an emotional response from their audience which will increase the level of commitment to their agenda. As well as being abstract and ambiguous, ethereal ideas are value-laden (see Chapter 9 for more on this topic). Viewed as supremely important in themselves, they come with a huge accumulated emotional baggage, and encourage a sense of superiority in believers.

The emotions

While the abstract nature of ethereal ideas allows their adherents to avoid focusing on difficult practicalities (like how to be sure what God wants, or when exactly freedom will have been achieved), these concepts are not detached from reality. Far from it: they gain their power by being linked to specific, highly emotive examples. Human brains tend to associate two stimuli perceived at the same time, and a skilled speaker will make use of this, trying for instance to associate a perceived or real injustice with an ethereal idea. Here is John Milton shortly after the English Civil Wars, linking a somewhat abstract constitutional question—whether Parliament had the right to execute King Charles I—to evocative images of war, destruction, and slaughter:

what hath a native king to plead, bound by so many covenants, benefits and
honours to the welfare of his people; why he through the contempt of all laws
and parliaments [...] after seven years' warring and destroying of his best
subjects, overcome and yielded prisoner, should think to scape unquestionable,
as a thing divine, in respect of whom so many thousand Christians destroyed
should lie unaccounted for, polluting with their slaughtered carcasses all the land
over, and crying for vengeance against the living that should have righted them?
Milton, The Tenure of Kings and Magistrates, p. 285

The consequences

Ethereal ideas are generally bloodstained. Valued more highly than human life, they also facilitate the processes whereby, firstly, ends can come to justify means, and secondly, people who don't accept the ideas' supremacy can be seen as less than human.[4] In other words, ethereal ideas encourage totalist thinking, as described by Robert Lifton (see Chapter 1). They therefore can be, and all too often are, used to justify acts of terrorism. To the victim, or to us who look on, it may seem unimaginable that human beings could do such things to others, could knowingly and calmly fly a planeload of people into a skyscraper, or bomb a hotel, or look a child in the eyes and then blow out its brains. Groping for explanations, we use terms like evil, mad, or—if we perceive a controlling agent—brainwashed. We also react with hostility and sometimes repression, providing a clear external threat which serves to strengthen the emotional commitment for terrorists.

It is noticeable that in England, a nation whose self-image (which may or may not be accurate) has long incorporated tolerance and a distaste for strong passions, the established religion has grown increasingly away from the kind of evangelical furore associated with grand visions. In that sense a distrust of big ideas has served England well: the last large-scale ideological conflict in which abstract religious ideals played a major role was in 1688, when Protestant William of Orange clashed with Catholic King James the Seventh (of Scotland) and Second (of England). The Church of England today is immersed in details. It acts alongside social services and government initiatives to support local communities in a huge variety of imaginative ways, from setting up centres in disadvantaged areas to teach computing and other job-related skills, to prison visiting and help for the very poorest in society. The result? England's established church, despised by many because of its lack of passion, does a lot of good (more than many of its critics). And it is exceptionally rare in England for someone to be killed for their faith.

As for religion, so for politics; at the time of writing Britain is in a phase where there are few major ideological differences among mainstream politicians. The country's leaders appear less concerned with grand visions than with the intricate technicalities of everyday management. Many people complain that this makes politics boring and citizens apathetic, that young people in particular find other outlets for their energies. Is this a bad thing? Maybe, but when politics becomes exciting the result can often be bloody. Swept up in the thrill of following a noble cause, people much more easily commit the kinds of atrocities which can lead observers to say: 'They must have been brainwashed!' Consider the last time politics became really exciting in Britain—the seventeenth-century Civil Wars, which killed thousands. Many would choose apathy any day over that kind of political engagement.

Unfortunately, peace is a pipedream for those numerous parts of the world in which religious or politically motivated groups inflict death, injury, and terror on others, and sometimes on their own members. To investigate in more detail the processes by which such groups gain their (often considerable) power, we need to look at specific examples. I have chosen two famous and archetypal instances of cults—groups in which religious and political motives, although not the only driving force, played a significant role. Both began with noble, even utopian ideals, and had their origins in the USA, land of the free and proud supporter of individual rights; they are not stories in which demonic others from alien cultures can be blamed. Both ended in murder, the disintegration of the cult, and a mess of misery and havoc for the relatives of victims. Both are so well known that I will describe them here only in outline. I have drawn heavily on Scheflin and Opton's description of the Manson Family in *The Mind Manipulators* and on Shiva Naipaul's book *Black and White*, which deals with the Jonestown massacre.

Small-scale cults: the Manson family

Charles Milles Manson had what is often euphemistically described as a troubled childhood. Born to a sixteen-year-old prostitute who paid him barely any attention even when she was with him and not in gaol, he was shifted between a series of unwilling relatives. Between the ages of nine and thirty-two he spent most of his time in reform schools or prisons which, though violent, provided a structure missing from life outside. He developed the toughness needed to survive, and he also acquired other skills: notably, an extreme form of a tendency most of us have to be social chameleons, behaving as the people we interact with want us to behave. (Who, looking back, has not been disconcerted by their deference in the presence of their boss, or their unexpected ability to be competent when competence was required of them?) As well as this interpersonal fluidity, Manson also developed interests in non-mainstream religion and philosophy: the occult, Eastern mysticism, Scientology.

Released in 1967 despite his pleas to stay inside, Manson found himself, at thirty-two, in the midst of the Sixties counter-culture. Suddenly there were people ready to love him, to welcome him, to hang on his every word (and his studies enabled him to lecture impressively on the subjects they wanted to hear). His skills in understanding what people wanted and giving it to them, honed in gaol by the pressures to survive and keep out of trouble, gave him a rapid mastery of the flower-children; his ability to read their thoughts seemed almost supernatural. Gathering a mainly female group around him, he evolved the Family, dedicated to free love and the unquestioning worship of its leader. He had used sex to initiate his female followers, but he also encouraged them to talk about themselves so that he could learn and exploit their weaknesses. Some of the girls, for example, had very difficult relationships with their fathers; Manson told them to pretend he was their father, then made love to them. This identification of him as 'loving father' not only distanced the girls from their previous lives (where sex with one's father was strictly forbidden), but also made Manson's approval hugely important to them. He supplied the love they had been lacking.

For a year, while Manson attempted to forge a career in popular music, the dream lasted. But his attempt failed. He was eventually to achieve, at least for a while, his goal of fame comparable to that of the Beatles, but he began to recognize that it would not be in the same field. Whether this contributed to the darkening of his vision is not known. What is clear is that he had contact with Satanist groups, that he began to talk of an imminent Armageddon, and that he began to use more violent controlling tactics in the Family. Isolated from the outside world, dependent on Manson for their emotional fulfilment, Family members accepted his authority over every aspect of their lives. He used drugs, aggressive interrogation, and constant repetition of his doctrines to reinforce that authority. He also began to identify himself explicitly with religious symbols—Christ, God, and the Devil—and to lead the Family in bizarre rituals which are said to have involved killing animals, drinking their blood, and simulating murder and violence.

At some point it seems that Manson decided the coming apocalypse was not coming fast enough and needed a helping hand. The concept of 'Helter Skelter'—the bloody revolution which would, he believed, give birth to the new world order—was born, and Manson set his Family the task of implementing it. Over two nights in August 1969 they started their campaign of violence with the ferocious murders of seven wealthy residents of Los Angeles, including a heavily pregnant woman, actress Sharon Tate.

Faced with stabbed and beaten bodies, the words 'PIG', 'WAR', and of course 'HEALTER SKELTER' [sic] written in blood, and evidence that the murderers had showered and eaten before leaving the crime scene, the public reaction was one of shock, fear, and incomprehension. When arrests followed, the lack of connection between killers and victims made what had happened seem even more bizarre. The sight of young women calmly reciting how they had butchered Sharon Tate and her unborn baby made people clutch at any straw in their search for explanations. In addition, the prosecution faced the problem that Manson had not actually been present at the killings. To argue that he had brainwashed his young female devotees into accepting a 'philosophy of death' seemed the obvious solution.

The prosecution's adoption of the brainwashing argument led it, however, into a dilemma. Its aim was to implicate Manson in the murders, as well as his followers, by arguing that his brainwashing of his followers was responsible for what they had done. Yet if the Manson girls were brainwashed, how could they be responsible for the murders which they had clearly carried out? At the time the prosecution fudged the issue, aided by the defence's failure to emphasize the dilemma and by the fact that the defendants presented no evidence of insanity or diminished responsibility. The California Court of Appeals, ruling on the case, took the same view as the courts at Nuremberg before it, stating that peer pressure, being a cult follower, or coming under the influence of a charismatic leader was not enough to relieve a person from criminal liability. It also agreed with holding the leader responsible. The defendants' convictions for first-degree murder were upheld, sending Charles Manson back to prison, this time for life.

Manson's interpersonal skills had been honed to a high standard, but without the group which coalesced around him it is doubtful whether he would have achieved such notoriety. Groups and intragroup mechanisms are central to religions and politics. We will explore the psychological mechanisms which underlie the formation and development of such groups. First, however, let us turn to the second of our case studies.

Large-scale cults: the Jonestown massacre

Jonestown was a community set up in 1977 by the Reverend Jim Jones in the isolated jungle of Guyana. The move was in response to deteriorating relations between his People's Temple, founded in 1956, and the community of San Francisco where it was based. Like Charles Manson, Jim Jones was charismatic and, at least to begin with, seen by those who followed him as full of love to a superhuman degree. The People's Temple preached brotherhood, communal living, the provision of social support, and a sense of belonging for the needy. In its early days it put many of its ideals into practice, running an impressive number of welfare support schemes. In self-reliant Cold War America, this socialist behaviour probably contributed to the suspicion with which Jones' organization came to be viewed.

To his followers, however, Jones was a messiah, sent by God to build utopia. And indeed, many of those outsiders who visited Jonestown following its creation in the summer of 1977 came away convinced they had glimpsed a heaven on earth. Even some of those who defected from Jonestown had high praise for the ethical standards of behaviour they had experienced. Life was hard as the fiery Christian preacher struggled to build his agricultural commune, but Jones had chosen his site well. Isolated and hard to reach, the commune was easy to control and the sense of external hostility, both physical and social, pressured occupants to stick together. And Guyana at that time was a place conducive to such experiments. Run by the increasingly dictatorial Forbes Burnham, it

31

professed ideals similar to those of the People's Temple. Yet in practice, as Shiva Naipaul suggests in *Black and White*, the Guyanan government displayed 'a peculiar sort of gangsterism that can contain within itself both corrupt cynicism of the highest order and ideological motivation', centred on Burnham's personality to such an extent that the government became little more than the institutionalization of 'his manias, lusts, and fantasies [...] a projection of his caprice'. One of those fantasies was paranoia: by the time of the massacre Guyana's military budget was four times as big as its health budget. Burnham welcomed the People's Temple to his country, and Jim Jones openly supported him in return.

There were others, however, who did not look so favourably on the new enterprise. Indeed, one of the chief features of the Jonestown story is how polarized the debate became. On the one hand, heaven; on the other an appalling kind of hell. Defectors and relatives of Jones' followers banded together to form the Concerned Relatives. Shiva Naipaul argues convincingly that the histrionics of this group, and their obsession with blackening Jones, were instrumental in escalating the sense of persecution within Jonestown. The defectors in particular felt securely in possession of the moral high ground, strengthened by the knowledge that, having been brainwashed, they bore no responsibility for anything they or anyone else had done in Jonestown (one wonders how they ever managed to defect). Rumours about the commune spread with avidity: Jones was a master of deceit and manipulation, with demonic powers of mind control; he tortured his followers; he had even acquired an atomic bomb and was planning to take over the world.

In November 1978, after months of increasing paranoia and escalating physical hardships, Jonestown had its back against the wall. Jones was seriously ill, and in the commune the talk was of death, of the atrocities committed by American society against its blacks and its poor, of exploitation, racism, and fascism. Amidst lawsuits, claim and counter-claim, and warnings from defectors that Jones was heavily armed and had planned for mass suicide, Congressman Leo Ryan led a delegation of Concerned Relatives and journalists on a visit to Jonestown. On 14 November the delegation's plane landed in Guyana. A truck full of armed men ambushed it; Congressman Ryan was one of those killed. Four days later, Jones implemented a well-rehearsed plan of self-destruction. Cult members, exhausted by bad diet, sickness, and intensive physical labour, may have felt that utopia was slipping from their grasp. Certainly few of them seem to have rebelled against Jones' decision to institute mass suicide via a sweetly flavoured cyanide soup. Over nine hundred people died.

The psychology of cults

Fanatics have their dreams, wherewith they weave
A paradise for a sect

John Keats, *The Fall of Hyperion*

Every cult, political or religious (insofar as these can be distinguished), is unique; and although it is arguable that the major world religions began as cults, most have become so institutionalized that they have lost many of their cultic features.[5] However, as our two case studies illustrate, there are some phenomena commonly found in both cults and religions (at least in their early days). These include a strict differentiation of leader and followers; rebellion against established authority; paranoia as the new movement seeks to establish itself; simplistic, dualistic thinking like that noted by Robert Lifton in Communist ideology (good/evil, believer/heretic, saved/damned); and a tendency towards utopian thinking. Finally, cults differ from religions and many other groups in the frequency and violence with which they self-destruct.

Leaders and followers

Jones, like Manson, was a charismatic leader who viewed himself (not without justification) as persecuted and who had a troubled background—that is, an experience of poverty, a disrupted family environment, discrimination, and other social disadvantages.[6] As time progressed both leaders seemed to teeter more and more on the edge of mental illness. Cults typically maintain an intense, isolated, and increasingly paranoid environment, fuelled by drugs and/or sex and powerful social forces. They experience the growing pressures of the discrepancies between the cult world (where the leader is God and everything is all right) and the world outside (where the leader is nobody and everyone is an enemy), as leader and followers drift further from reality. Cult followers typically consider their leaders divine or, at least, mandated by some supreme authority (God, fate, the forces of history, or whatever ethereal idea fits their particular world view) to change the universe.

Age, physical or psychological, is another factor relevant to cults. Many followers tend to join in their teens or early twenties, when they are still unformed adults—individuals not yet fully at ease in their own skins, seeking a sense of identity and security which the cult is able to provide. They are often described as lost, finding it difficult even to articulate, let alone satisfy, their needs. Moreover, many of these needs are embarrassing to older members of the rejected mainstream society: as Jonestown illustrates, many cult followers are idealists, genuinely and strongly seeking not only spiritual enlightenment but, also the chance to help other people. The cult is not only a path to redemption; it offers an opportunity to express goodness in a cynically hostile society. Unlike mainstream religions, it comes endowed with the thrill of establishment disapproval. Modern cults also differ from mainstream religions in two other ways. Firstly, cults often seem more youth-oriented, emphasizing their novelty and radicalism. This may be partly to do with their generally younger membership and partly with the modern fetish for youth, although there is a long tradition of appealing to the young which dates back at least as far as that archetypal cult leader the Pied Piper of Hamelin (the legend is medieval in origin). Secondly, cults generally operate much stricter information control. 'While a religion implies free, informed consent on the part of those who join it, people joining certain sects may be free when they join it, but are not informed, and, once they are informed, they are usually no longer free.'[7]

Rebelliousness and paranoia

Cults typically involve the rejection of established learning and authority (e.g. Manson's focus on alternative religions from Scientology to Satanism; Jones' dismissal of American capitalism). Since this rejection is associated with strong emotions (a Freudian might describe it as an Oedipal conflict, part of the process of defining oneself as an independent person), cult members often seem to assume that the rejected outside world will feel equally strongly, and strike back. This engenders a sense of paranoia which is highly cohesive and, in many cases (as in Jonestown), at least partially justified.[8] Families of members, for example, often go to great lengths to retrieve errant offspring, whether or not the offspring are legally adults. In the 1970s the process of deprogramming kidnapped cult members grew into a healthy industry, heavily criticized by observers for being even more like brainwashing than the actions of the cults themselves.[9]

Simplicity and purity

Cult members tend to demonize everything beyond the cult, thus justifying and even necessitating violence. They have an apocalyptic vision of society as evil and corrupt, a world which must be destroyed before the future they dream about can come to pass. Jones' followers worried about everything from cloning to sterilization to psychosurgery; all were potential weapons in the hands of the racist fascists they believed would shortly overwhelm America. The doomed world included everyone who did not share their beliefs—for a cult, all such people are impure. Thus in 1972, Jim Jones' Temple newspaper responded to a hostile newspaper article with the statement that 'nemesis would always strike down those who had the temerity to cross the Temple'.[10] Cult members, by contrast, are among the saved, virtuous as long as they remain members. The satirist Tom Lehrer, targeting folk singers who write protest songs, catches this attitude of smug conviction well:

We are the folk song army,
Every one of us cares.
We all hate poverty, war, and injustice
Unlike the rest of you squares.

Lehrer, 'The Folk Song Army'

Future-slanted thinking

Cults, like religions, typically hold out a promise: a utopian credo which urges that the present is unimportant in comparison with the glorious future available to God's Chosen People. Like many abstract ideas, cult visions are not only ambiguous but usefully untestable, unless of course the cult sets a specific date for the end of the world.[11] Utopian thinking, in other words, makes ethereal ideas even more ethereal, and hence more dangerous.[12] As Hannah Arendt points out, 'there is hardly a better way to avoid discussion than by releasing an argument from the control of the present and by saying that only the future can reveal its merits'.[13]

For Manson, as for Jones, the coming apocalypse became an obsession. He had, he felt, been chosen to start the revolution which would bring it about. But his conception of Helter Skelter was not original. Cult leaders often emphasize their supposed originality; in fact the same ideas resurface again and again. Indeed, when you compare Manson's murders with the fundamental Western template for apocalypse, the Bible's Book of Revelation (by which he was heavily influenced), they look pitifully small, a pathetic attempt to play God. In the original vision (from Revelation 16), which Manson hoped that Helter Skelter would usher in, we are promised 'noisome and grievous' sores, the seas and rivers becoming 'as the blood of a dead man', fire, pain and darkness, drought, thunder and lightning, a world-shaking earthquake, and a great hail. *That* is an apocalypse.

Violent finales

Finally, the tendency toward self-destructiveness is one of the most disturbing aspects of cults. Many human groups show a pattern of birth, growth, stability, and gradual decline; but some cults do not, ending instead in catastrophe. They are the best known; their death agonies bring them into the public gaze. The Manson Family's killings, the mass suicides and murders of Jonestown, the Ugandan 'Movement for the Restoration of the Ten Commandments of God', Waco, and the Order of the Solar Temple all made world headlines; all were largely unknown outside directly affected communities until they, in Waco's case literally, went up in flames.

The twentieth century gave birth to many horrors. It also gave us modern scientific attempts to understand them. With the development of the science of

35

psychology came research which for the first time applied psychological methods to the study of human groups. Since then, social psychologists have learned a lot about how groups are created and maintained, and the pressures which bind individuals together or drive them apart. This is not a social psychology textbook, and I will not attempt to do more than summarize some aspects of an immense literature.[14] But social psychology, although it has not yet considered brainwashing to any extent, has much to contribute to our understanding of it. Nowhere is this clearer than when considering groups such as cults.

Why are groups so important?

Individualism is a potent doctrine which has been extremely influential in the development of Western civilization. To see oneself reflected in its mirror is to admire a proudly independent being, a self as solid as a rock. Given this emphasis, and given how much I will be saying about the negative effects of some groups, it is worth asking why groups are not only important but essential, especially when it comes to dealing with ethereal ideas. The answer comes from one of the most influential arguments in modern philosophy, Ludwig Wittgenstein's criticism of the idea of a private language:[15]

Let us imagine the following case. I want to keep a diary about the recurrence of a certain sensation. To this end I associate it with the sign 'S' and write this sign in a calendar for every day on which I have the sensation.

The sign S is a word in my private language—the word for 'a certain sensation'. Only I know what it means. But how do I know what it means?

Can I point to the sensation? Not in the ordinary sense. But I speak, or write the sign down, and at the same time I concentrate my attention on the sensation— and so, as it were, point to it inwardly.—But what is this ceremony for? For that is all it seems to be! A definition surely serves to establish the meaning of a sign.—Well, that is done precisely by the concentrating of my attention; for in this way I impress upon myself the connexion between the sign and the sensation.—But 'I impress it on myself' can only mean: this process brings it about that I remember the connexion *right* in the future.

I know what S means because I am using it the same way that I used it previously—to refer to a sensation I am having. But how can I be sure that the sensation is the same both times? Sensations are notoriously ill defined, especially when they are evaluative. Does it even make sense to say that my brother's delight when he holds his daughter in his arms is the same on two successive days, let alone the same as my father's delight in giving me a hug? Just because our public language calls all three 'delight' does not mean my father feels exactly what my brother feels. Likewise, I cannot be sure that I'm remembering my sensation correctly and not using S in a different way each time. In other words:

But in the present case I have no criterion of correctness. One would like to say: whatever is going to seem right to me is right. And that only means that here we can't talk about 'right'.

To check whether I am using S in the same way every time, I cannot rely on my own judgement, because that standard may shift without my noticing. Only by comparing my usage against other people's can I find an independent criterion. Meaning is not some strange external imposition; words mean what we use them to mean. Language must be a shared, public enterprise, with each participant using others as a reference point. The same is true when we come to decide what we feel about ethereal ideas, which are after all linguistically expressed. We need to refer to what other people have said and thought about them, not only because one individual human being cannot match or even contemplate the knowledge accumulated by societies over centuries of moral debate (why reinvent the wheel?), but also because we cannot trust ourselves to remember our (evaluative) sensations accurately. This is why the dream of control is so lethal—for those it possesses as well as for their victims—when taken to extremes. We need to have things (and people) around us which are beyond our control, because their independence is the only way we have of making sure that we remain in touch with reality, of checking, as Wittgenstein says, that our thoughts and the words we use to shape them are still 'right'.

We need groups of ourselves to be able to trust our language, to assess and to remember our assessments of the ideas we barter using that language. However, as noted above, for our most powerful ethereal ideas the problem comes when groups reach conflicting conclusions over what these 'essentially contested' concepts mean. We do not need to enter the fictional world of *Nineteen Eighty-Four* to find a situation where 'war is peace' or 'freedom is slavery'; our own world is full of them. Sometimes the groups involved are deliberately trying to manipulate public opinion; but sometimes they fervently, and irreconcilably, believe their own descriptions. Often, confronted with such passion, we apply the label 'cult'.

The structure of a cult

As noted above, a cult is a hierarchical group: there is usually one leader and a number of followers (who may themselves have varying status, e.g. novice, adept, leader's favourite, and so on). Leader and followers bring very different needs to, and derive different satisfactions from, the group. In psychological terms, leaders raise the issue of charisma, followers that of dependence. Both are bound together in the group by a shared 'cognitive landscape': a commonwealth of ideas, beliefs, attitudes, and feelings. In later chapters we will look at leaders and followers in more detail. However, there are some psychological mechanisms which appear to operate in all sorts of groups, no matter how arbitrarily defined. There are also some mechanisms which are common to many cults. We need to consider the techniques which cult groups use to enforce conformity of belief among their members, and compare those with the totalist techniques used in brainwashing.

Ingroups and outgroups

East is East, and West is West, and never the twain shall meet
Rudyard Kipling, *The Ballad of East and West*

From our most low-level sensory processes to our treatment of other human beings, grouping things is one of the basic activities of human brains. Temporal coincidence or spatial proximity can be enough, as many visual illusions show. If we hear a sound about the time we see an object, we assume that the object is making the sound unless we have learned otherwise. We cluster, we classify, and over the course of a lifetime we acquire innumerable category concepts. We use these to speed up our interpretations of the world. If I can judge a novel object to be a member of the category 'cat' I immediately have access to all sorts of stored information about the new object ('eats meat', 'may scratch', 'could not comfortably be swung in my kitchen') without having to work it out anew. This gives me considerable savings in time and energy, and a definite survival edge.

Open up any popular neuroscience book and you will probably find some version of a statement extolling the immense complexity of the human brain. This intricacy makes human beings among the most complicated things that other human beings have to deal with. If we are not to grind to a stammering halt in our social interactions, we need short cuts. We will come back to these heuristics in the next chapter, when we see how advertisers have used them to part us from our earnings. For now, we can note that categorization is one of the strategies we reach for. If I define a person as a member of a group, my knowledge of that group will colour my responses to the person.

As Wittgenstein pointed out, a concept which has no conceptual borders, no possible counterexample, is spread so thinly as to be meaningless.[16] The word 'possible' is vital; actual counterexamples may or may not exist. I can define you as a member of the group of 'people who excrete' even though I know that in practice that group has no counterexamples: every human being produces waste matter. The concept of 'people who excrete' is meaningful because I can easily (i.e. without tying myself in logical knots) conceive of a human being who never excretes: movies are full of them. Similarly for groups, the very act of defining a group—us—implies the possibility, and usually the actual existence, of that-which-the-group-is-not—them. This tendency to define ingroups (us) and out-groups (them), thought by social psychologists to be at the heart of prejudice, seems so basic to human beings that they will group people as 'in' or 'out' on amazingly spurious criteria: not just sex, age, appearance, or beliefs, but even clearly arbitrary assignations made by experimenters in psychology laboratories.[17]

In general, natural groups (those *not* formed, like social psychology experiments, for investigative reasons) seem to encourage attraction between their members. This attraction is not restricted to romance or sex: we prefer to be with people who 'provide us with rewards'[18] and who 'are similar to us at a very basic level on such aspects as beliefs, interests, personal background, and values'.[19] We also tend to be attracted to people (or objects) who are physically or functionally (e.g. in cyberspace) nearby: the mere fact of repeated encounters with them seems to increase our liking for them.[20] Human beings engaging in social interactions tend to synchronize their posture, movements, vocalizations, and facial expressions, usually without being aware of doing so: this leads to both their behaviours and their moods converging, a process labelled 'emotional contagion' by Elaine Hatfield and colleagues in their book of the same name.[21] Contagion increases perceived similarity and hence mutual attraction.

Thus in cults we would expect to find that members often share not only their beliefs and interests, but their background and basic values as well. We would also expect to find that being a cult member fulfils needs—is rewarding—for both leader and followers. Detailed analyses of cults, for example Eileen Barker's *The Making of a Moonie*, suggest this is the case.

Whether the group is formed naturally or not, it can have considerable effects on thought and behaviour. People seem to consider group membership in terms of a cost–benefit ratio, weighing the rewards they receive from membership against the efforts they have to put into group activities. This can lead them to make huge efforts to join one group or to escape another. (Such efforts can affect how group membership is valued: groups which are hard to join evoke more commitment, which is why some groups have such fearsome initiation rites.)[22] Once people are members, they continue to be influenced by the group via group norms and roles. As Parks and Sanna point out in *Group Performance and Interaction*, 'Norms tell us what actions will and will not be tolerated by other group members.' For example, having sex at a university graduation ceremony is not specifically proscribed in the regulations, but everyone present knows it is not the done thing. Group members are also typically assigned roles

39

which specify sets of behaviours they are expected to carry out: for example, becoming a charity's treasurer. Both norms and roles serve the same heuristic function as the categories described earlier: they speed up and smooth out intragroup relations, making the group more efficient and more comfortable to be in.

Every human being is a member of numerous distinct groups, and these differ in the amount of their members' cognitive landscapes which they occupy: that is to say, the importance which they have for each member. Membership of the same amateur football team may be viewed very differently by the player with long-term ambitions and his colleague who just wants a little fitness training. Likewise, membership of two different groups may mean different things to the same individual. My sister-in-law would define herself as both 'an accountant' and 'a resident of Birmingham', but the former makes up more of her identity than the latter. Cults occupy much more of their members' time and energy than many everyday groups: they seem to loom large, even take over, their partici-pants' cognitive landscapes.

The self and its world

But man, proud man
Dress'd in a little brief authority,
Most ignorant of what he's most assur'd,
His glassy essence

William Shakespeare, *Measure for Measure*

This idea of the cognitive landscape—the psychological space which each of us inhabits—is closely related to the idea of our self. Just as we are members of many different groups, we define ourselves in many different ways. What the self may actually be has been an important philosophical question for centuries. René Descartes conceived it in the Christian tradition as a unitary mental object, a view I have labelled with the metaphor of 'diamond minds'.[23] Modern ideas about selves regard them as much more plural and changeable. I will return to this topic, but for now I will say only that the view of the self adopted in this book will be very much along the pluralist line: I will define it as the total set of all beliefs held in an individual brain. This means that normally we define ourselves only partially—as a 'scientist', 'British national', or whatever. This is deliberate; apart from the time it would take to list all our beliefs, we do not *want* to think of ourselves as people who excrete. But group memberships, whether acknow-ledged or not, make up a large part of our cognitive landscape, and beliefs about them constitute much of our self. This has an important implication: the more valuable the group to us, the more likely we are to behave as if the group is equivalent to our 'self', assuming that rewards or dangers to the group benefit or threaten us.

Among the best established findings in social psychology are those of 'self-serving biases'. We favour ourselves, consciously if we think we can get away with it, often unconsciously, whether we are sharing out resources or explaining actions. The same is true for those extensions of ourselves, our favourite ingroups. For example, we tend to attribute our own success (or that of ingroup members) to internal factors ('my skill got me that job'), but an outgroup member's success to external factors ('the interviewer plays golf with his father'). For failure, the story is reversed ('the interviewer was biased against me', 'he didn't get the job because he's lazy'). This favouring of the ingroup and denigration of the outgroup is seen most clearly in the lethal strength of some prejudices. In cults it can take an extreme form, with the ingroup being glorified as the 'saved' children of God, while the outgroup beyond the cult is demonized and damned so that being alien becomes a moral fault.

Evolutionarily, these mechanisms make sense. The group provides much of one's immediate environment; favouring group members therefore encourages goodwill and strengthens group cohesion, defined as 'the result of all the forces acting on members to keep them engaged in the group'.[24] Other members are more likely to help you in future if you have helped them in the past, so it makes sense to favour them over outgroup members. For Jim Jones' cult, the outgroup *was* hostile from early on in the cult's development. Jones' followers had committed their lives to him; it made no sense for them to waste time and energy building bridges with a world which, as far as they could see, was out to destroy them. People are often hostile to people whose ideas differ from theirs; as the fictional example of Robert Heinlein's *Stranger in a Strange Land* shows, even when a cult leader's differences seem initially to be accepted, intolerance readily erupts.

Group pressures

Groups are bound together by various factors, including the perceived success of the group in achieving whatever goals it may have set (or sometimes its failure to do so, as many football fans can testify), the group's value to its members and the extent to which group goals match individual goals, the mutual liking of members for each other, and external forces (the extent to which personal goals can be satisfied more easily outside, or inside, the group).[25] Once committed to the group, members often adjust their own beliefs and values to make them more similar to those of other members; differences grate on the nerves and threaten the impression of solidarity. This leads to one of the most common problems with cult thinking: reality drift. Lower-status cult members will tend to shift their beliefs towards the beliefs of higher-status members, and particularly the cult leader; the reverse is not the case. If the leader's beliefs closely match the way the world actually is, this will benefit the other members: their cognitive landscapes will more accurately represent reality. Unfortunately, leaders often have beliefs which are very far from matching reality and which can become more extreme as they are encouraged by their followers. The predilection of many cult leaders for abstract, ambiguous, and therefore unchallengeable ideas can further reduce the likelihood of reality testing, while the intense milieu control exerted by cults over their members means that most of the reality available for testing is supplied by the group environment. This is seen in the phenomenon of 'groupthink', alleged to have occurred, notoriously, during the Bay of Pigs fiasco. The US government's series of disastrous decisions ratcheted up tensions between the US and Cuba, tensions which would lead to the brink of nuclear war. The charisma of the American president, John F. Kennedy, the closed nature of the decisive meetings, the strong anti-Russian convictions of those making the decisions, and the importance of abstract ideas such as 'the future of the free world', all contributed to an assessment of the political situation which was deeply unrealistic and very nearly lethal.[26]

Cults are typically highly cohesive, with members sharing many beliefs, performing the same routines and rituals, sometimes even wearing the same clothes. The emotions generated by the cult situation, and the simplistic nature of many cult doctrines, make cult beliefs temptingly simple and the pressures to hold them very strong. When one has committed to a belief, renouncing it is unpleasant in any situation; one is renouncing part of one's own identity. Faced with the disapproval of close friends and revered leaders, it can be all but impossible to walk away. As the group becomes more cohesive, and its importance in its members' lives greater, the difference between the group and the outside world also increases. The group tends to practise increasingly strict boundary control to protect against intrusion by others. This can include 'deviant' behaviour—glazed expressions, xenophobia, or aggression—towards any outsider perceived as threatening. This in turn provokes hostility from the outgroup, which further enhances cohesiveness.

Group membership can provide two comforting sensations: that the member is not alone, and that he or she is not responsible. For highly cohesive groups, the group can become an entity in its own right with its own power of action, often personified by the leader, who takes on the role of supernatural protector and relieves the individual of the need to make his own decisions. This diffusion of responsibility through the group can be one of the most dangerous phenomena in strong groups, as it can lower the threshold for violent action by reducing the normal social constraints (e.g. fear of being blamed and punished) which would deter most individuals. Knowing intellectually that there are people out there who would disapprove of what one proposes to do is very different from living among people who are clearly showing their disapproval. The closed nature of the Manson Family in effect isolated its members from the immediate sensations of disapproval which they knew intellectually they could expect to receive if they committed murder. That stored information about what society would think of them, as killers, was outweighed by the message from their environment: that murder would gain them social credit and group benefits, that the prospective victims were not real humans (not one of us), and that they were not really, individually, responsible for the murders.

Are cults totalitarian?

Chapter 1 discussed criteria put forward by the psychiatrist Robert Lifton for assessing whether a belief system is totalitarian or not (see Table 1, p. 17). Using these criteria, we can see that many of the most dangerous cults can be described as totalitarian. Milieu control and mystical manipulation are typical features, facilitated by cult rituals and also by the physical isolation characteristic of many cults (Jonestown, deep in the Guyanan jungle, is a clear example). The demand for purity manifests itself in rituals, for example initiation rites, and in the sharp dichotomy between ingroup and outgroup. The cult of confession is a large part of many cult members' lives, for example through group prayer, and corresponding to this is the unchallengeable nature of cult doctrines: Lifton's sacred science. Loading the language frequently occurs, as even a short glance at cult literature can show, and all too often cult members are expected to give their lives if necessary for the preservation of the cult. This primacy of doctrine over person coexists with the dispensing of existence—the right granted to many cult leaders to determine the fate of their followers. Manson did not actually kill his Family, but Jim Jones made a choice which ended the lives of hundreds of his followers.

Are cult members brainwashed?

As Chapter 1 showed, brainwashing has a number of aspects: insult, process, symbol (ethereal idea), or concept of last resort. Cults, readily defined as outgroups by the rest of us, invite insults, and often we reach for the easy, lazy explanation when confronted with them, using terms such as 'brainwashed' that mark them as different but which we don't really understand. The very term 'cult' has acquired negative connotations, when in fact there is evidence that at least some cults can offer considerable membership benefits: reduced psychological distress and improved emotional well-being, less drug use, healthier diets, and less stressful lifestyles.[27] Of course, many cults increase their members' stress by making extreme demands for lifestyle change—giving up worldly goods, for example—but the cults also provide mechanisms which relieve distress, such as strong positive feedback from other group members.

Chapter 1 also noted several features often found in alleged brainwashing situations, including the use of emotions and the bizarre nature of the beliefs which may be adopted. In cults, belief systems unrelated to reality or disadvantageous for the believer are common: Manson's followers ended in prison, Jones' in suicide. The belief change involved often seems considerable (one reads, for example, of previously dedicated capitalists giving up all their possessions for a vision of a socialist utopia) although this impression may be superficial if there are deeper, unfulfilled needs which are satisfied by cult membership. Personality change, over a shockingly short interval, is often alleged by those outside the cult, as are the difficulties of communicating with members who are either hostile or impervious to argument. Strong emotions are used in many cults to increase members' commitment to their group. Once the cult is established, coercive techniques may be applied to keep members in the group (as the Concerned Relatives claimed took place at Jonestown). However, as Marc Galanter argues, cult members do not always adopt cult views against their will; rather, 'in voluntary conversions contact must be maintained in a subtle (or deceptive) way, without forcing the individual to comply with the group's views'. As noted earlier, cults differ widely. Some use coercion, some deception, some simply appeal successfully to certain people's needs. Most reflect the personalities of their leaders to some degree. A more paranoid leader, for example, increases the risk that the cult will be dangerous.

What about the technicalities: brainwashing as process? We have seen that many of the most terrifying aspects of cults can be addressed by social psychological research on group cohesion, emotional bonding, and diffusion of responsibility. There does not seem to be a particular process called 'brainwashing' which is distinct from these other psychological processes. That is, the forces that operate in extreme cults, such as the Manson family and Jonestown, seem to be simply more powerful versions of forces which can be found in many other human groups. Beliefs about groups are part of one's beliefs about oneself: the more important the group, the larger it looms in its members' cognitive landscapes. Such cognitive landscapes are a limited resource—even the most fine-grained and well-developed self is a finite treasury. This means that as the group takes over more and more of the self, members define themselves less and less as independent beings. When the group is all that matters, when personal responsibility is diffused across the group, then the leader can achieve a level of totalitarian control worthy of Big Brother. There is nothing magical about how this can occur. The nuclear attack on Hiroshima was described in awestruck, even religious terms by those involved (Robert Oppenheimer's famous reaction—'I am become Death, the destroyer of worlds'—was taken from the *Bhagavad Gita*, a Hindu religious text).[28] Yet the effects were predictable—and predicted—by the physicists who gave us atomic energy. There was no magic in the Hiroshima bomb; it followed the laws of physics. There was no magic in the air at Jonestown either.

As for the symbolic aspect of brainwashing, the dream of control, we certainly see this featuring in many cults. When the apocalypse comes, it is the cult which will survive and inherit the new dispensation; the rest of the world will be dead, or at best enslaved. In the here and now, the cult leader typically insists on increasingly severe control over his members' lives, often encouraging them to refer to him as God or God's representative on earth. Indeed, this tendency towards 'control creep' is characteristic of religions and political systems as well as the most violent and self-destructive cults.[29] In short, brainwashing as mysterious psychological technique is surplus to requirements when we need to explain cults. Brainwashing as control fantasy, on the other hand, remains extremely relevant.

What makes some groups turn nasty?

I distrust the incommunicable; it is the source of all violence
Jean-Paul Sartre, *What is Literature?*

The examples discussed above suggest a number of factors which contribute towards a group becoming dangerous to itself or to others. One is isolation, psychological or physical. A lack of feedback from the external world not only makes it difficult for group members to track drift in their moral norms, but also increases their sense of threat: as any child knows, the void of a room in darkness is much easier to populate with horrors than that same room with the light on and all its contents visible. To dangerous groups, the threat to the group's collective ego from the world outside can seem enormous. As the case of Jonestown shows, this paranoia is not always entirely unjustified; sometimes the group's perceived opponents really are out to get it.

Group size is also important. For humans, there appears to be a tipping point when the group acquires more than around 150 members. Robin Dunbar suggests that 'At this size, orders can be implemented and unruly behaviour controlled on the basis of personal loyalties and direct man-to-man contacts. With larger groups, this becomes impossible'.[30] It seems that 'once a community exceeds 150 people, it becomes increasingly difficult to control its members by peer pressure alone'. Instead, a formal management hierarchy must be put in place, or the group will split into competing subgroups, losing overall cohesion. Small groups are therefore more likely to act on their beliefs in harmful ways, as terrorists of all political persuasions have known for years. Many religious or political movements are structured as 'social comets': a small core group of dedicated believers trailing a cloud of less committed followers (the animal rights/animal welfare campaigns are an example). This suggests that one antidote to small group venom might simply be to boost the numbers and hope that infighting will solve the problem. Unfortunately, what tends to happen is that the group does split—but only into even more venomous subgroups.

Another relevant factor is the type of ideas which such groups often espouse. Both their goals and their demons tend to be ethereal, and hence heavily value-laden. Linked to strong emotions, they facilitate commitment. They also bolster the group's sense of superiority, of being saved when all around are damned. Yet that sense of privilege coexists with a vivid awareness of the threat inherent in being one small light in a sea of darkness. (In Chapter 5, this dangerous combination of high esteem and a threat to that esteem will reappear when we consider the characteristics of offenders who readily resort to physical aggression.) This sense of threat helps to bind the group closer together.

We are back to religion and politics, many of whose core concepts are ethereal, ideally suited to raising the emotional temperature of their believers. Perhaps this is why atrocities are so often associated with religious or political motives. However, it is the abstract, ambiguous nature of the ideas, *not* their specific content, which is so dangerous. Committed atheists often condemn religion for causing the deaths of large numbers of people, citing religious wars and fundamentalist terrorism.[31] Yet the worst mass killings in human history, those which disgraced the twentieth century, were fuelled by beliefs renowned for their atheist content. Joseph Stalin's reign of terror saw the widespread suppression of religious institutions, as well as millions of deaths. The Cultural Revolution, whose dead are also estimated in the tens of millions, was spearheaded by an atheist, Mao Tse-Tung; and the Khmer Rouge are remembered for their killing fields, not for their faith.[32] Which religion has this much blood on its conscience? These ideologies, Nazi, Soviet, Chinese, and Cambodian Communist, were lethal at least in part because their ideas were ethereal, not because those ideas were 'atheist' or 'religious'.[33] The same argument applies to politics. Those ideologies (groups, individuals) which rely on ethereal ideas, and hence facilitate totalitarian thinking, are more dangerous than those which do not.

Summary and conclusions

Groups are a fundamental aspect of human existence. Often they benefit and comfort their members: cult membership in the West, while espousing a way of life very different from the capitalist milieu, can sometimes provide such considerable benefits for both psychological and physical health that it might almost be seen as a rational choice to make, a valid antidote to capitalism. However, the fact that cults adopt such different narratives from the societies in which they live challenges the assumptions of those societies, and provokes what can be extreme hostility, especially in relatives of cult members. The anticult movement has found the term brainwashing, tainted from birth with the stench of propaganda, a useful stick with which to beat its enemies.

And the fears of anticultists are not without some justification. Sometimes groups, particularly small groups, can become extremely dangerous. This can occur particularly when they are highly cohesive, when group membership is extremely important to individual members (perhaps because of perceived or actual persecution by an outgroup), and when abstract, unchallengeable ideas are coupled with extremely strong emotions. Because abstract, ambiguous ideas and strong emotions are characteristic of religious and political belief systems, they are often particularly associated with dangerous groups—those whose members are prepared to attack or kill outgroup members. Such groups often show features of totalitarian thinking. They use a number of processes to attract and maintain new members. Some of these can be so apparently compelling that they attract the label of brainwashing, but all of them appear explicable in social psychological terms. Taking a closer look often reveals characteristic group mechanisms at work, and demonstrates the way in which being a member of such cults fulfils the deepest needs of both leaders and followers.

In later chapters we shall look at ways in which the dangers of such groups may be minimized. We will consider in detail the characteristics which make some people leaders and others followers; and we will return to the dream of control. First, however, it is time to consider allegations of brainwashing in two rather more commonplace situations: advertising and the media, and education.

Chapter 3: The power of persuasion

Sed nihil est tam incredibile, quod non dicendo fiat probabile
[Nothing is so unbelievable that oratory cannot make it acceptable]
Marcus Tullius Cicero, *The Stoic Paradoxes*, 'Preface'

In Chapter 1, we saw how intensive, personal, painful, and terrifying brainwashing can be when force is used in the quest for thought control, as for example in some cults. However, brainwashing has also been alleged in two very different fields of human endeavour: advertising and the media, and education. Both seek to change minds, though for different reasons, and both are thought to wield considerable power. Unlike brainwashing by force, however, they generally employ less coercive methods, relying instead on stealthier forms of persuasion. Both are framed within, and transmit, a set of beliefs about the world, an ideology. That ideology defines the social roles of individuals as State subjects, teaching them their proper place in the *status quo*. The ideology itself may never be explicitly stated, and the individuals who purvey the adverts or lessons may not even be aware that they are reinforcing certain beliefs, but the underlying message is all the more powerful for being covert. In other words, education and the media are part of what the Marxist philosopher Louis Althusser called the 'ideological apparatus' of the State; they maintain and reproduce (instil in younger members) the beliefs of those who dominate the State. Ideological apparatuses may use force or stealth, or both, to impose their messages; advertising and education, for example, have little recourse to coercion compared with brainwashing by force. Are they, then, brainwashing by stealth, or are they not brainwashing at all? To answer the charge we must look at each in turn.

Advertising and the media

Advertising may be described as the science of arresting human intelligence
long enough to get money from it
        Stephen Leacock, *The Garden of Folly*, 'The Perfect Salesman'

Dynasties are out of fashion in the West. The twentieth century was supposed to emphasize equality, merit over heredity, the power of the masses. Yet even as some old established dynasties collapsed a new one was taking shape. Two of its members would between them determine much of the profile of that century, and their impact continues in the next. Sigmund Freud gave us modern sex, while his nephew Edward Bernays gave us modern advertising. This is not a book on the history of advertising nor a detailed analysis of the techniques used by advertisers to seduce us into buying their products.[1] Instead, I will look at the persuasion methods used by salesmen, governments, and other compliance professionals—what the social psychologist Robert Cialdini calls 'weapons of influence'—in order to shed light on the allegation of brainwashing.

In his book *Influence*, Cialdini groups persuasion tactics into six types of weapons of influence (apart from naked appeals to self-interest, which he takes as given). Firstly, commitment and consistency traps make use of the fact that we prefer to appear consistent to ourselves. Therefore, if we can be persuaded to make a small commitment we will be much more likely to follow this with a bigger one, which we may not actually have wanted to make, if that larger commitment is consistent with its smaller predecessor. Cialdini gives the example of phone calls soliciting for charities where the caller begins by asking after your health. 'The caller's intent with this sort of introduction is not merely to seem friendly and caring. It is to get you to respond—as you normally do to such polite, superficial inquiries—with a polite, superficial comment of your own: "Just fine" or "Real good" or "I'm doing great, thanks." Once you have publicly stated that all is well, it becomes much easier for the solicitor to corner you into aiding those for whom all is not well.' Tests of the underlying theory, that people who have asserted their own well-being 'find it awkward to appear stingy in the context of their own admittedly favored circumstances', showed that the procedure was very effective.

A second weapon of influence uses reciprocity: our tendency to feel obliged to a person who gives us something, no matter how trivial or unwanted the gift. This leaves us open to persuasion by the giver, and to get rid of the feeling of obligation we may agree to giving back a much larger gift than we received. An example also discussed by the social psychologists Anthony Pratkanis and Elliot Aronson in *Age of Propaganda* is the Hare Krishna movement, who successfully increased falling revenues by having disciples first give a single flower to anyone they asked for a donation.

Two other widely used weapons of influence rely on the authority and the likeability of the persuader. An example of authority is the use of television actors who play doctors (but have no medical qualifications) to recommend medical products. Their authority is illusory, but they still shift stock. (I will return to authority in Chapter 4.) An example of likeability is the use of film stars, athletes, and big smiles to promote just about any product.

Cialdini's last two weapons of influence employ the principles of scarcity and of 'social proof'. The former makes use of our instinct that if something is scarce it must be valuable by artificially restricting availability, or emphasizing the scarcity of the product ('Limited Edition', 'Buy Now While Stocks Last', etc.). The principle of social proof is that, rather than think things out for ourselves, we often just follow the herd, working on the assumption that so many eager others can't be wrong. Despite some catastrophic failures (the history of Western stock exchanges is a good place to look for examples), this assumption often works well, as indeed do the assumptions underlying the other five weapons of influence. That is why they have developed: as heuristics, saving us the time and effort of thought. Sometimes, when we are sufficiently motivated, we stop and think about the influences we experience. When we do not we are open to exploitation.

The *Merriam-Webster Dictionary* gives two definitions of brainwashing. The first, similar to the *Oxford English Dictionary* definition given in Chapter 1, is: 'A forcible indoctrination to induce someone to give up basic political, social, or religious beliefs and attitudes and to accept contrasting regimented ideas.' The second is: 'persuasion by propaganda or salesmanship'. What this has in common with the first definition is the use of pressures to override the victim's capacity to think rationally about his or her situation and beliefs. This overriding of reason is what a good advertisement aims to achieve. Failure is giving the person time and space to think 'yeah very nice but I don't want or need that product'. The advert will therefore try and tap directly into emotions, hoping that they will bypass this more rational approach to the message being put across. Often the approach is to arouse a negative emotion (guilt, anxiety) and then present buying the product as the only, or easiest, way to remove that emotion. Alternatively, the product may be associated with a positive emotion, to encourage the assumption that buying it will lead to pleasant feelings. Loud music, bright colours, fast pacing, all these may be used to discourage critical analysis of the advert by distracting the viewer from the fact that it is only an advert, a way of selling a product. More sophisticated adverts use humour as a positive reinforcer: making someone laugh is a great way to make them feel sympathetic to your position. Whatever the exact method, the aim is the same: don't think about our product (or you may decide you don't want it), just absorb the message that having our product would improve your quality of life.

Does this exploitation of our emotions, and our laziness, constitute brain-washing? As I have already noted, force is not usually an option in advertising. The closest most advertisers can get to force is blanket coverage for their product, but this is not the same as having a captive audience. The watcher is, at least in principle, free to channel-hop, discard the brochure, get up and make a cup of tea. Many people do. Depending on the medium involved, the degree of freedom may be reduced (it's harder to avoid billboards, for example). But there is no overt compulsion either to look or to buy.

Brainwashing in fiction is often depicted as a coercive torture, but its conceptual heart, the deliberate and manipulative changing of belief, need not require force. Advertising is not coercive, but it is a deliberate attempt to change minds. Companies do not promote their products by accident, and their aim is primarily to increase their profits by removing money from customers. Frequently companies will claim to have identified needs for their products, and to be simply supplying those needs. Who could deny that needs ought to be fulfilled?

Yet we should be sceptical of this explosion in consumer needs. The ability of our brains to associate powerful emotions with abstract ideas means that it is relatively easy to associate a product with a basic desire. The need is not for the product particularly, it is for the fulfilment of the basic desire; but we accept the product as a proxy (and then wonder why, when we get it home, we may feel vaguely disappointed). A traditional example, rarer now in mainstream advertising, is the sales technique which promotes certain cars by draping semi-naked females across their bonnets (the target audience was assumed to be male and heterosexual). Cars are machines for transporting one comfortably and conveniently from A to B; most are really quite similar in design and construction. Having an attractive woman sprawled across the front could scratch the paintwork and would do nothing for the aerodynamics even if she took all her clothes off. Not that the eager buyer was likely actually to find such a vision in his local showroom. Rather, the advertisers assumed that their customers would associate one particular lump of metal and plastic with sexual desire. The implication is clear: buying this product will satisfy that desire and improve your sex life. Freud and Bernays come together—in a satanic embrace, some would say—in such commercials.

The link between advertising and the promised fulfilment of desires is not, of course, restricted to basic desires. New needs—as opposed to needs for proxy products—can be created. Indeed, the number of new human needs apparently identified in the twentieth century should reassure us that at the least human creativity is alive and well. An example, and one which certain companies have found extremely useful over the years, is that of biological cravings: addictions. Human beings, unless they are extremely unlucky, are not born with biological needs for nicotine, opiates, or other addictive substances. However, ingesting these substances can throw the body's biochemistry out of kilter, creating a need (to renew the balance) where none existed before. In this case, the products sold are not proxies: they directly fulfil the addict's needs. The strength of these needs, and the ease with which addiction develops, have made such products extremely profitable.

Advertising certainly aims to change belief. The advertiser wants to alter your cognitive landscape such that your previous indifference, aversion, or total ignorance vis-à-vis Brand X is replaced by a more favourable attitude towards it. Ideally, you rush out and buy the thing as soon as possible. Realistically, you may be a little more likely to buy it next time you see it in the supermarket; you may choose it over Brand Y, or you may 'just give it a try'. Theoretically, a successful advert will change belief over a very short time interval, resulting in your holding, consciously or unconsciously, the view that obtaining the product will fulfil a need of yours. This belief may be unrelated to reality (how much did buying that new car really do for your sex life?) and extremely disadvantageous for your bank balance. However, it is rare for an advert, even a successful one, to change more than a small number of beliefs; and there is to my knowledge no recorded instance of someone watching an advert and emerging with a different personality. Thus the global effects on the cognitive landscape described in cases of brainwashing are not matched by the power of advertising: we are talking erosion, not earthquakes.

Those who describe advertising as brainwashing, however, are not usually intent on singling out particular adverts. Rather they deplore the cumulative effect on our cultural environment of a large number of adverts over a period of time. The same argument is made about violence in television, cinema, and the news media. No single gory murder may be responsible for desensitizing modern youth, no single sugary advert for rendering it increasingly overweight, but the net impact of visual violence can be considerable. Is this a valid claim?

There is in fact considerable evidence that mass media models of the world we live in have a significant impact on us. These portrayals of 'real life'—which may, like a cultist's view of reality, bear little resemblance to the real thing—can shape our behaviour in ways we may not recognize. Studies in Britain and the United States, for example, consistently show a fear of crime which is out of proportion to the actual risks of being a victim, but which reflects the proportion of attention devoted by the media to crime. Television shows provide extremely distorted versions of reality. As Pratkanis and Aronson point out in the *Age of Propaganda*, in the world of television beautiful people are much more common than in real life, as are doctors and lawyers, while positive role models of scientists, the elderly, the disabled, or ethnic minorities are much less common. We all think we know it's not real, yet US studies have clearly shown that people who watch more television have a more distorted, racist world view than those who watch less. Television can affect behaviour as well as attitudes.[2]

This brings us back to the discussion in Chapter 1 about brainwashing as a method of changing belief, and specifically the observation that, to date, influence technicians have had to rely on indirect methods of changing beliefs by changing the victims' environments. What critics of advertising may be concerned about may be not so much the mystical—and mythical—power inherent in single adverts. There is no magic process which can condemn all who watch a commercial extolling Brand X to roam the earth unsatisfied until they get their hands on it. The fact that sometimes people behave as if only a certain product will make their lives complete (visit a toy store just before Christmas if you doubt this) is not due to magic, but to the operation of one of Cialdini's weapons of influence (in the case of the toy store, scarcity achieved by deliberately limiting stocks). No, what bothers the critics seems to be the idea that the environmental effects of advertising and the media are shaping our minds in subtle ways which we do not recognize. We can select any one of hundreds of magazines from our local supermarket—yet we rarely stop to ask why all those magazines contain so much about sex and physical attractiveness, why the faces on the covers are so unrepresentative of readers, why certain topics are covered in detail and others completely ignored. Someone makes those decisions, and makes them with profits in mind, but it certainly isn't us.

In other words, the critics fear that advertising and the media may be contributing to our immersion in an environment which is in fact becoming increasingly manipulative. Someone (or several someones)—the media, the government, or pick your pet bugbear[3]—is setting our agendas for us, dictating not what we think but what we think about. To borrow from Pratkanis and Aronson again, 'Consider someone who watches TV and repeatedly sees competing adverts extolling the virtues of Chevys and of Fords. It is unlikely (in most cases) that any given advert will cause that person to switch his or her preference for one car over the other. However, it is very likely that this heavy dose of car adverts will lead that person to want a car and to give little consideration to alternative modes of transportation.' Such dosing also primes the person with the sort of criteria on which, when they come to buy their car, they are likely to judge it. Such criteria apply well to the unrealistically open roads featured in many car adverts, but may not be so relevant to the congested traffic many car drivers are far more likely to encounter. Every such advert applies a little layer of bias against public transport, and these layers build up over time, helping to weld consumers firmly to their car seats.

Soma World

When investigating passionate opinions one often finds a fear at their roots. I think that the fear at the heart of 'brainwashing' criticisms of advertising and the media is of the same family which animates brainwashing itself: the terror of losing control, even identity. We have already seen, in Chapter 1, how George Orwell pictured this fear. Another famous novel of the twentieth century which crawled insidiously under our skins gave a name to the fear of the advertising critics. That name is *Brave New World*.

Like *Nineteen Eighty-Four*, the dystopia portrayed by Aldous Huxley's 1932 novel is totalitarian. But its totalitarian nature is not as upfront as in Orwell's world. Rather, it is disguised as freedom of choice. Orwell's inhabitants have their needs suppressed or channelled: Huxley's have theirs met. Like angels in heaven, they want for nothing. They can choose when to take soma, the perfect happy pill; they can choose, to some extent, their friends and activities. But their futures, their places in society, are determined by genetics before they are even born. They do what society requires of them, and most of them have lost the capacity even to imagine doing otherwise.

This potent idea—that if some agent can meet all our needs we will become its slaves—is reflected in one aspect of what so terrifies non-cult members about cults. As we saw in Chapter 2, part of the power which cult leaders exert over their followers is the power of meeting needs: individuals join cults because they find something there which is not available elsewhere. The same fear—that we may be approaching the placid 'Soma World' of Huxley's novel—can be found in critiques of advertising. As Huxley himself says in the foreword to his book, a 'really efficient totalitarian state would be one in which the all-powerful executive of political bosses and their army of managers controls a population of slaves who do not have to be coerced, because they love their servitude. To make them love it is the task assigned, in present-day totalitarian states, to ministries of propaganda, newspaper editors, and school-teachers. But their methods are still crude and unscientific.'

This, then, is the question raised by allegations of brainwashing directed against the media. Do we live, or could we soon be living, in Soma World? Are we at risk of emulating the Roman citizens disparaged by their contemporary Juvenal, giving up our powers to follow anyone who gives us *panem et circenses* (bread and circuses)?[4] Could all our needs (or enough to keep us docile) be met with happy pills, or if not fulfilled directly, directed into profitable consumption? Could information control even brainwash us into chasing certain desires (for a new car, the latest fashions, etc.) and forgetting other needs (for long-term thinking and autonomy of mind)? If we lived in such a world, would we be perfectly free or perfectly enslaved?

The first thing to say about this fear is that it is not a new one. We find it at the end of the nineteenth century in the form of H.G. Wells' beautiful, simple-minded Eloi, distant descendants of human beings living in a paradise where all their needs are provided for. Wells' protagonist, visiting in the time machine which gives Wells' story its title, learns to his horror that theirs is a poisoned idyll: the Eloi are harvested for food by the Morlocks, an underground race also descended from humankind. We find the same disgust in Friedrich Nietzsche about a decade earlier with Zarathustra's famous description of the future of our species:

Behold! I show you the *Last Man*.

What is love? What is creation? What is desire? What is a star? asketh the Last Man, and he blinketh!

Then will earth have grown small, and upon it shall hop the Last Man which maketh all things small. His kind is inexterminable like the ground-flea; the Last Man liveth longest.

'We have discovered happiness,'—say the Last Men, and they blink.

[…] Sickness and mistrust they hold sinful. […] A little poison now and then: for that causeth pleasant dreams. And much poison at the last for an easy death.

They still work, for work is a pastime. But they take heed, lest the pastime harm them.

[…] We have discovered happiness, say the Last Men, and they blink.

Nietzsche, Thus Spake Zarathustra, pp. 9–10

The second thing to say about fear of Soma World is that it centres on freedom. People in Soma World, like Nietzsche's Last Men, have achieved happiness. We are constantly being told these days that happiness is the great goal we should all be chasing, so why do these dystopias turn our stomachs? Why do we sympathize when Milton's Satan declares it 'Better to reign in hell, than serve in heaven'?[5] We seem to be predisposed to rank freedom as a higher goal than happiness, despite the attempts of modern authorities to persuade us otherwise. 'Life, liberty and estate', '*Liberté, egalité, fraternité*', 'Life, liberty, and the pursuit of happiness': these three great creeds, rallying cries for revolutionaries in England, France, and America, respectively, have shaped the modern West, and in all of them freedom is central. Erich Fromm argued in *The Fear of Freedom* that we dread freedom as well as desiring it (freedom can require effort or even pain), but an ambivalent attitude does not detract from the importance we seem to ascribe to this particular human value.

Does our fear of Soma World have any basis in today's realities? Are we approaching a subtle totalitarianism of the kind which so appals us in *Brave New World*? In Chapter 1 I looked at Robert Lifton's identification of eight themes—milieu control, mystical manipulation, the demand for purity, the cult of confession, sacred science, loading the language, the primacy of doctrine over person, and the dispensing of existence—which one might expect to find in a totalitarian environment (see Table 1). However, with respect to advertising we imme-diately hit a problem. Americans in Korea could point to the Chinese Communist system, and ultimately to Chairman Mao, as the source of their troubles. But where is our agent, our brainwasher, our Morlock chief?

Thought control without a controller

To imagine that all our sources of advertising answer to one controlling mind seems far-fetched.[6] Instead, what we seem to have is a situation akin to that of evolution: apparent design, but with an absence of designer (for creationist readers, evolutionary theory does not strictly specify that the designer must be absent, rather that He does not need to be present for the processes of natural selection to take place). This evolutionary analogy led the biologist Richard Dawkins to introduce the notion of memetics, a 'strong genetic' metaphor for cultural transmission, which views ideas as 'memes' able to replicate themselves and be transmitted by imitation from brain to brain.[7] Many people have adopted an evolutionary view of cultures and cultural ideas without specific reference to some of the more controversial claims of memetics, but meme is an irresistibly useful shorthand, so I will use it in this weaker sense of evolutionary analogy. What such analogies claim is that ideas can spread, change, converge, or diverge without the need for overarching agency. How does this absence of designer—of agent—affect Lifton's eight themes?

Very little. Milieu control becomes milieu standardization: instead of imposed control by the Party we see selection pressures on cultural products (newspapers, adverts, etc.) which tend to push them to become more similar over time. The fact that many of our media are increasingly global, ultimately controlled by an oligarchy of moguls who themselves have much in common, only accelerates this process. The need to sell makes media folk inveterate followers of fashion, and the desire of busy people for 'easy info', for news in a soundbite or a headline, leads to a demand for simplification which can be alarmingly similar to an ideology's demand for purity. Paedophiles, to take a topical example, are always evil and their victims always innocent. It is rare to find a tabloid taking seriously the idea that paedophiles, like 'normal' people, are influenced by their history and environments. And what of Lolita, Nabokov's provocative child? Nowhere in sight, in theory; but in practice she's roaming our high streets and the pages of our fashion magazines. The cult of confession is also popular, with 'real' people exposing their lives to the media, and being well-paid to do so. We have largely lost our right to remain silent, both when facing the police and when facing the cameras. Loading the language is particularly common in advertising, where words like 'new' and 'essential' carry a weight far beyond their original meaning (I frequently see 'essential' products advertised and I have never yet felt the lack of any of them). We also see elements of sacred science in those modern dogmas which mass culture rarely seeks to challenge, such as the idea that the British are especially tolerant, and mystical manipulation in references to abstract ideals which are supposed to make us jump through some emotional hoop as soon as we hear them (terms like sexism and multiculturalism are examples of this). Finally, we have governments with a considerable control over the dispensing of existence (as US residents of Death Row, or foreign nationals interned without trial after 9/11, could testify, if they were allowed to) and public media with a frightening control over the dispensing, if not of existence, then at least of reputation. The one potential exception is Lifton's seventh theme, the primacy of doctrine over person, and this is because in the West individualism is itself such a powerful doctrine.

What we seem to have, in short, is a difference not in kind but in degree; tendencies towards totalitarian thinking, but tendencies which at present are not as extreme as they could be. We may be on the road to Soma World, but we are not there yet. Voices still challenge commonly held beliefs and object to intellectual standardization. And many people resist the consumerist dream or treat it as only a part of worthwhile living. They view adverts with healthy scepticism, listen carefully to political arguments, and distrust most of what they read in the newspapers. Awareness of the manipulator's motives lingers at the back of their minds and keeps them careful. They may not have read Robert Cialdini, but they are nevertheless motivated to stop and think, and that, as we shall see in later chapters, is the basis of resistance to persuasion.

One of the limitations on the current power of advertising is that mass communication media are unable to target individuals precisely, for the simple reason that they do not know enough about their customers. Whether or not someone falls for a salesperson's patter depends on a number of factors. The most obvious is what is being sold. My reaction to an evangelical Christian trying to persuade me to come to church differs from my reaction to the representative who phones me offering deals on new kitchens, although both influence attempts are likely to fail. For the cold-caller, all I have to do to end the influence attempt is to say that I rent rather than own my flat. The evangelist, however, will be greeted with a lengthy list of my reasons for not attending church, because in the past I have thought about religion in depth. Buying a new kitchen is so irrelevant to a life spent in other people's houses that I rarely think about it at all, let alone in depth. The success of the influence technique depends on what is being sold, not in itself, but insofar as it is relevant to me. Even with apparently universal goods, such as money, the degree of relevance—and hence the success of the influence technique—will vary from person to person. Not everyone, even in the acquisitive West, would accept an offer of cash with no strings attached.

The targeted individual's personality and history will also affect responses to the method of influence used. Some people, for example, react negatively to the use of phrases such as 'must-have' or 'essential' in a sales pitch, preferring approaches which emphasize their freedom of choice. Some are more likely to respond to an authority-based approach ('buy this, it's good for you'), some to a charming salesperson ('buy this to please me; you'd like to please me, wouldn't you?'), some to an implied threat ('buy this or your health will suffer'), and so on. Indeed, the seller's personality is also very relevant to the success of an influence attempt. We may readily donate to the sweet old lady concerned about animal rights, while walking past the unshaven, unsmiling young man collecting for aid to Africa. Yet her money could be funding nail bombs, while his is probably saving children's lives. As Cialdini and others have noted, likeability is an important weapon of influence.

Case study: textual persuasion

What is being sold, in other words, interacts with the targeted individual's personality and history to exert influence (successfully or not). Whether we stop and think depends on a uniquely personal context which includes not only current stimuli but also easily accessible memories, allowing us to use the past to interpret the present. As an example, consider the following text:

the act of a woman driving her child to school and back is not seen as one of maternal care but rather as a unique demonstration of selfishness. For the good of society, for the good of the economy, for the good of her own children, the school-running mother must be persuaded to change her behaviour.

This excerpt is trying to sell me a set of ideas. But I cannot begin to interpret its message without accessing a lot of background knowledge. I need to know the English meaning of words like 'driving', and I need to understand that driving here means using a car, not a whip. I can also access memories of other texts, news programmes, debates with friends, or whatever which tell me that there is an ongoing debate in Britain about whether mothers who drive their children to school should reduce traffic congestion and improve their children's health by making the child walk or cycle to school instead. Before reading this excerpt I had not encountered the adjective 'school-running', but context makes its meaning perfectly clear. Having done the basic interpretation, I can now begin to assess the arguments in terms of what I think about the issue.

That assessment will be influenced by factors originating in my personal experience: my attitudes to children and to traffic, whether I live near a school or not, and how I'm feeling as I read the text. However, the text itself also affects me, though I may not always recognize this. One example in this excerpt is the contrast between, on the one hand, the well-vowelled warmth of 'maternal care' and, on the other hand, the spiky chill of 'unique' or the sibilance of 'selfishness', which subtly sways me towards the put-upon mother and away from those who would restrict her right to drive. Another is the emphasis on repeated generalizations ('the good of ...', 'society', 'the economy', 'the school-running mother'). Someone with a fondness for abstract nouns may enjoy a sentence full of them; the rest of us sense distance, depersonalization.

Finally, texts are not usually as isolated as this example. It was taken from an article in *The Observer* newspaper[8] which is clearly criticizing the position stated in the excerpt. I have read other articles by David Aaronovitch, and I have read *The Observer* often enough to know its liberal flavour. The article is in the Comment section of the paper, which I know is a licence for more opinionated prose, so I would expect a piece defending a liberal position. Furthermore, my cognitive landscape contains the belief, as Jacob Talmon puts it in *The Origins of Totalitarian Democracy*, that liberal thinking 'assumes politics to be a matter of trial and error, and regards political systems as pragmatic contrivances of human ingenuity and spontaneity'. Like Robert Lifton (see Chapter 1) and others, Talmon contrasted liberal pragmatics with totalitarianism's fondness for the abstract and absolute. I therefore interpret the excerpt's spree of abstract nouns not as referring to Aaronovitch's own (liberal) position, but as being used to represent (and subtly to denigrate) an opposing view. All of this background information, and more, is available to me as I read Aaronovitch's article, or any other text. You have a different though equally luxuriant background, unique to you. Explicit access to these cognitive databases, however, is probably the exception for both of us: life is too short, and stopping to think too effortful, to make a habit of spelling out connotations. More often the links remain unnoted except as a general sense of the text's tone or flavour, adding an emotional tinge—approval or disapproval—to the record filed in our heads under Aaronovitch, D. Emotions, in other words, serve as short cuts, summarizing the contents of our cognitive databases without the need for us to search them explicitly. We shall return to this important point in Chapter 9.

The message from experts on the psychology of persuasion is that, if motivated, adults at least can resist weapons of influence. We can dodge commitment traps, refuse to reciprocate, discount the effects of authority and likeability in those who want us to buy, decide not to acquire a product just because everyone else has or because the product's availability has been artificially limited in order to stimulate demand. Part of the fear inherent in the word brainwashing, alongside the terrors of losing control and losing one's very identity, is that the processes, whatever they may be, are overwhelming; that no one is safe. As far as individual influence attempts go, we are all vulnerable to the persuasion of advertising, but that power is by no means irresistible.

This comforting conclusion, unfortunately, does not apply to the wider ideological apparatus of which advertising is one small part: the media. Adverts inform us about products, and most are relatively honest about their aims. For information about the rest of the world, beyond the minuscule fragments we perceive directly, we rely crucially on the various systems of mass communication which make up today's extraordinarily powerful media. This is where the charge of brainwashing really begins to bite. Remember Lifton's eight themes. Milieu control is most visible after major news events such as the destruction of the World Trade Center, which saturate newspapers, radio, television, and the Internet; but it is more subtly present in the endless everyday repetition of tired themes and mind-numbingly similar formats (lifestyle magazines are a good example). The demand for purity and the simplification of complex arguments, the cult of confession, and loading the language are obvious features of any tabloid newspaper, and by no means exclusive to tabloids. As for sacred science, mystical manipulation, the primacy of doctrine over person, and the dispensing of existence, one has only to look at how the media treat those who query their hegemony. 'Freedom of the press' and 'the public interest' are held up as unchallengeable truths, individual privacy destroyed in the hunt for a story, and reputations torn to shreds. As we shall see in Chapter 13, the media can be potent weapons of mass control.

Education

We don't need no education, we don't need no thought control
Pink Floyd, *Pink Floyd—The Wall*

We come now to education, that process whereby a State establishes its grip on the minds of the young. Of course, formal education is only a part of the influences which shape a child into an adult: the messages from parents and especially peers, the media and advertisers, and their own genetic heritage all contribute to the eventual person. But education is, in theory at any rate, a standardized experience available to every child. It is also a public process. It has consequences for society as a whole, including those who participate in education to a minimal extent.

I shall spend less time on education than on advertising because I think they are in many ways similar. The fears of brainwashing, or 'thought control' as Pink Floyd called it, have the same basis, although the controlling agent—the State—is more clearly identifiable in education. Both education and advertising are mass belief-shaping processes, applicable across a wide age range, making copious use of our tendency to use heuristics to make life easier. In both we debate the motives and techniques of those who do the shaping.

Education differs from advertising in three important respects: developmental, structural, and motivational. The first is perhaps more a matter of presentation than actuality: education is aimed primarily at children, whereas advertising concentrates on adults. There are some restrictions on advertising to children, although they are not as tight as many would like; an example currently worrying experts is the high impact of adverts for sugary and fatty foods on children already at risk of obesity. Likewise, adult 'lifelong' learning has recently received more emphasis. Nevertheless, most education is experienced by children, and the majority of adverts target adults: car drivers, homeowners, holders of purse strings.

Education also differs from advertising and the media on a structural level. As we saw earlier, advertising often seems very standardized (cars on empty roads, women in eerily tidy houses, and so on). Yet this standardization has come about by an evolutionary process which uses trial and error, not active design; disastrous adverts still appear from time to time, to hearty lampooning from other corners of the media. Education is much more controlled—teachers frequently complain about just how controlled it is and the amount of time they spend on paperwork to satisfy government bureaucracy.[9] The aim is equality: all children should have a similar basic grounding to prepare them for their adult lives.

The third difference between education and advertising is arguably the one that matters most to those subjected to both: their motive. The main aim of advertising is to sell products. The advertiser is not primarily concerned with the benefits which the consumer who buys his product will receive, except in so far as emphasizing the benefits increases sales. The main aim of education is to process children into citizens, giving them at least in principle the skills they need to prosper and contribute to society ('creating opportunity, releasing potential, achieving excellence', as a current UK government slogan puts it).[10] Louis Althusser, his pupil Michel Foucault and many others have argued that schools, like prisons, are totalitarian environments.[11] (This can seem particularly true of boarding schools.) Tempting as it may be, however, to make snide remarks, such criticisms are only partially justified. The social environment of a school can indeed demonstrate that children make excellent totalitarians, nastily adept in their control of language and behaviour. The same psychological brutalities that sickened us in William Golding's *Lord of the Flies*, which can drive their unlucky victims to a suicide just as final as Piggy's murder, can be seen in playgrounds across the world. However, any school is only part of life. Indeed, Golding's children had no school, no adult ideologues, controlling their behaviour. All that was needed for them to start dispensing existence was to be members of a stressed and frightened group.

Education is about learning facts and learning rules. The facts build up a corpus of knowledge that will be more or less useful in adult life. The rules, however, give education its real power. This is because rules, unlike facts, can be generalized, that is, applied to new situations. Rules seem to be best taught by seeing how they work in practice, that is, by learning a number of facts to start with. Hence the traditional depiction of school as a boring place where students are drowned in facts.

Education and critical thinking

But education, at its best, teaches more than just knowledge. It teaches critical thinking: the ability to stop and think before acting, to avoid succumbing to emotional pressures. This is not thought control. It is the very reverse: mental liberation. Even the most advanced intellectual will be imperfect at this skill. But even imperfect possession of it frees a person from the burden of being 'stimulus-driven', constantly reacting to the immediate environment, the brightest colours or loudest sounds or most enticing adverts. Being driven by heuristic responses, living by instinct and emotion all the time, is a very easy way to live, in many ways: thought is effortful, especially for the inexperienced. But emotions are also exhausting, and short-term reactions may not, in the long term, be the most beneficial for health and survival. Just as we reach for burgers for the sake of convenience, storing up the arterial fat which may one day kill us, so our reliance on feelings can do us great harm.

The intellectual environment, in the West and in theory at least, aims to reduce the power of this social tyranny (I will return to this idea in Chapter 15). Its aims are essentially antitotalitarian: to give the child the skills it needs to prosper, to facilitate its growing independence, to enable it to assess competing claims for its attention, and to give it the ability to stop and think. Christians praise a God 'whose service is perfect freedom',[12] and we should, ideally, be able to view education in a similar light, as self-service, giving *us* more freedom to understand and act in the world. The UK National Curriculum, for example, requires its more advanced history students to learn not only British history (three studies are required), but European history (one study from before the First World War) and world history (one study from before and one from after 1900). The earlier option for world history includes:

Islamic civilisations (seventh to sixteenth centuries); the Qin Dynasty in China; Imperial China from the First Emperor to Kublai Khan; the Manchu invasion and the fall of the Ming dynasty; India from the Mughal Empire to the coming of the British; the civilisations of Peru; indigenous peoples of North America; black peoples of the Americas; the West African empires; Japan under the Shoguns; Tokugawa Japan; the Phoenicians; the Maoris; Muhammad and Makkah; the empires of Islam in Africa; the Sikhs and the Mahrattas; the Zulu kingdoms.[13]

According to the Curriculum, pupils are expected to 'show their understanding by making connections between events and changes in the different periods and areas studied, and by comparing the structure of societies and economic, cultural and political developments. They evaluate and use sources of information, using their historical knowledge to analyse the past and explain how it can be represented and interpreted in different ways.' When you consider the range of case studies on offer, and the critical thinking implied in learning about multiple interpretations of the past, it seems that modern Britain has grown up enough to realize that manipulating education for ideological reasons may be counter-productive—our fast-changing postmodern world leaves the inflexible patterns of totalist thinking exposed as maladaptive. So were Pink Floyd wrong, or were they unlucky in their childhoods?

The ideals of education are very different from the profit motives of the media: education aims to increase our freedom. Not just the illusory freedom to choose a wider range of cars, but the freedom to ask those questions the advertiser doesn't want asked: about public transport alternatives, the long-term health of drivers, the effects on the environment. We should have the choice to think, or not to think, and that means providing not just the information we need to make that choice, but also the skills we need to think it through. It is those skills which are most effective against influence techniques, from the mildest advert to the most vicious and coercive thought control; and it is those skills for which we should look to education.

Education and ideology

What we must look for here is, first, religious and moral principles; secondly,
gentlemanly conduct; thirdly intellectual ability

> Thomas Arnold, *Address to His Scholars at Rugby*

Unfortunately, education all too often falls far short of these noble intentions. Not only is it frequently ineffective in teaching thinking skills and critical analysis, it is inescapably vulnerable to ideological abuse, prompted by the temptation of moulding the minds of future citizens. An extreme example comes from the former Soviet republic of Belarus, as depicted in the *Irish Times* (14 August 2003). If you are still raking over the extracts from the UK National Curriculum, above, looking for evidence of ideological loading, then this should put your search into perspective:

President Alexander Lukashenko yesterday ordered 'ideology' teachers be
chosen from every firm in Belarus to educate state workers, in a move criticised
as Soviet-style indoctrination.

'To penetrate the soul and the mind of everybody is of course a most
challenging art form, a very complex work and people (working in these
organisations) must be qualified to the highest degree,' Mr Lukashenko said at
a government meeting on ideology.

This resplendently totalitarian attitude is not unique to President Lukashenko.
Some madrassahs train Muslim boys for the martyrdom of suicide bombing.
Some racists teach their children that black people should be removed from
Britain, by force if necessary. Some US schools object to the teaching of evolutionary theory because it contradicts the Bible's creation story. The relationship between education and religion is a frequent source of controversy, but
religion is only one particularly obvious instance of ideology. There are many
others. For reasons of space, I will give only one more example: the alarming case
of a neo-Nazi teacher.

The story is set in a school in Alberta, Canada. This in itself is surprising: if I
were to ask a random sample of my fellow citizens to name the nation they
thought most likely to have a totalitarian education system I would be unlikely to
garner many votes for Canada. Nevertheless, a charismatic Christian teacher
named Jim Keegstra was able to foist his extreme anti-Semitic beliefs on his high
school students so successfully that they adopted Nazi ideology wholesale. One
student 'wrote that Jewish-controlled thugs rode around in packs, bashing in
children's heads, raping and drowning women, and cutting open men's
stomachs so they would bleed to death',[14] before advocating the Nazi solution:
genocide. In *Canada*? When Keegstra was removed following complaints from
parents, his replacement showed the students pictures from Nazi death camps,
only to find that any evidence he presented was automatically assumed to have
been faked. One student had to be taken on a trip to Dachau before he changed
his mind. Keegstra was not even operating in the 1930s, when the full extent of
Nazi atrocities had yet to become clear, but several decades *after* the Second
World War. His case is a graphic illustration of the dangers of education when it
is used for totalist purposes.

Summary and conclusions

Brainwashing is a term often applied to advertising and education, both of which
are concerned with changing belief. Of course no single advert transforms a person from free-thinking individual to consumer zombie. However, the accumulated mass of consumer culture is awash with unexamined assumptions which
are often extremely stereotypical. We may think we are immune to such prejudices, but there is a wealth of evidence from social psychology to suggest that
we are not. And just because an assumption tends to escape scrutiny does not

mean that we should continue to ignore it. The basic assumptions of consumer culture—that wealth brings happiness, that every need can and should be satisfied immediately, that physical perfection is a right and even a duty—have become widely accepted in the West. Yet there is little or no evidence that we are happier or more secure than we used to be.

Where advertising seeks to make us good consumers, education seeks to make us good citizens. Its control of young minds in particular has made it an easy target for the charge of brainwashing, and there is no doubt that a society's ideological principles come through in education just as they do in advertising. However, although education may often fall short in practice, its aim is to increase the freedoms of the individual. Buying things can do this up to a point, but advertising, by portraying an impossible dream, can also weigh us down with overly high expectations. 'Buying this will make you happy' is the message; we buy, and find ourselves still as unhappy as before. Education, by contrast, does not promise happiness explicitly. Yet it aims to deliver more earning power, and therefore more access to the consumer playground. At its worst, it can warp and damage young minds; at its best, it delivers a crucial skill, the ability to stop and think, to examine assumptions. We are drowning in information, but without the power to understand, select, and analyse we cannot use that information well.

In the next chapter, I will consider another domain in which the charge of brainwashing has a potent resonance: the strange and disturbing world of psychology and psychiatry.

Chapter 4: Hoping to heal

Descriptive labeling does not provide causative understanding
Robert L. Taylor, *Mind or Body*

In Chapter 1 we encountered the metaphor at the literal heart of the term brain-washing: the use of water to cleanse and purify. We now turn to another, closely related metaphor: that of healing. From the time the word was born, analogies have been drawn between brainwashing and treating sick minds. Edward Hunter, for example, makes the comparison early on in *Brain-washing in Red China* when describing how he interviewed a Chinese student, Chi Sze-chen, who had undergone thought reform. Chi's descriptions trigger Hunter's memories of 'a most modern sanitarium' in America, where Hunter had gone to visit a sick friend. In particular, he recalls one of the psychiatrists:

He had just won a glorious victory—the fight for a man's mind—and he felt that he was now able to recommend his patient's release. [...] There had been a painful family scene in this man's childhood that the doctor knew about, although not from the patient. Unless the man were able to place his unhappy incident in its proper perspective, to fit the pieces together to make his mental mosaic whole, he could not be considered safely cured. Nobody else could do it for him; he had to do it voluntarily. There was no valid reason for the patient's concealment because he had disclosed far more revealing details. His 'cure' could come only by frankly recognizing facts—by 'being frank', by 'mind reform'. Those were all terms the Chinese student, too, was using in our interview. [...] The feelings that had come over me in that most modernized institution while talking to the psychiatrist were the same as those I felt as I listened to Chi's story: the same disquieting sense of probing into dangerous fields. Chi's experiences in North China had been similar to that of the patients in the American institution. It was as if that most advanced mental hospital with its staff of psychiatrists had stopped treating the insane and had begun treating only the sane, without changing the treatment.

Doctors and demons

This link between 'psychic healing' techniques in psychology, psychotherapy, and psychiatry and the coercive techniques of brainwashing and its ancestor, torture, has been highlighted by many commentators. The association also runs the other way: those who administer coercive persuasion may deliberately choose to justify their actions using a medical model, describing their coercion as beneficial to the 'patient' (i.e. the victim). This language of 'cure' and 'health' may be mingled with other models. A common one is the language of 'repent-ance' and 'sin' of evangelical religious conversion, where the goal is to save the patient/victim's soul. Another is the language of the battle exemplified in the quotation above, which is fought by the healer/brainwasher against the enemy forces (rival ideologies) which have taken over or corrupted the patient/ victim. Here the goal is to liberate the person from these false doctrines, in effect following St John's dictum that 'ye shall know the truth, and the truth shall make you free' (John 8:32). Needless to say, truth is a resource of which the brain-washer assumes a monopoly.

George Orwell, always superbly aware of the power of language, provides clear instances of how these 'virtuous' models (healing, saving, freeing) can be co-opted by abusers of power. In *Nineteen Eighty-Four*, for example, Winston Smith's tor-turer O'Brien uses an explicitly medical model to describe the Party's aims towards Winston. 'Shall I tell you why we have brought you here? To cure you! To make you sane! Will you understand, Winston, that no one whom we bring to this place ever leaves our hands uncured? We are not interested in those stupid crimes that you have committed. The Party is not interested in the overt act: the thought is all we care about. We do not merely destroy our enemies, we change them.'

The same medical model is used explicitly in Chinese Communism, from which the term 'brainwashing' first emerged. Edward Hunter describes a play called *The Question of Thought*, first produced for the Chinese public in 1949 and not intended for foreign hearers, in which thought reform is dramatically brought to life. In it the medical model of alternative ideologies as mental poisons mingles with the evangelical model of thought reform as a conversion process. For example, group leader Miss Tsao remarks:

The reactionaries have been defeated. Now the sick people are getting
treatment; and if they still do not own up, and if they still are not frank about
their past during this period of treatment, if they still do not want to save
themselves, and to repent their wrongs, then they cannot blame anyone else.
Hunter, Brain-washing in Red China, pp. 135–6

Those who use totalitarian influence techniques may wish to enhance their credibility by adopting one or more of these virtuous models; but, one may argue, that is surely distinct from *actually* healing (or saving, or freeing). Mental health professionals, in the vast majority of cases, take their duty of care very seriously and do their best to assist their patients using the best treatments available. Yet the social system which processes the mentally ill can have immense power over them. It is this capacity for coercion which has led to the allegation of brainwashing.

The anti-psychiatrists' challenge

Doctors have always faced criticism from within their profession. There are some members of the mental health professions who, confronted with Michel Foucault's rhetorical question: 'Is it surprising that prisons resemble factories, schools, barracks, hospitals, which all resemble prisons?'[1] would answer 'Not in the least.' To Foucault, and to anti-psychiatrists of the 1960s and 1970s such as R.D. Laing and Thomas Szasz, the processes of defining someone as mentally ill are not primarily about healing; rather they are about power exercised by the State against those individuals who behave in socially deviant ways.[2] The argument of these critics is that having to live in society puts pressures on some people with which they are unable to cope, leading them to behave in ways which are distressing to themselves and to others. Laing goes so far as to define schizophrenic behaviour as *'a special strategy that a person invents in order to live in an unlivable situation'*.[3] Ideally, 'curing' such people would mean reforming society to remove the harmful pressures; but it is easier to define the sufferers as deviant, mad, or sick. This language labels them as 'non-people', which as we learned from Robert Lifton (in Chapter 1) is a dangerous move. Not only *can* non-people be deprived of their rights, institutionalized and/or forcibly treated (theoretically for their own benefit, but mainly for society's convenience), but the demand for purity in the wider group of 'normals' *insists* that they be so removed. As Thomas Szasz puts it:

It is widely believed today that just as some people suffer from diseases of the liver or kidney, others suffer from diseases of the mind or personality; that persons afflicted with such 'mental illnesses' are psychologically and socially inferior to those not so afflicted; and that 'mental patients', because of their supposed incapacity to 'know what is in their own best interests', must be cared for by their families or the state, even if that care requires interventions imposed on them against their will or incarceration in a mental hospital.

I consider this entire system of interlocking concepts, beliefs, and practices false and immoral.

Szasz, *The Manufacture of Madness*, p. xv

Szasz is not saying that 'weird' behaviour doesn't exist. He is not even saying that people with weird behaviour may not want or need to be helped, to seek, as Shakespeare's Macbeth does, to 'Pluck from the memory a rooted sorrow, Raze out the written troubles of the brain.'[4] Szasz is careful to make clear that his critique is not directed at psychotherapy or 'contractual psychiatry', in which the patient freely enters into a contract and pays the therapist directly for mental health services, and where there are penalties for the therapist who uses force or deception. Szasz is targeting instead what he calls 'institutional psychiatry', in which 'the institutional psychiatrist is a bureaucratic employee, paid for his services by a private or public organization (not by the individual who is his ostensible client); its most important social characteristic is the use of force and fraud'. It is the coercion to which he primarily objects, the assumption that a person's unusual behaviour is justification enough for removing their liberties. As Laing comments, 'The perfectly adjusted bomber pilot may be a greater threat to species survival than the hospitalized schizophrenic deluded that the Bomb is inside him.'

Robin Dawes, writing a quarter of a century later, raises similar concerns in his book *House of Cards*, which argues that far too much of psychology and psychotherapy rests on scientifically dubious foundations. Discussing the process by which the American Psychological Association licenses its practitioners, he notes that:

professors and 'organizational' or 'industrial' psychologists who work for business organizations or government units are exempted. The rationale is that such people are not working for individual clients per se. That conception conflicts with the APA's Ethics Code, which specifies that the psychologist should be working for the individual being evaluated or treated.

Dawes, *House of Cards*, p. 177

Like Szasz, Dawes points out that such State employees can have considerable power over those they evaluate, up to and including the dispensing of existence, as for example when they assess convicted killers. As Dawes remarks, 'Psychologists who decide that murderers should be executed as "irredeemable" [...] can hardly be described as working in the best interests of these people.' They are working for a society which prefers excision (physically by capital punishment or socially by incarceration) to rehabilitation for those individuals to whom it denies, as Hitler denied to the Jews, any possibility that they can be redeemed. This is reminiscent of the totalitarian attitudes discussed in Chapter 1.

At the opposite end of the spectrum from the 'social power' hypotheses of the anti-psychiatrists lies the currently powerful biological/medical model of psychiatry, which argues that mental illnesses are a subset of physical illnesses.[5] This is undoubtedly true of some of the more than 300 conditions defined by

American psychiatry's official, and much-criticized, handbook, the *Diagnostic and Statistical Manual (DSM)*, or European psychiatry's equivalent, the World Health Organization's *International Statistical Classification of Diseases and Related Health Problems*.[6] As Dawes notes, like medical diseases some *DSM* conditions have 'a fairly well-understood cause, physiological nature, set of associated behaviors (symptoms), and course over time'. The psychotic symptoms which sometimes accompany the immune disorder lupus are of this kind.

Yet the current version of the *DSM* includes diagnoses which range from the familiar (depression, schizophrenia) to the frankly bizarre (e.g. body dysmorphic disorder, in which patients demand surgery to remove healthy parts of their bodies). Some 'disorders'—such as reading disorder, conduct disorder, and the personality disorders—have proved highly controversial. Many parents of children with dyslexia would object vehemently to the idea that their offspring should be given a psychiatric diagnosis, and many commentators on the person-ality disorders are concerned about defining an entire personality as an illness. In antisocial personality disorder (APD), for example (and its 'junior version', con-duct disorder), it is difficult to conceive of what the person would be like without their 'disorder'; this is not the case for, say, hallucinations in schizophrenia. Criteria for APD include deceitfulness, failure to plan ahead, aggressiveness, irre-sponsibility, and lack of remorse. Although APD is diagnosed on the basis of behaviour, and technically these terms are descriptions of *behaviour*, they sound to many people more like *character* traits, and of highly unpleasant characters at that. APD 'sufferers' (it is often not clear that they do suffer, at least until the law catches up with them) are sometimes called psychopaths, although psychopathy is a term 'defined by a cluster of both personality traits and socially deviant behav-iors'.[7] In other words, a psychopath may be assessed as having a cruel, ruthless, and deceitful character as well as behaving badly. It is not at all clear to what extent cruelty, ruthlessness, and deceit can be related to problems in brain func-tion, or treated with drugs or other methods, as the biomedical model implies. Treating someone with a personality disorder without their consent, 'by force or fraud', is perilously close to the enforced personality change associated with brainwashing.

Some commentators object to the strict distinction between sanity and mad-ness implicit in both the social power and biomedical models of mental illness.[8] Others have challenged the coercive use of treatments such as lobotomy[9] or the effectiveness of pharmacotherapy (drug treatments)[10] or psychotherapy.[11] The modern mental health movement has an array of critics in its ranks—yet it is flourishing as never before. Why is this? Many people place the blame firmly on 'authority', one of Robert Cialdini's weapons of influence described in Chapter 3. This is not to say that mental health professionals are out to pressurize and con their clients; a few are crooks, but the vast majority are well intentioned.

However, influence techniques need not be wielded with trickery in mind: authorities may be genuine (a doctor endorsing a pill) as well as false (an actor who plays a doctor in a famous TV series endorsing a pill). Mental health professionals view their authority as genuine, approved by the State and backed up by years of training. To quote Dawes again, we accept their authority because 'we have continually heard that they are experts, because we are prone to accept what people claiming to be authorities say'. To understand why authority is such a powerful weapon of influence requires us to revisit social psychology.

The power of authority

hoc volo, sic iubeo, sit pro ratione voluntas
[That is my wish, my *order*; my will is reason enough]
                                        Juvenal, *Satire VI*

The study of authority began early in social psychology, not least because many of the discipline's greatest names had moved to America to escape an authoritarian regime—Nazi Germany. Theodor Adorno and colleagues proposed the idea of 'the authoritarian personality' (measured by the Adorno F scale): a person who is excessively deferential to those in authority and unusually hostile to anyone not in the same group. They argued that overly harsh discipline from parents makes some children displace natural aggression onto weaker targets instead of displaying it directly to the parents. As these children grow, they become psychologically predisposed to submit to authority—seen as representing the parents—to need to be within a hierarchy, and to enjoy exerting authority over others. Although later work has cast doubt on just what the F scale actually measures,[12] the concept of authoritarianism has remained influential. Research by Milton Rokeach extended the personality type beyond adherents to right-wing ideologies (the 'F' in the F scale stands for 'fascism'). Not only did highly authoritarian individuals tend to score highly on ratings of dogmatism and prejudice, but they also did so whatever their secular or religious ideology. Father Simon, whose conversion to Communism was related in Chapter 1, was described by Robert Lifton as having an authoritarian personality. Rokeach argued that it is the type and structure of belief which is important, not the specific content.[13]

The personality theory of authoritarianism was soon challenged. Critics argued that, by allocating prejudice to the 'dynamics of the individual personality, it underestimates the importance of current social situations in shaping people's attitudes',[14] that it ignores sociocultural and historical factors which influence prejudice, and that, as a theory of individual differences, it fails to explain the high prevalence of authoritarianism in societies such as Nazi Germany. Moreover, if only certain personalities were susceptible to blind obedience, anyone fortunate enough to live in a properly free country, which encouraged liberal parents, could presumably set aside any threat of dictators in their neighbourhood.

And so indeed many people thought—until the arrival in Psychology's Hall of Fame of Stanley Milgram. In a series of famous experiments, he challenged the idea that only certain people are susceptible to authority, shifting the focus from personality to behaviour and showing that even highly educated and liberally minded American students (traditional contrasts to the authority-loving Germans) would be willing to inflict dangerous levels of electric shock on people, if instructed to do so by a psychologist. The experiments, which were ostensibly about learning, involved the subject being duped into thinking that he or she was giving electric shocks to another volunteer, the 'learner' (in fact, a confederate in the experiment who pretended to receive shocks). The subject gave a learning test to the confederate, and shocks were given when the confederate made a (prearranged) 'mistake'. If the subject hesitated, the experimenter instructed them to continue.

In terms of Robert Cialdini's weapons of influence, discussed in Chapter 3, we can see that Milgram was using not just authority, but commitment and consistency as well. The level of supposed electric shock was initially very low; it increased by degrees to dangerous levels as the experiment progressed. So the initial commitment to participate in the experiment, and even to step through the first few levels of shock, was a relatively easy one to make. But every time a participant agreed to increase the shock level he or she fell deeper into a commitment and consistency trap which made it harder and harder to refuse. This kind of entrapment is a favourite technique of influence technicians, which is why soldiers facing the threat of capture and interrogation are often trained to give their name, rank, and serial number—and nothing else.

Milgram asked 'Psychiatrists, graduate students, and faculty in the behavioural sciences, college sophomores, and middle-class adults'[15] to predict the number of subjects who would be fully obedient and administer the highest, potentially lethal, shock available. The answers were all around 1–2 per cent, not a bad guess at the number of sadists in the general population. Unfortunately, Milgram wasn't studying sadism. In the actual experiments, up to two-thirds of subjects were fully obedient. Rather than the problems of blind obedience being due to a minority with the 'wrong' kind of personality, Milgram argued that:

This is, perhaps, the most fundamental lesson of our study: ordinary people, simply doing their jobs, and without any particular hostility on their part, can become agents in a terrible destructive process. Moreover, even when the destructive effects of their work become patently clear, and they are asked to carry out actions incompatible with fundamental standards of morality, relatively few people have the resources needed to resist authority.

Milgram, *Obedience to Authority*, p. 24

Milgram's explanation of his findings centres on what he called the 'agentic shift'. He conceived of human beings (and other organisms) as being able to operate in two states: 'autonomous' and 'agentic'. When acting autonomously, humans are selfish and free; their actions are controlled by them and serve their needs. If society were entirely composed of such independent units, life would probably approach Thomas Hobbes' famous vision of the state of nature: 'solitary, poore, nasty, brutish, and short'.[16] Milgram argues that the very act of coexisting in the same territory requires such units to limit their own selfish behaviour; they must learn, for example, not to attack each other. This inhibition, he believes, underlies the individual conscience.

Humans live in highly complex groups, from which they derive considerable survival benefits. Once they become part of a complex social system, they can achieve jointly much more than they could manage individually. Social systems tend to organize themselves into hierarchies, as this allows a number of members to have their actions co-ordinated by a member higher up in the hierarchy. However, this co-ordination (control) can only be effective if each member sacrifices some personal autonomy, since otherwise individual control might conflict with systemic control. This would be uncomfortable for the individual and would damage group efficiency. So a shift in behaviour and attitude—the agentic shift—is required, as outlined by Milgram: 'Specifically, the person entering an authority system no longer views himself as acting out of his own purposes but rather comes to see himself as an agent for executing the wishes of another person.' An example of agentic thinking comes from the missile scientist Wernher von Braun, one of numerous Nazi scientists who went to work for the Americans after the Second World War, as satirized by Tom Lehrer:

'Once the rockets are up, who cares where they come down?
That's not my department,' says Wernher von Braun.

Lehrer, 'Wernher von Braun'

In the last few decades, Western countries have seen a trend towards challenging traditional authorities. Doctors, priests, public sector workers, and politicians have all seen their stock fall to some extent. As the domains of religion and the public sector have shrunk, as the many tentacles of the New Age movement have invaded medicine, so the power of traditional authorities has diminished. Yet authority, as well as being extremely useful to brainwashers, continues to be a widespread and necessary feature of societies across the world.

Obedience to authority is instilled (to borrow, as I did in the previous chapter, from Louis Althusser) via a wide variety of ideological and repressive state apparatuses, including but not limited to the family, the media, religious and political organizations, and the education and criminal justice systems. Being essential for the maintenance of all ideologies, obedience can therefore be viewed as 'meta-ideological', that is, above and beyond any particular ideology. Compliance is rewarded, often by promotion to a higher rank in the social system, 'thus both motivating the person and perpetuating the structure simultaneously'. Dissent is disapproved of and may be punished. Milgram observes that if we are to obey, we must regard the authority as legitimate and relevant: these are context-dependent judgements, and the commands from the authority are also context-dependent. 'Thus, in a military situation, a captain may order a subordinate to perform a highly dangerous action, but he may not order the subordinate to embrace his girlfriend.' Ultimately, authority will only be accepted if 'the overarching ideological justification' (for Milgram's experiments, the view that science is 'a legitimate social enterprise') is also accepted. Thus obedience to authority is *not* blind obedience: it depends critically on the psychological and social context and the beliefs of the person involved.

Milgram summarizes his work by listing a number of recurrent themes which characterize the 'agentic state' of an obedient person. The first is a tendency to concentrate on administration and technical details rather than the big picture or a moral point of view. Morality becomes centred on obedience, which is defined as good in itself. The individual tends to place a high value on discipline, duty, loyalty, and competence, virtues which 'are simply the technical preconditions for the maintenance of the larger system'. Language changes; euphemisms disguise the moral implications of actions. Responsibility is diffused up through the hierarchy, and organizations frequently split components of morally dubious actions between individuals: the Nazis ensured that the men who chose the death-camp victims were far away from those who manned the gas chambers. People tend to be treated as a means to an end, a move justified by appeal to 'some high ideological goal', and dissent, or even comment, is discouraged.

Familiar? These themes echo Robert Lifton's discussion of totalitarianism (see Table 1, p. 17): loading the language with euphemisms, the primacy of doctrine over person as individual autonomy is suppressed for the good of the system, the sacred science of ideology, accepted without question, and the dispensing of existence in which lethal shocks could (apparently) be given to innocent strangers. Milgram's 'agentic state', evoked by the recognition of legitimate and relevant authority, seems to be a powerful facilitator of totalitarian functioning. In other words, totalitarianism is not a bizarre aberration, but a constant risk arising from the same psychological mechanisms which allow us to have societies at all. Applying this conclusion to the central topic of this chapter leads to the following verdict: to the extent that the mental health professions depend for their influence on authority, they are therefore at risk of totalitarian thinking. Their business is changing minds. Are they therefore vulnerable to the charge of brainwashing?

Totalitarianism and brainwashing

The fear of brainwashing is the fear of losing control, even of losing one's very identity. This fear is expressed differently in each of the domains of human life where brainwashing has been alleged. Modern Western culture has provided powerful totems: *The Manchurian Candidate* (political), *Nineteen Eighty-Four* (media), *Brave New World* (pharmacological), and Pink Floyd's *The Wall* (educational). The mental health professions, with their labelling, controlling, and curing of deviants, provide another totem: Stanley Kubrick's iconic film of Anthony Burgess's *A Clockwork Orange*, whose young and violent protagonist is tortured by aversion therapy. As we have seen, the anti-psychiatrist movement of the Sixties and Seventies argued that institutional psychiatry, at least, *was* totalitarian: not only did it serve to propagate and maintain the ideology of those in power, but it also did so in ferociously repressive ways. Is this fair?

Robin Dawes argues, like others before him, that the mental health professions do depend too much on the power of authority, which when coupled with our predilection for defining ingroups and outgroups can produce a truly toxic social force. However, this may be more a natural consequence of human nature than an irrevocable fact about psychiatry and psychotherapy. Private therapy obtained voluntarily for a fee is exempted, for instance, from Thomas Szasz's criticisms: it is when compulsion sets in that he rings alarm bells. Institutional psychiatry can seem to show totalitarian features, but again, totalitarianism is a matter of degree, not a yes/no categorization. And the mental health professions are a widely variable bunch, ranging from mild, short-term therapy, with or without chemicals, through to institutionalization and forced surgery. One cannot simply argue that all therapies are totalitarian; some are more totalitarian than others.

In relation to education, I argued in Chapter 3 that, although the reality may often fall short of the ideal, the ideal of education is antitotalitarian: it seeks to increase, rather than reduce, personal autonomy and intellectual freedom. In his book *Thought Reform and the Psychology of Totalism*, the psychiatrist Robert Lifton makes the analogous argument for psychotherapy. While admitting that 'in its organizational aspects, psychoanalysis—like every other revolutionary movement, whether scientific, political, or religious—has had difficulty maintaining its initial liberating spirit', he argues that 'The ethos of psychoanalysis and of its derived psychotherapies is in direct opposition to that of totalism. Indeed, its painstaking and sympathetic investigations of single human minds place it within the direct tradition of those Western intellectual currents which historically have done most to counter totalism: humanism, individualism, and free scientific inquiry.' Psychotherapy's emphasis on human uniqueness is surely the very opposite of the stereotyping generalizations employed by totalist thinking. It is of course extremely effortful to think in such a way continually—stereotypes, after all, exist to make our brains' lives easier—so it is hardly surprising that psychotherapists, like educationalists, can fall short of their ideals.

A more modern example than psychoanalysis is provided by the technique of cognitive behavioural therapy (CBT), which aims to teach the patient effective ways of examining and altering unwelcome ideas, such as the 'automatic thoughts' which plague people with depression. These thoughts, so-called because they seem to just pop into the mind, are overwhelmingly negative, featuring guilt, worthlessness, self-loathing, and even suicide. CBT helps the patient to stop and think. Rather than negative thoughts being accepted unchal-lenged (and hence influencing mood and behaviour), the patient learns to regard them as a feature of the depression which need not be taken as seriously as 'normal' thoughts. Thus their influence on mood and behaviour can gradually be lessened. As we shall see later, the ability to stop and think is characteristic of all antitotalitarian 'intellectual currents' and of resistance to totalitarian regimes. CBT aims to enhance this ability, and hence to bolster the patient's sense of control.

Summary and conclusions

The mental health professions speak to us of what we try to ignore: the scary fragility of that accreted concoction of ideas we call the self. The strength of the fears they evoke explains why the charge of brainwashing has been fought with such viciousness on this battleground. However, as we saw in Chapter 1, brain-washing has many aspects as process, symbol, or concept of last resort. In this chapter we have seen that with respect to the mental health professions, social psychology has explained much, eroding the need for concepts of last resort. Our increased understanding of weapons of influence, particularly authority, and of social psychological phenomena such as the diffusion of responsibility means that we can replace a magical process of brainwashing with a collection of more scientific concepts which, while still not fully understood, have considerable explanatory and predictive power.

Understanding brainwashing, however, is about more than simply rational explanation. The terror at the heart of A Clockwork Orange is not the highly aestheticized violence of its thugs but what is done to one of them in the name of therapy. We do not understand ourselves, and the less we understand the more we fear our ability to maintain our freedoms in the face of those who may seek to limit them. Brainwashing symbolizes our helplessness in the realm of our cherished minds. It attacks our feeling that selves above all else are sacrosanct, our brains the one place where we can rest in peace. It represents the dread we all have of acting out of character or out of control, or of waking up to find we have done something awful, as loyal German citizens woke up after the nightmare of Nazism. Brainwashing represents the dark side of obedience, and while the mental health professions continue to rely so heavily upon authority the fear of brainwashing cannot be laid to rest. Indeed, this fear may be better *not* banished: it drives a healthy scepticism which encourages us to question authority, to minimize the use of force in psychiatry and to question the motives and methods when force is used, to restrict help to those who want or need help, and to leave the rest to the laws which bind us all. In so far as psychiatry and the psychotherapies help us towards an increased understanding of ourselves, they are antitotalitarian, and I believe that this liberal spirit is an honest motivation for many practitioners. As with education, which shares many of the same goals, the ideals of mental therapy are noble, even though the realities may fail to match them.

Chapter 5: 'I suggest, you persuade, he brainwashes'

Nature has left this tincture in the blood
That all men wou'd be tyrants if they cou'd
> Daniel Defoe, *The History of the Kentish Petition*

In the previous chapters I have considered allegations of brainwashing made against a variety of social practices: religion, politics, advertising, education, psychiatry, and psychotherapy. The institutions which embody these practices are all in the business of changing people's minds. They are all what Louis Althusser would call ideological and repressive state apparatuses; they attempt to promulgate, by force, stealth, or persuasion, a set of ideas which influences behaviour (an ideology). In this chapter, rather more briefly and drawing on ideas from previous chapters, I will consider two other social institutions: the military and the criminal justice system. A rather more in-depth discussion of that most basic of social units, the family, will use the example of abusive adult relationships to address the issue of one-on-one brainwashing. Finally, I will consider one of the most malignant of social practices: torture.

The military

The army ages men sooner than the law and philosophy; it exposes them more
freely to germs, which undermine and destroy, and it shelters them more
completely from thought, which stimulates and preserves
> H.G. Wells, *Bealby*

The armed forces of a State provide its primary means of defence and of aggression against those whom the State's ideology defines as enemies, whether internal or external. The particular ideological function of the military is to transform citizens—typically taught from childhood to regard killing as wrong—into agents willing to kill. To achieve this, the military emphasizes the importance of obedience to authority. As Stanley Milgram's experiments showed, persuading even highly socialized, liberal, and otherwise gentle people to harm others for a cause is frighteningly easy if the instructing authority is accepted. Elias Canetti remarks that this 'system of commands' is 'perhaps most articulate in armies, but there is scarcely any sphere of civilized life where commands do not reach and none of us they do not mark'.[1]

An established social role for the authority—granted to the military by virtue of its role in defending the State—facilitates its acceptance. Overarching justification is usually provided by the State rather than the military itself. Depending on the situation, this justification may be clear and concrete: for example, the need to defend territory, citizens, or citizens of allied powers. If concrete justifications cannot be found, more abstract ones, citing threats to freedoms, values, or 'our way of life', will be employed. When justifications are liable to be challenged—that is, when the authority of the politicians who defend them is not necessarily accepted—the more concrete they are the better. When political authority is strong, ethereal ideas suffice.

Knowing that actions are required and approved of by the State can help to increase obedience and reduce the stress associated with carrying out those actions. When things go wrong the justification of only following orders may be used, as it was by Nazi soldiers after the Second World War. Soldiers of a State usually operate in an environment where they can assume that their orders are set within a recognized legal and political framework whose rules are widely accepted. However, actions as extreme as killing, even in a war run according to the Geneva Convention, can still be extremely stressful for those who kill.

Military training has therefore developed a number of ways of reducing stress. As might be expected, such training emphasizes obedience, loyalty, and discipline—virtues which help to conserve and propagate the current ideology, and which allow the diffusion of responsibility through the military and political hierarchies. High levels of physical activity are also used during training, independent thought is discouraged, and personal freedom is restricted. In modern warfare, particularly, the use of, and heavy emphasis upon, technology can serve to distance the aggressor who pulls the trigger or drops the bomb from the victim who is shot or blown apart. The greater the distance, the more bloodthirsty the aggressor may be. Indeed, as the historian Joanna Bourke notes, a wide-ranging survey of American infantrymen during the Second World War found that 'servicemen who had not left America hated the enemy most, and men serving in Europe hated the Japanese more than did the men actually killing Japanese troops in the Pacific'.[2] Or, as novelist John Buchan put it eighty years earlier, 'You find hate more among journalists and politicians at home than among fighting men.'[3]

Technology also provides complicated activities which demand attention and skill. These give rise to what the social psychologist Roy Baumeister calls 'low-level thinking', which he describes as 'a very concrete, narrow, rigid way of thinking, with the focus on the here and now, on the details of what one is doing'.[4] Anyone who has been thoroughly engrossed by some activity has experienced this; Baumeister's description is reminiscent of Stanley Milgram's 'agentic state', discussed in Chapter 4. The nineteenth-century philosopher William Hamilton gives a number of examples in his *Metaphysics*, including a Greek mathematician who had the misfortune to be in Syracuse in 212 BC, when the city was attacked and stormed by the Romans.

Archimedes, it is well-known, was so absorbed in a geometrical meditation, that he was first aware of the storming of Syracuse by his own death-wound, and his exclamation on the entrance of Roman soldiers was,–*Noli turbare circulos meos* [Latin for 'Do Not Disturb', at least for geometricians].[5]

The psychologists Robin Vallacher and Daniel Wegner have set low-level thinking within a wider framework they call action identification theory. This theory begins with the observation that most actions are indeterminate, that is, they can be described in multiple ways, using different levels of description with different terminologies. I can speak of my finger movement, for example, in terms of joints and muscle contractions (a mechanical description, treating my finger as if it were a machine). Or I can describe the movement as a mouse-click (a functional description of the movement which indicates its immediate purpose—to interact with the mouse). Or I could say that I moved the cursor to the text I wanted to italicize (an intentional description, referring to my state of mind). These three descriptions are quite different, but they all describe the same activity.

Vallacher and Wegner argue that 'whereas people may think about any action in many ways, they typically think about an action in just one way'.[6] That is, I may in principle be aware of the many ways in which I could describe my finger movement; if pressed I could list a number of them. However, *at any given moment* only one description will be active in my thoughts, and only that particular description is relevant to my reasons for acting as I do. When I move my finger, I am thinking of where I want the cursor to be; thoughts of muscles and joints do not impinge.

Certain finger movements—for example when aiming a gun at someone—are associated with descriptions in moral terms ('killing people is wrong'). These descriptions depend on a view of people as ends in themselves, valuable independent entities, not simply means by which one's own aims can be achieved. If a moral description were active when I was about to move my finger, it would greatly reduce the chance of my performing the action, since my moral inhibitions are powerful where murder is concerned. If, nevertheless, I wanted to kill the person at whom I was pointing the gun, it would be necessary to activate another description in place of the moral one. Focusing on the low-level details of the action, rather than its high-level implications, would make it easier to pull the trigger. Wegner gives the example of a nervous burglar disturbed by a home-owner:

> Thus, an action that started out in the early planning stages as 'protecting myself' [carrying a gun] might be achieved in the heat of the moment merely as 'pulling the trigger' and understood only at some point later in terms of its larger meaning and moral overtones as 'taking a life'. Although the burglar may have done all the things that would allow his behaviour subsequently to be viewed as intended [carrying a gun, pulling the trigger], the explicit intention [to 'take a life'] may not have been in his mind beforehand or as the action was done.
>
> Wegner, *The Illusion of Conscious Will*, p. 160

This focus on details allows the killer to avoid thinking about the victim's human status. As Baumeister puts it, 'Not only does this way of thinking help them perform more effectively, but it also prevents any feelings of guilt' from interfering with the action. Hence, in Hannah Arendt's famous phrase, the banality of evil. An obsessive interest in technicalities and bureaucracy can make sending people to their deaths much easier, and the same is true for killings committed in war.

As Joanna Bourke notes, the story of military training is not simply one of mindless obedience. Soldiers are indeed trained to obey, but many of them insist on their personal responsibility for their actions and conceive of even unseen enemies in personal, human terms. To see why, one needs to remember that participation in the military is not always a coerced and negative experience, especially when service is voluntary rather than conscripted. For the successful soldier, the benefits include physical fitness, technical skills, status, and a sense of group identity and support which can be as strong as or stronger than that provided by cults. In the elite units particularly, members are trained to think of themselves as superior beings and of their unit as their family (sometimes providing more emotional support than their real families ever did). Bourke, in her detailed review of the First and Second World Wars and the Vietnam War, argues that negative emotions such as hatred were considered less effective in producing good soldiers than the positive emotions of love and friendship which were encouraged within military groups. Hatred impaired self-control and efficiency, being 'liable to make men's hands tremble when shooting at the enemy'; it also made soldiers less certain of the justness of their cause, which in turn increased uncertainty and psychological conflict. In contrast, Bourke notes that love for one's comrades was an excellent motivation, 'widely regarded as the strongest incentive for murderous aggression against a foe identified as threatening that relationship'. Analogies of fraternal, paternal, or even sexual love were used to describe the 'buddy system' between soldiers. These positive emotions could be extremely strong and, as for lethal cults like the Manson Family, an intense group environment with a clearly identified external enemy provided powerful motivations and justifications for killing.

Is military training brainwashing? Here again, as in previous chapters, the various uses of the term brainwashing are apparent: as insult, process(es), concept of last resort, or totalitarian ideal. Critics of military techniques usually have either a strongly pacifist agenda or are seeking to transfer power away from the military. Such critics are using brainwashing as an insult when it is applied to non-conscript armies, since brainwashing involves the denial of voluntary choice (one could conceivably volunteer to be brainwashed, but a successful act of brainwashing would remove freedom, placing choice under the brainwasher's control). Military training, though it may change people, does not turn them into robots; indeed, the role of personal autonomy and the degree to which decisions are left to individual soldiers are often considerable. In functional terms, the processes by which civilians are turned into soldiers have been intensively studied and are increasingly understood by social psychology, which in America at least has owed much of its funding to the military. The use of brainwashing as a concept of last resort is shrinking accordingly.

As for the conceptual usage of brainwashing as totalitarian ideal, it can be invoked as a warning to those who would extend military powers into the civilian sphere, reducing civil liberties and increasing State control. As long as it is not overused, it can provide an incentive for the population to stay alert to possible repression. In the West, the plethora of voices purporting to be guardians of our freedom is often more apparent than real; as was seen in Chapter 3's discussion of advertising, media opinion is often remarkably homogeneous, particularly in times of crisis. Keeping us watchful for encroaching ideology is probably no bad thing. Nevertheless there are many important ways in which Western states are not totalitarian.

Criminal justice

Let justice be done, though the world perish
> The Holy Roman Emperor Ferdinand I, *attrib.*

Another area where the State often seems to be encroaching on its citizens' liberties is the criminal justice system. Laws define criminality not only in broadly accepted terms (murder, rape, embezzlement) but sometimes in much more specific and controversial ways. A current example is given by the baffling British drug laws, which, largely for historical reasons, ban the widely used drugs cannabis and ecstasy while tolerating alcohol and tobacco. It is of course a caricature to argue that ecstasy makes you loving and cannabis makes you stare at the ceiling, while alcohol makes you aggressive and tobacco makes you sick. However, objective measures of death statistics make a similar point, as Richard Davenport-Hines demonstrates in his eloquent critique of Western drugs policy, *The Pursuit of Oblivion*. Criticizing an antidrugs pressure group for declaring in 1996 that 'Hundreds of Scots died from drugs last year',[7] Davenport-Hines notes that 'The actual figure for 1995 was 251, comprising 155 opiate overdoses and 96 suicides using analgesics such as paracetamol. This compared with 20 000 Scots who had died of tobacco-related disease and 4000 of alcohol-related disease.' In 1995, then, the number of deaths from drugs (including legal drugs) was less than 2 per cent of the number of deaths from tobacco and less than 7 per cent of the number killed by alcohol. Neither the year nor the country are unrepresentative:

In Britain there are around 100 000 deaths annually from tobacco-related illnesses, 30–40 000 from alcohol-related illnesses and accidents, and 500 from paracetamol. On average, heroin and solvent abuse each claim about 150 lives each year, while amphetamine's death toll is about twenty-five. In the first ten years of British rave, with, at its peak, 500 000 people taking E every weekend, it was implicated in approximately sixty deaths: an average of six per year.

Davenport-Hines, *The Pursuit of Oblivion*, p. 391

Figures like these lead to suspicions that the hysteria over illegal drugs derives from factors other than a rational appreciation of statistics. Such drugs are feared not only because they are mind-altering (alcohol is mind-altering), but because they are associated with many undesirable qualities: poverty, squalor, social exclusion, violence, and crime. They are often described in the kind of tabloid language usually reserved for hated enemies, serial killers, or lethal infections, stigmatized in the same way we still all too often stigmatize mental illness. Drug users are portrayed as dangerous and dirty; lacking the usual social restraints because they are 'high' or 'addicted', they are unpredictable and therefore terrifying. The only ways to deal with them are elimination, isolation, or, possibly, rehabilitation (certainly not legalization). All involve the loss of liberty and the assumption that drug users cannot be trusted to act in their own best interests. These are the characteristics of the ideologically-defined non-person, the outsider, who provides an acceptable focus for group antipathy.

A huge amount of effort has gone into the promotion of this view that illegal drugs are evil while legal drugs are not. Is this partly because problem drug users are overwhelmingly from the least powerful groups in society, and therefore a relatively easy target for State ideology? Like any other group, societies are more cohesive, followers more obedient, and leaders more secure when they have some well-defined opponents to abhor. The drugs laws are one aspect of the criminal justice system where the functions of protection, deterrence, and harm reduction seem unconvincing. This lack of conviction weakens support for the criminal justice system in general, because it leaves room for the argument that the system's main function is to increase control by the State of its citizens. Michel Foucault claims that 'The ideal point of penalty today would be an indefinite discipline: an interrogation without end, an investigation that would be extended without limit to a meticulous and ever more analytical observation, a judgement that would at the same time be the constitution of a file that was never closed.'[8] The more closely an individual's actions are regulated by the State, the more precisely that individual's behaviour can be predicted and the more efficiently the government can run its affairs.

Is such control brainwashing? As remarked in previous chapters, the fear at the heart of brainwashing is the fear of losing control; of having not only one's actions but one's very thoughts manipulated by some outside agency. Thoughts are slippery enough as it is; the closer we look the more uncertain we are as to our own dominance of what we call our self. But we long to be able to echo that epitome of Victorian self-confidence, W.E. Henley's *Invictus*:

I am the master of my fate:
I am the captain of my soul.

We do not want to think of ourselves as straws blown about on the winds of causation, but as rational agents steering a careful course. The world may not be fully predictable; our actions may not be fully predictable even by ourselves, but that is preferable to having everything we do predicted by another—especially since that other may use prediction to implement control, against our best interests. Human beings may be socialized from an early age into the idea of obedience, but if they are made to feel that their actions are predicted or controlled by someone else (particularly if that someone is not an accepted authority) they often react very negatively, a phenomenon christened 'reactance' by the social psychologist Jack Brehm.[9] However, for reactance to occur, the 'reactor' must feel that some kind of resistance is possible; otherwise a set of submissive, depressed attitudes and behaviours (learned helplessness) will be adopted.

These responses—resistance or learned helplessness—can be seen in the different Christian traditions dealing with predestination, the idea that God, the ultimate (omnipotent) controller, knows the fate of each of us all along. They can also be found in responses to the secular equivalent, the doctrine of hard determinism (predestination for atheists)—the claim that everything we do is determined by events which occurred long before we were born, tracing back ultimately to the beginning of the universe. Some Christians emphasize the loving kindness of God: 'Okay, He pulls all the strings, but He loves you and He's got your best interests at heart, and being omniscient He knows what's good for you a lot better than you do, so why worry?' Others place more importance on the idea of our duty of obedience to God as Authority (*not* in the sense employed and enjoyed in Philip Pullman's *His Dark Materials* trilogy, but as the genuine and unique source of all power), in effect demanding learned helplessness. The atheist—'There's no one pulling the strings, but we're still puppets'—finds it difficult to argue for beneficence, since causes and chance are not to be personified, and has traditionally resorted either to fatalism or to some version of compatibilism, the generic name for arguments which aim to reconcile free will and determinism. (I will return to this topic in Chapter 11.) All these traditions, however different, are responses to our fear of losing control, the terror at the heart of brainwashing.

Domestic abuse

So far, the situations considered in this chapter have involved social institutions and their relationship with individuals. However, theorists who discuss ideology often include the family, that 'school of despotism' (as John Stuart Mill described it), on their list of ideological apparatuses.[10] The various types of abuse which can be found in families can reduce the power relationship to its simplest case: power held by one human being over another.

This basic social interaction can be one of the most intense and damaging.[11] A skilled abuser can use every trick in the influence technician's repertoire, from authority to commitment traps to sheer brute force, building up even an initially small inequality in power into an imbalance so huge that the abused partner in effect becomes a slave. Such abusers achieve a degree of control over their victims which is closer to the traditional idea of brainwashing than any situation mentioned so far, with the possible exception of the most extreme cults. All that is required is the imbalance of need whereby the victim rates her partner's 'love' more highly than he rates hers, and is willing to compromise in order to keep him happy.[12] She may be used to social interactions in which a compromise by one partner is reciprocated with concessions by the other; she will probably also be socialized into behaving more deferentially with social superiors. The abuser will take care to act as if he is superior in whatever domain she respects: if she is proud of her intelligence, he will be cleverer; if of her salary, his will be bigger (or else he'll find a good reason why it isn't). He will also ruthlessly exploit her tendency to compromise, minimizing the value of her contributions and exaggerating any concessions which he makes.

Abuse clearly illustrates the gradual nature of psychological control techniques. Human brains are good novelty detectors, but they have thresholds below which they cannot detect a change, and they have to make a special effort when tracking perceptions over long periods of time. This means that they are bad at detecting long-term, cumulative change if each step of that change is very small. From the start, the abuser may exploit this weakness by testing his partner's tolerance in small ways, perhaps with a snide remark here or there. A victim of abuse may initially register each individual put-down as trivial ('He's tired, he's had a bad day, he didn't mean it'), and unless she has made that special effort and conceptualized the remarks *as* part of a whole (as a concerted campaign, whether planned or not, by the abuser) she will not keep track of them—or their cumulative effect on her self-esteem. Recall the urban legend of boiling a frog: if the heat's turned up slowly enough the frog will never jump out and will boil to death. The abuser likewise ratchets up control by slow degrees. Every time his victim does not object, does not set her tolerance boundaries and stick to them, the next slight will be that little bit more hurtful, slowly lowering the victim's belief in her own competence while building up her perception of the abuser's abilities. If he is physically stronger, she may adopt learned helplessness. Repetitive verbal abuse focusing on her weakness, worthlessness, and isolation will reinforce this behaviour. She may also come to depend on the abuser for everything, particularly if he has demanded, as some cults do, that she withdraw from ties with friends and family.

If the victim does object, the abuser will apologize, turn on the charm, and then, a little while later, try again. Or he may use threats: desertion, poverty, humiliation, violence to her or her children. If she threatens him, he will know how to play on her guilt; the helpless small boy act is often very effective. But as the relationship progresses, the chances of her being this proactive will decrease. The continual denigration of her abilities, coming from someone she may once have loved, or may still love, but has come to fear, will change her self-image until she no longer thinks of herself as someone who is capable of threatening. We *do* see ourselves as others see us. Telling a person that they are useless at their job, for example, is an effective way of reducing their performance.

Over time, an abuser can reduce his partner from a functioning individual to a trapped and terrified creature whose cognitive horizons have so shrunk that she cannot even comprehend the possibility of escaping her predicament. Abusers not only exert control using verbal or emotional abuse and/or physical force, but they also create an environment in which the victim's only experience of herself is as a helpless being. Outsiders may be amazed at what a victim will tolerate, but this does not mean that there is something extraordinary about how that woman, child, or man came to be a victim. It is surely a truism to note that we often think things extraordinary when we do not understand the processes that made them. A peacock or a coral reef is an astonishment, but if we could know their history and the history of their species we would accept each step of that long evolutionary story as unremarkable, though it leaves us, here and now, gazing at a natural superlative. What is true of peacocks and coral reefs is true of abusers and their victims too.

Abuse and brainwashing

As I have already noted in other contexts, the processes which underlie brainwashing can increasingly be explained by social psychologists. The need for a concept of last resort is shrinking; the mysterious process has become a collection of less mysterious processes. We still use brainwashing as a pejorative term, signifying our disapproval of an abuser's control over his victim, signifying also perhaps our incomprehension of the specific twists and turns by which the oppressive relationship evolved. We accept, however, that those steps could in principle be comprehended; there is no magic process of brainwashing involved.

Also recognizable are the similarities between the abuser's behaviour and that of the totalitarian regime, as described by the psychiatrist Robert Lifton (see Table 1, p. 17). By milieu control, the abuser seeks to dominate the victim's environment, the stimuli that reach her brain, and hence the content of her thoughts. Abusers often also make use of a cult of confession in which the victim is allowed no privacy and must render detailed accounts of actions and thoughts.

Totalitarian regimes are characterized by a specific and firmly held ideology. They practise mystical manipulation and loading the language, and insist on their demands for purity, their sacred science and the primacy of doctrine over person. The ideology is good, that which is opposed to it is bad. What, then, is the abuser's ideology? Like all ideologies, it is a set of beliefs, in this case centred on the abuser's superiority. The abuser will act to reinforce these beliefs, partly by maximizing the contrast between his power and his victim's helplessness, partly by demonstrating his control over her, by force if need be.

Roy Baumeister has argued that individuals are much more likely to be violent if they have a high opinion of themselves, *and that opinion is threatened*, than if they have low self-esteem (his book *Evil* discusses this thesis, which runs contrary to many people's intuitions, in detail). In other words, violence is a response to an ego threat, in which a person is presented with a view of themselves that unfavourably contrasts with their own self-image. For people with high self-esteem whose achievements are mediocre, the chances of meeting such an ego threat are great; the truly great, and the mediocre who accept their mediocrity, will not be so frequently threatened. This thesis implies that a disproportionate amount of violent crime will be committed by individuals whose self-esteem has reached psychopathic levels. To quote Robert Hare in *Without Conscience*, they have 'a narcissistic and grossly inflated view of their self-worth and importance, a truly astounding egocentricity and sense of entitlement, and see themselves as the center of the universe, as superior beings who are justified in living according to their own rules'. The implication is correct: experts estimate that psychopaths make up between one and two per cent of the population of North America and commit about half of the serious crimes. As Hare comments, 'the prevalence of psychopathy in our society is about the same as that of schizophrenia, a devastating mental disorder that brings heart-wrenching distress to patient and family alike. However, the scope of the personal pain and distress associated with schizophrenia is small compared to the extensive personal, social, and economic carnage wrought by psychopaths. They cast a wide net, and nearly everyone is caught in it one way or another.'

Psychopathy remains a poorly understood condition, but what seems clear is that the underlying traits which make up the syndrome can also be found to varying degrees in the general population, including abusers. Not all abusers may be psychopaths (although some are), but many of them have the characteristic high but vulnerable self-esteem noted by Baumeister, tendency towards exploitative behaviour (treating other people as ends, not means), and lack of empathy.

Returning to the analogy between totalitarian regimes and abusers, we can see that abusers, like regimes, practise forms of mystical manipulation, sacred science, and loading the language, and insist on their demands for purity and the primacy of doctrine over person. Ego threats, which are after all expressions of alternative ideologies, are minimized as much as possible (demands for purity). Totalist ideology condemns anything other than itself, and an abuser will often load his language with simplistic, pejorative remarks, often based on little actual knowledge, which denigrate not only the victim but her family, friends, background, and opinions. The victim's psychological and physical health are less of a priority than the maintenance of the abuser's fragile ego (the primacy of doctrine over person), and the victim is not allowed to challenge this situation even though the abuser may provide no rational justification for his behaviour. Like sacred science, his superiority is taken for granted, first by him and later by his victim, and he uses mystical manipulation to establish a status within the relationship which is as close to that of an all-powerful, supernatural being as possible. Finally, the dispensing of existence needs no analogy: abusers can use lethal violence against their victims, both adults and children. In England and Wales, for instance, government statistics show that approximately 79 children are killed by violence every year. Most of these murders result from domestic violence.[13]

To accept these arguments is not, of course, to deny that the causes of violent behaviour are many and varied.[14] Similarly, the ingenuity of human beings' attempts to control each other is as much of an astonishment as a peacock or coral reef, albeit less pleasant to watch. But issues of self and self-image, like issues of freedom, are at the heart of any discussion of mind control techniques. To understand the possibilities of mind control, it is essential to look more closely at these topics, and I will do so in Part II. First, however, to our remaining case.

Torture

In Chapter 1, the case of Thomas Cranmer showed how the techniques associated with brainwashing have evolved from those developed for use in torture, while Father Luca's experience showed the continuing use of torture techniques as part of brainwashing. As Peter Suedfeld points out in *Torture*, such techniques have a long history: 'Although by no means universal, the use of torture to extract confessions from suspected criminals has a history that goes back at least to ancient Egypt' and includes the Greek and Roman civilizations and medieval European law. The *Malleus Maleficarum* (Hammer of Evil-doers), published in or around 1486 and by far the best-known medieval guide to witch hunting, is replete with torture techniques. By the mid-eighteenth to nineteenth centuries, judicial (public) torture and public humiliation in general were declining (Foucault's *Discipline and Punish* describes these changes). As of 9 December 2002, the United Nations website records that three-quarters of the 193 nations listed are a party to, or have signed, the UN Convention against Torture.[15] However, torture is still used 'unofficially' today by many regimes. A 2002 press release from Amnesty International, one of the most high-profile organizations campaigning against torture and other human rights abuses, states that 'The Amnesty International Report 2002 (covering events in 2001) documents extra-judicial executions in 47 countries; judicial executions in 31 countries; "disappearances" in 35 countries; cases of torture and ill-treatment in 111 countries and prisoners of conscience in at least 56 countries.' Amnesty 'believes that the true figures are much higher'.[16]

It should also be noted that torture is a somewhat fluid concept. Although there is general consensus that its hallmark is the deliberate infliction of severe pain or discomfort, often by agents of the State, the classification of individual cases may vary considerably with perspective. A study of Communist interrogation techniques during the Korean War notes that many American prisoners of the Chinese Communists regarded the prison diet, and particularly the fact that they were expected to relieve themselves publicly during brief, specified periods, as 'fiendish tortures'. However, as Hinkle and Wolff point out in *Communist interrogation and indoctrination of "Enemies of the States"*, 'Open latrines and public defecation are the custom in rural China, and they do not seem to be regarded as unpleasant by most Chinese'. Likewise, 'the Chinese Communists intend to provide in their prisons a diet equivalent to that of an average Chinese peasant or soldier'.

Descriptions of the 'classical' paradigm of brainwashing, for example those given by the word's inventor, Edward Hunter, make the similarity with torture obvious. Various methods of psychological and physical torture were common, despite the fact that, as Hinkle and Wolff remark, 'The KGB hardly ever uses manacles or chains, and rarely resorts to physical beatings. The actual physical beating is, of course, repugnant to overt Communist principles, and is contrary to KGB regulations also. The ostensible reason for these regulations is that they are contrary to Communist principles. The practical reason for them is the fact that the KGB looks upon direct physical brutality as an ineffective method of obtaining the compliance of the prisoner.'

Physical beatings, however, are only one facet of physical torture. 'Another which is widely used is that of requiring the prisoner to stand throughout the interrogation session or to maintain some other physical position which becomes painful.'[17] Sleep deprivation, isolation, and restrictions on vision, movement, diet, and urination/defecation may also be used. Such practices blur the line between psychological and physical torture. Their effects can be catastrophic, as Arthur Koestler showed in *Darkness at Noon*. Hinkle and Wolff note that 'The chief features of the isolation regimen in China are the same as those of the Soviet Union: total isolation, utter boredom, anxiety, uncertainty, fatigue, and lack of sleep; rejection, hostile treatment, and intolerable pressure; and reward and approval for compliance', a list of factors blending physical and psychological elements. Of course, some techniques of psychological manipulation do not involve physical torture. Physical torture, however, has an undoubted psychological impact.

Torture is totalitarian: like brainwashing, its overall goal is domination of the victim. In his book about torture in three Western democracies (Britain, the US, and Israel), John Conroy lists the specific goals of the torturer as follows: 'to gain information, to punish, to force an individual to change his beliefs or loyalties, to intimidate a community'.[18] The third goal is the most reminiscent of brainwashing. The psychologist Ervin Staub notes that motivations to torture can be pragmatic, for example intimidation to enhance political control, or 'more psychological', such as 'revenge for real or imagined harm or the desire to establish one's superiority and elevate the self'.[19] Again, this emphasis on control is reminiscent of the desire for total conquest which characterizes the dream of mind control.

Torture, like other extreme forms of doing harm, can, Staub says, 'be analyzed on three levels. At one level is the psychology of individual perpetrators. At the

91

second level, perpetrators and decision makers may be studied as a group. [...] The third level of analysis is the exploration of the characteristics of culture and historical processes within a society that give rise to psychological processes and motivations that are likely to lead to extreme harm doing.' Staub goes on to discuss social psychological factors: obedience to authority, differentiation between ingroups and outgroups, the role of ideology, the diffusion of responsibility, and the gradual, evolutionary nature of becoming a torturer.

Conroy also emphasizes the social aspects of torture. For example, he discusses what he calls the 'torturable class': the set of members of society whose torture is judged socially acceptable. In theory, if asked, we might all say that no one should be tortured; in practice, however, people are more flexible. Conroy argues that 'it is easy to condemn the torment when it is done to someone who is not your enemy', that torture 'arouses little protest as long as the definition of the torturable class is confined to the lower orders; the closer it gets to one's own door, the more objectionable it becomes', that 'the class of people whom society accepts as torturable has a tendency to expand', and that 'in places where torture is common, the judiciary's sympathies are usually with the perpetrators, not with the victims'. In other words, many tortures are carried out in circumstances where the perpetrators know that the wider society in which they operate either explicitly approves of their actions or turns a blind eye. Often 'just-world' thinking is involved: bystanders assume that the torturing authorities must know what they're doing and are unlikely to be sadists—that is, that their behaviour is rational and just. Therefore, bystanders conclude consciously or unconsciously, the torture victim must have deserved such treatment; he or she is therefore worthy of contempt. This conclusion can lead to extreme hostility towards the victim, as the poet Robert Browning's traveller shows:

I never saw a brute I hated so;
He must be wicked to deserve such pain.
                    Browning, 'Childe Roland to the Dark Tower Came', lines 83–4

This devaluation of the innocent is a common, tragic side-effect of torture.

Summary and conclusions

As emphasized in previous chapters, brainwashing is very much a social event, requiring both an agent and a victim. All the social situations considered in this book have involved ideological agents, representing forms of power which are widely understood and accepted by society in general. Such social consent, tacit or explicit, provides essential support for the activities of influence technicians.

Brainwashing involves stealth or coercion rather than rational persuasion. It shares many similarities with torture, from which it evolved, and many descriptions of alleged brainwashing situations include psychological or physical torture. Both brainwashing and torture seek to dominate the victim. Torture may be less concerned for the victim's welfare than brainwashing, for example when the torturer knows in advance that the victim will be killed. Both, however, share the totalist mindset, regarding the victim bureaucratically, rather than personally, as an instrument to be manipulated. Both also aim at the elimination of the victim's independent identity. Such independence is incompatible with total control, whether of body or mind.

In the next chapter I will explore the different degrees of influence, persuasion, and coercion, looking at the ways in which mind control techniques can vary.

Chapter 6: Brainwashing and influence

The love of liberty is the love of others; the love of power is the love of ourselves

William Hazlitt, *Political Essays*, 'The Times Newspaper'

In previous chapters I considered the history and development of the term brainwashing and its relevance to a number of situations where minds get changed: religious and political groups (Chapter 2), advertising and education (Chapter 3), treatments for mental illness (Chapter 4), and forms of social control which can be found in the military, the criminal justice system, and even in personal relationships (Chapter 5). It is now time to try and draw from these examples some conclusions about the nature of brainwashing.

Chapter 1 differentiated four ways in which the term brainwashing appears to have been used over its half-century of existence. Its widespread political use as an insult was already being noted and criticized by the 1960s, and remains much in evidence today. Its use as a concept of last resort was arguably dominant to begin with, but has declined as social psychology has provided specific theories to explain those human behaviours which so baffled Edward Hunter. The media still reach for the term brainwashing in certain situations, for example reports on cults, to suggest a sinister, occult, and gratifyingly sensational activity; but most psychologists would probably say that brainwashing by itself is not an explanation. That is, there is no specific magic process called 'brainwashing'. Rather, the term is a collective one, a shorthand for a set of specific social psychological processes, some or all of which may be operative when 'mindcraft' is employed to influence a person or persons.

Types of brainwashing

As Chapters 2 to 5 show, this is not to say that mind-changing situations are all the same. Religious cults and political parties are usually hierarchical, with a leader and followers whose needs are often complementary. These social institutions rely heavily on the power of the group for their success; they can be highly coercive, and they can come to dominate the cognitive landscapes of both leaders and followers. They use what I have referred to as brainwashing by force, in which the interactions between brainwasher and victim are personal and highly coercive, whether the brainwasher is following his own agenda (as in partner or child abuse) or acting as part of a larger social system (as in Communist thought reform).

Advertising is much less about coercion. Where a cult may attempt to impose an entire ideological system on its followers, any given advert aims to change only a few specific (product-related) beliefs. Advertising also generally reflects and works within currently accepted ideology—most adverts on British television today assume a background of capitalism, consumerism, and individual freedom. The one-to-many social structure of advertising, a form of influence created by a few and aimed, even for sophisticated niche advertising, at a relatively undifferentiated mass audience, is very different from that of cults. This is brainwashing by stealth, where the influence attempts are individually weak but accumulate in huge numbers, over time, to form a largely unchallenged background. No one advertisement can be held responsible for consumer culture, for example, not when there are hundreds of them facing us every day. Yet take them together, and the underlying messages have powerful effects on our thinking and behaviour.

Brainwashing, by force or by stealth, is part of a wider array of influence techniques, from television to terrorism. Returning to the metaphor of the cognitive landscape, we can say that an influence attempt may change the inner world in many ways, from the lightest persuasion—a wind brushing the grass—to the catastrophic coercion of forceful brainwashing—an earthquake or volcano. Many ideological apparatuses employ both forceful and stealthy techniques: domestic abuse is an example. And, as previous chapters have illustrated, many personal and social factors affect the nature and success of any given influence attempt. They include the personality, attitudes, and behaviours of the targeted individual and the differences between these and the aims of the influence technician, the time and effort put into the influence technique, the background ideology within which the influence attempt occurs, and the social structures used to transmit influence. The amount and type of coercion will also make a difference, as will the relative social power of target and influence technician. Social psychologists have done an immense amount of research on influence and social power.

One well-known classification system is Robert Cialdini's weapons of influence (reciprocation, commitment and consistency, social proof, liking, authority, and scarcity), discussed in Chapter 3, which derives primarily from the domain of marketing and advertising. Another is John French and Bertram Raven's 'bases of social power', widely used in organizational/workplace psychology. French and Raven distinguish six sources of social power: reward, coercion, legitimacy, expertise, reference, and information. Raven explains these as follows:

> consider the bases of power that a supervisor might use to correct the way in which a subordinate does his or her job: Reward (offer a promotion or salary increase for compliance); Coercion (threaten some punishment such as a loss in pay for noncompliance); Legitimacy (emphasize that the supervisor has the right to prescribe such behavior and a subordinate has an obligation to comply); Expertise (the supervisor knows what is best in this case); Reference (appeal to a sense of mutual identification such [that] a subordinate would model his or her behavior after the supervisor); and Information (carefully explain to the subordinate why the changed behavior is ultimately preferable).
>
> Raven, 'Power/interaction and interpersonal influence', p. 218

Mindcraft may be aimed at beliefs, emotions, or behaviours; it may rely on power, stealth, or rational persuasion; it may entice or compel, leave its target feeling disgusted, resentful, helpless—or joyful, grateful, and empowered. What it always does is change the target's brain, as every stimulus does.

Brainwashing by force, as described by Edward Hunter, George Orwell, and others, relies heavily on coercion and emotions, on power inequalities, and on the intense interactions which can be generated in groups, particularly small groups. It is time-consuming and resource-intensive; this, as much as or more than ethical qualms, is a reason why it has not been widely used by Western governments. Small groups such as cults or terrorist cells, however, are able to use intense techniques because they can much more completely control a victim's environment. They can also use the external world as a large and ever-present threat with which to whip up fear and anxiety in the mind of the victim (liberal, peaceful, and secure democracies have to work harder to make such tactics convincing). Brainwashing aims to achieve behavioural change, but behaviour is secondary: its main goal is to change the thoughts of its victims to fit its preferred ideology. Change should be possible however resistant the victim and however different the victim's prior beliefs. Ideally the change in the victim's cognitive landscape is so huge that it affects not only those beliefs directly relevant to the imposed ideology but all beliefs, however trivial, so that every action and perception can be reinterpreted in the light of the new convictions.

The ideas behind brainwashing

The concept of brainwashing is, as psychologists say, both cognitive and affect-ive: it draws on both reason and emotion (a dichotomy which, as we will see in Part II, is by no means absolute). Emotions are important and can be extremely strong. Brainwashing evokes fears of losing self-control, of being used and domin-ated by another, and of losing one's very identity. In this it is similar to command hallucinations, the bullying inner voices which can so terrify patients with schizophrenia. Socially, it shares with intoxication the prospect of the target being blamed for actions which were very poorly controlled (though a drunk may believe at the time that he knows what he is doing). Unlike intoxication, brainwashing attacks not only the victim's sense of control, but also their very identity. The command to act is external, but in a successful victim of brainwash-ing it is not felt as such, and the victim will accept responsibility for the resulting actions. This contrasts with schizophrenia, where the demanding voices are often perceived as coming from outside sources (aliens, the CIA, the Devil, or whatever it may be).

Brainwashing also has a cognitive component: that is, it draws on a number of ideas we have about ourselves. These ideas have surfaced at intervals throughout the preceding five chapters, but I think it is worth collating them here, as they are central to our understanding of mind control and the problems it poses.

The idea of power
Power is variously defined, but definitions usually centre on an individual agent's capacity to act in a certain way. Power is therefore domain-specific, unless you are God; mere human beings can do certain things but not others. The concept of power is closely related to the concepts of control and influence and, as discussed earlier in the context of social power, may originate from a variety of sources. The influential psychologist David McClelland argues that power motivation, which he defines as 'the inner need or disposition to seek power or concern for having a strong impact on others', is one of the three basic motives underlying social behaviour (the other two are the need to achieve success, and affiliation, the desire to socialize and have friends).[1]

The idea of change
An individual's power depends not only on what he or she does, but on how the actions are received and interpreted by other individuals. Social power is the ability to impact on other people, that is, to change their beliefs, attitudes, and behaviours. Processes of mind control essentially involve change, simply because the world of human beings is never as co-operative as one might like.

The idea of causation

As the philosopher David Hume famously showed, causation is one of those concepts which we think we understand well and generally don't. Hume said that it is not our power to reason but merely the actual experience of 'constant and regular conjunction' which leads us to make inferences about cause and effect.[2] This particularly applies to prediction:

> These two propositions are far from being the same, *I have found that such an object has always been attended with such an effect*, and *I foresee, that other objects, which are, in appearance, similar, will be attended with similar effects*. I shall allow, if you please, that the one proposition may justly be inferred from the other: I know, in fact, that it always is inferred. But if you insist that the inference is made by a chain of reasoning, I desire you to produce that reasoning.
>
> Hume, *Enquiries*, p. 34

Daniel Dennett, writing well over three centuries later,[3] distinguishes a number of factors which we use to support claims about causation (such as the sentence 'Bill's tripping Arthur caused him to fall'). These include causal necessity ('had Bill not tripped Arthur, he would not have fallen'), causal sufficiency ('Arthur's fall was an *inevitable outcome* of Bill's tripping'), independence (it should be possible to conceive of Arthur falling as separate from Bill tripping him, so that one might exist without the other), and temporal priority ('A reliable way to distinguish causes from effects is to note that causes occur earlier'). Dennett also notes that other factors, such as physical contact between cause and effect, or our belief that the cause is an *agent*, 'may increase our confidence when we make causal judgments'. We may be less convinced about those judgements, for example, when an event has multiple causes, but we still rely on the concept of causation. Influence attempts depend on the idea that the behaviour of the person making the attempt will cause changes in the target.

The idea of responsibility

The capacity to be acknowledged as the owner or source of an action is vital and basic to our social interactions. Along with this sense of agency comes the concept of responsibility, through which human beings can be held to account for their actions. Responsibility is essential for the accurate assigning of credit and blame, reward and punishment.

The most analytical treatment of responsibility we are likely to encounter in everyday life is that used by the criminal justice system to decide whether a given action (or omission) is a criminal offence for which the defendant is responsible, and therefore liable (able to be held to account). British law distinguishes two components of an offence: the *actus reus* and the *mens rea*. Broadly speaking, the *actus reus* comprises 'external' elements such as the defendant's behaviour and states of affairs arising from that behaviour, while the *mens rea* refers to 'internal' elements such as the defendant's intentions and state of mind. The two components are not always easily separable, as for example when a defendant is accused of carrying an offensive weapon. A weapon is an external element, and therefore part of the *actus reus*, but a 'weapon of offence' is legally defined as 'any article *intended* by the person having it with him to cause injury to another person';[4] in other words, the intention (the *mens rea*) is crucial. However, though *mens rea* and *actus reus* may sometimes be interdependent, they are both usually required for an offence to have been committed. 'There is no criminal liability merely for possessing a particular state of mind.' Not in British law, or at least not yet, although the increasing medicalization of personality (as discussed in Chapter 4) has encouraged a trend in this direction.

The idea of the self

Responsibility and agency require a responsible agent. This evokes the problem of how to define such an agent. Human agency usually takes for granted the idea of a self, traditionally the recipient of perceptions and the source of both thoughts and actions. In the seventeenth century the philosopher René Descartes defined consciousness as the essential aspect of the self: pure, disembodied, and independent of the physical world. This is the view that our minds are pure and crystalline, like diamonds. More recently, philosophers and scientists have argued that, whatever the self is, it is much more like clay than like a diamond: malleable, interconnected, and dependent on physical reality, particularly the physical reality of the human brain. Social scientists, meanwhile, have argued that we define ourselves in large part based on our roles in the society we live in and our interactions with other human beings. The way in which the self is envisaged has considerable impact on the way attempts to change that self are conceived; diamond minds are much less changeable than clay ones. So the notion of self is an important one for brainwashing.

The idea of free will

Central to the notion of the *actus reus* is the requirement that the defendant had free will when carrying out the actions, or bringing about the state of affairs, which constitute the *actus reus*. In *Criminal Law* Jonathan Herring notes the 'fundamental principle that such action must be willed or voluntary', that is, 'that the defendant must have been able to prevent herself from acting in the way she did'. This requirement rules out accidental behaviour and physical compulsion by others (in the strictly physical sense of being pushed, not of being threatened with death), as well as automatism and insanity. Automatism refers to actions which happen outside the consciousness and/or control of the mind: examples include reflexive muscle spasms caused by a sudden event and actions carried out while concussed. Self-induced automatism (e.g. resulting from intoxication) is not an acceptable defence. Insanity is similar to automatism except that the causal factors are internal (e.g. disease) rather than external (e.g. a sudden noise or a blow to the head). What is not ruled out is provocation, the reaction to strong emotions associated, for example, with so-called crimes of passion. I will say more about strong emotions in Chapter 9.

As for the legal system, so for the rest of the social universe. Freedom, as we shall see in Chapter 11, is a basic human value. Historically minded philosophers comment upon the relatively recent (seventeenth-century) arrival of the term 'consciousness' in the English language; words for freedom have been part of that language at least since the ninth century. And the concept of freedom is much older than its English manifestation. Even today, free will is a hotly debated topic, lurking at the heart of theories of human behaviour like a singularity in an equation. Just as dividing by zero gives an infinity of possible values, so plunging into the cauldron of free will can leave one feeling adrift in a sea of confusing philosophical possibilities. Yet free will is central to our conceptions of ourselves, particularly in the modern Western world. It is central to, indeed constitutive of, the problem of brainwashing, since it is only if we have free will that severe forms of influence pose a potential threat. Otherwise we seem to be like beads sliding down a never-ending string of causes, and any form of influence is just one more cause among many in a causally determined world.

Summary and conclusions

The concepts described above cannot be avoided when discussing mind control. Some, like the idea of change, appear relatively unproblematic; others, like free will, have been puzzling great thinkers for centuries. However, present-day thinkers have one advantage over their forebears, an advantage which I think is a considerable one. That advantage is the increased scientific understanding of human brains and behaviours bequeathed to us by the twentieth century. Part I of this book has described many examples of how social psychology has improved understanding of behaviour, particularly group behaviour. Part II will turn to neuroscience, and the marvels of the human brain.

Part II

The traitor in your skull

Chapter 7: Our ever-changing brains

For there is no creature whose inward being is so strong that it is not greatly
determined by what lies outside it

George Eliot, *Middlemarch*

This Part will lay the scientific foundations required to put the 'brain' into brainwashing. In particular, much of this chapter will be devoted to the central mechanism involved in influence techniques—brain change—necessitating some
acquaintance with the findings of modern neuroscience.

Tantalizing science

Neuroscience, the investigation of brains, is a child of the Enlightenment, born of
the belief that nothing is out of bounds to science.[1] Like her sister, genetics, she
grew up in the twentieth century, overshadowed by their older sibling physics,
who has changed all our lives and has blood on her altar to prove it. Genetics
promises even greater accomplishments, boasting of how she will one day conquer the world. Compared to these showy teenagers, neuroscience is a quiet
Cinderella. But some say that she will outstrip her sisters, changing not only the
world we live in, not only the bodies we are born with, but the thoughts and
selves and cultures we create.

Neuroscience has already begun to tell us that we are not the kind of creatures
we thought we were; that some of our best-loved everyday assumptions about
our selves are misplaced. Many of our social interactions are based on two such
cherished concepts. The first is solidity: the idea that we have diamond minds,
that our personalities and memories, once formed, change slowly if at all. The
second is free will: the idea that we control, and can therefore be held responsible
for, at least some of our actions (those we call free). These assumptions have,

of course, not gone unchallenged by the world's scientists, philosophers, and writers. Even in this book we have seen plenty of evidence of how people can change and how they can be controlled. Yet ideas of solidity and free will retain colossal influence, particularly in the West. The British criminal justice system, for example, relies on the notion of free will when assigning responsibility and handing out punishment. It also assumes solidity: the person jailed for a murder is expected to be 'the same person' who killed, in that their personality has not drastically changed in the meantime. Brainwashing, which by inflicting massive personality change removes its victims' freedom to act but leaves them still believing they are acting freely, also draws power from these assumptions. To understand what happens in brainwashing, we need to look at them more closely.

Free will is the topic of Chapter 11; we explore the assumption of solidity later in this chapter. Before doing so, however, it is time to pay a visit to Neuroworld.

Neuroscience in a nutshell

Open a popular neuroscience book, and before you're very far into it you'll almost certainly find a sentence telling you how many billions of neurons there are in a human brain. A popular analogy relates the number of possible connections between these neurons to the number of atoms in the known universe. Given the difficulties most people have in conceptualizing such gigantic numbers, I shall not be making either of these statements. Instead, I shall try a different way of conveying the superabundant complexities in our skulls: the metaphor of planet Earth.

Science and computer graphics have helped us to imagine how our world began, coalescing into a naked, spinning rock with a core of molten iron. Baby Earth was a tortured creature, racked by earthquakes, volcanoes, and meteoric impacts, shaped by huge changes. But as it cooled, the violence of birth receded and the geography we see today became established. Meanwhile, whether borne from space or harboured in the deepest seas, a cluster of chemicals arose with a unique ability—to make copies of itself. Life has clung on ever since, surviving comets, ice ages, and everything else the universe has thrown at it. So far.

As for our planet, so for each human brain. Early changes are huge, shaping our still-fluid cognitive landscapes, determining the major patterns of our personalities. A meteor at this stage could have catastrophic effects on future development. Gradually things settle down, the fierceness of early emotions cools, the rate of change decreases. And, just as life took hold on the young Earth, each species carving out its own niche, so the miasma of culture settles over our landscapes, shaping them in innumerable ways. Thoughts, the inhabitants of the neural world, flourish in their millions. Some, like fossils, leave a mark; most die in silence. Like living things, they are clearly distinguishable into species, yet each is unique. And, like living things, thoughts can replicate, spreading from brain to brain as we may one day spread from world to world.

Some forms of life have gone so far as to develop complex bodies, brains, and social interactions. Only one, to our knowledge, has come up with language and an intensely developed culture, but many species lacking these faculties have nevertheless made a huge impact on the world around them. But the Earth itself, although greatly shaped by the existence of life, does not require it. If, as doom-mongers have been predicting since humans grasped the concept of doom, we someday cease to be and take everything living with us, the Earth won't give up in despair and go into a decline. It will simply spin on its axis as it has always done. As the writer Salman Rushdie puts it:

we look up and we hope the stars look down, we pray that there may be stars
for us to follow, stars moving across the heavens and leading us to our destiny,
but it's only our vanity. We look at the galaxy and fall in love, but the universe
cares less about us than we do about it, and the stars stay in their courses
however much we may wish upon them to do otherwise.

Rushdie, *The Moor's Last Sigh*, p. 62

The same is true of brains. They do not cease to exist if their mental inhabitants are removed, if thought and culture become extinct, or never get established. They simply lose almost all of what makes them interesting. All that remains is the same bleak message we receive from our desolate sister-planet Mars: a reminder of what was, or might have been, and of what we will be when our flourishing is at an end.

Imagine the job of exploring a new planet—of not only understanding the forces which shaped land and sea and weather but recording the species and explaining how they evolved—and you have some idea of the task facing neuroscientists. Like interplanetary pioneers, brain explorers bring tools and knowledge with them: neuroanatomists to map brain geography, neuropharmacologists, neurophysiologists, cell biologists, and neurogeneticists to study mechanisms, neuroimaging researchers to take beautiful pictures from space, and innumerable other specialists investigating everything from sex to serotonin. The explosion in research has brought inevitable fragmentation and makes neuroscience as a whole impossible to summarize. However, certain fundamentals are generally agreed upon, and it is to these that I now turn.

What are brains made of?

Brains, like the nerves in our bodies, are made up of cells known as neurons, specialists in transmitting signals to each other. Neurons contain a fluid (the cytoplasm) full of various molecules, as well as a central area (the nucleus) which contains essential machinery such as the DNA (deoxyribonucleic acid) of which the cell's genes are made. Each neuron can send signals via a long protuberance called an axon, while receiving signals from other neurons via shorter protuberances called dendrites. Usually each neuron has one axon and many dendrites, so it can receive thousands of signals from other cells, but can only send one signal at a time. Each neuron's axon stretches out to another neuron (the nerves which tell us our toes are cold have axons reaching across a metre or more, from foot to spinal cord). But the axon does not touch the recipient cell. A tiny gap, called the synapse, is left between them (see Fig. 7.1).[2]

Where do neurons live?

Neurons can only function because each cell lives and breathes and has its being in a teeming soup of particles, the cerebrospinal fluid (CSF). Some of these molecules are neutral, others, called ions, carry a positive or negative electric

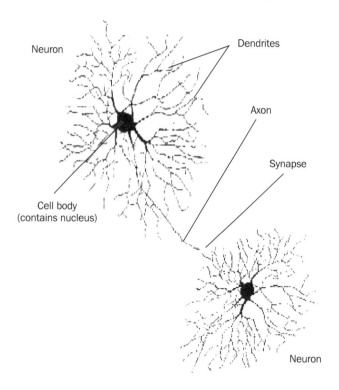

Figure 7.1 Neurons consist of a cell body—containing the machinery the cell needs to function—from which many dendrites and a single axon protrude. Dendrites receive signals from other cells. The axon, which can be a metre or more in length, allows the cell to send signals to other cells. Between the end of the axon and the next cell is a tiny gap (exaggerated in the diagram). This is the synapse, across which information passes from one cell to another.

charge. Sizes vary, from the smallest and simplest (ions like sodium, potassium, or chloride) to the larger and more complicated (like proteins, fats, drugs, or viruses). Brains receive the nutrients they need to function (like glucose and oxygen) from blood vessels lined with a specialized type of cell. This lining makes up the blood–brain barrier, a vital protection which controls what may and may not enter the brain (see Fig. 7.2a).

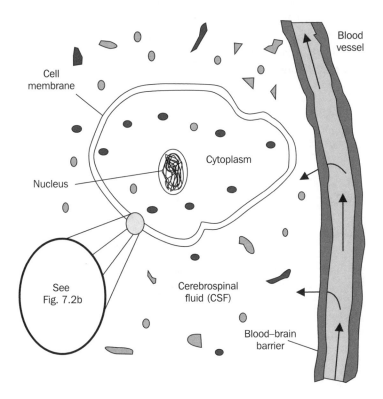

Figure 7.2(a) A schematic representation of a neuron (for simplicity, the axon and dendrites are not shown). The neuron is surrounded by a cell membrane which contains the cell nucleus and a fluid—the cytoplasm. The nucleus contains the cell's genes, the recipe from which proteins are built. The cytoplasm contains much of the machinery which runs the cell, producing energy, moving proteins from where they were produced to where they are needed, repairing damage, and generating the electrical signals which pass along the axon to the synapse. The cytoplasm contains many ions (electrically charged particles: represented by small filled shapes in the diagram). When the neuron is at rest (not signalling), the cytoplasm contains relatively more negative ions than the CSF in which the neuron lives. Any cell contains many varieties of both negative and positive ions as well as molecules with no overall electrical charge.

Inside and outside

The neuron's equivalent of skin is the cell membrane, a double layer of fatty molecules called phospholipids. Like a country's borders, it defines the shape of the cell and—at least in theory—keeps unwanted visitors out. In practice, most countries have many routes of access, some guarded, some not. Cells are the same: the phospholipid membrane is full of holes. Some are unguarded, but only allow certain molecules, like water and potassium, to leak through; others are guarded by mechanisms known as receptors, which must be activated by a specific signal (usually from another neuron) before the gate will open to let molecules into the cell (see Fig. 7.2(b)). There is a constant two-way traffic across the cell membrane and, like countries, cells have complex internal mechanisms for dealing with whatever enters them.[3]

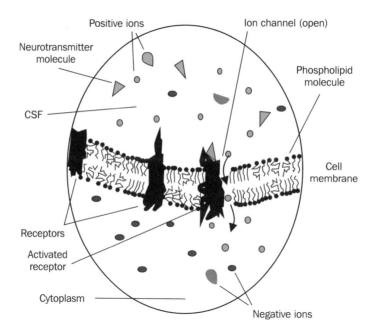

Figure 7.2(b) A section of the cell membrane, which is made up of a double layer of phospholipid molecules. Embedded in the membrane are receptors, complex molecules which can be activated when a neurotransmitter locks on. Each receptor responds only to a few specific molecules, and does so by changing shape. This can trigger a number of changes within the cell, including (as shown here) the opening of an ion channel. Because a neuron at rest has an interior which is negatively charged relative to the CSF, positive ions will tend to pass through an open ion channel into the cell. This is because they are repulsed by other positive ions—of which there are more in the CSF—and attracted by negative ions—of which there are more in the cell. The diagram shows positive ions (grey filled shapes, with direction of motion indicated by arrows) moving into the cell through an open ion channel.

How do neurons work?

All cells have evolved mechanisms known as ion pumps. Just as receptors regulate what goes into the cell, so ion pumps remove certain ions (like immigration officials ejecting undesirables from a country). Neurons have become particularly good at this ion trafficking, with the result that they can precisely control the difference in electrical charge between their environment (the CSF) and their innards (the cytoplasm). When they are not busy receiving signals, neurons' innards are negatively charged relative to the CSF. Signals activate receptors which let positive ions *into* the neuron, making it *less negative* relative to the CSF and starting an electrical wave—the cell's own signal—which spreads along the entire cell to the tip of the axon. Pumping *out* positive ions makes the cell *more negative* relative to the CSF, bringing the balance of charges back to the resting, negative state, ready to generate the next signal.

How do neurons communicate?

Synapses, in brain terms, are where the action is. Across these tiny chasms cells talk to one another. The language they use is a semaphore of spitting. When an electrical signal reaches the end of an axon, it triggers the release of tiny packets of chemicals, known as neurotransmitters (because they transmit between neurons). These molecules are spat out across the gap, and some of them reach the neuron on the other side. There they find receptors on the neuron's surface (the cell membrane), just waiting for the right molecule to come along. For the perfect partner, bonding is immediate: like a lock in a key the neurotransmitter plugs into the receptor molecule, causing it to writhe into a new position. As the receptor changes shape, a gate in the cell membrane opens and whichever chemical can enter through that gate does so, changing the electrical status of the cell and setting off a variety of secondary signals (known as second messengers). Its message delivered, the neurotransmitter detaches, to be recycled by specialized molecules (reuptake enzymes) lurking in the synapse; while the receptor returns to its 'passive' state to await the next contact (see Fig. 7.3).

Learning

Though the receptor may resume its former position, the cell in whose membrane it sits will never be quite the same again. Sometimes the change is minuscule, but often the bombardment of transmitter molecules can cause long-lasting changes, affecting not only the cell's electrical status (which may lead the cell to generate a signal of its own) but its genetic machinery. Genes can be switched on or off; the machinery which reads those genes and makes proteins can be urged to redouble its efforts or told to take it easy. Those proteins may be more receptors, to be shipped out to the cell membrane. Or they may have jobs to do within the cell. They in turn will affect the neuron's inner environment,

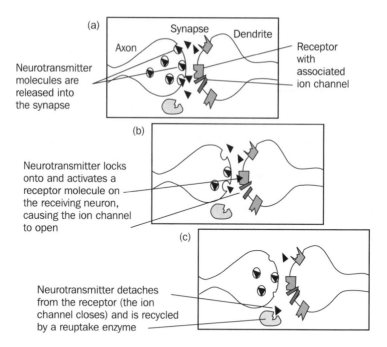

Figure 7.3 The process by which a neuron communicates with another neuron across the tiny gap between them, the synapse.

Figure 7.3(a) shows the axon of the communicating neuron (on the left) and the dendrite of the receiving neuron (on the right). The axon terminal contains a number of tiny spheres filled with molecules of neurotransmitter (black triangles). When a neuron's signal reaches the end of its axon, these spheres move to the cell membrane, where they empty their contents into the synapse.

The receiving neuron's cell membrane contains a variety of receptor molecules (three are shown here), some of which have associated ion channels (one is shown here).

Figure 7.3(b) shows one of the molecules of neurotransmitter (black triangles) locked onto a receptor on the receiving cell. The associated ion channel has opened.

Figure 7.3(c) represents the recycling of neurotransmitter. Once the neurotransmitter molecule has detached from its receptor, the ion channel associated with that receptor closes, allowing the receiving neuron to rebalance the electrical charges inside and outside the cell, ready for the next incoming signal. Meanwhile, the reuptake enzyme removes neurotransmitter from the synapse and transfers it back into the cell which sent the signal, so that the cell's ability to talk to its neighbour is constantly maintained.

which may cause other receptors in the membrane to open or close … and so on, in an illimitable mesh of cause and effect.

Why does this matter? Because the net effect is often to change the cell's receptiveness to future messages. Shipping out more receptors to the cell membrane, for example, will make a cell more sensitive to neurotransmitters, and hence more likely to respond with a signal of its own. Conversely, 'retiring' receptors from the cell membrane will make a neuron less likely to be activated by incoming signals. This ability of cells to alter the strength of the synapses between them is the secret of the brain's power to learn from experience. Generally, when two neurons are active at the same time the synapse connecting them will tend to strengthen. When one neuron is activated, having a stronger synapse between them will increase the chance that the other neuron is also activated. By linking synaptic strengths to how active neurons are, the brain sculpts its cognitive landscape according to the stimuli it receives. Just as water flowing over the ground carves out a channel, and thus over time flows more and more easily, so signals flow between neurons, strengthening connections between them, and making it easier for future signals to flow. The more frequent or intense an incoming signal is to some neurons, the stronger the connections between those neurons will become. This is why repetition is a central feature of brainwashing techniques.

Brain layout
Human brains are divided, like country mansions, into upstairs and downstairs. Below stairs are the subcortical regions, such as the cerebellum, thalamus, amygdala, and superior colliculus (more on these later), where a lot of the work gets done: heartbeat, breathing, temperature control, many aspects of movement, some learning, and a lot more of which we are usually unaware. There are many areas of subcortex: some process incoming (sensory) information, some outgoing motor commands, some information about the current position and state of the body (which contributes to the states we call emotions), and some have more complex functions. I will not be saying very much about subcortex: books have been written about individual subcortical areas, but reprising even a few of them here is beyond the scope of this book.

Upstairs is the cortex, where the glamour is—self, free will, consciousness, even 'the God module', are all alleged to live somewhere in this realm. The cortex is divided into two halves, the right and left hemispheres, each of which is split into four main regions, or lobes.[4] At the back of the head are the two occipital lobes. At the sides of the head are the less well-understood parietal lobes (towards the top) and the temporal lobes (towards the bottom), while the front of the brain, highly developed in humans, is taken up by the right and left frontal lobes (see Fig. 7.4). Every lobe contains many subareas, and the types of signals

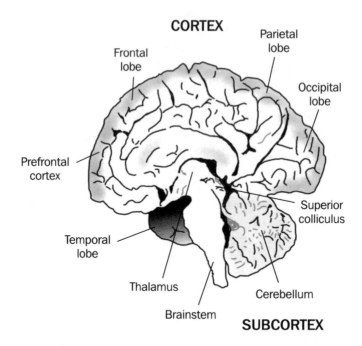

Figure 7.4 A medial view of a human brain, with the four major divisions of cortex (the frontal, temporal, parietal, and occipital lobes) labelled. Medial views represent the brain as if it had been split down the middle, with one half-brain removed so that the inner surface of the remaining half is visible. (Also common are lateral views (e.g. Fig 10.1(a), p. 168), in which the brain is seen sideways on, with the front end (frontal lobe) towards the left and the back end (occipital lobe) towards the right.) The cortex forms a wrinkled layer over the subcortex. Four subcortical landmarks—the thalamus, cerebellum, superior colliculus, and brainstem—are also labelled.

neurons receive seem to vary from lobe to lobe and from area to area. Signals from the eyes, for example, enter the cortex at the back of the brain, in the occipital lobes, while signals from the ears enter the temporal lobes. Neurons also differ in the signals they send. In sensory areas, cells send signals mainly to other cortical or sensory subcortical areas, while those areas in the frontal lobes which are concerned with the production of movements send command signals to subcortical output areas: groups of neurons with fast connections to the spinal cord, and hence to muscles.

The solid self

After that crash course, it is now time to return to the main topic of this chapter: the assumption of solidity. We all marvel at how quickly children grow up, and indeed the rate of change in a child's brain is dramatic. But we tend to assume that after a certain age our brains are basically fixed, barring accidents or disease. An example: when told that dyslexia is a brain-based condition, people with this learning disability often react with despair: 'So I'm stuck with it then.' It's in the brain; it's fixed for ever more. Scientists instruct us that selves are to do with brains; very well, then, selves must be fixed too, changing slowly (over years) if at all. The assumption of solidity can thus take two forms: one relating to brains, the other to selves. The former is modern; the latter much older. We adults know who we are: the source of our actions and the owners of our thoughts. Just because we can't give a philosopher's definition of self doesn't mean we don't have a strong sense of our own identity over time.

If we're lucky we'll never have felt those deep foundations shake, because such an experience can be among the most frightening in the world. The sense of inner death, of emptiness where a self should be healthily growing, gives depression its particular horror; while the splintering disintegration of self, whether slowly in Alzheimer's disease or catastrophically in florid schizophrenia, scares most people rigid. We fear anything likely to threaten our identity: drugs, illness, brain damage, new technologies. We especially object to attempts by other people to change us: social engineering, influence attempts (which at least are usually temporary), and brainwashing (whose effects might last for ever). Even when we want to change, submitting to therapists and gurus, chasing the dream of a shiny and bright new lifestyle, we are trying to change something about 'us', in the full expectation that 'we' (the same 'we' who signed up) will receive the benefits. The classic image of brainwashing is of a process which destroys that expectation; this is part of its horror.

With respect to brains, however, the assumption of solidity is simply incorrect. Brains change all the time: everything you perceive, every stimulus received by your senses, changes your brain. Sometimes the change can be dramatic. After limb amputation, for example, some unfortunate people develop a 'phantom limb'. Though imaginary, the phantom feels so real that its possessor can be tormented by pain from it; patients often say that the phantom is clenched tight and they cannot relax it. How does phantom limb pain come about? What seems to happen is that when the limb—a hand, for example—is removed, neurons in that part of the cortex which used to process signals from the hand no longer receive their usual input. Rather than have all those 'hand cortex' neurons lying idle (neurons have a rigorous work ethic), they are co-opted into the activity of other, neighbouring groups of neurons and start to receive the same inputs as their neighbours. Since 'hand cortex' is next to the area receiving input from the face, former 'hand' neurons become 'face' neurons. But the areas of the brain which receive signals from these neurons do not have any way of knowing about the neurons' change in input (from hand to face). As far as they are concerned, a signal from those neurons means something going on in the hand. This can lead to a bizarre result: touching the face of someone with a phantom hand can provoke the feeling that the *non-existent* hand is being touched.[5]

Not all brain alterations are as strange as phantom limbs. Some changes are tiny and short-lived, leaving, as the philosopher John Locke put it, 'no more footsteps, or remaining characters of themselves, than shadows do flying over fields of corn'.[6] But many changes, while small and unnoticed in themselves, are cumulative and their net effect longer-lasting. Consider how muscles adapt to the gradually decreasing weight of, say, a bottle of concentrated cranberry squash. The squash drinker takes so little at a time to flavour her water that each single change in the bottle's weight is imperceptible. Only when she reaches for a new, full bottle for the first time does she realize with a jolt that her brain is expecting the 'empty' weight. Just because we fail to notice a change does not mean our brains don't register it. In fact we don't observe the vast majority of what is going on in our brains at any given moment.

This gigantic blindness, which underpins the assumption of solidity, makes us unwisely conservative about what will and won't affect our brains. Drugs, disease, and damage we know about, but these are minority terrors, and even for them we are reluctant to acknowledge a change in our own identity ('he' may be a different person since he was brainwashed, but 'I' am the same as far as I'm concerned). Any other agent is assumed to have no effect on brains—and certainly none on selves—until proven otherwise. This conservative principle is associated with one of the most influential ideas in Western thought: Cartesian dualism, the doctrine I have labelled as diamond minds. Dualism is the philosopher René Descartes' notion that selves are 'thinking things', mysterious entities on the (posh) incorporeal side of a strict division between high mind and lower matter. If minds are as different from bodies as Descartes suggested, we wouldn't expect changes in bodies to have any effects on minds.

Even in the seventeenth century doubt was cast on this implacable dichotomy. The philosopher Anne Conway (1631–1679) suffered from debilitating headaches. She knew very well how body influenced mind, and said so in a much-admired critique of Descartes published (posthumously) in 1690:

Furthermore, why does the spirit or soul suffer so with bodily pain? For if when united to the body it has no corporeality or bodily nature, why is it wounded or grieved when the body is wounded, whose nature is so different? [...] But if one admits that the soul is of one nature and substance with the body [...] then all the above mentioned difficulties vanish; and one may easily understand how the soul and body are united together ...

Conway, *The Principles of the Most Ancient and Modern Philosophy*, p. 58

Descartes was dead by the time Conway's treatise was published, but he had been made aware of the question of pain by another highly intellectual woman, the Palatine Princess Elizabeth of Bohemia, with whom he corresponded. As Conway's editors note, 'Descartes never answered the question. He simply advised Elizabeth to spend only a few days a year on metaphysical matters, something he certainly never suggested to any of his male correspondents who queried aspects of his philosophy.'[7]

Yet it is Princess Elizabeth's argument—that pain is an exception to the dualist principle—which stood the test of time. Since the seventeenth century the history of thinking about selves, those fragile coracles each of us builds to navigate through life, has involved a growing number of such exceptions. Not only has neuroscience showed that pain, drugs, disease, and damage can affect both brains and selves, it has lengthened the list of agents far beyond these.[8] Genes, hormones, stress, the Earth's magnetic field, temperature, sunlight, electricity pylons, radiation, the food we eat, and even the air we breathe ... what vulnerable creatures we are, subject to so many outside influences, most of which we never even notice!

Ah, cries the critic, but 'I' am still basically the same. This tinkering at the edges, a pheromone here, an organophosphate there, doesn't affect the fundamental essence of me. This is the Cartesian view that we have diamond minds, pure and aloof, unsullied by the dirty world around us. Like diamonds, our minds may shatter under the extreme pressure of brainwashing, but lesser forces fail to warp their structure. Is the critic right to cling to the assumption of solidity? At what point does tinkering at the edges become an assault on identity? To consider this question, we need to look at some intermediate examples.

Feeding the brain

Recall the cell membrane, pictured in Fig. 7.2(b). The phospholipids of which it is made up were for a long time of little interest to neuroscientists who were having much more fun trying to sort out the different types of neurotransmitters and receptors by which neurons communicate. However, it now seems that phospholipids, too, are important for neuronal conversations. In particular, it matters which types of phospholipid are in the cell membrane. Some types are long and straight, and so can pack very tightly together; others are crinkly zigzags, which can only pack loosely together (look closely at Fig. 7.2(b)). Why do we care? Because the receptors sitting in the membrane need space to express themselves. If they are restricted by tightly packed phospholipid molecules, they will have difficulty changing their positions when the neurotransmitter plugs in. This reduces the efficiency and speed with which cells generate their signals, and hence the effectiveness of the entire brain.

In other words, changing the types of phospholipids can have quite an impact on how well the brain is working. What is needed is more of the crinkly phospholipids, and fewer of the long straight ones. To achieve this seems impossible if you truly believe that the brain is fixed and unchanging. In fact, it is easy. All you have to do is eat more oily fish.[9]

The lipid part of a phospholipid molecule is the (straight or crinkly) tail. This is made up of fatty acids (fats), which can be either saturated or unsaturated. Saturated fats, which are found in processed, long-life food, produce straight phospholipids. Unsaturated fats, which are found in oily fish, nuts, and green vegetables, produce crinkly phospholipids. The more unsaturated the fat in our diets, the less tightly packed the phospholipids in our cell membranes, so the better our cells can transmit signals. Since cell membranes suffer wear and tear like the rest of us, brains are constantly looking for new material to patch up their membranes; so changing the diet to include more unsaturated fats is an easy way to change your brain.

And the change can be significant. Taking unsaturated fatty acids has been shown to benefit children with attention problems and adults with depression or schizophrenia.[10] The high level of unsaturated fatty acids in breast milk is a major reason why breast feeding appears to be so good for children's development.[11] What you eat, especially when you are young, can have quite an impact on who you are in later life. Even in adulthood, eating differently can make a huge difference, as a research study by Bernard Gesch and colleagues showed. In a scenario reminiscent of *A Clockwork Orange*, they demonstrated that violence among convicted British criminals could be reduced by almost 40 per cent after a few months of treatment.[12] Burgess's protagonist underwent aversion therapy. The young men in this study simply took dietary supplements.

Lightning in the brain

My next example is more controversial still. It concerns the temporal lobes, those regions at the side of the head which are involved, among other things, in the processing of hearing, language, and memories. Sufferers from a type of epilepsy which affects these areas (temporal lobe epilepsy, or TLE) sometimes experience unusual creativity (the composer Dmitri Shostakovich, the writer Edgar Allan Poe, and the artist Vincent van Gogh are thought to have had TLE) or intense religious experiences (St Paul and Joan of Arc may have been TLEptics).[13] Epilepsy occurs when neurons become so overactive that they are continually firing off signals. However, both creativity and religious experiences also happen to some members of the general population. Although these people are not epileptic, they are thought to have temporal lobes whose neurons are unusually active, a phenomenon called 'temporal lobe lability'. Scientists think that individuals may have more or less excitable temporal lobes, ranging from very low lability (stolid inertia) to the high-lability frenzy of TLE.

Going further, researchers such as Michael Persinger have proposed that spiritual experience in general results from temporal lobe activity.[14] Of course, susceptibility to religious experience does vary from person to person. Some atheists, for example, have never had a religious experience (and may prefer to dismiss all such experiences, like a man born blind who refuses to believe in sunsets). Persinger's research implies that some people may simply be 'God-blind', perhaps for genetic reasons: their temporal lobe lability is so low that they are incapable of having—tuning into?—spiritual feelings.[15]

Research into temporal lobe lability has a further implication. Persinger reports being able to induce spiritual experiences in volunteers by applying complex magnetic fields to the right temporal lobe. This suggests that religious experience may be traceable to an interaction between brain activity and environmental magnetic fields. In time, the technology to provide such experiences on tap may become available, allowing people who may never have had a religious experience the chance to alter, by physical means, this fundamental aspect of themselves. Could they not seem as changed by such a challenge as a victim of brainwashing seems to friends and family? Who knows what other aspects of our selves technology may one day be able to change.

Shaking foundations

The critic who still wishes to cling to the assumption of solidity has a lot to explain. Our brains change all the time, and so do we, although we do not always notice. A determined critic must argue that the 'essence of me' remains the same whatever changes happen in my brain, whether from chemicals, magnetic fields, or anything else. Am I indeed the same person with and without attention problems? What about with and without chronic headaches, depression, religion, the schizophrenic delusion that I am God or (if I acquire Cotard syndrome) the belief that I am dead? Clearly, some aspects of brain function are more important than others in determining the essence of me.

What, then, is this essence, the mysterious self? Neuroscientists have tended to locate it in the gaps between neurons.[16] On this view, the self is the collective of all the strengths of all the synapses in a brain. However, it is not clear how much this tells us about the aspects of selves in which we are most interested: we feel, with apologies to George Orwell, that all synapses are equal but some are more equal than others. Having a self, as many psychologists have pointed out, is associated with specific phenomena. These include having a physical body, being able to exert influence upon that body and upon the world, being social (relating to others), and having self-awareness, the ability to be conscious of not only the world and body, but of one's own thoughts and feelings as well.

Beyond these essentials, the degree to which the self is considered a distinct psychological entity varies from person to person and from culture to culture, as shown in a landmark article by Hazel Markus and Shinobu Kitayama.[17] Western cultures involve 'a conception of the self as an autonomous, independent person' (an emphasis on individuality which appears to be a relatively recent development, as Roy Baumeister notes).[18] Americans, for example, are expected to think of themselves as individuals 'whose behavior is organized and made meaningful primarily by reference to one's own internal repertoire of thoughts, feelings, and actions, rather than by reference to the thoughts, feelings, and actions of others'. By contrast, many Asian and African cultures conceive of a more interdependent self, 'seeing oneself as part of an encompassing social relationship and recognizing that one's behavior is determined by, contingent on, and, to a large extent, organized by what the actor perceives to be the thoughts, feelings, and actions of others in the relationship'.

The importance of memory

The malleability of memory is becoming increasingly clear
Elizabeth Loftus, *Our Changeable Memories*

Ask someone, whatever their origin, how they know they are the same person as they were yesterday, and their answer will probably refer to memory. (In *The Manchurian Candidate*, the programmed assassin had no memory of being brainwashed.) We assume we are the same solid selves over time because our recollections of past selves suggest that not much has changed. We rely heavily on memory and are painfully aware of some of its inadequacies—time spent looking for lost keys or the glasses on one's nose; the acquaintance whose name refuses to come to mind. We may have read about the patient H.M.—made famous in neuroscience circles by an operation for epilepsy which removed most of his temporal lobes and with them his ability to form new memories—or we may have seen the film *Memento*, in which an amnesiac tries to uncover the mystery of his own existence. Such people do not recognize the doctors they saw half an hour earlier, though they may recognize a childhood friend: memories from before the time of the brain damage are intact. More recent events, even catastrophic ones like being told of the death of a parent, wash over the brain and are gone. Those of us whose memories only fail occasionally dread the idea of losing them altogether, whether that loss takes a bizarre form, like H.M.'s amnesia, or follows the gentler and more common path of Alzheimer's. We grow used to imperfection in our memories as everywhere else, but we don't regard the odd lapse as a threat to the self.

As the neuropsychologist Daniel Schacter points out, memory lapses come in various flavours. He details seven 'sins of memory': transience, absentminded-ness, blocking, misattribution, suggestibility, bias, and persistence. The first three are, in Schacter's terms, 'sins of omission', the sorts of memory lapses we are used to and often complain about. Transience 'refers to a weakening or loss of memory over time';[19] absentmindedness occurs when we were not concentrat-ing on, and so failed to remember, information we later find we need; and block-ing involves the frustrating feeling that the memory we are trying to retrieve 'is lurking somewhere, seemingly poised to spring to mind with more prodding, but remains just out of reach when needed'. The final sin, persistence, is the reverse of transience. Memories, usually of unpleasant or traumatic events, refuse to leave us, much though we would like them to. In extreme cases they can intrude as sensory 'flashbacks', sometimes so vivid that the sufferer feels he or she is reliving the original trauma.

Schacter's other three sins are also common, but they are not what we usually mean when we talk about memory failings. Sins of commission, they reflect badly on the assumption of solidity, which may be one reason why we prefer not to talk about them. Schacter describes them thus:

The sin of misattribution involves assigning a memory to the wrong source: mistaking fantasy for reality, or incorrectly remembering that a friend told you a bit of trivia that you actually read about in a newspaper. Misattribution is far more common than most people realize, and has potentially profound implications in legal settings. The related sin of suggestibility refers to memories that are implanted as a result of leading questions, comments, or suggestions when a person is trying to call up a past experience. Like misattribution, suggestibility is especially relevant to—and sometimes can wreak havoc within—the legal system.

The sin of bias reflects the powerful influences of our current knowledge and beliefs on how we remember our pasts. We often edit or entirely rewrite our previous experiences—unknowingly and unconsciously—in light of what we now know or believe.

Schacter, *Seven Sins*, p. 5

Sins of omission can be dismissed as failures of an imperfect memory system. We speak of blocking, for example, as if memory were a library whose staff had annoyingly failed to find us the book we required. Sins of commission are differ-ent: they may happen without our awareness, but they are neither accidents nor failures. The sin is ours, because it is we ourselves who, like the Party in *Nineteen Eighty-Four*, rewrite history, link and blur events which were originally separate, or create memories of things that never happened. To imply that we might be capable of these sins criticizes not only our memory but also our judgement—not only the library but also the person who ordered the book—and as the writer

La Rochefoucauld sardonically noted, 'Everybody complains of his memory, but nobody of his judgement.'[20] Given the sin of bias, it is no wonder that we feel we are the same from day to day. Our brains are constantly reshaping our memories to maximize exactly that conviction.

The schematic self

Psychologists have also remarked on the flexibility of individual selves, agreeing with Shakespeare's Jaques that 'one man in his time plays many parts'.[21] We seem to have a variety of different personae which we adopt in different social situations. These personae, usually referred to as roles or schemas, include not only a set of behaviours but also the thoughts, attitudes, and feelings which go with them.[22] Acquired by past experience in certain situations, such as talking to the boss, a schema can be triggered every time the situation recurs, acting as a short cut which spares us the effort of working out all over again how we should behave. Human beings activate well-learned schemas without realizing. Indeed, they can find themselves disconcerted when an honest intention to break the mould ('It's time to tell my boss the truth about his management skills') ends up being overridden by a schema ('He's still the boss, even if I'm leaving to-morrow'). Stressful situations are particularly good at evoking schemas and suppressing more thoughtful behaviour.

Human beings are also extremely good at compartmentalizing, keeping different schemas well apart so that, for example, boss-related schemas do not get confused with baby-related schemas. This allows for very different sets of behaviour to be performed at different times, with minimum conflict. Thus officials at the Nazi death camps were able to activate schemas concerned with duty (and anti-Semitic propaganda) while watching children go to the gas chambers, and then go home, activate their fond parent schemas, and cuddle their own children.

It seems likely, moreover, that there are individual differences in the ability to compartmentalize. Some people can keep their schemas tightly boxed, such as the serial killer whose neighbours say 'I can't believe it! Such a *nice* man, wouldn't hurt a fly!'. Others are more fluid, their schemas less clearly distinguished from one another. If two schemas share components, as often happens, activation of one can lead to activation of another. A famous example from psychiatry is that of a woman with schizophrenia who, asked to list the members of her family, came up with 'Father … Son … Holy Ghost': her family schema overlapped with her Holy Trinity schema. Most of us would be able to ignore such unwanted associations, but her illness rendered her unable to do so.[23]

Sometimes two schemas can contain incompatible beliefs—for example, if they relate to very different situations. If one is active and the other is not, the incompatibility will not be noticed. Thus Peter may activate schemas concerned with the importance of human rights in his job as a criminal lawyer, but fail to activate them when abusing his wife at home. Unless something, or someone, happens to activate both schemas at the same time, Peter will never notice the hypocrisy of his behaviour. (Even if it is pointed out to him, he may find a way round the problem, for example by arguing that his wife has forfeited her human rights by her actions.) We are only ever aware, at any one time, of a tiny minority of the available schemas in our repertoires, and even the most reflective individual will not have uncovered all the connections between them, or untangled all the knots where schemas clash. As the poet Walt Whitman said:

Do I contradict myself?
Very well then I contradict myself,
(I am large, I contain multitudes.)

Whitman, Song of Myself, lines 1325–7

Alas for the assumption of solidity. The 'essence of me' seems to have gone from Descartes' single pure stream of consciousness to innumerable schema-trickles, acquired collections of thoughts, feelings, and behaviours. One such set will be active at any given time, comprising our 'active self'. Other schemas lie dormant, ready to take charge when they are needed—when we change from professional to parent, from regulated number to expressive individual. Given this flexibility and capacity for variation, even internal contradiction, perhaps the changes alleged to occur in brainwashing are not quite as extreme as they appear. If our minds are like diamonds, brainwashing is a shattering, all-or-nothing force: we resist, or it breaks us in pieces. But if our minds are more malleable, more like clay than diamond, then brainwashing becomes a matter of degree, as subject to psychological explanation as any other form of influence.

The schem(a)-ing brain

How do schemas translate to the language of neuroscience? Easily. Brains are organized so that any given neuron is activated (fires off signals) in response to the inputs it receives. However, those inputs do not carry information about entire objects, but about aspects of things in the world: colour, sound, movement, physical feel. In other words, an individual neuron does not respond to, and thereby in the brain's language represent, an 'object', but one or more features. Thus, in the visual cortex, some neurons fire when a stimulus moves across the field of view, while others do not; some fire when it moves to the left, but not the right; some fire if it is blue, but less or not at all if it is red. Representing an entire object, such as a tiger, requires the simultaneous activation of a group of neurons, often in different areas of the cortex: some will respond to the animal's colour, some to stripes, some to roaring noises, and some to the signals from subcortical areas of the brain which indicate that the body is now going into a state of high alert.

Those experienced with tigers will have a well-learned 'tiger schema'. Psychologically, this will comprise a set of beliefs about tigers ('they are large, stripey cats', 'they roar', etc.), attitudes (e.g. 'fear!'), and behaviours (e.g. 'run!'). In brain terms, the groups of neurons which respond to tiger-type perceptions will have become linked to other groups, some responding to emotional signals from the subcortex, others which signal to muscles involved in running. As the links between all these neurons strengthen, the schema as a whole becomes more clearly defined and more easily activated. Of particular importance are the strengthening connections between sensory areas, towards the back of the brain, and areas in the front of the brain where movements are generated. They have enormous survival advantages for prey, for whom fractions of a second can make a life-death difference, because strong schemas do not need every member neuron to be activated before a behaviour can be produced. Thus protective action can be taken earlier. From an evolutionary viewpoint, the risk of mistakes (the rustle of bushes being taken for the steps of a predator) is preferable to getting eaten while you wait for every schema member to be activated ('It's large, it's stripey, I don't hear any roaring ... uh oh, too late'). Better to have strong links between neurons in the schema. Then the perceptions of 'stripey' and 'large' will be enough by themselves to activate the 'run!' behaviour. This is why in emergencies people often report reacting extremely fast and not being conscious of fear, shock, or pain (or sometimes even the stimulus to which they are reacting) until after their response has taken place.

Schemas—learned patterns of thoughts and behaviours—therefore seem to have a neuroscientific incarnation as patterns of connections among neurons. The stronger those connections, the more automatically the schema will be triggered when some stimulus activates one or more of the schema members, and the faster-evoked will be the thoughts or behaviours associated with that particular schema. As noted earlier, connections between neurons strengthen when they are both active at the same time: more frequent and/or intense activating stimuli lead to stronger connections.

Every self—thought of in neuroscience terms as the total of all connections between neurons—includes a collection of more or less well-learned schemas (particular patterns of connections which are activated in specific situations). The stronger (better learned) a schema, the more it contributes to our overall sense of self. Weak schemas are not used often and may involve conscious attention being paid to them. The strengths of their connections are low, and easily changed, and a change to such a schema would not make us or our friends feel that we have become a different person. The strongest schemas are used frequently and often without conscious thought (many prejudices, built up over years, are of this type). Their connections are very strong and extremely difficult to change, so if a strong schema were suddenly to alter we might suspect a change in identity—a change, moreover, achieved by some kind of outside agency. It is changes perceived to affect a person's strongest schemas which are likely to evoke allegations of brainwashing.

Summary and conclusions

We are back to the difference between brainwashing by force and brainwashing by stealth described in earlier chapters. Stealthy methods, such as an advertisement for washing powder, may change a few peripheral beliefs, perhaps slightly strengthening the weak schema which associates that particular washing powder with vaguely beneficial sensations. This may strengthen a few synapses in our heads, but we do not feel it as a change in self (though overall, advertising does affect us greatly). Brainwashing by force, on the other hand, is feared because it threatens the strong schemas, the core features which mould our cognitive landscape. The brainwasher's claim is that our strongest beliefs, the thoughts and attitudes which we find most familiar, and most difficult to change, can be wrenched into strange new shapes. If advertising is erosion, brainwashing by force is an earthquake or comet strike: explosive interference with our inner world. In Chapter 14 we will explore what neuroscience tells us about whether such profound alterations are actually possible. Before that, however, we must look in more detail at beliefs, emotions, and how we change them.

Chapter 8: Webs and new worlds

A golden mesh t' entrap the hearts of men
Faster than gnats in cobwebs

William Shakespeare, *The Merchant of Venice*

Brainwashing is about changing beliefs. To understand brainwashing, therefore, it is necessary to understand what beliefs are and how they change. In the previous chapter I set out the argument that mental activities are represented by highly changeable patterns of connections between neurons in the brain, and that over time these patterns can become grouped, by repeated co-activation of member neurons, into schemas. What does this view of brain function tell us about beliefs? I will begin by considering beliefs in the traditional fashion, as mental (rather than neuroscientific) constructs, asking what psychology has to say about beliefs. How do they form, what factors influence them, and how do they relate to behaviour?

What are beliefs?

Belief is one of those deep-rooted concepts we intuitively grasp but find rather hard to define. Beliefs are about objects or situations and involve the believer accepting the truth of statements about those objects and situations. If I believe, for instance, that my boss has the management skills of an electric eel, I am taking this evaluation, however metaphorical, as a valid representation of the way my boss behaves. This belief is dependent on other beliefs I hold—about what constitutes good management, about my boss's past behaviour, and about the behaviour of electric eels. Over time, on the basis of experience, I may have built up a highly complex network of such beliefs.

The complexity of that network, however, is of course no guarantee that the beliefs which comprise it are true. New information may require me to modify or even abandon one or more of those beliefs. For example, my assumption that electric eels spend their time thrashing around all over the place—on which the metaphor about my boss's management technique depends—may not survive watching a natural history programme which tells me that electric eels are in fact accurate and effective predators. If I accept the findings of the programme, I will have to change not only the belief about electric eels but the one about my boss as well.

In other words, any change to one belief may increase the overall level of inconsistency across the network of which that belief is a component. The modified belief ('electric eels are efficient') now conflicts with other related beliefs ('my boss is like an electric eel'), creating the stressful situation which the psychologist Leon Festinger christened 'cognitive dissonance'.[1] Humans are of course quite capable of maintaining incompatible beliefs—otherwise how could many people oppose abortion while supporting the death penalty, or vice versa?[2] Nevertheless, we tend to become uncomfortable when the incompatibility is forced on our attention, especially if the beliefs involved are important to us. Dissonance created by conflict between strong beliefs can be a major motivating force which may require changes across the network if overall consistency between member beliefs is to be regained. And consistency is a highly desirable commodity. The assumption that our world is, if not rational, at least not blatantly contradictory is a basic necessity which has served *Homo sapiens* extremely well over the centuries. So if we notice that our beliefs—which we do after all take to represent the way the world is—contain contradictions, then we can be justified in assuming that something has gone wrong with our representations of reality. Inaccurate beliefs can be very dangerous to their possessors, as many cult members and their families have found to their cost. So humans will often go to some length to remove inconsistencies among their more deeply held beliefs.

For less valuable beliefs the effort required to change the network is not a problem. Such weak beliefs tend to have relatively few links to other beliefs (I don't know much about electric eels and I don't spend much time thinking about my boss). The greatest degree of change involves the affected belief itself (I must reverse my unflattering opinion of electric eels) and those directly related to it (I must find another description of my boss). As one moves away from this focal point the degree of adjustment required decreases quickly (I don't have to change my theory of what constitutes good management skills, or my opinion about whether my boss has such skills). Weak beliefs are therefore subservient to reality, in the sense that if new information comes in which requires them to change, change they will, without much effort on the believer's part.

However, if the belief under threat (being challenged by new information) is a strongly held one the outcome may be very different. Strong beliefs are strong because they have been reinforced on many occasions, or by very intense stimuli, or both. They tend to be deeply embedded in the cognitive landscape, enmeshed in a web of connections with other beliefs. A devout believer in God does not hold this conviction in isolation from all his other beliefs; rather, it provides the emotional bedrock for much of his existence. Such beliefs can be extremely hard to change. In extreme cases believers may actively reject reality if it forces change upon them, retreating into psychosis, into new worlds woven from dreams. The analogy of a web is an appropriate one here. Discarding a weak belief is like cutting a thread at the edge of the web: it makes little or no difference to the body of the web itself. Changing a strong belief is like cutting one of the main supporting strands: the entire structure of the web may be changed or even destroyed.

A digression: terminology

So far in this chapter I have used three terms to describe patterns of connectivity between beliefs: links, networks, and webs. The reader will no doubt have noticed the similarity of these descriptions to those of schemas in the previous chapter. Schemas, like beliefs, relate to objects or situations; they represent aspects of the world—or ourselves—which we may want to affect, together with methods of affecting them (action plans). Both beliefs and schemas are embodied in patterns of connectivity between neurons, the totality of which makes up our cognitive landscape. What is needed is a more general term which incorporates both schemas and beliefs: a term for the connections between mental objects (beliefs, action plans, and so on). I will adopt the web metaphor (simply from personal preference: to me 'web' has a more organic, less technological feel than 'network') and use the term 'cognitive web', or 'cogweb' for short.

Strength of belief

Understanding why strong beliefs are so hard to change requires investigating what makes a belief strong or weak. Like a schema, a belief is as strong as the connections between its components. These components are represented by the signalling activity of neurons receiving input, either from other neurons or from a brain's many interfaces with its body and the external world. Neural signals flow from sensory inputs through our brains to the outputs whose signals command behaviour from our muscles. For neuroscientists, the classic and most-studied paradigm is that of the visual stimulus provoking a response. An apple reflects light, which falls upon Eve's two retinas, causing signals to race up her optic nerves; these signals are processed by areas in her brain, interpreted as representing an apple (as opposed to just a coloured pattern), and transmitted to motor areas, which in turn send signals to the muscles, resulting in a reaching action.

However, there is much more to input and output than this example suggests. Inputs may reach the brain from external sense organs (like the eyes), from internal sensors (such as those which maintain balance or tell us where we have put our arms and legs), or from more diffuse sources like our bloodstream. Hormones, drugs, foods, or chemicals released by our immune system can all reach the cerebrospinal fluid (CSF) in which neurons bathe, and hence affect brain activity. Similarly, outputs may control our limb muscles, or the deep muscles surrounding organs such as the gut and lungs, or the organs themselves: directly via the nerves which infiltrate these organs or indirectly by releasing chemicals such as growth hormone from the brain. Both inputs and outputs, in other words, may consist of chemicals, which can bind to receptors on neurons and thereby affect them, or of neural signals—which are themselves also chemical—carried by neurotransmitters as discussed in Chapter 7.

This ability of neurons to be influenced not just by neurotransmitters but also by other molecules in their environment means that connections between neurons, and hence cogwebs (beliefs, action plans, and so on), may vary depending on the state of the body as well as on signals from the world. Emotions, as we shall see in Chapter 9, are manifestations of inputs from the body, but less overwhelmingly noticeable bodily states may also have an impact. An example is the relationship between stress hormones and cognition. The glucocorticoid hormones, which affect perceptions of stress and the ability to perform complex tasks, fluctuate throughout the day in ways which vary between individuals. Some people ('larks') are at their best in the morning, some ('owls') peak later in the day. Experiments have shown that owls forced to make social judgements early in the morning are more likely to rely on stereotypes and prejudices than if the judgements are made in the afternoon or evening. Likewise, larks make more thoughtful judgements in the morning and more prejudiced judgements in the evening.[3] In other words, which beliefs we call on (and therefore reinforce) in a situation can vary depending on the levels of hormones in our bloodstreams.

Connections between neurons depend on the timing of their inputs: as noted earlier, neurons must be activated together if the connections between them are to be strengthened. Connections also depend on the frequency and distinctiveness (or 'salience') of the inputs those neurons receive. Salience is a relative rather than an absolute quantity. Neurons signalling in response to a bright light do not signal the absolute brightness of the stimulus in the way a photographer's light-meter would. Rather, they use their many connections with neighbouring neurons to signal relative brightness—the difference between the light and its background. The greater the difference, or contrast, the more salient the stimulus. This allows our brains great flexibility: we can read the faded text of an ancient manuscript in a shaded library, or peruse a novel while lying in the noonday sun. We can also fall prey—and regularly do—to salespeople who exploit contrast. Robert Cialdini gives the example of selling clothes:

> Suppose a man enters a fashionable men's store and says that he wants to buy a three-piece suit and a sweater. If you were the salesperson, which would you show him first to make him likely to spend the most money? Clothing stores instruct their sales personnel to sell the costly item first. Common sense might suggest the reverse: If a man has just spent a lot of money to purchase a suit, he may be reluctant to spend much more on the purchase of a sweater; but the clothiers know better. They behave in accordance with what the contrast principle would suggest: Sell the suit first, because when it comes time to look at sweaters, even expensive ones, their prices will not *seem* as high in comparison.
>
> Cialdini, *Influence*, p. 13

Frequency, salience, timing, what's in our CSF ... the strengths of our synapses are subject, like ourselves, to many influences. One factor I have not yet mentioned is technology—artificial attempts to change synaptic strengths. I will return to this topic in Chapter 14. Also important is the current strength of a cogweb's synaptic connections, since weak cogwebs tend to change more than strongly established ones.

Another similarity between cogwebs and human beings is that both live in communities. Cogwebs are heavily influenced by their environment: their activation—by stimuli or other cogwebs—depends on what's around them. (It is this relativist tendency for everything to influence everything else which makes science in general, and brain science in particular, so fiendishly complicated.) Consider an unfinished work of art, a painting or symphony. Some areas are finely detailed (they have a high density of paint molecules, or notes), while some are roughly sketched out (little paint, or just a few orchestral parts). In the cognitive landscape, density is determined by the number of related beliefs. In high-density areas (such as, in my brain, those related to neuroscience) the landscape is well defined, with tightly clustered, thickly overlapping cogwebs providing plenty of detail. In low-density areas (e.g. those containing beliefs about electric eels) only a few cogwebs sketch out the territory.

Density is important because when input signals reach a cogweb they may also activate neighbouring cogwebs in the cognitive landscape. The nearer these neighbours, the more likely they are to be activated. And the more often cogwebs and their neighbours co-activate, the more similar their connection strengths will be. Just as in landscapes the gradients are mostly gradual (gentle slopes, rolling hills, and slow inclines are more numerous on our weathered

Earth than cliffs), so in the cognitive landscape the gradients of connection strength mostly change by small degrees. Large differences between neighbouring connections are most likely to be found in low-density areas, where not many beliefs have built up. These are the darker, less-explored corners of our minds, places where mental weathering has not had much effect.

Mental weathering: neural activity and the role of consciousness

the formation of a habit may be thought of as analogous to the formation of a water-course

Bertrand Russell, *Religion and Science*

The next question which arises from the analogy of the cognitive landscape is: How is that landscape shaped? What are the mental equivalents of the forces of weathering and erosion? The answer is simple: neural activity carves out our cognitive world just as water has shaped our planet.[4] But this simple statement has some remarkable implications. To see them requires taking the analogy between neuronal activity and water flow a little further, using five commonplace observations about water and how it flows. These observations relate to the size of the channel through which the water flows, how smoothly it flows, the number of channels available for it to flow through, how neighbouring channels change over time, and the shape of the channels.

Channel size

Imagine a reservoir which has been filled with water and which has one exit channel (e.g. a pipe or a hole in the reservoir wall). If the channel is narrow (has a small cross-sectional area), water will flow faster than if the channel is larger (just as squeezing a garden hose, which makes it narrower, results in the water coming out faster). Imagine further that the channel is made of a material which is eroding, the channel walls slowly washing away as more and more water passes through. Over time the channel will get larger, and the rate of water flow through it will therefore decrease. But as the water flows more slowly, the rate at which the channel gets larger (as its walls erode) will also slow down until eventually the water will no longer be flowing fast enough to have any noticeable effect on the channel walls. In other words, there is a trade-off between size and rate of flow. Larger channels change less than smaller ones, given the same rate of flow. If there are two different-sized channels leading out of the reservoir, water will flow more strongly through (and hence be more likely to erode) the smaller one. This is why deepening rivers (e.g. by clearing away accumulated silt) is a common strategy in flood prevention.

Channels in the water-flow metaphor correspond to cogwebs, channel size to cogweb strength, and erosion to the brain's methods of increasing synapse strength. When activated by a stimulus, stronger cogwebs are less likely to change, and will change less, than weaker ones. I may completely change my impression of electric eels after one short television programme, without much effort and with no great grief. But it would take a great deal to convince me that my opinion of my boss's management skills, an opinion built up over years of observation, should be revised.

Smoothness
As water flows over the ground it wears away obstacles, creating a smoother flow. The equivalent is true for neural activity. Neurons activated at the same time change the synapses between them so that signals can flow smoothly from input to output. This process, known in the Neuroworld jargon as 'automatization', is how we acquire skills, from writing to driving. The stronger—more practised—a cogweb, the more easily and quickly signals will flow through its component pathways.

As we shall see in Chapter 10, the brain has specific mechanisms for facilitating smoothness by channelling the flow of signals to particular areas, the cognitive equivalent of putting a thumb on a hose to blast away encrusted dirt. A young girl learning to write focuses attention on the careful and conscious formation of individual letters, the way her hand feels, and the marks she is making. For the strongest cogwebs, however, the flow through them is so swift and smooth that it may lead to action with little or no conscious awareness. The adult woman writing a word is thinking about other things—the meaning of the whole sentence and how it advances her argument, what she would rather be doing, or what she needs to do next. She is not interested in how the word is being written. In a more extreme example, skilled drivers are notorious for being able to listen to a radio, conduct conversations, or even drift into sleep for a second or two, all while piloting an inflammable metal hulk along a busy motorway at eighty miles an hour. The skills required for motorway driving have been automatized to such an extent that the processes involved rarely require conscious attention. Indeed, focusing attention on what one is doing can disrupt the smooth flow from input to output, turning a smooth, skilled movement into a clumsy, disjointed effort.

One of the implications of this metaphor is that intense, simple stimuli are likely to evoke faster responses than weaker or more complicated stimuli. As we shall see in Chapter 10 when we come to look at how brains link perceptions to movements, the simplest stimuli can evoke such a swift response that there is no time for other areas of the brain even to register that the stimulus has occurred; we can trigger a rapid eye movement without being conscious of either the stimulus or the movement itself. Intensity and simplicity mean speed, and the same is true of beliefs. Stronger and simpler beliefs are harder to challenge because their cogwebs are often activated without reaching conscious awareness. They are like short straight channels through which the water flows so fast that it is gone before the flow can be blocked.

We rely on this ability of our brains to take care of most of our affairs without bothering the top management. Most of what we do is done unthinkingly, if 'thinking' means thinking consciously. As we learn a new skill, or a new idea, it becomes automatized—the amount of time it spends in consciousness decreases, leaving the top management in prefrontal cortex free for other challenges. Again, influence technicians have developed many ways to exploit automatic thinking, the rules we have learned to save us the effort of reviewing every situation anew. (This may be one reason why Pratkanis and Aronson's list of eight sales-boosting words includes 'quick' and 'easy'.)[5] Scarce = valuable; likeable = trustworthy; said-by-expert = true; these and many other heuristics keep us from drowning in the complexities of today's information-rich world. However, they are also exploited every day by retailers, politicians, and other influence technicians who would prefer us not to think carefully about their claims.

Number of channels
If there are only a few channels leading out of the reservoir, less water can be transferred from it in a given time. Since how fast the water flows out through the channels depends on how much water is in the reservoir, water will flow faster through the channels if there are only a few of them (because more water stays in the reservoir for longer) than if there are many of them (because more channels can remove more water from the reservoir faster). This is why providing alternative flow routes (more channels) is a common strategy in flood prevention. Over time, therefore, the rate at which the channels erode, which depends on how fast water flows through them, will be slower if there are many channels and faster if the number of channels is small.

Again, as for water channels, so for cogwebs. Signals transmitted by strong cogwebs will reach their outputs faster than signals of the same strength passing through weak cogwebs (but weak cogwebs will change more). However, the number of cogwebs in that area of the cognitive landscape (cogweb density) is important: the more cogwebs available to pass on a signal, the weaker the flow of activity through each cogweb, and the less the change in cogweb strength. Psychologically this makes sense. Given new information, I am more likely to change my beliefs in subject areas in which I am not an expert (where my cogwebs are weak), areas in which I have few current beliefs (i.e. few cogwebs available as routes for signal flow). Areas in which I am an expert have a high density of long-established beliefs; when input flows into these areas it may activate a large number of related cogwebs, but it will change each of them relatively little. A half-hour natural history programme on electric eels could reshape that entire region of my cognitive landscape, whereas reading another book on neuroscience, though it may take me several hours, is very unlikely to exert such seismic effects.

Neighbouring channels

Consider water flowing from a reservoir with two exit channels. If one channel is larger, water will tend to flow more slowly through that channel and more quickly through the other, smaller channel. The smaller channel's walls will therefore erode (increasing its size) more quickly, so its flow rate will slow down sooner, because of the trade-off between channel size and flow rate mentioned earlier. In other words, the large channel will widen slowly, while the small channel widens faster (catching up). Eventually both channels will end up similar in size and with flow rates so slow that no noticeable further erosion takes place.

Cogwebs can approach a similar equilibrium, a strongly established state in which their connection strengths no longer change much. Over time, neighbouring cogwebs will tend to become more similar in their connection strengths, resulting in a smoother cognitive landscape. Consciously reflecting on beliefs enhances this process, facilitating overall consistency. If Edward has believed for years that homosexuals are disgusting perverts, and then finds out that his adored and respected elder brother is gay, he will have some hard thinking to do to rationalize the resulting conflict (the cognitive dissonance) and smooth out the jagged edges in his cognitive landscape. But he almost certainly will be able to rationalize it one way or another, perhaps by creating a subtype category of 'exceptional homosexuals who are okay' into which he can put his brother. Indeed, the motivational imperative to reduce inconsistency will probably prevent him from thinking about much else until he has managed to resolve the dissonance.

Intricacy

Imagine water flowing from one (full) reservoir to another (empty) one through a single connecting channel. As we have already seen, how quickly and efficiently the water is transferred will depend on the size of the channel. However, the shape of the channel also matters. A simple straight line, covering the shortest distance between the two reservoirs, allows for fast-flowing water to move efficiently from one to the other, quickly filling the second reservoir. If the channel is convoluted, water from the first reservoir will take longer to reach and fill the second one. If the channel has many branches, cracks, or holes, then water will leak away, causing the rate of flow to fall, and again the second reservoir will take a long time to fill. In other words, the more intricate the channel's shape, the more weakly and slowly water will tend to pass through it. Imagine, as before, that water erodes the channels through which it flows. Simple channels, which have a faster flow rate, will tend to erode more—and, over time, become wider—than their more intricate counterparts.

Like channels, cogwebs can vary in their intricacy. Simple ideas with only a few components and with few associations linking them to other ideas require relatively simple cogwebs. As an example, consider my currently active belief about one of my favourite phospholipids (I trained as a scientist, remember; not every stereotype is entirely false in every case). I believe that, though normally referred to as platelet-activating factor (PAF), my favourite's name can also be written as 1-O-alkyl-2-acetyl-sn-glyceryl-3-phosphorylcholine. This belief of mine is extremely weak, as for some strange reason I find '1-O-alkyl-2-acetyl-sn-glyceryl-3-phosphorylcholine' almost entirely impossible to remember. The number of associations in my brain linked to the cogweb which encodes '1-O-alkyl-2-acetyl-sn-glyceryl-3-phosphorylcholine' is minuscule by brain standards (I can dredge up two at the moment), and the cogweb itself, despite appearances, is a relatively simple one—as becomes clear when I compare it with, say, my cogweb for 'brain-washing', a complicated, richly meaningful idea full of associations. Thinking about brainwashing triggers an abundance of other cogwebs; thinking about '1-O-alkyl-2-acetyl-sn-glyceryl-3-phosphorylcholine' triggers very little except a sense of fatigue. That particular cogweb is also short-lived in the sense that it can become active only when I actually look at the name, because of my inability to remember it. This is not the case with the two cogwebs associated with it. One of these is my PAF cogweb, which is intricate, as I have studied PAF in some detail. The second is a much vaguer entity—'that long thing with all the hyphens, you know, the other name for PAF'—which stands in for '1-O-alkyl-2-acetyl-sn-glyceryl-3-phosphorylcholine' whenever I don't actually have it in front of me.

The more complex the concept, the more intricate the cogweb that represents it, which implies that our strongest beliefs will tend to be simpler than our more weakly-held convictions. This fits with experience. The abstract belief that all asylum seekers are dishonest is simpler, and can be more strongly adhered to, than the more complicated—but more accurate and less abstract—belief that some asylum seekers are dishonest and many are not. Simpler beliefs are easier to represent and retain in cogwebs, just as headlines are easier to remember than philosophical arguments, and sometimes the attraction of simplicity can outweigh the attraction of accuracy. This is why the British National Party has been able to make progress in recent UK council elections despite its extreme views (see Chapter 9 for a further discussion of BNP propaganda). The messages it conveys are simple and (to some people) attractive; their simplicity makes them easier to accept.

Stronger, simpler, more abstract cogwebs also tend to have a much greater impact on behaviour. To see why, let us return to the metaphor of water flowing between two reservoirs through a connecting channel. In this metaphor, the water in the first, full reservoir represents the amount of brain activity triggered by a sensory stimulus, such as a flash of light. The second, initially empty reservoir represents the brain systems which directly control behaviour. An action in response to the stimulus begins when water reaches this second reservoir. If there are two connecting channels, the first short and straight and the second highly intricate, then the second reservoir will get its water (i.e. the behavioural response will be triggered) from the short straight channel (i.e. the simpler cogweb).

Hypothesis testing

Exploring the metaphor of water flow provides insights into what makes cogwebs in general, and beliefs in particular, stronger or weaker. The cognitive landscape is a reflection of the world we live in, shaped by that environment as well as by the patterns of gene activity in every cell. But the brain is a very strange mirror, distorting some aspects of the world, ignoring others, and filtering every input it receives on the basis of what it has previously experienced. Mirrors have no memory, but a brain's history is embedded in its very structure, continually influencing its guesses and predictions, its interpretations and speculations, its actions and reactions, even what it sees and doesn't see.

Evidence suggests that human brains constantly create predictions—hypotheses—about the world around them, based on experience. They derive these expectations of how the world is likely to be in the near future in part from knowledge of what their actions have achieved in the past. When I drop a glass I expect it to fall towards the ground. Such expectations may or may not be conscious, but that makes them no less influential on behaviour. My body flinches automatically, braced for the crash, before I hear the sound of breaking glass.

Cortical hypotheses are created when the outgoing motor command signal is sent from motor cortex to the spinal cord and muscles. Simultaneously the same signal is transmitted back to sensory and intermediate areas of the cortex, particularly those in the parietal lobe which maintain representations of the body's position in space. This information about the upcoming action is used to create a representation of body position *as if* the action had already occurred, a prediction of where the body will be which can then be compared with signals from the body itself once the action has occurred. If the signals match, no problem. If they do not then alarms will go off, and the brain will be provoked to investigate what has caused the mismatch (more on this in Chapter 10). As it is for the body, so it is for the world. Our brains are constantly monitoring and predicting vision, hearing, and all the other channels through which we receive information about our environment.

Much of the brain's 'hypothesis testing'—comparing what is actually incoming with what it expects to be receiving—appears to take place very early in the process of receiving sensory input, before that input even reaches the cortex. Sensory information initially passes from our eyes, ears, fingertips, etc. via nerves to the brain, and specifically to the thalamus, a collection of nuclei (cell clusters) in the core of the brain whose name derives from the Greek word for a bedroom or inner chamber. From the thalamus signals are farmed out to various areas of sensory cortex for further processing, and these areas in turn send signals back to the thalamus, comparing and commenting on the inputs they are getting.[6] This process of comparison acts as a continual filter, tweaking preconceptions generated in the cortex so that they converge with incoming signals from the subcortical thalamus, and simultaneously tweaking inputs so that they better match the cortical hypotheses. This smoothing and modifying also takes place at the level of the cortex itself as its numerous areas engage in ceaseless conversation. Input signals undoubtedly change the brain which receives them, but they themselves are changed in the process, adjusted so that they are a better match for the contours of the cognitive landscape. As discussed earlier, the aim is overall consistency: a smooth flow from input to output with minimal disruption.

Returning to the analogy of water flow, we see that water seeks the easiest path, and will flow through available channels before carving out new ones. Signals coming in to the brain likewise tend to flow through the cogwebs already present. This does not mean, of course, that new cogwebs are never created. Rather, there is an overspill effect: if the match between the new input and the current brain structure is poor, there will be little information flow through available cogwebs. Either the cogwebs will adjust, or new cogwebs will form to carry away the surplus, or the input signals will be modified (by adjusting subcortical filters, for example) until they are a better fit for the brain's expectations. Which outcome occurs depends on the connection strengths of the available cogwebs. Weaker cogwebs tend to change in response to challenging input; as discussed earlier, they are subservient to reality. Stronger cogwebs tend to lead to more input change—and may lead to the formation of new cogwebs to explain away the new information. Here reality is subservient to expectation. People appear to differ in the ease with which they will accept challenging information (it also depends, of course, on what is being challenged), but overall the tolerance threshold seems to be lower than we might like to expect. Humankind cannot bear very much reality, it seems.

As many psychological experiments have shown, people often really do see what they expect to see. They can also be astonishingly ingenious in explaining away unwelcome facts. Have you ever had to talk your way out of a sticky situation? Have you ever faced an unexpected challenge from, say, a work colleague, and found yourself amazed at the fluency with which you rose to the occasion, came up with some new and effective arguments, and routed the enemy? The human ability to tell stories is basic to all cultures, and the urge to construct coherent narratives—another aspect of consistency—appears to be a universal species trait.

Like other traits, it can be extreme in some cases. After brain damage, some patients show an extraordinary capacity to make up stories, a process known as 'confabulation'. This rather unkind term—such patients are not deliberately lying—refers to what can be extraordinarily complicated, implausible explanations which the patient derives when confronted with difficult information. Patients with certain kinds of strokes, for example, can suffer a syndrome known as 'anosognosia', in which they fail to comprehend the extent of their injuries, even when these may include paralysis. Confronted with a situation where they cannot avoid facing the consequences—for instance, being asked to walk by their doctor—they will immediately produce all sorts of reasons why they should not oblige. Another example of confabulation is well illustrated by the neurologist Oliver Sacks in his description of a man with Korsakoff's syndrome, in which alcohol abuse causes brain damage particularly affecting the memory.[7] The patient, having no memory of the doctor (whom he had seen before), repeatedly misidentified him, leaping to a dizzying range of erroneous conclusions about Sacks' identity and occupation. For each conclusion he had a narrative readily available, and he did not remember any of the previous mistakes he had made.

The current shape of our cognitive landscapes not only moulds the inputs we receive, it also influences the ways we react to those inputs. A brain's filtering of information does not begin in its subcortical relay stations, but much earlier, with the protective behaviours we all engage in to keep our worlds the way we like them. As philosophers say, beliefs 'function as reasons for action'.[8] Whether or not we recognize the reasons why we act, beliefs and other cogwebs provide those reasons. We spend time with like-minded people in preference to those whose ideas challenge our own, get our news from sources we approve of, read some books but 'can't be bothered' with others, and ignore or avoid information which might poke holes in our carefully constructed cogwebs.

Implicit beliefs and fallible convictions

Conceiving of beliefs as cogwebs can shed light on various aspects of brain function. The distinction made in Chapter 7 between active and implicit (dormant) selves, for example, can now be understood as a distinction between those cogwebs through which neural activity is currently passing and cogwebs not currently activated. This active–implicit distinction also applies to beliefs. When you communicate by telephone, you believe that the voice coming out of your receiver is that of the person you think you're talking to: cogwebs formed during past experiences with that person will be active in your brain. You also believe that putting down the receiver will not cause a dragon to erupt from your left nostril, but this belief remained implicit until reading this book caused you to articulate it for the first time.

One important point is that beliefs, like other cogwebs, can form—and affect behaviour—without their owner's awareness. Many influence attempts exploit exactly this feature of human brains to try and form beliefs by stealth. The idea is that while your attention is distracted by the salesman's chatter or the advertisement's bright colours, your brain is forming new cogwebs or strengthening old ones, cogwebs representing associations between the product and some desirable quality such as beauty, wealth, status, or sex appeal. Many prejudices also form in this way, from repeated experience of how family, friends, colleagues, or the media react to the target of the prejudice. If the social cues are strongly salient (e.g. their source is highly respected), or associated with powerful emotions, the associated cogwebs can become extremely well-entrenched. However, the prejudiced individual is likely to have noticed the cues and will therefore be aware of her negative feelings (she may or may not, of course, conceptualize them *as* a prejudice, i.e. as a disreputable aspect of her character which she would prefer to do without). If the cues are not strongly salient, but are extremely frequent (or if the prejudice forms at a very young age), the prejudiced individual may not be aware of (or later remember) the cues, and so may not be aware of the prejudice. Such stereotypes can be particularly difficult to change, since it is necessary not only to change embedded beliefs, but also first to convince the person involved that they do have a prejudice.

Another implication of this approach is that beliefs and memories, which are both instances of cogwebs, are made of the same kind of stuff: connections between neurons. Beliefs should therefore behave like memories. For instance, beliefs should be susceptible to the 'seven sins' of memory discussed in Chapter 7, and indeed this is the case. Beliefs do tend to fade over time if they are not reinforced (transience); but very strong beliefs, set up, for example, by traumatic experiences, can remain disabling (persistence): a child attacked by a dog may continue to believe that dogs are dangerous even after having met several friendly and unthreatening dogs. Misattribution, suggestibility, and bias can also affect beliefs, as the tragedy of false memory syndrome has shown: children and even adults can come to believe things that are not true, and could not possibly be true, on the basis of questioning by others. Even absentmindedness and blocking can occur for beliefs as well as for memories. An example is the unnerving experience of knowing that you have an opinion about something but not being able to bring that opinion to mind. Belief and memory, in situations like this, are indistinguishable.

The power of faith

In Chapter 2, I introduced the concept of ethereal ideas, abstract, ambiguous, and often highly dangerous because of their capacity for multiple interpretations and their association with powerful emotions. Ethereal ideas are encoded in cogwebs which, however different the specific concepts involved, share one feature. Their direct connections with inputs external to the body are few or non-existent, but they receive powerful signals from sources within the body, signals which the brain interprets as emotions. In the next chapter, we will look at emotions in more detail. For now, the take-home point is that ethereal ideas gain their strength from signals which may have little or nothing to do with the way the world is at the time (the emotions may relate to memories or daydreams, for instance), rather than from signals deriving directly from that world which could act as a useful reality check. As such cogwebs do not rely for their potency upon external information, arguments based on that information will have little or no impact. It is this 'Certum est, quia impossibile' quality of faith, impervious to reason and reality, which makes ethereal ideas potentially so lethal, and so attractive to would-be brainwashers.[9]

Modern scientific commentators on religion such as Richard Dawkins and Susan Blackmore assume that faith, as described above, is synonymous with religion. They view the latter as a particularly virulent form of thought control, a mental illness or cultural virus our species would be better off without.[10] Blackmore, for example, asserts in The Meme Machine that 'The history of warfare is largely a history of people killing each other for religious reasons', and argues that science is superior to religion because 'at the heart of science lies the method of demanding tests of any idea. Scientists must predict what will happen if a particular theory is valid and then find out if it is so.' In other words, ideas in science are prevented from becoming too ethereal, held in check by their reliance on hypothesis testing. Religions, by contrast, 'build theories about the world and then prevent them from being tested': their ideas are so essentially ethereal that any contact with the real world is a potential threat. Science functions like a well-regulated brain, religion like a psychotic one. It is a passionate accusation. In considering it, I shall set aside (as I have throughout this book) the obvious dangers of overgeneralizing, since science and religion both encompass a huge variety of practices and beliefs. Is the accusation fair?

No. Much religious practice is not concerned with abstractions, but with real life, testing out new approaches to social problems, experimenting with novel solutions, learning and applying ideas from around the world. The core ideas are certainly ethereal—how could we test the idea that God exists?—but this need not mean that the believer is detached from reality. As I noted in Chapter 2, many religious people are embedded in the grittier areas of the real world, helping the vulnerable and the socially excluded. Many find their religious convictions altering over time: some lose faith, some gain new insights. If religious faith were altogether ethereal, altogether independent of reality, how could it ever be changed, as it often is, by experience?

And consider some of the core ideas in neuroscience: that brains process information, that brains generate every aspect of mental life, and that therefore science will eventually be able to provide a physical treatment for anything—and everything—we don't like about ourselves. What experiment would disprove the idea that brains process information, or demonstrate an aspect of ourselves which brain science could not (in principle, eventually) change? If someone came up with a mental capability—process X—which they claimed occurred independently of changes in the brain, they would not be hailed as the founder of a new scientific paradigm. In fact, given the conservative nature of most scientific journals, it would be most unlikely that their research would even get published. They would be told that they were wrong, or mad, or both; that process X did not exist; or, if they had very strong evidence for X, that 'actually brain changes do occur during process X, but current technology can't detect them'. Neuroscience has its core, unchallengeable ideas, just as religion does. It has to take some sacred concepts for granted in order to be able to develop. Ethereal ideas are found in other heads than those of religious fundamentalists. Even atheists and scientists are not immune.

As demonstrated in Chapters 1 and 2, what matters is the nature of the idea—the structure of the cogweb—not its particular content. Moral or political, religious or scientific, every belief has its bigots. Blackmore's history of conflict appears to have stopped at the turn of the twentieth century, but since then, as I argued in Chapter 2, we have had Maoism, Stalinism, and the Khmer Rouge, among others: ideologies not known for their religious fervour which have racked up millions of deaths between them. Bertrand Russell may have defined Nazism and Communism as 'new religions'[11] but he was stretching semantics so far—to fit his vigorously atheist agenda—as to warp the word 'religions' completely out of shape: these creeds have no gods, no spirits or souls, no afterlife. Nor is excessive adherence to an ideology restricted to politics. It is not unknown for scientists to form intense emotional attachments to their pet theories, resulting in a sense of conviction quite unjustified by the evidence available. Symptoms of this very human condition include downplaying conflicting evidence by attacking those who present it, reacting to criticism with aggression rather than reason, and making grandiose statements about topics (like religion) which offend the speaker's point of view (often revealing a level of ignorance that would be unforgivable in the speaker's own speciality). Ethereal ideas are a common consequence of the way human brains are built. If they are a failing, they are one to which we are all susceptible.

I say if, because abstraction and ambiguity in themselves are not always undesirable. Any mathematician could argue for the merits of abstract thinking. As for ambiguity, therein lies the fascination of many of our favourite cultural products, from the Mona Lisa's smile to M.C. Escher's impossible buildings to Henry James' *The Turn of the Screw*.[12] Ethereal ideas, including (but again not limited to) those derived from religion, have provided much that is life-enhancing. They have also in many cases given their possessors the strength to resist oppression and torture, to survive terrible situations, to rebuild when the chance arises, and even to forgive. A world without faith would have much less colour to delight us, as well as much less pain. A world without religion would probably not be all that different from the present variety, since secular ideologies, and the urge to believe in them, would still exist.

Faith, in the sense of ideological conviction, and religion are not at all the same thing. Tolerance and dogmatism can both be found as easily in a lab or university as in a church, mosque, or synagogue. Nor does the scientific method guarantee immunity against ethereal ideas and the excesses they can lead us to. Challenging the old gods where they do harm is fine, but not if the result is that science itself gets set up as a replacement deity. Because of its exaltation of human reason, its divorcing of facts from values (see Chapter 13), science-as-authority makes two dangerous claims: that morals are irrelevant, and that scientists have the strongest claim to truth. Easy then to extend this authority to whatever prejudices the scientists happen to hold, because (since morals are irrelevant, and no other viewpoint is worthy to challenge theirs), there is no longer pressure on them to examine their beliefs. Hence come scourges like 'scientific' racism, sexism, and what one may christen 'psychism'—discrimination against people with mental health problems. Science relies on a method whose results depend on its input, and most experiments are complex and very open to interpretation. If the ideas providing the input (the theory being tested) evoke strong emotional commitment, the interpretation is likely to be in their favour. Science-as-authority, worshipped without the moral restraint, self-knowledge, and humility which most religions are old and wise enough to demand (if not always receive) from their adherents, lets scientists off the Socratic hook of self-examination and allows them to treat their personal bigotries as accepted truths.

Individual differences: 'one man's faith is another man's reason'

From the point of view of a book on brainwashing, one of the most interesting implications of what neuroscience and psychology tell us about beliefs is the idea of individual differences. Just as some people have better memories than others, so certain individuals may form new beliefs, or change their beliefs, more easily than others. Beliefs, like memories, come with differing degrees of conviction. However, there are some people whose entire personalities seem highly dogmatic—they are predisposed to believe (anything) more strongly than their neighbours. Variations in dogmatism could result from differences in the function of particular synapses, perhaps due to genetic variations. If so, this raises the possibility that in future conviction may become manipulable. Genes affecting belief strength? The idea conjures up fantasies of a pill for fundamentalism, a cure for extremists of all and any persuasions.

In 1960 the psychologist Milton Rokeach published an influential book called *The Open and Closed Mind*. Subtitled 'Investigations into the nature of belief systems and personality systems', it discussed dogmatism, or closed-mindedness. Individuals scoring highly on tests of dogmatism were resistant or even hostile to new ideas, more anxious about the future, less tolerant of ambiguity, more concrete in their thinking, and less flexible in their problem-solving behaviour than individuals low in dogmatism. Dogmatism was found to show little or no correlation with intelligence, but a strongly negative correlation with creativity. Highly dogmatic individuals are often able to resist influence attempts because their own cogwebs are so strong: Robert Lifton noted that one of the most successful and least traumatized of his group of Chinese and Western thought reform survivors was the Westerner Hans Barker, a devout Catholic bishop.[13] Highly dogmatic individuals may also appear extremely charismatic to others because of their strong sense of self. Their high confidence in their beliefs is attractive to others with weaker convictions, especially those who are actively seeking security.

Low-dogmatism individuals, by contrast, will display creativity, openness to new ideas, an intuitive and flexible thinking style, and greater tolerance of outgroups. Such individuals should also exhibit increased suggestibility and susceptibility to influence attempts. Their sense of self will be weaker, their faith more open to doubt and questioning. If they appear charismatic, it is because of creativity, not certainty, the sparkle of ideas rather than the blaze of self-belief.

It is tempting to attach evaluations to these two ends of the dogmatism spectrum, to agree with Yeats that 'The best lack all conviction, while the worst/Are full of passionate intensity'.[14] Yet the situation is more complex than these statements imply. Highly dogmatic people can appear extremely charismatic, and on occasions, particularly at times of great uncertainty, that charisma may prove extremely useful. (Winston Churchill may have changed the course of history in 1940 by swinging the British Cabinet from its hesitant pro-peace stance into clear opposition to Hitler, leading to the rejection of Germany's offer of a truce.)[15] However, it is just as much of a caricature to say that high dogmatics get things done while low dogmatics think about doing them. Many people who have worked in teams recognize the stereotype of the brilliant thinker, full of ideas, to whom 'deadline' seems an entirely alien concept. If they can be forced into making a useful contribution these scatterbrained intellectuals can change the world; but they may drive their colleagues to screaming point in the process. Neither dogmatism nor creativity, of course, should be thought of as context-independent. They come together with circumstances, and the person's other personality traits, to achieve the end result: absent-minded professor or charismatic cult leader, firm administrator or boring obsessive. Both extremes, and all the flavours in between, have advantages and disadvantages.

Summary and conclusions

This chapter has presented a view of belief—a view from Neuroworld—which is, I believe, exciting in the insights it can offer. However, it may also appear somewhat unnerving. Are we really as much the prisoners of our past, driven by our history and our current perceptions, as this viewpoint seems to suggest? What about free will, that singularity at the heart of so many theories about human nature? I will return to this most potent of objections in Chapter 11.

Brainwashing scares us because it proposes the idea that our strongest beliefs—the guide ropes which hold our minds together—can be twisted or even destroyed, without our consent, by other people. Is such mind manipulation possible? To find out, we must investigate two more aspects of human brain function: emotions, and the power to stop and think.

Chapter 9: Swept away

A dark weight in the air.
I am suffocating.
My heart labours and staggers.
My blood has thickened.
Some horror is close. Some evil
Settling cold on the skin.
Knowledge of it
Is weakening my whole body.
I cannot argue it away, or escape it.
Common sense, plain reason
Cannot get oxygen.
Trying to wake up
In the waking nightmare, I cannot wake up.
I am still sleepwalking in it

Aeschylus, *The Oresteia: Agamemnon*

Emotions are one of the most potent tools in a brainwasher's armoury. As we saw in Chapter 2, arousing strong emotions can glue a group together, make dubious ideas desirable, and sometimes lead to lethal consequences. Even in weaker forms of influence emotions have an important role to play. What is it about emotions which makes them so useful to influence technicians? To answer this question, we need to investigate what emotions do to brains.

Universal feeling

Look back at the quotation, cited above, from *The Oresteia*. Even before the prophetess Cassandra warns of the dreadful events about to overtake Agamemnon and his family, the Chorus knows that something is wrong. Aeschylus wrote his tragic masterpiece almost 2500 years ago, yet the emotions it describes are instantly recognizable. Twenty-three centuries later, Edgar Allan Poe was to become famous for stories such as 'The Pit and the Pendulum' and 'The Fall of the House of Usher'. Again we have no difficulty in knowing what his characters are feeling:

I at once started to my feet, trembling convulsively in every fibre [...]
Perspiration burst from every pore, and stood in cold big beads upon my forehead.

Poe, 'The Pit and the Pendulum',
The Complete Tales and Poems of Edgar Allan Poe, p. 248

I endeavoured to shriek [...] but no voice issued from the cavernous lungs, which, oppressed as if by the weight of some incumbent mountain, gasped and palpitated, with the heart ...

Poe, 'The Premature Burial', Complete Tales, p. 267

Why, then [...] did the hairs of my head erect themselves on end, and the blood of my body become congealed within my veins?

Poe, 'Berenice', Complete Tales, p. 648

A pounding heart, a chill on the skin, a sense of suffocation, of blood thickening or congealing. This is fear, described in very similar terms by two human beings at opposite ends of human history. Both descriptions closely match the 'racing heart, high blood pressure, clammy hands and feet' noted by a neuroscientific expert on fear research, Joseph LeDoux (in *The Emotional Brain*). In other words, fear is associated with certain physiological symptoms (including facial expressions) which seem to be so distinctive and unchanging that the emotion can be recognized across huge gaps of time and culture.

Other emotions such as anger and disgust also seem characterized by particular bodily effects. These symptoms are so consistent that researchers from Charles Darwin onwards have proposed that some emotions—at least fear, anger, disgust, and joy, and perhaps sadness and surprise as well—are universal features of the human species. The situations in which they are expressed may differ—Japanese people, for example, suppress emotional displays in situations in which Americans would have no such inhibitions—but the ways in which emotions are expressed are much the same for all the races. In the 1960s, Ekman and colleagues showed photographs of Western facial expressions to members of pre-literate tribes (the Sadong in Borneo and the Fore in New Guinea) who had had little previous contact with the West. They were able to identify the Westerners' emotions, and when asked to make a face typical of an emotional situation (e.g. 'Your child has died', 'Your friend has come and you are happy'), their facial expressions were easily recognizable by Westerners.[1]

For these basic emotions, many of the associated bodily responses seem to be shared not only across humanity, but also by other animals, as Darwin proposed

148

in his 1872 book *The Expression of the Emotions in Man and Animals*. Angry dogs and angry men both snarl with bared teeth, while a frightened cat's hairs 'erect themselves on end' just like the hairs on the head in Poe's description. Given these similarities, and the very young age at which infants start to express emotion, it seemed to Darwin that the external aspects of basic emotions might be innate reactions. In other words, emotions are intimately bound up with bodily changes. As William James, a founding father of modern psychology, put it: *'If we fancy some strong emotion, and then try to abstract from our consciousness of it all the feelings of its bodily symptoms, we find we have nothing left behind,* no "mind-stuff" out of which the emotion can be constituted, and that a cold and neutral state of intellectual perception is all that remains.'[2]

Feelings and physiology

The observation of universality in at least some emotions hints at a profound and long-debated question. Does the feeling of an emotion come first, and trigger the bodily responses, or is it the other way round? The Cartesian view would be that events in the mind cause effects in the body—and since causes precede effects, the feeling comes first. However, modern psychology has veered towards the opposite view. William James was clearly of this opinion:

My theory, on the contrary, is that *the bodily changes follow directly the perception of the exciting fact, and that our feeling of the same changes as they occur* IS *the emotion.* Common-sense says, we lose our fortune, are sorry and weep; we meet a bear, are frightened and run; we are insulted by a rival, are angry and strike. The hypothesis here to be defended says that this order of sequence is incorrect [...] that we feel sorry because we cry, angry because we strike, afraid because we tremble, and not that we cry, strike, or tremble, because we are sorry, angry, or fearful, as the case may be.

James, *Principles of Psychology*, pp. 1065–6

The neurologist Antonio Damasio has written extensively on emotion in his trilogy *Descartes' Error*, *The Feeling of What Happens*, and *Looking for Spinoza*. He agrees with James that, where emotions are concerned, outward expressions precede the mental events.[3] Damasio reserves the term 'emotion' for external, bodily changes, using the term 'feeling' for the internal consequences of these changes. Some thinkers have argued that conscious feelings are mere side-effects of brain activity, as devoid of function and influence as a slug in the path of a truck.

Damasio demurs. He argues that emotions help us to evaluate the world around us by providing quickly accessible positive or negative labels for our thoughts and perceptions. Damasio calls these labels 'somatic markers'—markers 'from the body'—because he argues that they arise when we associate a particular bodily state with a particular mental event. Just as a child stung by a wasp tends to develop negative feelings about wasps, so a person who has, for example, been angry when confronted with a colleague's incompetence develops a cogweb linking that colleague with not only the concept of incompetence, but also the physical symptoms of anger: raised heart rate, tension in the jaw, and so on. The next time that particular colleague is encountered, the cogweb will be reactivated, raising the heart rate, tensing the jaw—and influencing the way in which the colleague is treated. We often speak of reliving our memories, and this is particularly apt for memories of emotion: remembering our anger, we find ourselves enraged all over again. In the case of the inept colleague, remembered emotion may put someone on guard against future incompetence, but it can also mediate against establishing a good relationship.

Short cuts and memos

Emotions, in other words, are short cuts—in the language of social psychology, they are heuristics. They encourage, or warn against, behaviour, reminding us that the last time we encountered this particular situation our body felt this particular way. We may consciously experience, reflect on, analyse, or even be overcome by emotions; or we may be guided by their input without even realizing. Experiments have shown that people can be affected by emotional stimuli even if those stimuli are not consciously perceived. When shown some abstract symbols which they had never seen before, for instance, people's judgements of how much they liked the symbols was affected by whether a sad or a happy face was flashed briefly before the presentation of each symbol. Although the faces appeared and disappeared too quickly to be consciously perceived, people liked the symbols better when they followed a happy face.[4]

Much of our emotional life occurs at this unrecognized lower level. The process of emotional contagion discussed in Chapter 2, for example, allows people to synchronize their movements, facial expressions, and conversation extremely quickly and to a high degree of precision. Because these bodily changes are associated with—and, according to James and Damasio, precede—the feeling of an emotion, participants in any social interaction will find their emotions affected by those of the person with whom they are communicating. Yet most people are unaware of the extent to which they catch, mimic, and reflect each other's emotional states. Such sharing of emotions acts as a social pressure, facilitating conformity and a sense of belonging. Shared emotions also feed off each other. Social expression of emotions is neither random nor irrational; it serves extremely useful purposes.[5]

As with beliefs, the frequently inaccessible nature of our emotions assists our efficient functioning in the world. We do not have time to reflect on every feeling, just as we do not have time to analyse every perception or cognition— short cuts prevent us from grinding to a perplexed and fatal standstill. However, as every manager knows, delegation can have risks as well as benefits. Similarly, trusting to our emotions can lead us astray from reality and may even be danger- ous—especially when there are people around us who know how to manipulate those emotions to their own advantage. An instance of such manipulation can be found in this manifesto commitment from one of Britain's less mainstream political parties:

While the dumping of asylum seekers on our communities is fundamentally
the fault of the Government, BNP councillors will do everything in their power
to prevent asylum seekers being dumped in our areas [...] Whilst we do not
believe that the current wave of asylum seekers have any right to be in Britain,
while they are here we will insist that benefits provided by the local
community are repaid by asylum seekers being put to work to clean up the
streets and carry out other tasks on behalf of the local community. This must
not be at the cost of cleaning jobs at present held by local labour—there is
plenty of squalor to be tidied up. Such employment should not be taken to
mean they have any legal grounds for residential status.

British National Party, *Manifesto for the UK Council Elections*, May 2003

Setting aside the sentiments, consider the words in the light of what we have learned about cogwebs and how they form. Chapter 8 noted the importance of the timing, intensity, and frequency of stimulation for strengthening these mental associations. In the above short extract, the term 'asylum seekers' occurs four times; the only words which occur more often are 'the', 'of', and 'to', com- mon words to which we usually pay minimal attention. At the same time, the reader's brain is receiving some emotive verbal stimuli. Positive words like 'we', 'our', 'local', and 'behalf' draw the reader into the BNP ingroup. Negative words—'dumped', 'squalor', 'fault', 'cost'—push the outgroup, asylum seekers, further away. Note how the metaphor of rubbish is emphasized, at the beginning by using words like 'dumping' and 'dumped', later on more explicitly by insisting that asylum seekers should do menial cleaning jobs, tidying up the squalor pre- sumably created by good white British people. Note also the presence of ethereal ideas: 'power', 'community', 'legal', and 'asylum seekers'. No attempt here to differentiate crooks from doctors, economic migrants from torture victims. What we have is a piece of prose which is doing its damnedest to slip you a cog- web encoding the idea that all asylum seekers are garbage. (You may wish to analyse this paragraph in terms of my attempt to do the opposite.) The emotions triggered by certain words serve to strengthen that cogweb. In other words, even the weak emotions aroused by reading a text can serve as cogweb-boosters. The emotions generated during forceful brainwashing, for example in a cult, are far more intense; their power to strengthen cogwebs is therefore much greater.

Emotions derive from states of the body. Such states are often changed by events such as the release of hormones. Adrenaline, for example, is released in response to stressful or threatening situations, priming the body to fight a rival or escape a predator. However, although hormones can be released very quickly, they have a half-life, like radioactivity, which means their effects do not disappear immediately. This is why after a violent row we can find ourselves still shaking long after the other participant has stormed out. This is also how much propaganda works. The effects of the emotive words linger after we have read them, colouring our perceptions of nearby words (such as 'asylum seekers') in much the same way as unperceived sad or happy faces colour people's judgements of abstract visual symbols. This slippage in time can lead to mis-associations, cogwebs linking thoughts or perceptions with how we felt at a particular time—which may or may not have been caused by whatever caused the thoughts or perceptions. Any cogweb which is activated while we are still experiencing the emotion can become tinged with it: in this sense our feelings are indiscriminate.

If people feel uneasy about emotions, however, it is usually not because they worry about developing unduly negative perceptions of asylum seekers. What concerns us with emotions is their power. We have returned to the same fear that animates the spectre of brainwashing: the fear of losing control. A man in a jealous rage can kill the woman he adores; shame and fear can drive a mother to smother her illegitimate child; the despair of depression leads to the heartbreak of suicide. No wonder that the Greeks portrayed emotions as wild beasts trying to escape the chains of reason, or as Furies driving men to their destruction. Our fear is the fear of being swept away, of finding ourselves in a state where, as *The Oresteia*'s Chorus complains, 'Common sense, plain reason / Cannot get oxygen', in which we may wreak all sorts of havoc on our rational self-interest.

Why do some emotions seem to be so compelling? Part of the answer is probably that, as Darwin noted, the basic emotions are evolutionarily old. They serve as override switches for emergencies, for times when we cannot afford to process all the information fully, when speed of reaction may cross the gap between extinction and survival. In the grip of a strong emotion, we cannot think of anything else, cannot decide not to feel or to set the emotion aside until a more convenient hour. Negative emotions, such as fear, are particularly demanding. As the psychologist Alexander Bain noted, 'When we are under a strong emotion, all things discordant with it keep out of sight [...] the flood of emotion sometimes sweeps away for the moment every vestige of the opposing absent, as if that had at no time been a present reality.'[6] To return to the metaphor used in the last chapter, the emotion is like a torrent bottled up inside our heads. Action releases the flow, eases the flood waters, and reduces the dissonance created by strong emotions.

The relief of stress accompanying this catharsis can itself be a pleasurable sensation—one reason why so much of our culture has developed for the purpose of stimulating our emotions. This is often done in a moderate and controlled fashion, which is just as well: the physiological changes which underlie emotions are designed to be brief. Evolutionarily, emotions were for emergencies. To get out of a dangerous situation was worth risking the negative effects of a sudden jump in blood pressure, for instance. When the emotional response becomes chronically stimulated, however, those effects can cause accumulating damage. People who tell you that stress is bad for you are right: high levels of stress increase the chances of depression and infections, and are associated with a worse prognosis in conditions such as coronary heart disease. We run less risk of being eaten these days, but because of our ability to associate strong emotions with abstract concepts, we can experience a stressful response to events or objects our ancestors would not even have understood.

Stressing the brain

What happens when we become stressed? Physiologically, stress is a multifaceted phenomenon. When a person first encounters a stressful stimulus their brain responds by activating nerves throughout the body, raising the heart rate, and triggering the release of adrenaline and noradrenaline. These hormones prepare the body for 'fight or flight' by increasing blood flow to the muscles and brain, making neurons more sensitive to incoming signals, and dilating the pupils so that the eyes can better detect approaching dangers. Blood flow to other areas such as the skin and gut, whose metabolic demands are not so urgent, is reduced to conserve resources. Then comes the release of glucocorticoid hormones, which alter metabolism to release more energy from fat stores and allow more glucose to reach and energize the brain. All this activation is extremely useful for dodging predators. If the stressful stimulus is ongoing, however, the continuing high levels of adrenaline and glucocorticoids can damage the heart and muscles, raise blood pressure, and weaken the immune system, leaving the person more vulnerable to infections.

In the brain, as already mentioned, stress increases vigilance, placing neurons on high alert for any incoming signal. Brains normally filter out a great deal of information before it reaches the cerebral cortex, but during a stress response these filters are opened up so that more signals pour in. Neurons, however, have limited processing capacities. Faced with an ongoing state of high alert, they tire out, responding less and less to incoming signals (a phenomenon known as habituation). This is the downside of our brains' appetite for change and novelty—neurons tend to get especially excited by changes in their inputs, but keep the signal static and they lose interest. News, as the US President sings in John Adams' opera *Nixon in China*, has a kind of mystery. Advertisers have known the attraction of newness for centuries and still make use of it today: Pratkanis and Aronson note in *Age of Propaganda* that 'Ads that contain the words *new*, *quick*, *easy*, *improved*, *now*, *suddenly*, *amazing*, and *introducing* sell more products.' Of these eight words five—'new', 'improved', 'now', 'suddenly', and 'introducing'—catch our eye by explicitly emphasizing change.

Too much novel information, however, leaves us feeling overloaded, especially if it is continually present. The body's fight or flight responses did not evolve to cope with severe chronic stress, but with short-term dangers. The prefrontal cortex, which is thought to be heavily involved in regulating stress responses, is particularly vulnerable to severely stressful events such as abuse, especially early in life. This is highly relevant to brainwashing, which relies on inducing stress, because as we shall see in Chapter 10 prefrontal areas provide important defences against influence techniques. The stress induced in brainwashing can help to break down those defences.

Commentators on brainwashing have noted that some victims are better able to cope than others. This is because individual stress responses vary greatly from person to person.[7] These differences are due to both genetic variation and personal experience; from the womb onwards genes interact with environmental factors to influence development. Early stress in particular (even as early as a mother being highly stressed during pregnancy) can increase the sensitivity with which brain areas such as prefrontal cortex respond to stressful stimuli in the future, setting the baseline for anxiety levels throughout life.[8] A stark example of individual differences in stress sensitivity comes from research into antisocial personality disorder (APD). In a brain imaging study of APD and non-APD male volunteers, for instance, participants were given a social stressor (being asked to prepare and deliver a speech in four minutes) while researchers measured basic stress responses, such as heart rate, and the size of the prefrontal cortex.[9] APD participants had significantly smaller prefrontal cortices and were significantly less stressed: on average, their heart rate was more than eight beats a minute slower than their non-APD peers'.

Despite the physiological harm that they can do, the power of strong emotions to overwhelm reasoned reflection has sometimes been seen as a benefit in itself. Thinking too much can paralyse decision making and in some cases bring on depression. Strong emotions narrow the focus of consciousness to the immediate, encouraging short-term thinking and blanking out longer-term, often more negative thoughts—the disadvantages of casual sex, the dangers of smoking, the problems which will accrue if you do actually thump your boss. If I don't want to be bothered with the consequences of my actions, getting emotional is a good way to avoid thinking about them. This is not to say, of course, that all emotions have this blinkering effect. Moderate emotions may bolster prejudice, but they can also provide useful guides to colour and inform the cognitive landscape. Damasio's book *Descartes' Error* is built around the theme that emotions often aid rationality and are essential to effective social functioning. Robots, computers, and androids are often held up as ideals of logical processing, but not many people really want to be a robot, a computer, or an android. We believe, correctly, that emotions are a vital aspect of our lives.

The emotion excuse

The propensity of emotions to make us lose control and do things we don't want to do (i.e. wouldn't do in our more sober moments) is so well known that it is often employed as a justification for dubious actions. Are such justifications valid? At this point, it is worth considering the role of hindsight and hermeneutics in our assessments of our own emotional states. A manager forced to justify the verbal abuse of his secretary may look back on his irritation at the time and reinterpret it, under the pressure of social disapproval, as a spasm of blazing fury. He may simply be lying, but—because recalling emotions can actually strengthen them—he may genuinely come to believe that he was enraged. Whether he believes that he was overwhelmed, and so could not stop himself abusing his secretary, will depend on whether he believes that emotions can, and do, overwhelm all rational restraints.

The social psychologist Roy Baumeister has this to say about the notion of an 'irresistible impulse' and its modern companion, the faulty gene or genes which can make one obese, an addict, a criminal.

Our culture has lately become increasingly fond of notions of 'irresistible impulses' and genetic causes of addiction. But in research on self-control, one conclusion stands out over and over again: People *acquiesce* in losing control. In other words, they let themselves lose control, and they become active participants. Whether it is a matter of breaking a diet, going on a drinking binge, or abandoning an unpleasant task, usually the person somehow allows it to happen. The same applies to violence. The concept of an irresistible impulse is somewhat misleading, because most violent behavior is not truly the result of irresistible impulses. People allow themselves to lose control. And they do so in part because they learn to regard certain impulses as irresistible [...] For example, people speak as if an eating or drinking binge were simply a matter of being overwhelmed by strong impulses that rendered them passive and helpless. Yet during these binges, they continue to procure food or drink, prepare it for consumption, put it in their mouths, and swallow it. These are active, not passive actions. Resisting the impulse may have been too difficult for them, but they have not simply quit resisting, they have become active accomplices in indulging their desires.

Baumeister, *Evil*, pp. 274–5

With respect to self-control, Baumeister is arguing that when giving in to supposedly irresistible impulses we somehow 'choose to lose', to ignore or set aside the normal restraints, or to put ourselves in a position where we will be forced to lose control. Of course, the weaker those restraints are, the easier they are to ignore. How restraints are implemented in the brain, how they may be strengthened, and whether we do possess the power to choose, will be important themes of the next two chapters of this book. In the meantime, suffice it to say that although we often cannot control our emotions, we may have more control than we think over the actions which tend to flow from them. But exerting such control requires complex, long-term thinking, planning ahead, avoiding the situations which may lead to strong emotions, and bearing in mind the consequences—all capacities which are impaired when our strong feelings insist that we focus on the here and now. This narrowing of focus to the immediate present can be created by deliberately inducing emotions, a strategy attractive to influence technicians because it suppresses many of the second thoughts their victims might otherwise have.

Flooding the brain

What happens in the brain when we feel an emotion? From what has already been said, it seems that emotions derive from bodily events. So we would expect the subcortical areas of our brains to be involved in bridging the gap between body and cortex, transmitting information about the body to the cortex. First of all this requires a subcortical area or areas which will be linked both to cortical areas and to output control areas at the lowest levels of the brain—in the brainstem. Such areas can represent specifically emotion-related information, so I shall refer to them as emotional representations, or ERs (see Fig. 9.1).[10]

ERs receive incoming information from the world which notifies them of detected stimuli, such as approaching predators. A rough, preliminary signal arrives at high speed from the thalamus; slower, more highly processed versions come from sensory cortical areas. ERs also receive and represent input from the body, telling them about heart rate, blood pressure, hormone levels, and so on. Some of this input is neural, that is, it comes via nerves which connect the internal organs to the brain. Some is endocrine (hormonal): some neurons have receptors which can be activated by hormones, allowing those cells to monitor hormone levels. ERs send output to the brainstem, allowing them to regulate heart rate, breathing, gut function (hence the unfortunate effects that can result from extreme fright), and other body functions which we normally don't think much about, but which we need to have on full alert when there's an emergency to deal with. ERs also send signals to the pituitary gland, a small bulge at the base of the brain, which regulates hormone levels. ERs send information to

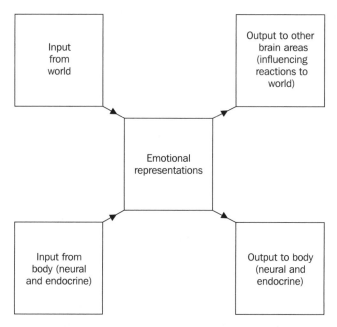

Figure 9.1 A schematic representation of the inputs received by emotional representations (ERs) and the outputs to which ERs send information. Arrows indicate the direction of information flow, although this is highly simplified; in practice neural communication is largely two-way.

other brain areas as well, particularly to the frontal lobes of the cortex, thereby providing the basis for the fully conscious, interpreted experience of an emotion.

Feeling what we think we ought to feel

Why do I emphasize that last point? Because research has shown that how we interpret our bodies depends not only on what they tell us, but also on what we happen to be thinking at the time. In 1962 the psychologists Stanley Schachter and Jerome Singer published the results of an experiment which, despite being extremely controversial (see below), would become a classic of the literature.[11] Participants who were told they were testing the transient effects of a vitamin compound were in fact given injections of either adrenaline or a placebo (a substance with no physiological effect). Some were told the injection would make them more alert (as indeed adrenaline does), some that it would make them more tired (which adrenaline certainly does not), and some were not informed of potential side-effects.

What happened? Those participants who received adrenaline felt aroused. If they had been told that the drug would arouse them, they had no need to look elsewhere to explain their feeling of alertness: 'the drug dunnit', and that was that. But if they had not been told anything, or if they had been (falsely) told that the drug would make them tired, then they couldn't blame the drug. They had to look for another explanation for what their bodies were telling them.

Schachter and Singer cleverly provided alternative explanations by relying on the human capacity for picking up emotions from other people. Participants were with a confederate, someone the participants didn't realize was actually working for the experimenters. The confederate pretended to be either very happy or very angry. Schachter and Singer expected that the presence of an apparently happy or apparently angry person (whom the participants thought had been given the drug just as they had) would allow the participants to explain their own sensations. 'He's had the drug, and he's happy; I've had the drug, so what I'm feeling must be happiness.' And it worked. The participants' interpretations of the confederate's behaviour interacted with internal signals from their bodies (resulting from the drug injection) such that the participants interpreted these signals as *either* happiness *or* anger. What we think affects what we feel, and vice versa.

Schachter and Singer's experimental results were ethically and scientifically dubious, as many social psychologists since have pointed out.[12] Yet their study remains a staple of social psychology textbooks. One reason for this continuing popularity may be its linking of two domains traditionally seen as separate: cognition and emotion. When we feel an emotion, the stimuli which trigger that emotion and the responses they elicit in our brain and body interact with our stored 'history inputs' to produce an ongoing process of appraisal and interpretation. We use this emotional hermeneutics to determine how to classify our sensations. Physiology and psychology interact and affect each other to produce the overall feeling we experience.

Emotion systems

If the feeling of an emotion results from bodily changes interacting with cognitive interpretations, and because we know that thinking about an emotion can bring it on, we would expect the communication between ERs and cortical areas involved in emotion processing to be two-way. Because we know that we have at least some control over our emotions, we would expect the cortical areas involved in emotion processing to be able to restrain, that is inhibit, the activity of the lower, subcortical areas. Moreover, emotional responses are complicated, involve many different behaviours, and occur at different times—from initial changes in heart rate to the slower adjustments of the facial muscles which result in a snarl or a smile. This calls for a complicated, overlapping set of controls: no simple input–output circuit could be flexible enough to cover all these options.

And indeed, that is what neuroscientists have found: multiple interactions between different areas of the brain from the cortex to the brainstem, all in aid of a finely tuned system of expression. Simple circuits evolved in simple organisms to help them tell predator from prey; more complex organisms could learn that sometimes a predator was out of range, or prey unreachable. We humans cannot merely tell a threat from a promise, we can grasp a thousand subtle shades of desire and terror, hope and deceit, love and fury. We have become prodigious mind readers—not in the sense of telepathy, but in the sense of being able to tell the difference between the smile that means 'I love you' and the smile that means 'I love you, but ...'. To learn a little more, we must turn to the ERs themselves.

Feeling brains

Deep in each half of the brain, lying beneath the temporal lobe, is a roughly almond-shaped cluster of cells, the amygdala. Strange things happen when the amygdala is damaged—accidentally, in a few unfortunate people, or deliberately, in experiments on monkeys. The victims become oddly fearless; they may also engage in more social and sexual behaviour. A monkey with amygdalar damage is a very friendly monkey, and it is so brave that it will reach calmly past a rubber snake for a grape and then reach back again to explore the snake. Monkeys without this damage would be hard put to grab the grape, and would never touch the snake. Damage to the amygdala seems to prevent monkeys (and people) from associating objects with emotions. Their vision is normal, but they do not seem able to grasp the emotional significance of what they have recognized.

The tragic circus of neurology gives us a second demonstration of why the amygdala matters. Capgras syndrome is a rare and dreadful condition in which the sufferer believes that his or her nearest and dearest are in some sense no longer authentic, that they have been replaced by robots or impostors.[13] What seems to happen in Capgras is that damage affects the connections from the amygdala to the cortex of the temporal lobe (which processes visual images, including faces). The Capgras patient can recognize people as normal. But when a loved one appears, the usual glow of affection—the meaning which makes that face so special—is absent: the emotional signal never reaches the cortex. The patient sees someone who looks—but doesn't *feel*—familiar. Like the participants in Schachter and Singer's adrenaline experiments who interpreted their feelings based on other people's facial expressions, the Capgras sufferer explains his or her bizarre sensations by referring to something familiar: the concept of the actor, impostor, or robot. Patients with schizophrenia also use cultural explanations to account for puzzling symptoms, such as the sensations that their actions are not their own or that their bodies are being controlled by an external source (delusions of control). In earlier times God and the Devil were the usual sources cited as exerting this control, but in the modern West they face stiff competition, notably from the CIA and aliens.

Interconnected with the amygdala is the hypothalamus, which in turn connects to a gland at the base of the brain, the pituitary. The pituitary gland, stimulated by the hypothalamus, releases a variety of hormonal signals which regulate, among other things, growth and development, sexual development and the menstrual cycle, hunger and thirst, and the release of adrenaline from the adrenal glands. Like a nerve which signals to a muscle, the pituitary gland acts as an output signal from the brain, a signal carried by hormone molecules rather than by a nerve axon. Damage to the hypothalamus can seriously disrupt the regulation of the body's hormonal systems and can lead to a wide variety of destabilizing effects, from changes in appetite to rage.

Both the amygdala and the hypothalamus are connected with the picturesquely named periaqueductal grey (PAG). This area sends direct signals to circuitry in the brainstem which controls many body functions: it is the output station for neural information going to the body. Stimulation of the PAG in human patients undergoing brain surgery (which is often done on conscious patients) results in feelings of intense fear and distress and the dread of imminent death, emotions which are not simply due to the experience of undergoing brain surgery. The amygdala, the hypothalamus, and the PAG are all linked to clusters of cells located towards the middle of the thalamus. These cells send information to the cortex, which in turn projects back to the thalamus, hypothalamus, amygdala, and PAG (see Fig. 9.2).

Signals from midbrain ERs such as the amygdala do not go only to the motor circuits in the brainstem. They can also regulate the activity of certain brainstem nuclei which are involved in wakefulness and sleep, mood, general alertness, and vigilance. These nuclei send widespread projections throughout the brain using the neurotransmitters dopamine, noradrenaline, serotonin, and acetylcholine (many mind-altering or mood-altering drugs are related to these neurotransmitters and influence these wide-ranging pathways). This is one reason why emotions are so pervasive and hard to ignore—and hence such useful tools for influence technicians. When something provokes an emotional reaction, most of the brain may be mobilized to deal with it, leaving fewer resources free for second thoughts.

Neuroimaging studies, which can look inside a living human brain while it is doing a task, often provide pictures of brains in which a few bright spots glow against a darker background, like the lights of insomniacs in a town late at night. In reality, patterns of neural activity in most tasks—even the simplest—change all over the brain. To make sense of the complexity, scientists set a threshold which bars all but the most notable changes from consideration, consigning everything else to darkness. Talk of 'brain areas involved in ...' is therefore a

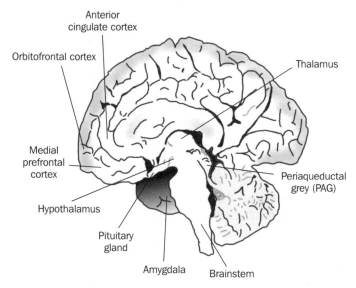

Anterior
cingulate cortex

Orbitofrontal cortex

Thalamus

Medial
prefrontal
cortex

Periaqueductal
grey (PAG)

Hypothalamus

Pituitary
gland

Amygdala   Brainstem

Figure 9.2 A medial (inner) view of a human brain, with the approximate locations of major areas involved in emotional processing shown.

shorthand for 'brain areas especially strongly activated in …'. It does not mean that other parts of the brain are not involved, only that our technology at present is not subtle enough to illuminate more than a fraction of the detail available. This is particularly true of subcortical areas: the vast majority of neuroimaging work is done on the cortex.

With this caveat in mind, what are the main cortical areas involved in emotional processing? This is a question which is by no means answered; there are currently several promising candidates. Although in recent years a huge amount of research has investigated the neuroscience of emotion, the roles of cortical areas in the brain's understanding of emotions are not well understood. I will not attempt more than a very brief summary here.[14]

The cortical candidates

The gap between the two halves of the brain—the left and right hemispheres—is bridged by a broad central band of nerve fibres known as the corpus callosum. Curled around this massive feature of the brain's architecture is the cingulate gyrus, whose front end comprises the anterior cingulate cortex (ACC). During its distinguished history this area has been linked with just about everything the brain does, from wanting to urinate to the feeling of self-generated action. Suggestions as to what the anterior cingulate does have included error monitoring, attention, action planning, regulating motivation, and the resolution of conflicts between other brain areas. It may help to resolve incompatible desires so that action doesn't grind to a halt, leaving us starving to death because we can't decide between the korma and the tikka masala.

In front of the anterior cingulate is the prefrontal cortex (PFC), another home favoured by neuroscientists for brain capacities not yet assigned elsewhere. Towards the middle of the prefrontal cortex is the medial prefrontal cortex (mPFC), which seems to be particularly involved in emotional processing. Like many prefrontal cortical areas, the mPFC may regulate the activity of lower areas, such as the amygdala. It is thought to specialize in learning associations between actions and outcomes, allowing experienced rats, for example, to take it for granted that the bell means an electric shock is coming and to concentrate on getting out of the way. The mPFC is particularly important when situations change; when it is damaged, rats have problems learning that a bell which once meant shock now means food. Fast, basic responses are mediated at the sub-cortical level; more flexible behaviour is achieved as additional layers of brain circuitry are overlaid.

Also located in the prefrontal cortex, just above the orbits, or sockets, of the eyes, is an area called the orbitofrontal cortex (OFC). It is also closely inter-connected with the amygdala. This area was damaged by the metal rod blown through Phineas Gage's head, an injury which transformed him from a hard-working, reliable man to a feckless ruin who exhibited himself as a circus freak (see note 16, on lobotomy, in Chapter 1). In *The Emotional Brain*, Joseph LeDoux notes that OFC damage appears to affect 'short-term memory about reward information, about what is good and bad at the moment, and cells in this region are sensitive to whether a stimulus has just led to a reward or punishment. Humans with orbital frontal damage become oblivious to social and emotional cues and some exhibit sociopathic behavior.' The OFC, in other words, appears to represent the value of a stimulus in terms of reward and punishment, and to facilitate complex choices between different rewards (or punishments). Very young children, if offered the choice between a small piece of chocolate now and a larger piece in a few minutes' time, cannot wait. Adults with OFC damage show the same inability to delay gratification: they want it all, but most of all they want it now.

The anterior cingulate, medial prefrontal cortex, and orbitofrontal cortex are all heavily interconnected with the subcortical areas which control emotional alterations in the body (Fig. 9.3 shows some of the major links between cortical and subcortical areas). Damage to, or stimulation of, the subcortical areas affects fast, automatic emotional responses. Interfering with the areas of the cortex produces more subtle effects on the interpretation of emotion, the slower, more deliberate aspects of emotional expression, and the flexibility which changes

162

responses when circumstances change. As Karl Marx might have said, emotions, like societies, involve power from the base (of the brain) and control from the superstructure. As was noted earlier, the areas I have discussed are not the only ones involved in emotion processing. Other regions (like the insula, thought among other things to process painful stimuli) also play a role, but what that role is remains to be fully understood.

What is clear, however, is that emotions involve interaction between cortex and subcortex, between body and brain, at a number of interconnected levels. Simple stimulus–response circuits have you freezing before you know why; more complex cogwebs identify a badly lit street or the sound of footsteps; the most intricate associations link darkness to the terrors of childhood, approaching steps to horror films or crime dramas. An undamaged brain is as permeated with emotional information as a well-made lemon soufflé is with lemon. In the words of

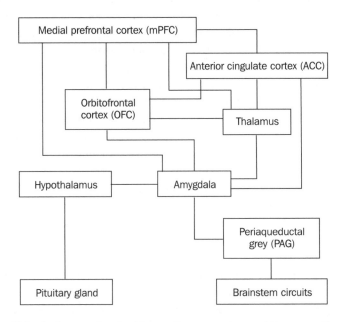

Figure 9.3 Major brain areas involved in emotion processing, and the connections between them. Their functions are not fully understood, but are thought to be along the following lines: the medial prefrontal cortex (mPFC) forms associations between actions and their results; the anterior cingulate cortex (ACC) is involved in motivation and conflicting desires; the orbitofrontal cortex (OFC) represents stimuli in terms of their value as punishments or rewards, and the amygdala learns the emotional meaning of stimuli, or retrieves it when the stimuli are familiar. The amygdala receives information about stimuli from the thalamus and the cortex, and sends outputs to the hypothalamus and to the periaqueductal grey (PAG). The hypothalamus in turn triggers the pituitary gland, changing hormone levels, while the PAG sends signals to internal body organs such as the gut and blood vessels.

Antonio Damasio, 'Feelings of pain or pleasure or some quality in between are the bedrock of our minds [...] the unstoppable humming of the most universal of melodies.'[15]

The all-emoting brain

People are most susceptible to propaganda when already in a high state of tension

Edward Hunter, *Brain-washing in Red China*

Emotions—particularly negative emotions—are all-pervasive. Different brain areas seem to emphasize different aspects—the orbitofrontal cortex is concerned with reward and punishment, the medial prefrontal cortex with linking actions and outcomes, and the amygdala with connecting objects to their emotional meanings, for example—but usually the intricate webs which bind these areas (and others) guarantee a unitary experience: hot fury, icy calm, black grief, or incomparable joy. Once associated with such an experience, an object or thought has the capacity to influence both brain and body, exerting a pressure for action which less intense cognitions cannot match. Musing on relativity theory may rouse some cortical areas, but it can't match the impact of seeing your child in danger. However, emotions are also indiscriminate. Physical changes can be interpreted very differently, depending on the situation and the person; and because emotional changes can take longer than thoughts to ebb and flow, the link between a thought and its value can be blurred as that same emotional value also becomes associated with other active cogwebs.

Herein lies the threat. Humans have evolved extraordinarily complex ways of communicating with each other. Facial expressions, gestures, and, of course, language allow us to stimulate each other's cogwebs very precisely. We can also evoke an emotion, flooding the brain, while ensuring that a certain concept-encoding cogweb is activated at the same time; this will develop a link between the two. Rats easily learn to associate the sound of a bell with an electric shock. Manipulating the emotional associations of words, playing the brain's cogwebs like a harp, can teach humans more complicated connections: that women are inferior, Jews dirty, black people stupid, or asylum seekers garbage. The emotions of fear or disgust are imprecise: they don't remain confined to the words which first evoked them, but leak, contaminating other words. Indeed, we can go further, as Schachter and Singer did, using words or situations to evoke changes in a person's body and then providing that person with a ready-to-wear interpretation of what those changes mean. That interpretation may or may not have anything to do with the way the world actually is.

Summary and conclusions

These features of emotions—their tendency to linger, their ambiguity, and the pressure they exert—are what give them their manipulative power. Certainly no competent brainwasher would want to be without them. Linked to ethereal ideas, whose abstract and ambiguous nature cushions them against discomfiting contradiction from the world beyond the brain, emotions can be devastating, overriding all contrary ideas, ignoring or suppressing any evidence which does not fit, distorting reality to match the contours of cogwebs massively strengthened by the energies flowing through them. We need emotions—what good is a lemon soufflé without any lemon? But we also need to avoid the demons conjured by their misuse. Self-control, touched on earlier in this chapter and intimately bound up with the story of emotions, provides the traditional mechanism for dodging such demons. In the next chapter, I will look at the region of the brain which seems to have the most responsibility for self-control—the prefrontal cortex—asking what we can learn from that mystery of mysteries about how human beings shape and change their own behaviour.

Chapter 10: The power of stop-and-think

The highest possible stage in moral culture is when we recognise that we ought to control our thoughts

Charles Darwin, *Descent of Man*

As previous chapters have suggested, influence attempts come in many varieties—and do not always succeed. A sufficiently motivated person can often stop and think before succumbing, recalling their reasons not to buy, not to believe, and thereby resisting the influence attempt. In the case of brainwashing, however, the pressure is overwhelming. Somehow a brainwasher must be able to bypass his victims' self-control so that they can no longer stop and think. To understand how this could happen, we need to understand how brains implement stop-and-think capacities. The area of cortex most intimately involved with stop-and-think is the bulge which lies immediately beneath our foreheads: the prefrontal cortex, or PFC for short.

Managing the brain

Researchers studying the PFC often compare its function to that of the chief executive of a big company. The analogy is meant to relate to leadership (and I will pursue the management metaphor later in this chapter), but I think it can be taken further. Both PFC and CEO have a hint of glamour, excitement, and power. Both consume large proportions of overall (metabolic or financial) resources relative to other brain areas/company employees. And in both cases most of us don't have the least idea what they actually *do*.

The prefrontal lobes are located at the front of the brain.[1] Crowning a cortex greatly enlarged in human beings compared with our nearest primate relatives, they are the most mysterious and intriguing of all brain areas. Anything humans

167

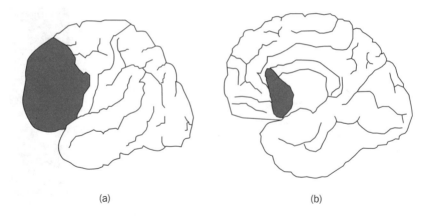

(a)   (b)

Figure 10.1 A human brain, schematically rendered. (a) Lateral (outer) view, showing approximate location of the PFC. (b) Medial (inner) view, showing approximate location of the anterior cingulate cortex.

do which neuroscientists don't understand, any function or capacity not pinned down by lesions, needles, or imaging to somewhere in the rest of the brain, tends to be assigned to the PFC or its close anatomical associate, the anterior cingulate cortex (the two are often grouped together). Consciousness, drive, free will, the self, decision making, complex thoughts and emotions, self-control, and moral thinking are just some of these 'glory-hole' functions.

The anterior cingulate receives input from, and sends signals to, many of the emotion-processing areas of subcortex discussed in Chapter 9, such as the amygdala, periaqueductal grey (PAG), and hypothalamus. Hence the cingulate has a short chain of command to the nerves and hormones which give the human body its powers of response and expression. These powers, while sometimes regulated by conscious control, often seem disconcertingly able to escape it, as any sufferer from panic attacks can testify. Bodily symptoms can also be strongly motivational—pain is an obvious example—providing a powerful impetus to action. The cingulate seems to serve as a bridge between subcortical areas processing this drive and the PFC. Using the Marxist metaphor from Chapter 9, it channels power from base to superstructure and control from superstructure to base.

The PFC's role has been described in many ways. It appears to be involved in ordering, structuring, and guiding behaviour, particularly in challenging or novel situations. It is thought to mediate choosing between alternative options, interpreting possibilities, and modelling potential futures. The urge to thump your boss may from time to time be extremely tempting, but you also want to stay in work. A well-trained PFC will save your career, forcing you to stop and think before you swing that punch. This ability to stop and think, so essential for a civilized existence, seems to require an intact prefrontal lobe. Stop-and-think also allows us to resist influence attempts. Any would-be brainwasher seeking to practise mindcraft on a victim must first get past that victim's prefrontal guard.

The PFC's importance is reflected by what happens when it fails to function properly. Damage to prefrontal areas does not result in clearly observable problems in the way that, say, damage to the visual cortex results in blindness. A patient with prefrontal damage can perform well on standard tests of brain function. Phineas Gage, part of whose PFC was damaged by a workplace accident (see note 16, on lobotomy, in Chapter 1), remained conscious and rational: the doctor who first examined him was able to ask him what had happened. However, as his doctor was later to observe, 'Gage was no longer Gage.' As described by Antonio Damasio in *Descartes' Error*, before his injury Gage 'had a sense of personal and social responsibility [...] was well adapted in terms of social convention and appears to have been ethical in his dealings. After the accident, he no longer showed respect for social convention; ethics, in the broad sense of the term, were violated; the decisions he made did not take into account his best interest, and he was given to invent tales [...] There was no evidence of concern about his future, no sign of forethought.'

Like brainwashing, PFC damage changes the personality, generally for the worse and without the victim's realizing. Depending on which area is damaged, the effects can be extremely variable. Phineas Gage suffered damage to his orbitofrontal cortex (the underside of the PFC, just above the eyes). Patients with damage to other parts of the PFC may show problems with working memory, planning ahead, or adapting to a change in circumstances. Sometimes they cannot stop and think before acting (impulsivity); sometimes, once they have begun to act, they cannot stop (perseveration). The ability to stop and think provides flexibility. It makes us actors, rather than stimulus-driven responders. In a complex and constantly changing world, flexibility may not be essential (spiders don't show much of it, and they're still around). But long-term survival, and that Darwinian imperative, passing on the genes, are undoubtedly facilitated by a flexible brain. Human beings are in charge of planet Earth; spiders (thank goodness) are not.

The PFC does not communicate directly with the outside world, but it does receive inputs from all over the brain. It appears to act as a meeting-point, or integrator; as neuroscientist Elkhonon Goldberg puts it, 'the only part of the brain where the inputs from within the organism converge with the inputs from the outside world'. Like Marx's superstructure, it is concerned with control, with the management of powerful forces. Just as the superstructure embodies ideology at the level of society, so the PFC implements the brain's ideology, takes the major decisions, and balances competing drives and inclinations.

To comprehend what prefrontal areas do, it is necessary to understand how their interactions with other brain areas affect the pathways which turn perceptions into behaviour. In the next section I will describe these interactions, using as an example the simplest of all body movements: moving the eyes.[2] (Similar arguments apply to more complicated behaviour, such as moving an arm or changing facial muscles.) Tracing the paths from input to output will involve considerable detail, but bear with me. Only by setting the PFC in its neural context is it possible to grasp what brain leadership is all about. We shall see that the old Cartesian model of 'diamond minds' misleads us: instead of the simplicity of diamonds we find a world of astonishing intricacy, change, and beauty. By focusing on the pared-down paradigm of eye movements, I hope to convey some of the flavour of this mystery.

Dancing eyes: how brains delegate in eye control

Non-blind human beings rely heavily on being able to see. The back half of our cortex is thought to contain over thirty separate areas devoted to processing visual information, some specializing in colour vision, some in depth perception, and so on. Balancing this sensory processing is the system which controls the way we move our eyes. Because we cannot usually identify objects unless we are looking straight at them, we need to make an awful lot of eye movements.[3] And we do: over ten thousand an hour when we are awake. Someone startled by a sudden flash of light will automatically look towards it, using an extremely rapid eye movement known as a saccade (from the Old French verb *saquer*, to jerk or pull). If you have ever watched someone looking out of the window during a train or car journey, you will have seen their eyes flicking rapidly back and forward (reflex saccades); but if you yourself were looking out of the window, you would not be aware of those eye movements: the passing countryside would seem smoothly and continuously visible to you.

In other words, we are not normally aware of many of the saccades we make. However, this does not mean that we cannot control our eye movements. Human beings are experts at the saccade game: we can move our eyes anywhere we like, when we like.[4] How does a human brain achieve such mastery? As in a well-managed organization, the secret is effective delegation.

Consider an adult human brain (with the rest of the adult human attached in the usual way) in a visual neuroscience laboratory. Visual stimuli are presented on a computer screen and the resulting eye movements are recorded. Simple stimuli, like a bright spot, can evoke an extremely rapid saccade. More complex stimuli, like landscapes or faces, lead to slower responses. What is happening in between to produce these differences?

First stop: the little hill

When the retinas at the back of the eyes register a stimulus, information is transmitted up the optic nerve to visual processing areas in the thalamus, and from there to the visual cortex. As discussed in earlier chapters, a good deal of processing has already occurred by the time the information reaches the visual cortex. Inputs to the thalamus are compared with hypotheses (generated at the cortical level) about what the brain is expecting to see next, and both the inputs and the hypotheses are adjusted depending on the discrepancy between them. No discrepancy, no problem. However, the thalamus is not the only recipient of information coming from the eyes. Input also reaches another subcortical area, the superior colliculus (named from the Latin word for 'little hill').

The superior colliculus (SC) represents the visual world in two dimensions, like a landscape picture does. However, while a landscape artist represents each location in the world using colour (sky = blue, grass = green, and so on), the SC takes a different approach. Locations in its picture are represented in terms of the eye movements required to reach them. Stimulating the SC with electrodes produces saccades whose size and direction change smoothly as the electrodes are moved across the SC. Thus every point in the SC's representation codes for a different saccade, with nearby points coding for similar saccades. The SC is the

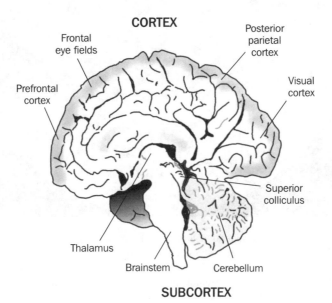

Figure 10.2 A medial view of a human brain, showing the approximate locations of the major brain areas involved in making rapid eye movements (saccades).

brain's major output centre for eye movements. From it signals go to the brain-stem neurons which directly control the muscles around the eyes.

When a stimulus activates the retina, and hence the SC, SC neurons will be activated which represent the saccades needed to move the eyes towards that stimulus. If the stimulus is a very simple one, like a bright spot on a dark back-ground, then SC neural activity will be large at one place (the place representing the eye movement required to point the eyes at the spot) and negligible every-where else. That's easy: just point the eyes at the spot. A rapid saccade is trig-gered, the gaze jumps to the new location—everything is taken care of before the person has even consciously noticed the spot. In other words, simple information gets processed faster. This is why demagogues, cult leaders, advertisers, and brainwashers try to keep their messages as short and simple as possible: by doing

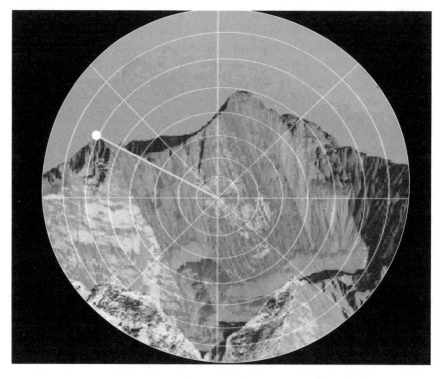

Figure 10.3 Neurons in the superior colliculus (SC) represent eye movements in terms of their size and direction. The figure shows a schematic representation of this map superimposed upon an image, as if the person were looking directly at the centre of the image (where the vertical and horizontal lines cross). The target location, to which the upcoming eye movement will be made, is indicated by a white filled circle, and the eye movement required to reach that target is indicated by a thick white line. Neural activity in the SC is greatest for neurons which represent saccades at or around the target location.

so they increase the chances of triggering a fast, automatic response before their target has time to stop and think.

Complex stimuli, however, present a problem. Imagine that the person in the visual neuroscience laboratory is presented with a picture of the view from my window: my neighbours' garden wall, with a climbing rose and a ceanothus spilling over it, roses and trees beyond, and one of their cats on the lookout for birds (see Fig. 10.4(b) for a cartoon version). The SC activity map will have peaks all over the place, corresponding to all the different locations which could be looked at: leftwards for the climbing rose, straight ahead for the ceanothus, right-wards for the cat, up a bit for the roses, and up a bit more for the trees. But the eyes can't move to more than one place at a time. The result is a paralysing conflict: all the SC neurons are competing for control of the eye muscles, but none of them has control. So, given that our universe consists of more than just bright spots on dark backgrounds, how do we ever manage to move our eyes? Put another way, if suddenly all we had to think with was the SC we might take so long to make any interesting decision that even the most patient influence technician would give up in disgust.

Lateral inhibition

The way out of this quandary is neuronal negotiation. The SC uses a mechanism called lateral inhibition to resolve conflicts among its member neurons, deter-mining who gets to move the eyes. Every SC neuron sends an inhibiting signal to every other neuron. The more active the neuron, the more it damps down the activity of other neurons. When a simple stimulus produces a single sharp peak in the SC activity map (see Fig. 10.4(a)), the active neurons effectively shut down all the other neurons who want to move the eyes to locations nowhere near the stimulus, quickly winning the competition for control of the eye muscles. If there are many peaks (as for the complex stimulus shown in Fig. 10.4(b)), the largest (corresponding to the most distinctive part of the stimulus) will over time tend to suppress its competitors more than they suppress it, persuading them in effect to withdraw their objections to the eye movement which it is encoding. Just as cult leaders suppress conflicting points of view, so the largest peak will eventually come to dominate the SC landscape, but the process of generating an eye move-ment will take much longer. To summarize, information about a stimulus rapidly reaches the SC. If the stimulus is simple, a fast saccade results. If the stimulus is more complicated, no movement occurs. Instead the SC begins the consultation process of lateral inhibition, letting member neurons fight it out until a clear winner emerges.

Mercifully, we don't have to wait until the SC has resolved its conflicts before looking around, or we would long since have lost the evolutionary battle for

(a)

(b)

Figure 10.4 (a) A bright spot on a dark background, an extremely simple visual stimulus which is likely to evoke a rapid saccade. (b) A more complicated visual stimulus: a cartoon representation of a cat on a garden wall.

survival. A typical saccade, even to a very cluttered visual scene, takes only a fraction of a second to programme and perform. This is because while the SC committee is meeting the visual stimulus which caused it to be convened is also being processed elsewhere. Colour, depth, outline, size, motion ... early sensory processing in the thalamus and visual cortex resembles a collection of committees, all concentrating on slightly different aspects of the incoming information. These committees pour out their findings into two gigantic processing streams, which neuroscientists have traditionally labelled the 'what' and 'where' pathways.[5] We shall concentrate on the 'where' pathway, which is more concerned with eye movements. First, however, a little about the 'what' route.

What's 'what'?

The 'what' pathway sends information from the visual cortex into the temporal lobe. Here the information undergoes many further analyses by more committees of neurons. Simplifying greatly, their overall task is one of recognition: identifying and classifying what the eyes are looking at. As the neural signal spreads along the temporal lobe, it represents increasingly sophisticated guesses about the nature of the visual stimulus. And at every stage, those guesses are made available to, and influenced by, reports from other brain areas.

When something is wrong in a company—low efficiency, poor morale, or suchlike—people often blame poor internal communications. Certainly, the brain's astonishingly efficient reactions are due in part to its internal communications, which are excellent. The amygdala, a major recipient of temporal lobe information, does not have to wait for a final report confirming that the object in the left field of view is indeed an oncoming car (colour, make, and registration number supplied). The first indication that it might be, however skimpy the evidence, triggers avoiding action (and an overwhelming sense of fear). Cars have not been around for much of our evolutionary history, but dangerous predators with an ability to conceal themselves up to the moment of attack stalked our ancestors until relatively recently (in some parts of the world they still do). Brains which could trigger fast action on the basis of very few clues ran the risk of flinging their owners about for no reason now and then; but they also spotted danger earlier, and were therefore more likely to survive. Full identification was a leisure activity, carried out in safety.

Second stop: the wall

Enough about 'what'; what of 'where'? From visual cortex, the next stop in the 'where' pathway is the posterior parietal cortex (PPC, named from *paries*, the Latin word for a partition-wall), which contains areas specialized for the control of rapid eye movements. Like the SC, the PPC encodes the visual world: its neurons represent locations in space in terms of how to reach them by moving the eyes. Unlike the SC, the PPC receives highly processed information, not only from the visual cortex but also from many other areas of the brain. This is a committee with a packed agenda.

From the frontal lobes, for example, comes information about the most recent saccade, a copy of the last command to move the eyes. The language areas in the temporal lobes provide information about verbal commands (e.g. an experimenter's instruction to move the eyes to the left). The first guesses as to what the eyes are looking at arrive from visual temporal lobe areas and start to trigger stored associations about objects and how the person relates to them ('that dark splodge towards the right could be a cat; I love cats'). Meanwhile emotion-processing areas (see Chapter 9) give notice of how the person is feeling at the time ('Being in this visual neuroscience lab is really stressful; I wish I could relax'). These and other inputs will all affect the PPC activity map. Some (such as feelings of stress) will have similar effects on all PPC neurons. Others (such as the experimenter's instruction to move the eyes leftward) will increase activity in neurons coding the plan to move leftwards, and will suppress activity in neurons coding plans to move up, down, or to the right.

Recall that, as discussed in Chapter 8, neurons in the thalamus carry out hypothesis testing, comparing incoming signals from the eyes to signals from the cortex which encode what the brain is expecting to see. The same matching process occurs in the PPC, comparing incoming signals from visual cortex ('there's something on the left') with signals from other brain areas ('go right, why not, wind up the geek in the white coat'), and sending back reports to both on the difference between them so that they can adjust their activity accordingly. Just as in the thalamus, the result is to increase the similarity between activity patterns in the PPC, the visual cortex, and the other brain areas activated by the stimulus.

The initial signal which reaches the SC can have many locations worth looking at. These multiple targets confuse the SC, resulting in no immediate saccade. However, by the time the visual signal reaches the PPC the process of hypothesis testing will have ruled out some of these targets while enhancing the appeal of others ('I'd like to stroke the cat, but not the climbing rose'). Lateral inhibition between PPC member neurons will further sharpen the PPC activity map. Meanwhile the PPC is sending signals to the SC, adding its more refined contribution to the SC's deliberations. Once again inhibition is important. PPC neurons triggered by leftwards stimuli increase the activity of SC neurons coding for leftwards saccades, and decrease the activity of SC neurons which encode movements in other directions. Sometimes this change can be decisive, triggering a saccade.

The SC is like a team of sales personnel in a large company, whose task is to decide which one of a range of new products (i.e. saccades) they should be selling, based on market research. Unless the market research is very much in favour of one product and against all the others, the members may be unable to decide between the products. Their next step is to make recommendations to their immediate superior, the group leader (the PPC). If the group leader says, 'Product G's the one to go for', Product G it is. If not, the group leader will consult with his or her superior. The information will continue up the management hierarchy until a decision is reached.

Third stop: output command

The same is true within individual human brains. If the PPC's contribution is not enough to trigger an eye movement, the signal passes forward to an area of the frontal lobes called the frontal eye fields (FEF). Here once again the processes of matching and lateral inhibition help to sharpen the signal, reducing still further the number of targets. By this stage the reports from the temporal lobe will be more refined ('guess it could be a cat all right'). Among the associations triggered by these reports will be cogwebs encoding object-appropriate beliefs and action-plans. 'Stroking cats is soothing'; 'Reach out and stroke it'; 'Look at it first to make sure it is a cat'; 'Look at it carefully, make sure it wants to be stroked.' These activated cogwebs will begin adding their voices to the evidence considered by the FEF committee (as well as contributing to the ongoing deliberations of the PPC and SC). If the cat-related cogwebs are more active than the other cogwebs (i.e. if the person's past experience has given them the kind of brain which finds cats more interesting than walls, flowers, or trees), then the FEF vote will probably be to move the eyes towards the cat. Once again, lateral inhibition will be playing its part, and the FEF output will affect the SC much as the PPC output did, pushing it towards triggering a catwards saccade.

At every stage in the process of eye movement control, from SC to PPC to FEF, the SC will either trigger a movement or not. Whether it does will depend on the activity of its neurons and the effects of lateral inhibition, as described above. However, lateral inhibition occurs *between*, as well as *within*, the PPC, FEF, and SC. Just as a leftwards saccade-coding neuron in the SC inhibits all other SC neurons, so leftwards neurons in the PPC *inhibit* all PPC, FEF, and SC neurons coding for other directions, and *excite* leftwards FEF and SC neurons. And vice versa. If the patterns of activity in the PPC and FEF are similar (in other words, if the incoming information closely matches what the brain is expecting to see), the signals these areas send to the SC will be unambiguous, and a rapid saccade will result. If the patterns are not sufficiently similar, negotiations between the PPC, FEF, SC, and other areas will take place using lateral inhibition, with each area tweaking its activity to more closely resemble the activity patterns in other areas. The longer this takes, the slower the saccade will be.

Last stop: PFC central

If visual information has flowed through the visual cortex to the PPC and FEF, and no movement is yet forthcoming, then it's time to consult the top management. By the time the PFC is activated, information from the temporal lobe will have activated numerous cogwebs encoding stored knowledge. This knowledge relates to the objects in the current visual scene, but it also includes a great deal more, much of which never reaches consciousness. How to behave in a neuroscience lab; how to react when the experimenter says 'Look left'; why instructions from scientists should be obeyed; why picture-cats can't be stroked; attitudes to cats—all this knowledge, and more, becomes available as the relevant cogwebs are activated. Past experience has set up the connections which link stored knowledge (our personal history inputs) to current input. The PFC acts as a filter, allowing what we know already to influence what we are about to do. Humans with prefrontal damage can often retrieve information about how to behave in a given situation. But they can't apply it. The link between knowledge and behaviour has been severed.[6] As a neurologist who works with such patients has commented:

It is quite disconcerting to hear one of those patients reason intelligently and solve successfully a specific social problem when the problem is presented in the laboratory, as a test, in the form of a hypothetical situation. The problem may be precisely the same kind the patient has just failed to solve in real life and real time. These patients exhibit extensive knowledge about the social situations that they so egregiously mismanaged in reality. They know the premises of the problem, the options of action, the likely consequences of those actions immediately and in the long-term, and how to navigate such knowledge logically. But all of this is to no avail when they need it most in the real world.

Damasio, *Looking for Spinoza*, pp. 143–4

Once again inhibition weeds out some possible eye movement targets and encourages others. Once again the process of matching tests the brain's hypotheses, expectations, attitudes, and memories (history inputs) against the incoming signals from the PPC and FEF. If the history inputs are signalling strongly—for example, if the person looking at the picture has remembered that the experimenter told them to look towards the left—then the PFC signal will facilitate leftwards representations in the PPC, FEF, and SC, suppressing other neurons. If, however, the person is feeling rebellious, or has forgotten, or really likes cats, then the incoming information will dominate, encouraging a rightward saccade

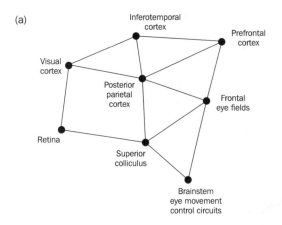

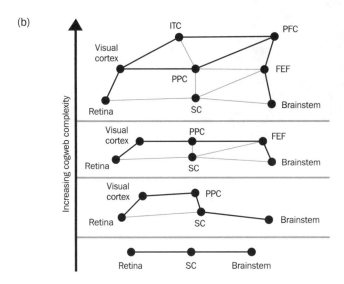

Figure 10.5 (a) A schematic diagram of the major areas involved in the formation of rapid eye movements. Saccades are generated via a series of overlapping input–output pathways. (b) Shows the pathways separated out (the vertical arrow on the left represents the direction of increasing cogweb complexity, and increasing time to process and respond to a visual stimulus with a saccade). The fastest saccades are generated when information about a visual stimulus reaches the SC and triggers an eye movement. This can happen when the stimulus is very simple (as in Fig. 10.4(a)). It can also happen when the person is expecting the stimulus and knows in advance where to look. Slower saccades occur when signals from the retina do not trigger the SC immediately. The visual information then has time to reach cortical areas—the visual and posterior parietal cortex, frontal eye fields, inferotemporal cortex (ITC), and prefrontal cortex. Which of these areas are activated depends on the visual stimulus: its complexity, and whether or not it matches what the brain expected to see.

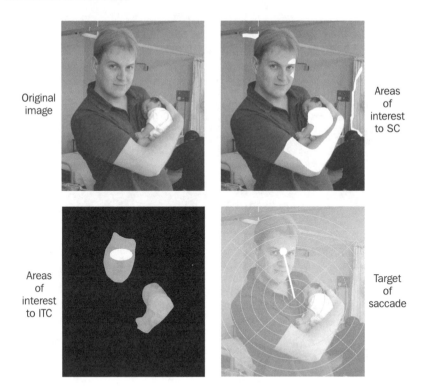

Original image

Areas of interest to SC

Areas of interest to ITC

Target of saccade

Figure 10.6 Illustrating the important role which past experience can play in deciding where to look. The upper left photograph shows a father cradling his new-born child. The image is a complex one, with many potential targets for saccades. The next picture (upper right) shows how the visual image might be represented in the SC, whose neurons respond strongly to bright light. Areas of the SC map where neurons are highly active are shown in white; areas with inactive neurons are shown in black. The brightest areas of the original image are the father's arm and part of his face, the light above his head, the baby's clothing, and (to a lesser extent) the rest of the father's face and the curtain at the right of the picture. Clearly, no saccade could reach all of these targets at once.

The lower left picture shows the areas of the original image which are of interest to—most strongly represented by—neurons in the ITC, an area of the temporal lobe which is involved in storing past experience of visual images. The ITC responds strongly to human faces and is particularly interested in the eye region, an emphasis which reflects the fact that (unless we are autistic) we use other people's eyes as a primary source of social knowledge. Neural activity is likely to be highest, therefore, in areas processing the face, and particularly the eyes, of the father's image (the baby's features are less visible). The ITC signal will therefore vote for a saccade which focuses the eyes on the father's face, allowing more detailed processing of his expression. This vote is likely to tip the balance of SC neural activity in favour of a saccade towards the father's eyes, as shown in the lower right picture (in which the target location is represented by a white filled circle and the upcoming saccade by a thick white line).

(towards the cat). Expectations and memories will vary accordingly: 'I want to look at the cat'; 'Left is so boring'; 'Time to remind this nerd just who's in charge'. Eventually, negotiations (to which, by this time, most of the brain can contribute), will achieve sufficient consensus to generate an eye movement. But few situations in our everyday lives give us this much trouble. Most of the time decisions emerge at the level of the SC, PPC, or FEF.

Stop-and-think: all-over function

The PFC is often described as implementing the brain's ability to stop and think: inhibiting movement to allow time for the consideration of further information. It mediates the active retrieval and application of stored knowledge, meanwhile holding back the urge to act. However, what the PFC does is the tip of an iceberg of similar functions carried out by other brain areas such as the PPC and FEF. Prefrontal areas can call on more information from our personal history; they respond later, and—because of the many areas from which they receive input— their activation by a stimulus tends to be particularly prolonged (see Fig. 10.7).

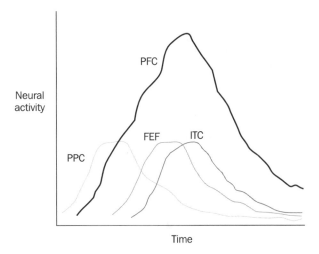

Figure 10.7 An approximate representation of the neural activity (vertical axis) over time (horizontal axis) in four cortical areas (the posterior parietal cortex, frontal eye fields, inferotemporal cortex, and prefrontal cortex) involved in eye movements. The posterior parietal cortex (PPC) is the earliest of the four to be activated by visual information. Activation results in a rapid rise in neural activity followed by a slower return to baseline levels. Similar patterns of neural activity are seen in the frontal eye fields (FEF) and the inferotemporal cortex (ITC), but these are activated later. All three of these areas, however, send signals to the prefrontal cortex (PFC) from the moment of activation. Because they respond at different times, the resulting PFC activity, to which they all contribute, is prolonged.

It is this prolonged activation which forms the basis of short-term memory, allowing the brain to keep conscious track of salient information (e.g. a phone number) until an action (e.g. finding a notepad, or dialling the number) can be carried out.

There is, however, no difference in kind (only in timing and inputs) between what the PFC does and what the FEF or PPC do. Neurons in all three areas activate corresponding SC neurons (via connecting synapses honed by experience), while suppressing the activity of neurons coding for different locations in the visual scene (PPC neurons) or movements to those locations (FEF neurons). The SC prevents an eye movement from simply being triggered by the most active neurons. Instead they must first convince their fellow neurons to shut up (i.e. shut down).

This need for consultation, which stops our eyes twitching maniacally from point to point, is a basic form of stop-and-think, relying primarily on the qualities of the immediate visual input. Sometimes that input is enough to evoke a saccade, if the target is compelling (a bright spot on a black background, for instance). If not, further processing (as neuroscientists call it) or thinking (as other people call it) will take place. The input reaches visual cortex, then flows across the brain from back to front in two great rivers, the faster 'where' pathway, which determines the next eye movement, and the slower 'what' pathway, which mediates object recognition. These pathways terminate in the prefrontal lobe, but they communicate at every synapse en route, sharing their increasingly refined guesses about how the eyes will move ('where') and what they will be looking at ('what'). The PPC may focus the incoming signal enough for its output to the SC to trigger a movement. If not, stop-and-think will continue long enough for us to notice, as the flow of neural activity reaches the FEF and then the PFC.

Effort and adaptation

I have described the process of eye movement control in such detail in order to illustrate that there is nothing particularly magical about the way the PFC works. It does what other brain areas do, only more slowly and with better information, allowing our past experience to play more of a role in determining our current behaviour than would be possible with a less-developed prefrontal lobe. This ongoing impact of past upon present, increasing continuity of perception across time, may be one reason why the human sense of self appears so solid. However, for much of our everyday behaviour intensive PFC activation is not required: we are far more reliant upon automatic routines than we may like to think.[7] Well-developed cogwebs elsewhere in the brain, strengthened by practice, channel the flow of neural activity from input to output. No need to trouble the top brass with mundane technicalities like breathing, walking, or driving when these can be assigned to subcommittees of specialized cogwebs.

Where the PFC is important is in dealing with novelty and challenge. Studies show that it is most active when learning a new task. As automatization takes place, making the task easier, PFC activation decreases. This is because the cogwebs at lower levels (e.g. connecting the PPC to the SC) strengthen at a greater rate than higher-level cogwebs. Recall Chapter 8: simpler cogwebs strengthen more than more complex ones, while more frequently used cogwebs strengthen more than less frequently used ones. Lower-level cogwebs are simpler than those including the PFC (since fewer brain areas are involved), and are activated more often, because many routine tasks will activate the PPC but not the PFC. Over time, therefore, the PFC will be less and less involved in the activity flows generated by increasingly familiar tasks.

As discussed above, when activated the PFC sends signals to other areas of the brain. These signals facilitate activity in corresponding cogwebs (i.e. those linked together by past experience) while suppressing activity in other cogwebs. Returning to the analogy of water flow of Chapter 8, we see that this suppression reduces leakage. Instead of activity dissipating through a myriad connections, it is focused in a smaller number of cogwebs, allowing these to strengthen faster. Thus, as described in Chapter 8, the PFC can act like a thumb on a hose, temporarily boosting the flow through selected cogwebs so that they strengthen more quickly. In this sense, the PFC is self-limiting: its aim is to reduce its own activity. This is also true of other brain areas. Human brains, in other words, behave as if they had been designed to minimize the amount of work they do.

Prefrontal activity is tiring; it uses up a lot of brain resources. Influence technicians instinctively understand this, which is why a favourite sales technique is to use novelty to engage the PFC before bombarding it with so much stimulation that the weary target agrees to buy just to relieve the pressure. The same principle was used effectively by interrogators in Communist China, as we saw in Chapter 1. Robert Lifton describes the not untypical experience of a participant in his study, Charles Vincent, whose stay in a Chinese 're-education center' began with chains and a week without sleep. Interrogations, lasting for hours, were mostly held at night; during the day Vincent was 'struggled' by eight other prisoners, a process involving continuous verbal abuse and physical humiliation. Eventually, 'overwhelmed by fatigue, confusion, and helplessness, he ceased all resistance'[8] and made the first of many false confessions.

Consciousness

As well as being active during mental effort, PFC activation is believed by many neuroscientists to play a vital role in conscious thought. This of course raises the question of how consciousness is defined, a problem which has puzzled thinkers for millennia. Rather than plunge into the morass which is consciousness theory (the details of which, while fascinating, are not essential for my purposes), I will adopt a simplistic position which is probably not too far off that held by many brain researchers.[9] This position divides consciousness into two types, which I will call awareness and monitoring.

Awareness is a consequence of brain activity, is continuous, and is characteristic of many other species than ourselves.[10] It does not involve a specific sense of self, but rather the absence of self, and has thus been prized by religious traditions, such as Buddhism, which regard overt self-consciousness as problematic. It has also been highly valued by influence technicians: recall the agentic state described by Stanley Milgram (see Chapter 4), which allows a person to become absorbed in details at the expense of reflecting on the wider implications of their actions. Certain stimuli, especially if they are familiar or highly repetitive, seem to be particularly good at triggering a state of awareness. T.S. Eliot's description of 'music heard so deeply / That it is not heard at all, but you are the music / While the music lasts' captures the essence of this state.[11]

Monitoring is a more specialized process associated with prefrontal lobe activity. It is intermittent rather than continuous, dipping into and sampling the most active parts of the stream of awareness when triggered to do so by a novel or challenging situation. Stimuli which are so complex that they have time to activate the brain's history inputs will tend to evoke a monitoring response; simpler or highly familiar stimuli will be less likely to do so. It is consciousness in this sense of monitoring which is associated with prefrontal activation, raising the intriguing idea that the function of consciousness may be to minimize its own existence.[12] Monitoring allows us to chop thought up into manageable chunks which can then be manipulated, combined, and recombined, providing the potentially infinite variety characteristic of human symbol systems like language and mathematics.

This ability to sample is especially useful for memory. Awareness, the flow of neural activity through the brain, changes the cogwebs through which it flows without the need for conscious interference, thus leaving a continually changing record of its presence. This is the basis for implicit memory, by which we can learn a new skill, or adjust to the changing weight of a bottle of cranberry squash, without even noticing. However, we also have explicit memory, for learning facts, memorizing words, or recalling specific situations. All of these require the ability to sample. When my flatmate tries to improve her Italian vocabulary, she wants to remember the words, and only the words. She does not need a detailed recollection of the sofa on which she was sitting, the smell of chrysanthemums in a nearby vase, or the sound of a neighbour's lawnmower. She needs to be able to focus attention on one component of awareness, shutting out everything else. If she is sufficiently motivated, then the history inputs which relate to the task of learning Italian will be signalling strongly to her PFC and her attention will be so tightly focused that she may not even hear me asking if she'd like a drink. If not, she may find her consciousness sampling more of the neighbour's gardening than the Italian verbs.

The personal brain

If monitoring is associated with prefrontal lobe activity, then the extent to which monitoring occurs should vary greatly from brain to brain. Some people may be more conscious, more of the time, than others, even if their sleeping patterns are similar. The prefrontal lobe only completes its development in late adolescence, and, like muscles, works better the more it is used. Also like muscles, it can be trained to function more efficiently, increasing concentration and short-term memory. Education and an ongoing active mental life facilitate its development, as does exposure to new experiences and complex environments. Age stacks up layers of stored knowledge, giving the PFC more history inputs to play with. Just as exercise hones muscles, improves health, and protects against disease, so using the prefrontal cortex refines cogwebs, improves mental flexibility, and protects against influence techniques.

There is some evidence of a gender difference in prefrontal capacities, with PFC function developing earlier in females than in males. There is also evidence of individual differences. For example, the neurotransmitter dopamine, which plays a critical role in the PFC, varies significantly depending on which form of a certain gene an individual has.[13] Human beings already use drugs like amphetamines, which boost prefrontal dopamine levels, to improve their mood and help them think. Perhaps as we come to understand genetics and neuroscience better, more selective and effective cognitive enhancers will be developed. Perhaps in the future insurers will demand brain scans to assess prefrontal function before issuing policies, while influence technicians will routinely use neuroscientific research when planning their campaigns (the term neuromarketing has already been coined, although research in this area to date is minimal). In the meantime, however, the study of how the PFC differs from person to person is only just beginning.

Summary and conclusions

How the PFC works is of critical interest to the study of brainwashing. At the beginning of this chapter I said that this most fascinating of cortical regions implements the brain's ideology. It does this by mediating between past and present, allowing the development of complex behaviour which is not simply stimulus-driven, but which also reflects the influence of accumulated knowledge. The influence of past experience helps to generate an impression of continuity over time, contributing to the sense of solidity discussed in Chapter 7. A healthy PFC, well oiled by education and wide experience, allows us to think ahead, to resist temptation (sometimes), and to see past the immediate gratification to the long-term consequences. These are all capabilities inimical to would-be manipulators. Ideally, a brainwashing technique would bypass or usurp the PFC's role, channelling neural activity to cogwebs implementing the desired beliefs while weakening or erasing the victim's former convictions. Could such a technique ever come close to the astonishing machine lying coiled at the forward end of the human head? I will explore this possibility in Chapter 14.

First, however, to a problem so gigantic that it has stimulated thought for over two millennia, and still lurks like a black hole at the conceptual heart of both neuroscience and psychology. In this chapter and its predecessors, I have described the brain in purely causal terms. Input flows in, producing effects (in the PFC and elsewhere) which in turn produce responses. The synaptic mechanisms which underlie neural activity are not yet entirely understood, but there is no sign whatsoever of room for magic. Yet we humans feel that there is something magical about us. We call it freedom, and some of us value it so highly that we die for it. At the heart of freedom is the sense of self-control, discussed in Chapter 1, which we call free will: our belief that we are in some way, however imperfectly, the masters of our fate. This sense of mastery is at the heart of brainwashing. Without it, we would find nothing surprising or terrifying about the dream of mind control, since attempts to manipulate us would take their place among a panoply of causes. Yet if everything we do is caused, how can we be free? In the next chapter I will attempt an answer to this question.

Chapter 11: That freedom thing

I wish I knew how it would feel to be free

Nina Simone, *song title*

At the end of Chapter 6 I discussed six ideas central to brainwashing: power, change, causation, responsibility, the self, and free will. Brainwashing involves exerting power over a victim or victims, causing changes in both thought and behaviour. These changes may be so profound that they affect victims' strongest beliefs, the core of the self. Brainwashed people no longer have free will: they must act as the brainwasher commands. Yet successful brainwashing leaves victims unaware of their new-found slavery; they still regard themselves as free, responsible agents. Unless their brainwashing becomes a matter of public knowledge, society will make the same judgement. This is the essence of brainwashing: the idea that our every move and thought could be controlled by someone (or something) else, without us even realizing. The power and freedom to act we assume we have would then be illusory, our sense of control a sweet but ultimately empty mental construct.

The problem of free will

Brainwashing may seem an unlikely terror. We may feel ourselves manipulated by advertising and the media, but we know what's going on when we watch an advert. We can go out and buy books by social psychologists which tell us the tricks to watch out for, and even if we do find ourselves buying products we don't really need, we're still fundamentally free. Aren't we?

One might think that the answer to this question is obviously yes. After all, we pin so much on freedom! Even the verbs in our language seem to imply the power to act—or to refrain from acting. The words 'I can' are among most children's favourites, an attraction which doesn't cease with childhood. We learn early to control our own bodies, and they initiate us into the magic of agency, so that seeing the new toy, we desire it, and lo! our hand is there, a willing servant, reaching out to grab. From then on, power is our default assumption—and life one long series of frustrations. We believe we can until we find out that we can't, and as our knowledge of the world expands, so does the list of restrictions on our freedom. Most of us, most of the time, accept most of these restrictions, with good grace or bad. We develop other values—from security to status, lawfulness to love—and reduce our freedom in order to fulfil these other desires. We can even train ourselves to despise what we have given up. Yet freedom remains one of the world's most potent ethereal ideas, its blood-drenched banner waving above the remains of countless men and women who thought it well worth dying for.

There is also the issue of responsibility. If freedom is an illusion, how can we be judged accountable for our actions? As noted in Chapter 6, concepts of freedom and responsibility are essential components of our judicial system: this is why the brainwashing claim used by Patty Hearst and against Charles Manson's followers aroused so much interest and comment at the time. The old lady mugged by a teenager believes her attacker was acting freely and could have chosen not to hurt her. The judge who orders the boy to do community service is inflicting punishment, an action which seems meaningless, even cruel, if the youngster was not acting freely.

Freedom inspires us. We rely on it when assigning responsibility. Yet the idea that freedom is an illusion has an ancient and distinguished pedigree. To understand why people make this claim we need to turn to a discipline which has devoted much attention and effort to exploring it: philosophy.

Freedom and determinism

The Moving Finger writes; and, having writ,
Moves on: nor all thy Piety nor Wit
Shall lure it back to cancel half a Line,
Nor all thy Tears wash out a Word of it.

And that inverted Bowl we call The Sky,
Whereunder crawling coopt we live and die,
Lift not thy hands to It for help—for It
Rolls impotently on as Thou or I

The Rubaiyat of Omar Khayyam, trans. Fitzgerald

In religious thought the idea that freedom is an illusion appears in the guise of predestination, which attributes control of human fates to a god or gods. In philosophy it is referred to as 'necessity' or 'determinism'; in popular culture 'Shit happens' or 'So it goes'. Until quantum mechanics appeared to unsettle us all, it was the foundation-stone of science. In the large-scale world with which most scientists (and the vast majority of human beings) are concerned, it still is, underpinning the assumption that the world is consistent and therefore comprehensible.

Determinism holds that the universe operates according to rules, rules which in principle can be understood by human beings and used to predict the future. If every rule were known, the prediction would be one hundred per cent accurate, because everything which happens in the universe is caused to happen by preceding events. As the philosopher Peter van Inwagen puts it, determinism is the thesis that 'there is at any instant exactly one physically possible future'.[1] That future is causally determined by everything which has gone before, and therefore could not be otherwise than it actually turns out to be.

If this is the case, then what happens to our sense that we are free, that we could have done otherwise? Commentators on free will have tended to answer this question in one of three ways. Determinists reply that free will is an illusion, whether we like it or not. Libertarians deny determinism, arguing that some of our actions are not part of the causal net. And compatibilists try to show that both free will and determinism can be true at once.

There are good reasons for believing determinism. They have been well reviewed recently by a number of authors, but I do not have the space to go into detail here.[2] Suffice it to say that the concept of causal determinism is a hard one to throw away. We rely on the universe behaving itself. Even in the domain of thought and action, we predict, explain, and guess using the assumption that causes are necessarily followed by their effects. After all, we do not want our actions to have *no* causes. If my leg starts moving and I don't know why, I don't rejoice in the thought that I'm free of the nets of necessity, having finally proven determinism false. I wait for it to happen again, to make sure I wasn't imagining it. Then I look very hard for a cause, and if I can't find one I go and see my doctor, not a philosopher.

Freedom does not reside in uncaused action—this is why quantum theory is not the saviour of free will that some libertarians would like it to be—but in actions caused by me.[3] When my leg moves, I like to think that it does so for a reason, namely that I wanted it to move. I had the desire, I had the power, and lo! *fiat motus*. Being free is being able to fulfil one's desires, to back up 'I can' with 'I do'. An action of mine is free if I could have chosen not to do it. 'Ah,' says that annoying determinist, 'but your choices, your desires, were themselves entirely determined by a set of causes which, should you trace it back far enough, would take you back to the beginning of the universe. You were always going to make the choice to act.' In which case, where can we find free will? Why, if it is an illusion, do we find it so potently believable? And what happens to moral responsibility, and everything which goes with it?

To answer these questions, and hence understand how brainwashing impacts on freedom, we first need to look at the idea of freedom itself.

A brief history of freedom

While freedom has been a concern of human beings throughout their history, it has been conceptualized in very different ways. The Stoic writers of the ancient world, for example, argued that a citizen was free if he (women were not generally considered full citizens) was good and reasonable, even if he lived in slavery. This was because freedom consisted of being able to will what is good and reasonable, that is not being enslaved by bad, unreasonable desires.

Some classical writers, however, saw this as a convenient way of justifying a status quo which they saw as deeply unjust. Freedom, they insisted, required at the very least the absence of coercion. Others went further, arguing that freedom was not just absence of coercion but absence of dependency. If a man was dependent on the goodwill of, say, a patron, even if in practice he was able to do what he liked, then he was not truly free. He had no control over the patron, who might change his mind at any moment. True freedom lay in self-sufficiency. It did not entail lawlessness, rather living according to laws which one had oneself helped to shape. This required a form of democracy much more intense and immediate than anything we have today, with every free citizen contributing directly to new legislation.

As the historian of political thought Quentin Skinner has compellingly argued, this 'neo-roman' theory of liberty was taken up again in the Renaissance, notably by the hugely influential Italian thinker Niccolo Machiavelli.[4] It became particularly popular in England, where it was used by writers like John Milton to criticize the behaviour of Charles I.[5] However, neo-roman ideas fell out of favour with the Restoration and the gradual ascendancy in political thought of their great opponent, Thomas Hobbes, who argued that freedom lay merely in the absence of coercion, not dependency.[6] Moreover, changing economic circumstances made self-sufficiency increasingly impractical as society became more complex and interdependent. Although neo-roman ideas have formed a continuing strand in political thought—the work of eighteenth-century political philosopher Jean-Jacques Rousseau is an example—their influence has waned in recent times.

As the definition of freedom has shrunk, from the neo-roman absence of *possible* compulsion (e.g. by a fickle patron) to the Hobbesian absence of *actual* compulsion, so its range has expanded. In the classical world, laws and the reach of government applied in principle to every aspect of behaviour. Today, some theocracies and dictatorships still fit this pattern. However, many governments have accepted the notion of the 'private sphere', an area of thought and behaviour over which government has no jurisdiction, as long as the rights of others are not infringed. This notion leads to the modern opposition of classical liberalism and authoritarianism (which in extreme form becomes totalitarianism). Liberalism tends towards expanding the private sphere, keeping government out wherever possible unless a citizen's behaviour threatens other citizens. Authoritarianism argues that human institutions represent the wisest, most considered aspects of individual self-control (government as society's prefrontal cortex).[7] They may therefore know what is good for us better than we do. This view tends to shrink the private sphere (in totalitarian regimes, to zero).

The liberal–authoritarian dichotomy is probably better conceived of as a spectrum of individual–group relations, ranging from political systems (or thinkers) which glorify individual liberty (like John Milton's) to those which emphasize the authority of social institutions (like Thomas Hobbes's). Where on the spectrum a society settles depends on the prevalent view of human nature. Totalitarian regimes uphold the primacy of doctrine over person (see Table 1, p. 17); they see individuals as relatively unimportant compared to the stability of 'society', an ethereal idea whose preservation becomes an overriding goal. Self-control becomes externalized in the political institutions, because individuals cannot be trusted to act for the overall good. The personal self shrinks to a meagre entity whose privacy is non-existent, as the cult of confession demands. Ideally, every cogweb in every citizen's head has been set up by agents of the State—using milieu control, mystical manipulation, loading the language, and other totalist methods—and every stimulus which activates those cogwebs is likewise under State control. Keeping citizens busy helps keep them stimulus-driven, minimizing the chance that they will form additional—potentially subversive—cogwebs; unsupervised leisure (for others) is not generally a favourite of dictators. The need for centralized State control, however, makes many totalitarian regimes bureaucratic and inflexible, stifling economic growth and reducing citizens' quality of life.

Liberal regimes expect more from their citizens. Their governing ethereal idea is individual freedom. The self is bulked out, with imagination, creativity, and privacy all highly valued. Restraint is internalized to the individual, whose cogwebs are his or her own, as long as other people are not threatened. In return for this freedom, citizens are expected to be able to control their own behaviour.

Which view is correct? Are we independent beings or manipulable machines, solid or shadow selves? For compatibilists, for whom free will can and does coexist with a causal world, a liberal position is still available. But for determinists, for whom free will is an illusion, it doesn't make sense to elevate the ethereal idea of freedom to prime position, glorifying something they don't believe we have. We would therefore expect determinism to be associated with a more authoritarian political position. This seems to be the case. As science gained ground in the nineteenth and early twentieth centuries, the impact of deterministic thinking on politics increased. Karl Marx's deterministic theory of historical forces led to the totalitarian nightmares of Communism, while biological determinism, which insisted that race was a fixed determinant of character, gave anti-Semites the additional venom which contributed to the Holocaust.[8]

Just because determinism can facilitate crimes against humanity, however, does not mean that it always will—or that it should be discarded as a philosophical position. If free will is an illusion we may simply have to reorganize our politics to avoid terrible excesses, if that is possible. However, that conclusion is something of a last resort, as it depends on compatibilism being false. The next step, therefore, is to look at whether free will can really survive in a causal universe.

Free will and determinism: the hope of togetherness

A well-known recent defence of a compatibilist position on free will is Daniel Dennett's *Freedom Evolves*. As the title suggests, Dennett argues that freedom is not an all-or-none absolute but a graded capacity of organic life on planet Earth, a capacity which evolved from humble beginnings just as humans did. He acknowledges its importance to our lives, but says that it does not have to be a moral absolute in order to be held in high esteem. Indeed, it is this black-and-white, totalist view, pitting abstraction against abstraction, which is, Dennett argues, the source of the problem. If instead we view freedom as a product of evolution, the old, sterile debate between free will and determinism breaks down into a set of smaller, more answerable questions:

How, then, can our inventions, our decisions, our sins and triumphs, be any different from the beautiful but amoral webs of the spiders? How can an apple pie, lovingly created as a gift of reconciliation, be any different, morally, from an apple, 'cleverly' designed by evolution to attract a frugivore to the bargain of spreading its seeds in return for some fructose? If these are treated as rhetorical questions only, implying that only a miracle could distinguish our creations from the blind, purposeless creations of material mechanisms, we will continue to spiral around the traditional problems of free will and determinism, in a vortex of uncomprehending mystery. Human acts—acts of love and genius, as well as crimes and sins—are just too far away from the happenings in atoms, swerving randomly or not, for us to be able to see at a glance how to put them into a single coherent framework. Philosophers for thousands of years have tried to bridge the gap with a bold stroke or two, either putting science in its place or putting human pride in its place—or declaring (correctly, but unconvincingly) that the incompatibility is only apparent without going into

the details. By trying to answer the questions, by sketching out the
non-miraculous paths that can take us all the way from senseless atoms to
freely chosen actions, we open up handholds for the imagination.

Dennett, *Freedom Evolves*, pp. 305–6

According to Dennett, freedom lies in the ability to predict the future. This capacity allows an organism to see what is coming and, if harm is threatened, avoid it. Avoidance is possible because organisms such as humans have evolved the capacity 'to change their natures in response to interactions with the rest of the world'. This changeability is at the heart of freedom.

Predictions must be made on the basis of knowledge. Being able to store and retrieve the contents of our capacious memories gives us a wealth of information on which to base our judgements about what will happen. Memory also stretches the time zone over which causes can affect us far into the past. A glass breaks because I drop it, but the causes of human behaviour can be events occurring many years earlier (childhood traumas, for example). With all that past, the influences on our behaviour are hugely enriched. We are no longer simply beads sliding down a string of causes, stimulus-driven, every action determined by an immediately preceding event. We are caused to yelp when someone treads on our foot, certainly; but no single cause makes us have a drink, lie to a friend, or fall in love.

Being able to garner knowledge means that we can change ourselves in response to intricate, long-term predictions of the future. Precisely because the world is deterministic—orderly, predictable—we are able to observe its regularities and use them to predict what is likely to happen. This power to predict evolved; organisms which happened to develop it were more likely to survive and reproduce than organisms which did not. Organisms able to predict the future are no longer entirely stimulus-driven, because as their internal models of the future (predictions) become more developed, the cogwebs of which those models consist become more likely to influence behaviour (via their connections with areas such as the posterior parietal cortex and prefrontal cortex, as described in Chapter 10). In other words, the predictions themselves become causes affecting behaviour. Such an organism no longer lives in a state of constant surprise, but operates at least in part on the basis of its expectations. Thus the power to stop and think, the heart of our resistance to brainwashing techniques, is born.

The psychologist George Ainslie, in his fascinating book *Breakdown of Will*, refers to this interaction between present and future as 'intertemporal bargaining'. It takes place within a self which is not unitary, but which resembles an 'internal marketplace' of often competing interests.[9] Recall my discussion of active and dormant selves in Chapter 8. The active self at any given time is the set of all cogwebs whose member neurons are activated at that time. However, at any moment other—even contradictory—cogwebs may become active. An example of switching between contradictory cogwebs is provided by the Necker cube, a visual illusion in which two mutually incompatible cogwebs are activated in quick succession (see Fig. 11.1(a)). One can see the cube angled up and to the right (Fig. 11.1(b)) or down and to the left (see Fig. 11.1(c)), but not both at once.

Active and dormant cogwebs implement Ainslie's 'interests'. Sometimes these interests co-operate in the pursuit of shared goals (like survival). Sometimes they compete: one will be active at one point ('I'm giving up chocolate because it's bad for me'), only to be supplanted by another ('she's offering me a sweet, it would be rude to say no'). Since interests relate to anticipated rewards (e.g. long-term health or short-term gratification), they can be thought of as agents whose goal is to ensure that behaviour brings about the desired reward. The long-term interest in health wants abstinence from chocolate; the short-term interest wants chocolate—now. During the period when the long-term interest is active, it must, to gain its desired reward (long-term health), be able to affect behaviour in such a way as to minimize the chance of a defection (from the long-term interest to the short-term) whenever chocolate sails into view. As Ainslie puts it: 'Ulysses planning for the Sirens must treat Ulysses hearing them as a separate person, to be influenced if possible and forestalled if not.' In effect, the currently active self (which incorporates the long-term interest) makes a contract with future selves that they will not defect. Without the power to predict the future, intertemporal bargaining would be impossible, because long-term interests would never even enter the competition (you can't care about long-term health if you've no conception of the long term). The power to stop and think allows our long-term interests not only to enter, but to win.

Of course, they do not always win. Failures of will occur when this process of negotiation between present and future selves fails to prevent short-term interests from grabbing the reins of behaviour. However, temptations can sometimes be resisted. Much of the time we are stimulus-driven, responding to our

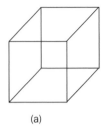 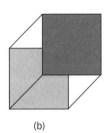 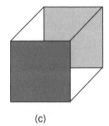

(a)   (b)   (c)

Figure 11.1 (a) The ambiguous Necker cube. (b, c) The two possible views of this illusion, which cannot be seen simultaneously.

environment without noticing what we are doing. Sometimes, however, what I referred to in the last chapter as our history inputs become activated, dominating proceedings and determining how we will act. It is these cogwebs, set up not by the current situation but in our (sometimes very distant) past, which implement Ainslie's intertemporal contracts. If a currently active self, using the focusing power of prefrontal cortex, can strengthen the cogweb which encodes the diet interest sufficiently, then that cogweb will become activated very easily, and strongly, in future. When a chocolate appears on the scene, the active, strengthened diet cogweb is a reminder of the contract set up by a predecessor self. If the strengthening has been effective, even a particularly delicious chocolate will not be able to activate competing cogwebs strongly enough to override the hunger for health.

A person at a given time, therefore, can—*if* he or she has the power of prediction—foresee how future selves are likely to behave. If sufficiently motivated, they can implement intertemporal contracts which aim to bind those future selves to certain actions. It is in this power to change our future selves that Dennett and Ainslie think we should look for freedom. Of course, there is no guarantee that the contracts will hold (the chocolate might prove just too irresistible). With freedom comes uncertainty: our predictions are not one hundred per cent accurate.

Is this type of freedom compatible with determinism? Yes. A current self is caused to set up an intertemporal contract, just as future selves are caused to take that contract into account when determining their behaviour. Relevant causes include cogwebs activated directly by stimuli in the environment (representing, for example, the size, shape, and smell of a chocolate), history input cogwebs activated indirectly by a stimulus (e.g. representations of past chocolates, knowledge of chocolate's unhealthy consequences), and cogwebs representing how the body feels (e.g. hungry, satiated).

All these neural pathways and more contribute, as discussed in the last chapter, to the eventual behaviour. The obvious cause—your friend waving that chocolate under your nose—causes a huge number of events inside your brain, which in turn cause your behaviour. However, the gargantuan number of such events gives us a vast range of possibilities, all neatly tucked under the cranial bone in a manner reminiscent of the space inside Doctor Who's *Tardis*. Mechanisms such as matching and conflict resolution provide the means by which this noisy sea of probabilities collapses, like Schrödinger's wave function, into a single determined outcome.

That outcome is *often* predictable (your friend may know perfectly well that you can't resist chocolate). However, because of the complexity of the neural contributions involved, it is *not always* predictable. (This is why behaviourism—the doctrine that if you want to understand minds then input and output, stimuli and responses, are all you know and all you need to know—was a useful theoretical model for simple stimuli but hopelessly inadequate in more complicated situations.) Sometimes the stimulus will cause the predicted behaviour (you take the chocolate). Sometimes it won't (after yesterday's depressing encounter with your bathroom scales, you've promised yourself you'll never touch another sweet). On some occasions, neither you nor anyone else may know why you did—or didn't—take the sweet. That does not mean your behaviour was not caused. It just means that the causes were complicated and not all available to consciousness. As I noted earlier, we don't want our free actions to be uncaused, we want them to be caused by reasons internal to us. If you say: 'I took the chocolate because I wanted to', or even 'because I couldn't resist it', you acknowledge that your desire for the chocolate caused you to take it. Does that mean that you didn't act freely? If so, then you are only acting freely when you have *no* reasons for acting, no desires or inclinations one way or the other. If you say instead that 'I wanted the chocolate' is entirely compatible with 'I took the chocolate freely', then actions can be caused by your desires, and yet be free. Your desires, likewise, arise from complex combinations of events in your brain, caused in their turn by a huge variety of factors, from the smell reaching your nose to your history of encounters with chocolates of various kinds. Would you have it otherwise—and find yourself acting at random, a baffled puppet? Redescribing desires, beliefs, or other reasons as brain events doesn't make them any less yours, or the actions that proceed from them any less free.

But don't those reasons have to be conscious? Not at all, unless you identify self with conscious self and believe that you cease to exist when you go to sleep at night. A cogweb which never reaches consciousness can still control behaviour, and sometimes (for example in the delusions of control seen in schizophrenia) conscious cogwebs can be interpreted as not-yours, so consciousness is no guarantee of authorship. In healthy brains, however, the default assumption is that an action is yours until proven otherwise. Just because I wasn't conscious of taking a spoon from the cutlery drawer at breakfast doesn't mean someone else put it in my hand. It simply means my conscious mind had better things to think about.

How does this idea of freedom mesh with the everyday conception of free action: 'All things being equal, I could have done otherwise'? Strict determinism denies this, since it claims that 'there is at any instant exactly one physically possible future'.[10] If a friend offers you a chocolate, and you take it, then if that exact same situation were to arise again, your response would be the same: so you could not have done otherwise.

The condition 'All things being equal, I could have done otherwise' renders the concept of freedom unusable in the real world, for the simple reason that no two situations are ever exactly the same. Even if the external events could be made to repeat themselves, you have changed in the meantime. You have a memory of the first occasion, and your ability to make predictions has allowed you to learn from your experience. Foreseeing your weakness for chocolate, you may have strengthened certain cogwebs—those implementing the intertemporal contract which is your resolution to eat more healthily. If you should find yourself in a chocolate version of *Groundhog Day*, facing the same sweet temptation over and over again, you will learn from experience, as Bill Murray did in the film. 'I could have done otherwise' really means 'I could have done otherwise if I'd wanted to', but this violates the requirement of 'All things being equal' (you didn't want to do otherwise then; you do now). So perhaps it would be better to replace 'I could have done otherwise' with 'Next time, I could do otherwise' (because I have changed in the meantime, and the change may have consequences even I cannot predict). The first statement gives us nothing useful; the second gives us freedom.

Freedom, in other words, resides in predictability and changeability. You take the chocolate freely if you could (in the past) have altered the cogwebs in your skull so that (now) you politely refuse. If you could have made (but didn't make) changes which would stop your current self taking the chocolate now, then the action of taking it was changeable. Similarly, you may or may not be able to make changes now which will prevent you from taking a chocolate the next time it's offered. The desire to make those changes is itself caused—by the myriad interwoven cogwebs in your head. Some of these may be active but irrelevant (the ones which help you keep your car on the road while thinking about something else). Others, however, remind you of what you saw in the mirror this morning, the numbers which leapt shrieking from your bathroom scales, your desire to impress a potential partner, and so on. These are all reasons—your reasons—for giving up chocolate. Whether they determine your actions only time, your brain, and the world beyond will tell. If the person offering the chocolate suddenly pulls a gun and tells you to eat it or die, even the strongest intertemporal contract may be overridden by other considerations (unless of course you are prepared to be a martyr to your principles).

The ability of a current self to influence future ones also explains the fact about self-control noted by the psychologist Roy Baumeister (and quoted in Chapter 10): that we 'choose to lose', putting ourselves in situations where we could expect to find ourselves being stimulus-driven and then saying, when those situations duly materialize, 'I just couldn't help it!'. Just as we can set up an intertemporal contract which we hope will influence our future selves, so we can arrange our circumstances so that an intertemporal contract is more likely to be broken (e.g. choosing a route to work which we know leads past our favourite chocolate shop). Intertemporal contracts may be set up by long-term interests or short-term ones, beneficial to the organism, or—as in the case of addictions, actively harmful. Our ability to form them, which largely depends on how well our prefrontal cortex works, will itself change with, among other things, age, experience, and the amount of recreational chemicals we ingest.

Causes come in many different flavours. Some are clearly external, and equally clearly restrictions on our freedom to act as we choose: torture, bullying, repressive laws. Some are internal, but we nevertheless regard them as outside ourselves, like brain disease or the effects of drugs. However, causes which are ours are the reasons why we choose to act as we do. They do not restrict our freedom; without them freedom would be meaningless. This is why brainwashing is so frightening: it fools us into thinking the new beliefs are actually ours. Of course, what we define as ours can vary. 'If you make yourself really small you can externalize virtually everything'[11] so that even your desires become external, no longer yours, instead restrictions on your freedom. Addictions and some illnesses, like anorexia, are often regarded in this way: the self shrinks, abdicating freedom and thereby evading responsibility. The risk of overdoing this shrinking process is that the self is reduced to a Cartesian spot, an irrelevance, blown about on the winds of fate and contributing little or nothing. But it doesn't have to be this way: there is nothing in the doctrine of determinism that forces us to be Cartesian dualists.

Freedom and responsibility

What are the consequences for moral responsibility of this account of freedom? Nothing catastrophic. Adult members of society make the default assumption that other adults have certain intertemporal contracts (principles) which influence their actions. Which principles are assumed to hold will vary from person to person, but certain principles will be a matter of common consensus. As drivers, for example, we assume that the driver behind us will have taken care to ensure that he is not drunk; that is, that he has a principle of self-preservation which prevents him drinking heavily when he knows he will have to drive. These consensus assumptions—some of which have been legally formalized—make social interactions possible and underpin much of our everyday life. We expect every adult to be aware of these principles and have the appropriate intertemporal contracts installed, whether by formal education, upbringing, or other experience. We predict, on the basis of this expectation, that adults will behave in accordance with consensus principles, and in the vast majority of cases our predictions are correct.

When they are not correct, the reason why is often obvious. Brain disease or external compulsion, for instance, can cause an intertemporal contract to fail, a failure which the person involved could have done nothing to avoid. That person is not thought to have acted freely, so is not held responsible for their actions.

When the reason is not obvious, we assume that internal reasons determined the action. That means that the person could have predicted the consequences of their action, consequences which would have caused 'any reasonable person' (in the law's famous phrase) to change their behaviour so as not to commit the action. If they could have changed, and didn't, we hold them responsible unless they come up with a convincing explanation of why they could not have made the relevant change.

Responsibility involves a social judgement, and like other social judgements it is susceptible to bias. Social psychology has shown that our tendency to attribute responsibility (in a case where no obvious reason for action is apparent) depends on the person and the action involved. Someone we like will be judged more responsible if the action is praiseworthy, and less responsible if the action deserves blame. For someone we don't like, the reverse is the case.[12] The law, of course, is supposed to be neutral about those who come before it as defendants. However, since one of the factors which determines how much we like someone is their similarity to us, one wonders whether this neutrality can always be achieved (for example when the judge is elderly, white, conservative, and male, and the defendant is a young, liberal, black woman). Attempts to make the judiciary more representative of the people facing judgement are therefore a welcome advance.

The feeling of freedom

Digesting Dennett's or Ainslie's expositions may leave a reader with a vague sense of unease. The arguments are attractive, the prose persuasive, and yet, and yet ... All this talk of prediction, of intertemporal bargaining and contracts between selves at different times, it's all rather dry and, well, *cognitive*. 'I don't *think* I'm free, I *feel* free—or not.' If the reader's intuition is correct, then humans have a sense of freedom which is, in effect, an emotion. As we saw in Chapter 9, emotions can have a cognitive component, but they also have an affective part: the feeling which provides the motivational drive. What might give rise to such a feeling in human brains? Does it make sense to view our feeling of freedom in this way, and if so, what purpose does having such a feeling serve?

Here I must venture beyond my sources into a more speculative realm. I believe that our sense of freedom can indeed be usefully viewed as an emotion. I believe that neuroscientists in the not-too-distant future will be able to identify the physiological conditions which accompany the sense of freedom, as they have already begun to do for the emotion of fear. I predict that those conditions will involve a state of relaxation that is inherently rewarding, overlaps heavily with other positive emotions such as happiness, and may be mediated by the same brain mechanisms. (Perhaps the activity of these mechanisms is interpreted as 'feeling happy' on one occasion and as 'feeling free' on another, depending on what else is going on at the time.) This implies, among other things, that freedom can be addictive, and begins to explain why people accustomed to freedom often fight so hard to keep it, while people who have never known freedom may not fight at all.

Freedom is rewarding because it implies control. We become extremely stressed when our sense of control is threatened; freedom, therefore, involves the absence of stress. Here it is necessary to distinguish between subjective and objective freedom. As noted previously, from early on in life our default assumption is that we are free—that we can control. Because our universe is at that time so small we can objectively do very little; but we have not yet begun to do much, and therefore have not yet learned about all the things we can't do. Our subjective sense of freedom is therefore high. One of civilization's greater achievements is the trick of teaching us to adopt other values, like social status, thus devaluing our sense of freedom so that we more readily accept its loss. Of course, not everyone gives up the urge to control so easily.

Like other rewards, freedom tends to promote its own increase, because the brain acclimatizes to a certain level of freedom just as it does to a certain level of crack cocaine. However, the urge to accumulate freedom is not as strong as the urge to defend against its loss, an urge known as reactance (see Chapter 5).[13] People react very negatively to loss of freedom, just as they do if their drugs are taken away. In both cases, their reaction often includes seeking alternative sources of satisfaction. An employee suddenly told he can no longer smoke at work may bolster his sense of freedom by sending personal e-mails during office hours. Ostensibly, smoking and sending e-mails have nothing to do with each other. In fact, the employee's defiance makes him feel free—he has thwarted his employer's interests as his have been thwarted—thereby assuaging the reactance provoked by the employer's diktat.

What, then, is the sense of freedom for? Would organisms with it have an advantage over those without it, and if so what is the nature of that advantage? Speculating again, I think the answer is that the sense of freedom serves as a safety signal. It tells us everything's under control, or if not everything, at least enough for us to feel able to relax for the moment. Since if we can control our environment we can change it, the sense of freedom signals changeability. If we feel that we acted freely, that sense of freedom tells our brains that it is possible for them to change so as to prevent, or encourage, future similar actions (which type of change occurs will depend on whether the action produced a reward or a punishment). Rather than having to undergo the effort of consciously computing some measure of changeability, our brains record the outcome of every occasion when we tried to carry out a certain action. The greater the number of successful outcomes, the more likely we are to think that this type of action is one we can carry out freely.

The sense of freedom is balanced by a sense of reactance. This is a threat signal: something is out of our control. It arises whenever our predictions don't work out, for example when the employee's expectation of being able to smoke comes up against a new bureaucratic reality. When we act, our brains generate a prediction that we are about to act. That prediction forms a hypothesis which is then tested against incoming information. If the prediction doesn't match, an error signal results, calling up the resources of additional brain areas to find out what has gone wrong.

This error signal is the sense of reactance.[14] It is aversive, just as the sense of freedom is rewarding. If everything goes well (if there is no error signal), we are not troubled by reactance and regard ourselves as free. This is why I can believe that I acted freely when I took my spoon from the cutlery drawer at breakfast, even though at the time I was conscious only of my plans for the day. If, as has happened once or twice, my hand emerged from the cutlery drawer clutching a fork, my brain would signal a prediction failure: the expected visual input does not match what I'm actually looking at. At that point, my (rather sleepy) prefrontal cortex would intervene, calling up those of my history inputs which store information about why forks are not appropriate for cornflakes and setting in place an action plan that sends my hand back to the drawer. At the same time my brain would be developing a reassuring explanation of why I got a fork first time round, dissipating the sense of unease (the reactance) aroused by my discovery that the world (at least, the world of forks and spoons in my cutlery drawer) was not as I predicted it should be.

That the sense of freedom, and its complement, reactance, are good candidates for being acted on by evolution is clear. An organism which persistently thought itself in control when it wasn't, and vice versa, would be less likely to survive than an organism with an accurate awareness of what it could and couldn't change in the world around it. Better to have a quickly accessible, accurate changeability signal formed on the basis of experience—or, more precisely, a reactance signal warning of possible unchangeability (unexpected lack of control).

Quick accessibility saves our brains from wasting time and effort in the conscious recollection of individual experiences. If the sense of freedom can be viewed as an emotion, it will speed up decision making just as other emotions do. If, for example, you were to find yourself in the path of an oncoming car, your sense of fear would save you having to recall the actions you took the last time this happened, movies in which you saw other people reacting to oncoming cars, and so on. Similarly, your sense of freedom tells you that the last time you got a sales call you were able to put the phone down at once, while your sense of reactance tells you that the last time your boss rang up you were left feeling stressed and overworked. You don't need explicit recall of either experience to feel your mood drop when you next take a call from your boss.

An accurate signal has two benefits. It reduces time spent trying to alter the unalterable (this would happen if the reactance signal were too low, so that the organism mistakenly thought it was in control). Accuracy also allows the organism to take chances which would otherwise be missed (if the reactance signal were too high, in which case a situation which was in fact controllable would be judged unchangeable). An accurate sense of freedom, in other words, helps its possessor to maximize opportunity while minimizing wasted effort.

If our sense of freedom is indeed an emotion grounded in the brain, several conclusions follow. The sense of freedom (and its converse, reactance) will differ from person to person, just as some individuals are happier, or more prone to angry outbursts, than others. Perhaps this is why Stanley Milgram found that, while the majority of his experimental volunteers obeyed the instruction to deliver what they thought were severe electric shocks, there were always some who refused.

An obvious point is that the sense of freedom will become associated, on the basis of experience, with some situations but not others. The same individual may feel free at home and trapped at work, or vice versa. Freedom, like other emotions, is also a graded experience rather than an all-or-none sensation. Our conception of how free we are overall derives from totalling up all our experiences of freedom (or reactance), just as our conception of how happy we are overall depends on the number and nature of happy and sad experiences we have had. Thinking of freedom as an emotion also recalls the findings of Singer and Schachter, discussed in Chapter 9, in which the same affective sensation (due to an injection of adrenaline) was given different cognitive interpretations depending on the social situation. Similarly, we may interpret the same emotion as, for example, relief (if we have just left a medical check-up with a clean bill of health), or a sense of freedom (if we have just left prison).

Our ability to change ourselves also allows us to learn to value some freedoms more than others, like the employee banned from smoking who decides he was about to give up anyway. The more used we are to being in control of a situation, or the more we value a freedom, the bigger the sense of reactance when that control or freedom is threatened, and the more vigorous our response is likely to be. Social factors are hugely influential in setting the levels of freedom an individual experiences, and there is some evidence that these factors are particularly important in early childhood, while brains are still undergoing rapid change. Social experience may serve to set the baseline level and range of many personality variables. Early trauma may result in later fearfulness (a high 'fear baseline'), for example. Similarly, early restrictions on behaviour may result in a lower general expectation of freedom, and hence less reactance.

Another consequence of grounding freedom in the brain is that changing the brain may affect our ability to feel free. Abnormal brain function has already been associated with some disorders of free will, such as the delusions of alien (or CIA, or demonic) control experienced by some people with schizophrenia, and the rarer alien hand syndrome. In this bizarre neurological condition, a patient's hand, or sometimes another limb, makes movements which are experienced as purposeful but beyond the patient's control. It may, for example, grab a door-knob and have to be prised loose, tug at clothes, or even try to strangle its owner.[15] Syndromes like alien hand and delusions of control raise the possibility, already implied in this chapter, that deliberately damaging, or otherwise manipulating, a person's brain might affect their sense of freedom. In particular, if identifiable brain regions contribute to the sense of reactance, reducing the activity of these areas may increase suggestibility, since the signals which normally warn of threats to freedom would no longer be available.

Some brain scientists have already begun to investigate issues of freedom and agency using modern neuroimaging technology. One group, for example, used hypnosis to explore what happens in the brain during the experience of alien control, that is, when people feel that a movement they have made is not theirs.[16] The scientists did this by hypnotizing healthy subjects and inducing them to attribute an arm movement they themselves had made to an external source (a pulley to which their arm was attached). Brain scans showed that areas of parietal cortex, cerebellum, and prefrontal cortex were more active when subjects mistakenly thought the movement was due to the pulley, compared with when they thought they had made it. In other words, it seems that relating features of brain function to the experience of alien control in a consistent and reproducible way may be possible. This is a step on the road to understanding how our brains provide us with our feeling of being free agents. But only a step. There are many difficult technical and conceptual issues to resolve, and the road looks set to prove a long one.[17]

Summary and conclusions

God grant me the courage to change the things I can
The serenity to accept the things I cannot
And the wisdom to know the difference

Anon, The Serenity Prayer

If the world and everything in it is causally determined, can we be free? Thinkers like Daniel Dennett and George Ainslie say we can, if we conceptualize freedom in terms of the ability to change our future selves as well as the world around us, an ability which depends on predicting the future. Freedom, however, is more than just cognition (predictions, intertemporal contracts); it is an emotion, arising out of patterns of brain activity. *The Serenity Prayer*, though clichéd, is nonetheless apposite: our sense of freedom is an emotional signal which gives us the wisdom to know what things we can and cannot change. It is this emotional force which gives the ethereal idea of freedom its power to topple dictators, inspire revolutions, and send human beings to their deaths.

We are back to brainwashing, to the dream of mind control, because if freedom is an emotion then it can be manipulated just like other emotions. If, as I have suggested, our sense of freedom is tarnished by the presence of a threat signal (reactance), then artificially reducing that signal could make us feel ourselves free when we were not. Conversely, enhancing reactance can stimulate a person into acting in ways they normally would not in order to defend their freedom against the perceived threat, a trick well known to every demagogue worth the name. Judgements of freedom, like judgements of whether or not we are happy, are not absolute yes/no issues. Rather they will depend on circumstances, on our overall mood, on who is asking us to make the judgement, and so on.

Manipulations (whether to increase or to suppress reactance) may be social, as in the case of a woman buying the headache pills she saw advertised, or the explicit requesting of consent to, say, a further sales call (which not only soothes reactance but also acts as a commitment trap). As previous chapters have shown, there are many ways in which social manipulations can exert influence, from the vivid headlines of a newspaper to the savage coercion of torture. Some of these techniques are extremely powerful. But they developed by trial and error over centuries, rather than from a detailed understanding of how brains work. Many of the techniques used in brainwashing situations, for example, derive from methods used in torture.

In recent years we have begun to move away from dependence on trial and error. New technologies have allowed neuroscientists an unprecedented level of insight into how brains work. Of course, a huge amount remains to be done, but one thing can be guaranteed. Those among us who, for whatever reason, yearn for the powers of mind control will not wait for total understanding before they attempt to use the findings of science to manipulate their fellow human beings. The dangers of brainwashing are not going to go away. As Chapter 14 will show, they may well get worse.

In Part III I will look at what we can do, as individuals and societies, to minimize these dangers.

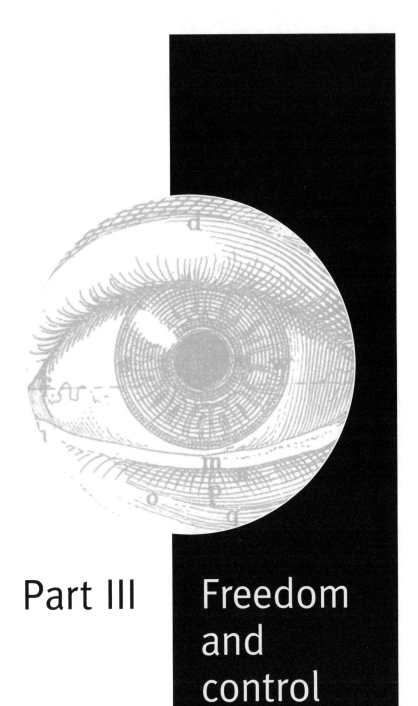

Part III Freedom and control

Chapter 12: Victims and predators

He that would governe others, first should be
The Master of himselfe

Philip Massinger, *The Bond-Man*

Time to recap. So far we have looked at the history and usage of the term 'brainwashing' since Edward Hunter created it in 1950. As brainwashing necessarily involves brains, we have also delved into neuroscience, psychology, and philosophy, replacing the old Cartesian 'diamond mind' with a much more flexible and composite construction. We have learned about how brains and their beliefs can change suddenly, or slowly over time. Sudden change can occur when the energy from strong emotions pours into the cogweb encoding a concept, strengthening it from mere idea to deep conviction. Slow change occurs by imperceptible degrees, like learning a habit. We have also seen that brains keep a record of what they can and cannot change in the world about them, and that this changeability signal provides the basis for our feelings of freedom and its negative counterpart, reactance. Reactance, which warns of an imminent threat to freedom, is the greatest challenge facing influence technicians. Whenever we feel we are being manipulated reactance triggers stop-and-think, the prefrontal basis of our resistance to influence attempts. A sudden change which is strong enough, such as the emotional battering of brainwashing by force, overwhelms this resistance by coercion, while the slow change of brainwashing by stealth uses more deceitful methods to bypass our awareness of being influenced.

Part III will apply our findings so far to answering five important and interrelated questions about brainwashing. The first question concerns victims of brainwashing: what makes some people particularly vulnerable while others seem better able to resist? The second question relates to methods of brainwashing: what can we learn from neuroscience and psychology about which techniques—

and individuals—are likely to be the most effective? These questions will be addressed in this chapter. The third question (the topic of Chapter 13) concerns the possibility of mass mind control. In Chapter 14 I will consider the future of brainwashing and the potential impact of new technology, asking the fourth question: could the current gap between the dream and the reality of mind control ever be bridged? Finally, in Chapter 15, I will look at the fifth question: how can brainwashing be resisted and its dangers minimized?

We're all individuals

One of the themes of this book has been the importance of individual differences. Brains, like the selves they generate, vary widely in shape and size, as well as in the numbers and types of synapses and cogwebs.[1] No two brains are the same, either in their structure or in their patterns of activity. To begin with, this variety comes from having different genes. The effects of genetic variation, however, are hugely magnified by the fact that genes switch on and off at different times and in different areas of the brain. Two cells in an embryo have the same DNA. Yet one may give rise to skin cells, fathering generations of dandruff, while the other's progeny end up as neurons, firing in response to a lover's kiss.

These cells owe their contrasting fates to the way in which their genes are used. A switched-on gene leads to the creation of a protein which may have a number of effects in the brain, including switching other genes on or off. Genes may also be switched on or off by the environment: chemicals, electromagnetic stimuli, or the stimulation of our senses entailed by living in a world full of objects, people, and ideas. Chemicals may enter the brain, for example, as a result of eating or drinking, taking drugs, hormone changes in the body, or infections. These chemicals may have many different effects in the brain and body.[2] Since nerve cells rely on electricity, they and the genes they contain may also be affected by electromagnetic emissions.[3] This is the rationale for using electroconvulsive therapy (ECT), which administers electric shocks to the patient, to treat very severe depression. Finally, our brains receive stimuli which not only activate neurons but change the genes within. Nature and nurture are inextricably entangled.[4] With so much variability, it is hardly surprising that the human brain is not a standard package.

Suckers and cynics

This variability holds for psychological traits as much as for physical structure—including the traits which predispose to, or protect against, susceptibility to influence. Some people can emerge unbroken from torture or unfleeced from a brush with a conman. They have an ability to say no which makes them the envy of friends and the despair of charities and salesmen. If such people had encountered Stanley Milgram, they would have balked at his procedures early on (as indeed a minority of his experimental subjects did). They have an inner strength, a self-belief, which insulates them from these forms of social pressure.

Most of us lack that protection. Although we may think we're immune, reality is constantly proving us wrong. We fall prey to conmen, subscribe to dubious offers, buy things we don't want or need, give money to charities about which we don't really give a damn. If we are honest, our suggestibility should make us agree with the expert on compliance techniques Robert Cialdini, whose introduction to his (highly influential) book *Influence* begins:

> I can admit it freely now. All my life I've been a patsy. For as long as I can recall,
> I've been an easy mark for the pitches of peddlers, fund-raisers, and operators
> of one sort or another. True, only some of these people have had dishonorable
> motives. The others—representatives of certain charitable agencies, for
> instance—have had the best of intentions. No matter. With personally
> disquieting frequency, I have always found myself in possession of unwanted
> magazine subscriptions or tickets to the sanitation workers' ball.
>
> Cialdini, *Influence*, p. ix

Influence attempts are as old as the minds they target, so it is hardly surprising that today's techniques have evolved as excellent matches for the brains they target. Influence and attempts to resist it, in other words, can be seen as opponents in an evolutionary arms race. The latest step in the arms race may be our predilection for buying and reading books by social psychologists like Robert Cialdini, but even that is no guarantee of protection against weapons of influence. We do not always remember that we are independent beings with minds of our own; sometimes we are too tired, too busy, too lazy, or too weak. But often we do—and for many influence attempts it doesn't matter anyway. I don't care which brand of washing-up liquid ends up beside my sink as long as it works; so I reach for the one I've seen most adverts for, provided it isn't noticeably more expensive. A detailed consideration of the relative merits of all available washing-up liquids would be well within my capabilities—and an exquisite waste of time. Who cares, as long as the dishes end up clean?

Changing beliefs

But sometimes it does matter. Sometimes we are manipulated into acting against our own best interests, whether that means plunging into debt to buy something we don't really need or strapping on explosives in pursuit of martyrdom. The aim of brainwashing is to control both thought and deed—ideally, to get inside the target's head. In Chapter 14 we will see how modern neuroscience can make that literally possible. However, the vast majority of influence techniques cannot change brains directly, so instead they change the environment in which those brains are immersed.

This need to operate at a distance puts two obstacles in the influence technicians' path. The first is the amount of time and effort it takes to change belief, especially if the change is to be significant and long-lasting. Whipping up strong emotions can help, but the new beliefs must still be reinforced, again and again, until they become so habitual—so automatized—that the chance of their being challenged is greatly reduced. Until they are safely below the threshold of consciousness, these new cogwebs will not fit comfortably into the rest of the target's cognitive landscape. And until they stop sticking out and attracting attention, there is always the danger that the target may be prompted to doubt them.

This is one reason why cults, for example, often isolate their followers from their previous lives. By minimizing the likelihood that friends, family, or former circumstances will activate old cogwebs inconsistent with the new dispensation, they reduce the power of old ideas to challenge the new ones. Recall that when making decisions, for example about where to move the eyes, brain areas negotiate among themselves so that their activity patterns tend to converge. Most simplistically, if area A is voting to move leftwards and area B is voting to move downwards, their consensus will likely converge on a diagonal saccade moving down-and-to-the-left. More strongly activated cogwebs have more voting power in this process of adjustment; if activity in area B is stronger than that in A the saccade will be more down than to the left. So when a new set of (cult-related) beliefs is imposed on a (sometimes very different) pre-existing pattern, the success of the brainwashing will crucially depend on how much stronger than the old cogwebs the new ones are. Isolation reduces the voting power of older cogwebs and allows the intense emotional and psychological manipulation of the cult environment to operate to maximum effect.

The second problem faced by influence technicians is that, unless they know their target well, they are working in the dark to some extent. Their aim is to get their preferred beliefs accepted by the target, a task which is much easier if those beliefs are not inconsistent with what the target already believes. Better-fitting cogwebs are more acceptable because they provoke less thought and are hence less effortful. The more similar my cogwebs to yours, the more we will have in common and the better we are likely to get along. The better you know me, and the more closely our ideas match up, the more influence you will be able to exert. A frequent comment from converts to a new religious or political movement is that its leader said exactly what they were thinking. This perception of meshing minds can itself be a potent source of shared exhilaration, adding to the emotional glue which binds the movement together and makes it a coherent entity, a group, tribe, or cult rather than just a number of people.

Influence technicians, however, often do not know the state of their target's cogwebs in advance. Some will guess on the basis of their background knowledge (the cold-caller who offered me a cut-price kitchen was unlucky: most of my neighbours do own their homes). Some will try and probe the target with well-directed questions; but this can risk the target's becoming alerted, triggering reactance, or bored, triggering withdrawal. In the myriad individual confrontations which make up the influence arms race both sides have their victories.

In extreme cases, however, brainwashing using force may overwhelm resistance. And the gradualism of brainwashing by stealth may slip past even the most watchful prefrontal guard. Even so, some people are clearly more watchful, or more resistant, than others. What are the features which make some brains more vulnerable and others more able to defend themselves against influence? Our findings from Part II suggest that a brain's resistance to acquiring new beliefs comes from three main interrelated sources: the number of cogwebs already present, the strength of those cogwebs, and the capacity to stop and think. Let us look at each of these in turn.

Changing cogwebs

Number of cogwebs
A rich cognitive landscape, filled with cogwebs and able to process stimuli in varied and flexible ways, makes it harder for a brainwasher to impose new beliefs. Using the water-flow metaphor from Chapter 8, we can see why this might be the case. If water has only a few channels through which to flow, the flow through each channel will be strong and the effects of erosion—which increases channel size—will be considerable. If more channels are available, the flow through each channel will be less and channel size will increase more slowly. Likewise for cogwebs. The more alternative paths there are available for the flow of neural activity from input stimulus to output response, the weaker each individual synapse is likely to be.

This is why age, education, creativity, and life experience, all of which enrich the cognitive landscape, tend to protect against influence techniques. The number of connections between neurons in a human head is not fixed; active cogitation can grow new synapses, which is why 'use it or lose it' applies as much to brains as to muscles. In a younger, less educated, less creative, or less experienced brain, the balance between incoming information and information stored in memory—the history inputs described in Chapter 10—gives greater weight to incoming information, as the individual has less personal history available. He or she is therefore more likely to be stimulus-driven, reacting to the immediate environment rather than stopping to think about it. Older, better-educated, or more experienced brains have more history inputs to compete with the demands for action made by goings-on in the immediate environment. Emotions may also be less painful, and needs less demanding—if only because many have already been met—in an older person. Perhaps this is why travel is thought to broaden the mind: what matters is not the act of travelling, but the variety of new experiences en route. (Going to Ibiza to get drunk and have sex probably doesn't count unless drinking and sex are beyond the pale at home.) A mind enriched by varied experience, in which history inputs have a large role, is a more subtle and differentiated mind, harder to pressure with incoming stimuli and therefore harder for mindcraft to control.

Having more cogwebs available can help a targeted individual to resist even the most extreme forms of mindcraft. Torture victims often react to their coercion by activating a particularly cherished cogweb—religious belief, or the image of a loved one—clinging to it for dear life, and gaining support from it. This is why sophisticated coercion often alternates brutality with kindness. Love is the great antidote to torture, as to so many kinds of harm, and apparent concern can break a victim's resistance more effectively than pain. One American prisoner of war in Korea described how he was repeatedly brought 'to death's door' before being revived. Despite the fact that his captors were responsible for almost killing him, he said that after a while 'you were thankful to them for saving your life [...] when you were about to die, they saved you. They did this often enough for it to consume your whole thinking process, until you were grateful enough to do anything they wanted.'[5] Over time, being saved from death was more effective a weapon of influence than being threatened with it.

Strength of cogwebs
Paradoxically, a brain with fewer cogwebs can also be harder to brainwash than the average. This is the case if its cogwebs are particularly well established: strong convictions of one's own provide at least some protection from belief merchants. Here again individuals vary. Some hold strong beliefs, but their level of what psychologists call 'need for control' is low. They are secure enough in themselves not to feel their own beliefs threatened when they meet others with differing views; they will listen tolerantly, but they are unlikely to change their own beliefs. Some people seem sceptical and unconvinced even by beliefs held widely within their community; they do not commit strongly to any ideology. And some combine the tendency to firm convictions with the need to impose their opinions on others. Such individuals have a strong sense of self—their beliefs are strongly held—but their need for control is also high. As the social psychologist Roy Baumeister has argued (see Chapter 5), their high but vulnerable self-esteem can make these highly dogmatic people prone to react aggressively to any challenges to their point of view. However, a sufficiently powerful method of influence can impose a new belief—which will then be fiercely defended.

Prefrontal abuse: bypassing stop-and-think

… but pity the perplexèd state
Of troublous and distressed mortality,
That thus make way unto the ugly birth
Of their own sorrows, and do still beget
Affliction upon imbecility

Samuel Daniel, *Certain Epistles*, 'To the Lady Margaret,
Countess of Cumberland'

The capacity to stop and think

How efficiently we detect and challenge influence attempts depends, as discussed above, on the richness of our cognitive landscape. It also depends on how strongly activated our cogwebs are: when energy from an intense and simple stimulus, or from strong emotions, is pouring through them an action may be triggered before we can stop ourselves. As Part II made clear, one thing a human brain is not is a perfectly rational computing device, aware of its own best interests and choosing accordingly. Even *Star Trek*'s Vulcans, held up as paragons of logic, have their emotional interludes; and humans are considerably less skilled than Vulcans at mastering their passions. That this deficiency often acts to their advantage may be due to the fact that *Star Trek*'s writers are human rather than Vulcan, but it nevertheless reflects our growing comprehension of how and why emotions matter to us.[6] As Chapter 9 suggested, they are essential components of successful human function. In excess they can be problematic—all things in moderation, as the proverb goes—but without them decision making can grind to a halt.

However, relying upon emotions can mislead us. Their function as short cuts to action can weight decisions in favour of short-term indulgence rather than a greater but more long-term benefit. Emotions are also somewhat indiscriminate. Their ability to flood the brain, causing changes in many interrelated areas of cortex and subcortex, is linked to their relatively slow timescale. Feelings linger where thoughts do not (we speak of grasshopper minds, not grasshopper hearts). As discussed in Chapter 9, this mismatch between emotional duration and the quicksilver precision of thought and language allows the feelings evoked by one thought (word, phrase, image) to become associated with another, perhaps quite unrelated, concept, a mismatch often exploited by influence technicians.

Individual differences in how brains process emotions are therefore relevant. People show a wide variety of emotions—and of emotional baselines. Some people are more or less sensitive, more placid or prone to temper, more laid-back or easily offended, braver or more fearful than their neighbours. Part of the challenge of forming a new relationship is learning your partner's set points. Some of this variation is due to genetic differences, for example in the levels of neurotransmitters such as serotonin which are thought to modulate anxiety, but there is also evidence that early experience can affect the baseline setting of many emotions.[7]

A much-studied example is sensitivity to stress, which as noted earlier is known to vary greatly from person to person. Influence technicians often make use of stress: by arousing some kind of negative feeling in the target—guilt, fear, cognitive dissonance of some kind—they can then present the behaviour they want to evoke as the way to get rid of all this emotional pressure. They know that stressed people are more likely to react reflexively, using stereotyped thinking, than if they are given time and leisure to consider their situation.

Individual variety is also found in our sense of freedom, and its complement, reactance, which function as emotions, as I argued in Chapter 11. These baselines may be set when a child is around two years old, the age at which the human animal discovers its sense of freedom—and generally becomes obnoxious. As Cialdini has observed, 'Most parents attest to seeing more contrary behavior in their children around this period. Two-year-olds seem masters of the art of resistance to outside pressure, especially from their parents. Tell them one thing, they do the opposite; give them one toy, they want another.'[8] The 'terrible twos' bring the beginnings of individualism and autonomy, as the child starts to understand itself as separate from the world around it, and to develop its mastery of its own body, with all the sense of agency that entails. Part of this process of self-definition requires a detailed understanding of the social environment. Much of the necessary information is gained by trial and error: testing the limits of caregivers' tolerance in order to learn what is and is not acceptable. (This is one reason why consistent behaviour is often recommended in parenting classes. A child attempting to comprehend social rules will learn them more easily if the examples it is given follow an obvious pattern.) Limit-testing involves an often infuriating degree of reactance, as the child hones its initial nihilist assumption that everything is permitted into a more realistic match for the way the world is.[9]

Some children, like some adults, accept restrictions meekly. Others are slow to give up the dream of control, though most 'unmanageable' children will settle down eventually, given a chance. The behaviour of peers and caregivers is crucial in determining whether a child hangs onto the dream into adulthood, viewing the rest of the human race as material ripe for exploitation, or whether other freedoms come to compensate.

Manipulating our sense of freedom can increase our susceptibility to influence techniques, which is why approaches emphasizing personal choice can slip past otherwise robust defences. Gaining a new freedom does not seem to affect us as much as a threat to our current freedoms; we generally prefer being coaxed, having our sense of control unobtrusively flattered, to being bullied into changing our behaviour. And this preference is no lightweight inclination. Like any emotion, freedom/reactance does not exist in isolation from either brain or body. The sense of control which characterizes freedom and whose loss triggers reactance is, like other positive emotions, associated with better physical and mental health. Reactance triggered by losing control, like other negative emotions, can induce disease and even sudden death in humans and animals.[10]

The subtle influence technician understands that once reactance is triggered, a target is primed for opposition and much harder to control. He or she may therefore attempt to make the victims feel that they are in charge, for example by explicitly requesting their consent—'May I just take a moment of your time?'—or adding phrases like 'your decision', 'you choose', and 'it's up to you' to the sales pitch. Often the degree to which freedom is trumpeted reflects the degree to which it is actually being restricted. Talk of freedom is easy to find in the sayings of dictators.[11] A less extreme example is the much-vaunted freedom of choice provided by the media in Britain and America. In principle, someone wanting to know the latest news can choose from an exciting variety of newspapers, television, radio, websites, and so on. In practice, any major news event reveals the essential similarity of these apparently different sources. Certainly we can choose how our information is flavoured—liberal or conservative, national or international, highbrow or facile. What we can't normally do is set the agenda which determines what is classified as news, and therefore the options from which we make our choice.

Your susceptibility to brainwashing (and other forms of influence) has much to do with the state of your brain. This will depend in part on your genes: research suggests that prefrontal function is substantially affected by genetics.[12] Low educational achievement, dogmatism, stress, and other factors which affect prefrontal function encourage simplistic, black-and-white thinking. If you have neglected your neurons, failed to stimulate your synapses, obstinately resisted new experiences, or hammered your prefrontal cortex with drugs (including alcohol), lack of sleep, rollercoaster emotions, or chronic stress, you may well be susceptible to the totalist charms of the next charismatic you meet. This is why so many young people baffle their more phlegmatic elders by joining cults, developing obsessions with fashions and celebrities, and forming intense attachments to often unsuitable role models.

Prefrontal abuse, however, is not restricted to the young. Maturity, and the immunization it can bring against weapons of influence, is within the reach of most of us—but we must choose to make the effort to achieve it. Extending the metaphor of the cognitive landscape, we can say that growing a brain is much like growing a garden; from an initial wilderness the aim is to create a pattern pleasing to oneself and others. In our early years the gardeners are those around us, the caregivers, siblings, and friends from whom we take our earliest imprints. As the years pass we become increasingly able to take over, to conceive of ourselves, uniquely among Earth's species as far as we know, as *self-gardeners*. We seek out the people and experiences who will help us to become what we want to be; we avoid temptations, distractions, and digressions by learning reasons why they are not really all that interesting. Age helps, as things tend to matter less.

Of course, the awakening which reconceptualizes us as self-changing beings does not always occur. Some gardeners are asleep all their lives, and can place a gigantic burden on those around them. But not all. And it is easier for another gardener, should one try to take over your spacious plot, to impose his or her preferred pattern on a chaos of weeds than on a previously well-kept garden. As for gardens and gardeners, so for brains and brainwashers—although it is worth adding that brains are unimaginably more complicated than any garden. Even the best-regulated cerebrum will never come anywhere near the stifling neatness found in our more ferocious horticultural endeavours.

We have discussed the importance of emotions in influence attempts, and we have seen how in general a richer mental world can be protective. But there is also a third factor: self-knowledge, the awareness that we are clay, not diamonds. If we know that we can change ourselves, we know that we can cultivate our cogwebs, shaping them as we would shape a garden. Understanding that brains can be changed is the first step in resisting change imposed by others. This, incidentally, is why chickens can be hypnotized by a line drawn along the ground in front of them or by swinging a finger back and forth in front of them, while humans generally cannot.[13] Although anyone who has seen an attractive woman walking past some schoolboys may doubt the validity of this evolutionary gap, most humans are harder to hypnotize than most avians. We know in advance that we are changeable; chickens do not.

The power hunters

Having considered what factors make us vulnerable to brainwashing, we can now ask the complementary question: what makes a good influence technician? The first, most obvious answer is motivation: influence technicians must want to change the minds of others. Here the need for control—the baseline setting of a person's sense of freedom—is relevant. The higher that setting, the greater the sense of reactance when freedom is infringed, and consequently the greater the need to control the environment—especially the human environment. Perhaps this goes some way to explaining why people who fight vigorously for freedom can so easily, once their revolution is achieved, transform into harsh dictators.

Because simpler things are easier to feel in control of (compare leading a child with leading a government) high levels of need for control tend to go with cognitive simplification: what Robert Lifton refers to as 'totalist thinking'. Simplicity is highly attractive to those who are themselves confused—of whom there are many—so projecting a simple message is often easier than selling complex arguments. For individuals, just as for societies, the overall impact they make on others is far greater if all their competing interests can be lined up behind a single clear identifiable message. In practice, most individuals, like most societies, are already too highly structured for the imposition of a single, simple message to be feasible. Those who govern us use other strategies: mission statements, manifestos, and of course the retreat to ethereal ideas, whose ambiguity is calculated to increase their mass appeal. But in situations where chaos—personal or political—is the governing principle, the clarity of vision which goes with totalist thinking can seem like a lifeline out of an abyss.

Charisma

As we saw in previous chapters, leaders often owe much of their influence to clear, simple visions. Charisma—'A gift or power of leadership or authority; aura. Hence, the capacity to inspire devotion or enthusiasm'—can be greatly enhanced by perceived power, Henry Kissinger's ultimate aphrodisiac.[14] Charisma is also enhanced by a strong sense of self, the impression of single-mindedness and purpose. Recalling George Ainslie's description of each human brain as an arena of competing interests, discussed in Chapter 11, we can see how appropriate the term 'single-mindedness' is. Although interests compete—'take the chocolate' versus 'stick to the diet'—they are also forced to co-operate at times because of the limited resources; we humans only have one set of limbs. (Is an octopus brain, which has more limbs to play with, less co-operative than ours?) The higher the degree of co-operation—the more interests aiming at a single goal—the more single-minded the person, and the more compelling they can seem to other people. Those with more divided minds may envy the sense of purpose, the apparent absence of tedious internal bickering, displayed by people with a strong sense of self.

However, clarity of vision is not enough to generate charisma: one also needs enough social skills, and self-belief, to inspire followers with devotion and enthusiasm. Without this interpersonal fluency the result is lonely obsession, as any Oxford college can testify. And even this may not be enough. As noted earlier, charismatic leadership depends not only on personality but on circumstance: the leader must ride the zeitgeist. Chance and timing play a large part in determining whether a would-be cult leader, for example, ends up as Manson or Moses. As Anthony Stevens and John Price argue in *Prophets, Cults and Madness*, sometimes what circumstance requires is a fresh perspective—a new way of looking at a tired situation or problem. This ability to take information and reorganize it in a novel way is part of what makes us human. However, some exceptionally creative individuals are particularly good at what Anthony F.C. Wallace calls 'mazeway resynthesis', recombining elements of their current ideas about their culture (the mazeway) into a new and dramatic form which seems to promise solutions to previously insoluble problems.[15] These people may also be prone to experiencing feelings of paranoia, strong spirituality or belief in the paranormal, and unusual visual and auditory experiences (such as hearing a voice when no one is actually present). These are milder forms of symptoms seen in schizophrenia, and indeed, high creativity has been linked to an increased risk of psychosis and perhaps bipolar disorder.[16]

Highly creative people seem to think differently, relying less on traditional logic and more on intuition. They see connections that others do not, and this flexibility leaves them better placed to undertake the huge internal shake-up which is mazeway resynthesis. Neuroscientifically, high creativity has been linked to high temporal lobe lability (unusually active neurons in that area of the brain; see Chapter 7). It may also be that highly creative people have, not necessarily larger, but more highly connected brains—more synapses linking neurons together—which might facilitate their ability to link ideas in unusual, original ways. Creativity, however, is not sufficient for charisma: many highly creative people are not very charismatic. Once the new mazeway has been synthesized, its creator must have the passion to adopt his or her new ideas and pursue them rigorously—single-mindedly—as well as the ability to understand and meet the needs of others (and thus attract followers).

Although in the long term reality tends to catch up with totalist thinkers, forcing its unwelcome presence on all but the most obdurate, in the short term they can be devastatingly persuasive. The best demagogues take care to stay in control, never forgetting the ultimate goals they are aiming for, intimidating or inspiring by the appearance of confident purpose, the aura of power. If they have fewer scruples than the rest of us, and readily see us only as means to their ends, such people can be extremely dangerous. An effective brainwasher knows how to apply pressure, to wind up stress and fatigue, pain or isolation, the force of the group and the pressure to comply, to overwhelm our stop-and-think resources and send us back to our instinctual basics.

Summary and conclusions

How your brain develops, which ideas it absorbs, which fads it follows, and which dreams it disdains—all this is deeply personal to you and you alone. Slight variations in our susceptibility to stress, the concepts we encounter, or our treatment at the hands of others early in life can inflate, over time, into profound differences in adult personality. Our differences as adults are shaped by our genetic heritage, by our past experience, and by the cogwebs which populate our brains.

But many of the ideas which influence us are not merely personal. To a greater extent than we tend to realize, they—and we—are shaped by our social interactions and cultural context, the groups and gatherings in which we spend our lives, the sea of ideas in which we swim from birth.[17] In the next chapter I will take a look at these wider societal influences, asking how they encourage, or discourage, attempts at mass mind control.

Chapter 13: Mind factories

just as the good of the race is better than the good of the individual, so also the good of the universe takes precedence over the good of any particular creature
Malleus Maleficarum

For 'universe', read 'society' in the epigraph above, and you have a succinct statement of totalitarianism … dating from fifteenth-century Europe. The claim that racial or species survival justifies any amount of individual suffering is a social version of consequentialism, the doctrine that the end justifies the means. This idea is notoriously associated with the Italian Renaissance thinker Niccolo Machiavelli (1469–1527), but although he was vigorously denounced for it, he was not its first proponent.[1] The word 'totalitarian', by contrast, has graced the English language only since 1926 (according to the *Oxford English Dictionary*). Yet consequentialism found its harshest expression in the proponents of totalist thinking: twentieth-century super-dictators like Hitler, Stalin, and Mao.

That same century also gave us 'brainwashing', a whisper of hope for dictators everywhere. Brainwashing held out the promise that reliable, scientific methods could be found to enforce the full control of human minds. Long before modern technology was available, however, the high priests of control were making inventive use of a range of techniques, from rhetoric to torture, to impose their various ideologies on others. Confident that they alone had the key to the ultimate Good which mankind was required to pursue—whether by God, Aristotle, the forces of history, or some other authoritative icon—these influence technicians shaped the climate of ideas in which they lived. As I have argued, their attempts at changing belief continue to resonate today.

Much of our investigation so far has focused on what I have referred to as brainwashing by force, the kind one might find in a cult or a prison camp. However, I have also discussed a more insidious form of manipulation, brainwashing by stealth, typically used by States to spread the ideas with which they hope to control their citizens. To understand brainwashing by stealth requires that we understand why ideas are so important to those who dominate societies, how they spread, and why they are so powerful. Those questions provide the focus of this chapter.

Infectious notions

The greater the lie, the greater the chance that it will be believed
Adolf Hitler, *Mein Kampf*

The doctrine of memetics discussed in Chapter 3 compares ideas to viruses and emphasizes the human susceptibility to cognitive infection. Memetics is a recent articulation of the much older metaphor of idea as disease, which complements the metaphor, discussed in Chapter 4, of brainwashing as healing. The Qur'an, for example, repeatedly describes unbelievers as having a disease in their hearts (see, e.g., Sura 2:10). Of course, humankind has always been afraid of illness.[2] Modern societies remain particularly terrified of infectious illnesses: even out-breaks which kill relatively small numbers can make headlines around the world.[3] Although evolution does provide instances of beneficial symbiosis between humans and micro-organisms, our gut bacteria don't get the publicity accorded to their deadlier relatives, so the concept of infection remains, overall, a strongly negative one. Consequently the idea-as-infection metaphor, even in the form of supposedly neutral meme science, continues to carry heavy pejorative over-tones. The memes which infect us, the diseases in our hearts, are all too often ideas with which those discussing them happen to disagree. Religion is a prime example of a meme, according to the atheist who gave us the term memetics. Unbelief is a disease of the heart, according to the sacred text of one of the world's major religions. Surprise, surprise.

The idea-as-infection metaphor gives some scientific authorities a way to dis-guise ideology as science and some religious authorities a way to disguise it as truth. However, it also serves to emphasize the importance of ideas in human culture. The concepts we hold in our heads are not merely doodles produced by bored neurons; they influence the way we act—and interact.[4] Many of the cogwebs which settle in our skulls are communal notions. They are uniquely inflected by the brain in which they live, just as no cat is quite like any other cat, but from brain to brain they share enough features to make them members of a species.

One highly variable characteristic of cogwebs is their ability to command adherence. Some beliefs can be classed with John Betjeman's 'faint conviction'.[5] Others, however, can be as deadly to those they infect as any virus, if not more so. Should you unluckily happen to share an aeroplane with someone infected with the Ebola Zaire virus, for instance, you may not become infected; and even if you do the survival rate is roughly ten per cent.[6] Share the flight with a suicide bomber dying for his creed and your odds of survival effectively drop to zero.

Ideas matter

Cogito ergo sum
[I think therefore I am]

René Descartes, *Discourse on the Method*

The ideas that we acquire from the world around us, or build when links form between previously unrelated cogwebs, form threads in a rich tapestry woven by that 'enchanted loom', the human brain.[7] This is the cloth from which we are cut; what ideas we have is part of who we are. Beliefs are not epiphenomena, mere accompaniments to the synaptic song-and-dance; all too often beliefs call the tune. This is particularly true of ethereal ideas, with their ability to tap our emotional energies. As discussed in Chapter 9, emotions can serve as short cuts, emergency action plans to override our stop-and-think functions. (Even top management responds to a fire alarm.) Linking a strong emotion to an ethereal idea provides, in effect, a false alarm. The manipulated brain reacts as if to an emergency, not stopping to think, simply choosing the most obvious course of action.

Often that course of action is the correct one in the circumstances: we draw back from fire and run from predators. But sometimes the course of action is obvious because it has been made obvious by the manipulator who installed the false alarm in the first place. Influence technicians raise alarms in order to pressurize their victims into acting in a certain way (which may or may not be in the victims' interests). Long before Adolf Hitler, people infected with the ethereal idea of anti-Semitism didn't simply argue that Jews were dirty. They suggested, and in many cases implemented, solutions to the 'problem', as the shameful history of Jewish ill-treatment in Europe (including Britain) demonstrates. The vituperative anti-Semitic claims which inspired the Nazis are ridiculous: full of logical holes, or lacking in evidence, or both. A few brave voices pointed this out at the time. Most Germans, however, believed what they wanted to believe. Their emotions had already been primed, engaged to such an extent by the widespread anti-Semitism of their culture that for them the ethereal idea of Jewishness was irredeemably tainted (largely by fear and disgust). Nazi propaganda fell on fertile ground.[8] Even the most forcefully presented of rational arguments would have struggled to stem the tide.

Societies, like individuals, always need some motivating factor (whether recognized or unconscious) to stop and think. If the balance of motivations is in favour of *not* pausing to reflect, as in Nazi Germany, then an ethereal idea can drive forceful action even when the idea itself is flatly contradicted by personal experience. German Jews were not invisible. Many were clearly respectable professionals: clean, honest, trustworthy. But the negative stereotype of the dirty, diseased, and wickedly grasping Jew had become so widely held, so much part of the culture, that it could override individual counterexamples. Either they could be consigned to a different area of the cognitive landscape ('my friend Daniel isn't a *typical* Jew'), or they could be ignored and contact with them minimized (using ghettos, for instance), thus avoiding encounters which might challenge the stereotype. Nazi activists went much further, reducing quality of life to such an extent that Jewish people could no longer maintain even the most basic appearance of respectability. Forced to look dirty, often succumbing to disease, they reinforced the Nazi idea of Jewishness, further strengthening their persecutors' convictions, a vicious spiral of intensifying dehumanization which ended in mass murder. And not just murder, but a search for purification which required the complete erasure of the contaminant using burial and fire, the two traditional methods for dealing with disease. For devout Nazis, Jewish emigration was not an appropriate option; only obliteration could remove the source of the infection.

When there are strong motives for believing an ethereal idea, its cogweb can become so strong that it distorts the cognitive landscape, a warping effect analogous to that of a black hole in space-time. Since established cogwebs play a large role in filtering incoming stimuli, new information will tend to be interpreted in support of the ethereal idea; the stronger the cogweb, the more it affects how the world is perceived. Action may even be taken to generate supporting— or suppress contradictory—evidence. It isn't only the Beatles' *Nowhere Man* who just sees what he wants to see.

Societies and shared ideas

I do not want to be *I*, I want to be *We*

Mikhail Bakunin, *letter*

Ethereal ideas are as fundamental to a society's self-image as they are to an individual's. Probably more so, since an individual has many more alternative sources from which to draw beliefs, such as a physically limited body and well-defined modes of action. Societies, which are less secure about their own embodiment, tend to resort more readily than individuals to the attractive apparent simplicity of ethereal ideas: freedom, justice, equality, and all their blood-soaked kin. Societies whose governmental and other institutions are less well established are at particular risk; older or more secure societies need not depend so much on a multitude yoked by strong emotions. This is in part because security contributes much to quality of life, and as their quality of life improves people are less desperate to change their lives. Reactance and other negative emotions are not as intense; influence technicians must work harder to whip them up. Greater security, whether at the individual or the societal level, also facilitates the tolerance of alternatives—leading to a greater diversity of ideas which enriches the (personal or societal) cognitive landscape.

Increased exposure to alternative possibilities may help to explain a puzzling fact about terrorism, a phenomenon often linked with brainwashing. Western politicians frequently denounce terrorists as irrational, poorly educated, and ignorant, but research in the Middle East suggests that, if anything, education correlates positively with support for terrorism.[9] Education shows people alternatives to their present circumstances: in their admittedly different ways, a Western secular education and a religious education both emphasize highly desirable visions of a better world. The visions may differ in detail, but many of the ethereal ideas involved are the same. (Islam, for example, extols justice, compassion, and charity, all dear to the hearts of Western liberal democracies.) When such ethereal ideas are made available, the contrast with everyday life can be more painfully obvious than it was before, especially if that life is lived in a heavily controlled or corrupt society. Reactance, the brain's signal of a mismatch between idea and reality, can be an extremely powerful motive for action. Shaped and targeted by cogwebs already present, or by influence technicians (whether religious or secular), dream and desire come together with inflammatory results. Without the dream, the desire may remain unfocused; without the desire the dream can have no venom. Giving people goals without providing them with the means to achieve those goals is a recipe for protest; frustrating protest is a recipe for violence, and controlling violence requires you to make yourself seem less human to those you are trying to control—which in turn makes it easier for them to think of you as subhuman and increase the ferocity of their violence against you. Not giving people goals in the first place, by restricting education and access to the global media, is one possible response, but in our shrinking and interconnected world it is increasingly unlikely to succeed. It also conflicts head-on with many of the most cherished ideals of both liberal democracies and the world's great religions (although this need not always be a problem: as we have seen, one of the advantages of ethereal ideas is their flexibility).

Many societal ideas are transmitted directly from person to person, sometimes explicitly, sometimes implicitly. For example, if teachers and pupils discuss the death penalty, the pupils will learn a number of explicitly stated facts (e.g. 'The last woman hanged in Britain was Ruth Ellis in 1955'). However, the discussion will also reinforce a number of pervasive assumptions: that crime should be punished (whether or not by death), that the State can legitimately harm a person (whether or not to the extent of killing that person), and so on. These may be stated explicitly—a good way of causing children to question them—but often they are left unspoken. These societal cogwebs are ideas which are widely, though not necessarily universally, held by a society's members (the extent to which an idea is societal depends on how many people's brains it has invaded). They may be explicitly set out in a constitution, or rarely if ever expressed; either way the degree to which they are accepted makes them powerful. Acceptance is encouraged by apparatuses such as the family, which transmit ideology from one generation to the next (discussed in Chapter 5).

The media-tors

Virtually any belief, valid or invalid, supported by cogent reasoning or by prejudice, can be inculcated and be widely accepted as realistic through deliberate manipulation or through unintended exploitation of prevailing institutions

Murray Edelman, *The Politics of Misinformation*

In modern societies, cogwebs are also transmitted by intricate global networks of mass communication: printed media, radio, 'moving pictures', and the Internet. An influence technician seeking to brainwash the masses needs to be able to control these media, and totalitarian states devote much of their efforts to this task (witness the pressures applied to privately owned media organizations in Serbia during the dictatorial rule of Slobodan Milosevic). However, as societies become more complex they tend, like cells, to become more responsive to external influences, and hence more permeable to new ideas. This much-discussed effect of globalization (itself an effect of increasing complexity) makes control more difficult, if only because there are more sources of ideas to be monitored, censored, or blocked. Energies devoted to a society's immune system are energies diverted from its metabolic functions, and totalitarian economies have a tendency to stagnation which can do more to hasten their demise than any amount of enemy propaganda.[10]

This is not to say that easy access to information cannot help to destabilize a totalitarian State; political events tend to have more than one cause. Like education, the media can introduce people to new ideas, provide alternative visions (for instance, of life in the glorious West), increase knowledge, or challenge the received wisdom of authority. Whether this actually happens will depend on the motives with which the info-largesse is purveyed. Crudely, State-owned media will tend to reflect the attitudes of the State and its desire for control, while privatized media reflect the attitudes of their owners and their desire for profit.

The myth of neutrality—the notion that there is such a thing as a naked, uninterpreted fact—is a favourite post modern target. At least since the glory days of Heidegger and Wittgenstein, thinkers have queued up to attack the notion that, in Terry Eagleton's words, 'Facts are public and unimpeachable, values are private and gratuitous.'[11] Eagleton phrases his challenge as follows:

> There is an obvious difference between recounting a fact, such as 'This cathedral was built in 1612,' and registering a value-judgement, such as 'This cathedral is a magnificent specimen of baroque architecture.' But suppose I made the first kind of statement while showing an overseas visitor around England, and found that it puzzled her considerably. Why, she might ask, do you keep telling me the dates of the foundation of all these buildings? Why this obsession with origins? In the society I live in, she might go on, we keep no record at all of such events: we classify our buildings instead according to whether they face north-west or south-east. What this might do would be to demonstrate part of the unconscious system of value-judgements which underlies my own descriptive statements. Such value-judgements are not necessarily of the same kind as 'This cathedral is a magnificent specimen of baroque architecture,' but they are value-judgements nonetheless, and no factual pronouncement I make can escape them.
>
> Eagleton, *Literary Theory*, p. 13

Statements cannot be considered in isolation; they always have a social context. Sometimes the actual content of the statement is clearly less important than its communication of non-verbal information. When we decipher the statements of a friend—or a newsreader—we are relying on numerous non-verbal social cues, all of which are assessed in evaluative terms. Even when reading we read between the lines (as illustrated by the discussion of the British National Party's manifesto in Chapter 9). The information which reaches our eyes, ears, or (if we are Braille readers) fingertips is destined to pass through the minefield of our experiential filters, so thoroughly screened by prior expectations that it may never reach the heights of consciousness. Whatever information does get through to cortex will be used to generate a series of sophisticated guesses, hypotheses which may be unconsciously influenced by all sorts of factors, from the placing of emotive words to the burgeoning virus in our bloodstream that is about to give us food poisoning. Naked facts never parade across our cognitive landscapes without a layer of hermeneutics to preserve their modesty. Sometimes we make that layer as diaphanous as possible—mathematics is an example—but thin or thick, it is always there, inescapably evaluative. Philosophers are fond of saying that you can't get an 'ought' from an 'is'; but abstraction can travel the reverse route, to 'is' from 'ought'. By ignoring all the background circumstances, by comparing many examples and extracting common features from them, we can arrive at a dry symbol, a 'fact'. In other words, perhaps an 'is' is simply an 'ought' with (almost) all the emotional juice sucked out.

No one, not even the most scrupulous editor, can escape his or her own point of view. Should we then conclude that every source of news is biased, and that as long as we are aware of their bias we can somehow take it into account and thereby compensate for it? Well, no, according to media studies theorists, because there is more to selective interpretation than simple bias. John Street, for instance, distinguishes the idea of bias from the idea of a 'frame'.[12] Bias is a systematic tendency to selectively highlight, or even misrepresent, information. A right-wing newspaper, for example, may repeatedly report stories about poverty in negative terms in order to support an ideology which blames the poor for their own misfortune. Precisely because it is so systematic, bias is easier to detect: which newspaper someone reads may tell an observer more about them than the clothes they are wearing.

Bias is also easier to remedy if one has access to alternative media sources, as in societies with a diverse and competitive privatized local and national media whose owners have a wide range of social backgrounds. Even so, pressures to simplify, standardize, and agree with popular opinion (or that of one's owner) are potent forces which operate to reduce diversity, as discussed in Chapter 3. Totalist thinking is not the sole preserve of overweening governments. One reason why media regulation should not, as some have argued, be left in the invisible hands of the market is the number of factors which reduce the chance of that market being a free one. The great Scottish economist Adam Smith, from whose masterwork *The Wealth of Nations* modern capitalists select many of their justifications, would probably not have approved of modern advertising, journalists' networks (with each other and with politicians) so cosy as to be almost incestuous, the amount of power in the hands of a few global media moguls, or many other features of today's British media.[13]

Frames are more subtle and more difficult to detect than bias. They are also often more consistent between media sources. Street suggests that 'Although frames are devices for seeing the world in a particular way, they differ from the notion of bias in the sense that they do not presume a single ideological position.'[14] Instead, media studies emphasizes that 'news stories' are exactly that, stories. Like other stories, they have a selective narrative structure which draws on deeply held assumptions (e.g. about cause and effect, morality, and social relationships), and which leaves out inconsistent or irrelevant information. Storytellers, including those who report the news, have a number of templates at their disposal and will use whichever best fits to organize the story they are telling: 'brave hero', 'bureaucratic incompetence', 'intractable conflict', and so on. Each template—or frame—has a particular language associated with it. If a child dies from illness, for instance, it is likely to be referred to as brave, tragic, and above all morally virtuous, a source of joy to its now-grieving parents. No doubt at times it screamed, sulked, or walloped its little sister—children do—but that commonplace observation does not fit the frame, and so tends not to feature in such reports. If a child is killed by a stranger the elements of tragedy and moral virtue are present, but instead of bravery we have innocence, and the corresponding dehumanization of the killer.

Frames and biases are shared societal extensions of individual ways of viewing the world. Indeed, personal and social viewpoints interact with and influence each other. The media claim to reflect the views of their audiences: for private enterprises with plenty of competition the profit motive ensures at least some degree of matching between source and audience, and even for State-owned media there must be some correspondence or they will become a laughing-stock, as happened in many Eastern European countries under Communism. As discussed in Chapter 3, however, the media also shape audiences' opinions: differential exposure to television, for example, can produce significant differences in attitudes.

Street suggests that news, in the sense purveyed by the media, 'is a product of the need to trade'.[15] Trade is an ancient facet of human interactions; the economist Haim Ofek argues that 'the antiquity of human exchange can be traced back to an early time range of 1.5–2 million years ago'.[16] The complexity of modern trading arrangements, however, is matched by the complexities of information management. Exchange presumably began as face-to-face interactions within a small social unit where each individual relied on the group for protection or even survival. Any motive to cheat would be tempered by the inability to avoid one's victims, and their revenge, in future, as well as by the threat of punishment from other group members. In addition, participants in exchange could use non-verbal cues and rituals to assess each other's trustworthiness. Although the tradition of face-to-face interaction survives to this day (political summit meetings are an example), many exchanges are either indirect, requiring no human contact, or involve encounters with people we will probably never meet again. Living in much larger clusters, as most Westerners now do, has weakened the hold of group upon individual, making cheating a more interesting option. It has also increased our reliance on information and those who provide it.

Uncritical reliance on media sources is a necessity. We simply do not have the resources to check every statement for ourselves, and so we either trust or, if trust is challenged, react with a blanket cynicism which is often no more than skin deep (in practice, disbelieving *everything* would simply incapacitate us). News organizations know the importance of trust, which is why they take pains to present themselves as credible, impartial authorities, while pointing out the biases of their rivals.[17] However, as Street suggests, 'reporting is a form of rhetoric, it is about *persuading* us—the readers, the viewers—that something happened'.[18] As such, the information we receive from the media comes pre-abstracted. Like the water in a city dweller's taps it has already been through someone else's system—probably several someones'. We may choose the bias of our paper, but we don't choose the frame for a particular item. We may not even notice how information has been shaped and slanted to appeal to our preconceptions. Indeed, we are not intended to notice, as noticing might trigger reactance and thus be counter-productive.

Charisma for groups

Being a gang member may satisfy needs that do not get satisfied elsewhere, like the need for security, positive connection to others, a positive sense of self, or a feeling of effectiveness

Ervin Staub, *The Psychology of Good and Evil*

In the previous chapter I discussed the idea that charisma may in part relate to an individual's perceived single-mindedness. People whose efforts all appear devoted to a single clear goal may be admired or loathed depending on the nature of the goal, but their simplicity and purpose are often envied by those of us with more plural, disunited minds. Life in black and white can look so easy to an observer overwhelmed by shades of grey. Why not just take up the creed and give your long-suffering cortex a well-deserved rest? 'Because you are not terminally brain-lazy, grossly self-indulgent, or nauseously stupid' is part of why not, but only part. Some people are driven to simplicity not just by laziness, selfishness, or idiocy, but by fear, fury, or frustration, negative emotions provoked by a threatening world. Natural, or social, disasters can be good for church attendance; weak government can leave space for a popular uprising; economic problems bolster support for extremists. When the environment is unstable, whether politically, economically, or physically, the lure of simplicity is heightened.

Simple, clear doctrines, set out with conviction, can impress others and often attract many followers, especially if those followers have no vehement convictions of their own. A charismatic leader who appears to believe wholeheartedly in those doctrines probably has a better chance of convincing others than a leader who thinks through every detail and dwells on snags and complications. The same is true of societies. Simple, well-publicized ideas give the impression of unity, and hence of strength of purpose. Ethereal ideas, such as truth, justice, tolerance, and freedom, are particularly useful for enhancing a society's charisma; their covert ambiguity widens their appeal and they can be stated in a few compelling words.

The media form a prime mechanism by which a society reinforces its own self-image. The appearance of consensus, especially in privatized media where a certain amount of variation is the norm, can therefore have a considerable impact on the citizens who consume the media's products, facilitating social conformity and increasing the government's ability to control its people. A loyal, united front can also be useful on the international stage. (Unity and loyalty, the group's favourite virtues.) Most of the time most of the nonsense that is talked in the media about ethereal ideas may not be too obviously detrimental. Where it can matter enormously is when it reflects bitter social division. Talking in stereotypes is rarely much help when it comes to solving complex political problems.

Consider the following statements: 'Islam is truth'; 'Men are superior to women'; 'The United States is the land of the free'; and 'Communism is a noble creed'. All of these, if accepted, bolster the positive image of their respective constituencies. All can be countered by equally abstract claims: 'Only Jesus shows us the way to truth'; 'Women are kinder than men'; 'The USA was built by slave labour'; 'Capitalism is best'. If your only concern is to make your constituents feel better about themselves (and incidentally more committed to you), then statements like these can serve that purpose well. If, however, you are trying to reconcile, say, communists and capitalists, you will need to move away from ethereal ideas. Not freedom, but perceptible improvements in personal freedoms; not one unassailable truth, but the acknowledgement that truths come in many colours, that both sides have at times abused human rights and compromised their own ideals. Even one human brain, whose competing interests are strongly forced towards co-operation by the limitations of a single human body, can contain incompatible ideas, as we have seen. Societies, even when polarized by years of conflict, are far less constrained. In the Middle East, for instance, it is possible to find Israelis who hate what their government is doing to the Palestinians, Palestinians who grieve for Israelis killed by suicide bombers, and members of both communities working together on reconciliation and education projects. The same variety of opinions can be found in other arenas of conflict such as Northern Ireland, Sri Lanka, or the Sudan. But these contrapuntal voices are not often heard. They do not fit the 'intractable conflict' frame on which the stories are usually hung.

Brainwashing the masses

Chapter 1 began with a dictionary's definition of brainwashing: 'The systematic and often forcible elimination from a person's mind of more established ideas, especially political ones, so that another set of ideas may take their place.' Throughout the book I have noted the political nature of the concept of brainwashing—in the most fundamental sense of politics which deals with the relations between individuals and the groups they form. With respect to influence techniques, four combinations are theoretically possible: individuals influencing other individuals, individuals influencing groups, groups influencing other groups, and groups influencing individuals.

Brainwashing is traditionally associated with coercion, but force brings its own particular problems. Applying force to someone triggers vigorous reactance, engaging the victim's emotional instincts to defend the threatened freedoms. Although the brainwasher may be able to apply enough force to overcome this resistance, the victim may be left so traumatized as to be both dysfunctional and, more importantly from the brainwasher's point of view, unreliable: American prisoners returning from Korea had high rates of mental illness. Large-scale belief change achieved by force may occur, but it cannot be trusted to be stable on a long-term basis without the close supervision—and continuing coercion—of the victim. For individuals, this requires a huge amount of time and effort on the brainwasher's part, and although the victim may suppress his or her previous opinions there is no guarantee that they might not re-emerge, should the coercion be lifted (in this respect brainwashing differs from its progenitor, torture, which requires only short-term violence, often ending in death, and aims at evoking certain types of behaviour rather than belief change). This kind of interaction does occur—domestic violence offers us examples. But at present the amount of work it takes is a considerable deterrent. Even if the task of coercion is shared among members of a group it still requires appreciable resources to control and monitor one person, let alone many. As for the last of the four combinations, individuals influencing groups, forcible influence is unlikely, simply on resource grounds.

There is, however, another option: stealth. Under this wide banner I include the subtleties of advertising and the media, the false utopias spun by charismatic leaders, and proposed technologies of mind manipulation (of which more in the next chapter). Stealth, if successful, has a great advantage over force: it avoids the problem of reactance. The risk, of course, is that the victim may inconveniently notice the deception, triggering an outraged backlash. Stealthy influence technicians often gamble that by the time this happens they will have achieved their goals and departed for pastures new and other sheep to fleece. Their aim, therefore, is to make sure their victim doesn't conceptualize their behaviour *as* an influence attempt.

Stealth is an easier option than force, especially when the belief change need be only temporary. It need not be conscious; in fact success is made more likely if the deceiver believes what he is saying—or can convincingly appear to. This is not the raw dichotomy it seems: there are speakers who when arguing a case feel a firm belief in what they are saying. Their conviction may or may not last beyond the debate's conclusion, once the fire of emotion has cooled; but while in that flame they are entirely sincere. Human beings have developed sophisticated lie detection facilities, but they are by no means infallible. Detecting people who believe, if only for the moment, the lie on their lips can be beyond their victims' capabilities.

Stealth, however, has its difficulties for a brainwasher intent on mass control. The dangers of being discovered are magnified in a population of varying backgrounds, beliefs, and desires, more so if that population has access to alternative sources of information. In even the most restricted societies today there is rarely only one fount of truth. Ideally, a brainwasher (whether State or individual) would prefer the target population isolated. If this is not practicable, it may still be possible to make them feel isolated, for example by playing up the danger from external threats (i.e. defining or reinforcing outgroups). A clearly labelled enemy (e.g. 'Communists', 'Al-Qaeda') is always handy, especially if the enemy agents themselves are not always clearly identifiable: their presence among the target group can then be suggested, stirring up further unease. A brainwasher will want to keep the target masses stressed, or busy, or both, as this will reduce the likelihood of stop-and-think objections.

To change belief on a mass scale, given the size of modern societies, is almost certainly out of the question for an individual without group support. To attract this support, an influence technician will use methods discussed throughout this book. He will lace his rhetoric with ethereal ideas, cleverly using language to hook the relevant associations into his victims' brains, making sure that his doctrines are simple and memorable. Like Socrates in the dialogues reported by Plato, he may seek his victims' consent at every stage of his attempt to change their minds.[19] Although his aim is to make his victims feel more unhappy, so that they are looking for the 'help' he is ready to offer, he will do his best to appear likeable, humorous, and human, suppressing challenges to his point of view by derision rather than force, and emphasizing what he has in common with his audience. He may also give the impression of healthy debate, even self-criticism (for example, by using his followers in staged discussions); but the message actually delivered will always be the same even if he is appearing to say the opposite.[20] He will also be careful to avoid any impression of uncertainty, enhancing his charisma by an appearance of single-minded confidence. In all these ways he will hope to gain publicity for his cause, achieving regular access to the media, getting people talking, persuading respected authorities to refer to his ideas as if they are not only reasonable but entirely taken for granted.

Human brains are tuned for detecting changes, mismatches between their stored experiences and the information they are currently receiving. Influence technicians can and do use this to attract attention by presenting themselves as new, unique, different. The downside is that too big a gap between the ideas they hope to impose and those in present occupation of the target brains will lessen the chance of the new ideas being accepted. Small steps, on the other hand, will be easier to swallow. (Take enough small steps, and a respectable middle-class citizen can be transformed into a cold-blooded murderer.) Knowing the target audience also helps to shape the style of presentation. As well as using the brain's reactions to stress and to change, a brainwasher will want to use existing social pressures to his advantage. By associating his chosen outgroup with socially unacceptable, group-threatening characteristics, such as selfishness, treachery, dirt, disease, and pestilentially large numbers, he both increases the sense of threat and reassures his audience that they themselves are not selfish, untrustworthy, foul, or a plague on the face of planet Earth.[21] All this applies to groups as well as individuals, and depending on the circumstances, stealth may take a panoply of forms.

Summary and conclusions

Whatever the exact technique, stealth, like the use of force, has its limitations. Using stealth tends to have the unfortunate side-effect of increasing one's own suspiciousness of others (if you're cheating, why shouldn't they be?). Stealth may therefore lead to force as control increases—in an attempt to move from deceit to high-impact coercive brainwashing and thereby to guarantee subservience—because stealth alone can never fully assuage paranoia. Another problem is that though stealth may work for a while, or for changing a tiny region of the cognitive landscape, it seems unable to achieve the systematic transformations traditionally laid at the door of brainwashing over similarly brief time periods. And, as we have seen throughout this book, even those—impressive though the change may sometimes be—can be explained in social psychological terms. Brainwashing as belief change can certainly occur; what we have not found is evidence of brainwashing as a magic bullet.

Brainwashing as a magic bullet, however, is exactly what is needed for the dream of control, particularly mass control, to become reality. Although some scientists and technicians have undoubtedly been complicit in the worst atrocities of the modern world (not a recent trend; Archimedes and Leonardo da Vinci both worked on weapons of war), all their skill has failed to come up with a guaranteed technique of mind control—apart, of course, from physical obliteration, a method understood since Cain slew Abel. However, there is hope for would-be brainwashers. Science has only lately begun to unravel the mysteries of human brains; and knowledge, at least potentially, is power. Perhaps a magic bullet may still be found.

In the next chapter, I will look at what brain science may be able to offer, perhaps even in the not too distant future, to those who dream the dream of mind control.

Chapter 14: Science and nightmare

People are manipulated; I just want them to be manipulated more effectively.

B.F. Skinner, *interview*

In *The Search for the 'Manchurian Candidate'*, first published in 1977, the investigative reporter John Marks describes how the US government's Central Intelligence Agency spent years—and vast amounts of taxpayers' money—searching for foolproof methods of brainwashing people. Despite acknowledging that much CIA research into mind control was far ahead of its academic counterpart, the behavioural sciences, Marks concluded that to the best of his knowledge the search had failed—so far. 'Spurred by the widespread alarm over communist tactics, Agency officials had investigated the field, started their own projects, and looked to the latest technology to make improvements. After 10 years of research, with some rather gruesome results, CIA officials had come up with no techniques on which they felt they could rely.'[1]

The United States' ability to recruit world-class researchers and give them space to flourish had proved its worth during the Second World War with the Manhattan Project, which achieved what many at the time thought impossible: the creation of a usable atomic bomb.[2] Yet all the talents and energies focused by CIA resources over a much longer period had been unable to crack the challenge of thought control. Perhaps the challenge was insuperable after all, in which case the fears raised by brainwashing could safely be set aside. In 1977, however, John Marks was not ready to relax. 'A free society's best defense against unethical behavior modification is public disclosure and awareness [...] it is now too late to put behavioral technology back in the box. Researchers are bound to keep making advances.'[3]

Although the CIA's investigations of brainwashing may have failed in their ultimate aim—gaining total control of a human being's thoughts and actions—

the Agency had studied and applied many techniques along the way: mind-changing substances such as LSD, hypnosis, sensory deprivation, even 'depatterning' experiments which involved 'intensive electroshocks, usually combined with prolonged, drug-induced sleep', the goal being to turn the subject's mind into a blank slate upon which new beliefs could then be imposed. Some of these tortures were abandoned—occasionally for ethical reasons, more often when they failed to prove reliable. Depatterning, for example, could erase memories and leave its victim confused and passive, but imposing new beliefs proved harder than expected. Other techniques, like drugs, hypnosis, and sensory deprivation (e.g. the hooding of prisoners), are still with us. Moreover, since Marks' book was written, the scientific understanding of human brains has greatly increased. Could future, or even current, research in the neurosciences give influence technicians the tools they need to turn the dream of mind control into reality? That question provides the topic for this chapter.

Back to brains

As we saw in Chapter 7, the basic units of any brain are its neurons. These tiny cells, continually bathed in fluid (the CSF), receive, combine, and transmit electrical signals. Neurons communicate by spitting packets of chemicals (neurotransmitters) across the gaps (synapses) between them. These chemicals interact with specialized molecules (receptors) on the surface of the recipient neuron, thereby affecting its behaviour.

In other words, neurons—and therefore brains—are electrochemical entities. They can be influenced both by many kinds of molecules and by electrical stimuli (and therefore also by magnetic fields since, as Michael Faraday and James Clerk Maxwell showed in the nineteenth century, electricity and magnetism are aspects of an underlying unity). In practice, brain-changing influences tend to be subdivided into a number of categories which reflect traditional scientific demarcations. Physical influences include radioactivity, electromagnetic radiation (encompassing visual images, temperature changes, magnetic fields, and so on), and more recently proposed quantum effects. Technically part of this grouping, but usually thought of separately, are the mechanical and organic influences: surgery, damage, and disease. The latter two are not always easily distinguished: a brain tumour, for example, may wreak its havoc by altering levels of chemicals, or by physically crushing neurons as it grows, or both. Chemical influences include neurotransmitters, hormones, foods, and drugs (with the obvious proviso that these labels often overlap). Some of these agents act directly on neurons; others are converted to their active forms within the body. Some affect the balance of electrical forces between a neuron's innards and the CSF in which it bathes; some affect the cell membrane, and some can pass through the cell membrane and change the neuron's inner workings. When those inner workings include the neuron's genes, the agents responsible are usually classed as genetic influences. Finally, there are social influences: the catch-all description for language, culture, personal relationships, and suchlike.

Like genetic influences, social effects are thought to be mediated by changes in brain electrochemistry. In both cases, however, it can be impossibly cumbersome (or, given our present state of knowledge, just plain impossible) to spell out in full how that mediation occurs. When a cell biologist speaks of a gene 'switching on', he or she is glossing a highly complex mechanism uncovered over years of patient experiments (and still not fully understood). When a neuroscientist speaks of 'theory of mind' or 'face recognition', the gloss covers more assumptions and has less empirical support, because social neuroscience is more complicated and less well-developed than genetics. Nevertheless, until someone comes up with an empirically testable counter-claim, the assumption that *all* brain-changing influences act, at base, by changing brain electrochemistry is likely to remain secure.

Physical influences

As already noted in this book, influence technicians attempting to change a brain have in theory had two options available: direct operations on the brain itself, or indirect operations on the brain's immediate environment. In practice, most of the effort devoted to changing minds has involved changing environments. Many of the CIA's attempts at mind control are of this more indirect type: sensory deprivation, interrogation techniques modelled on Soviet methods, and so on.[4]

One obvious change to our environments which (unlike sensory deprivation experiments) has the power to affect a large number of people simultaneously is the growth of mass media such as television and the Internet. These technologies are applications of physics that have had a huge impact on modern life. In her book *Tomorrow's People* brain scientist Susan Greenfield speculates that the further development of mass media technologies into the realm of sophisticated virtual reality could create increasingly infantilized, stimulus-driven, and asocial consumers whose every need is anticipated and provided by endlessly watchful information technologies.[5] Change the world, Greenfield argues, and you change the selves which live in it. The changes we in the rich West are contemplating could fundamentally alter human nature.

In the twentieth century, the CIA's technological achievements did not include the systematic synthesis of fake worlds. Some of its most controversial efforts, such as depatterning, took the alternative tack of direct intervention. Ever since neurosurgeons such as Wilder Penfield discovered that applying electrical currents to their patients' brains could evoke sensations, movements, or memories, the idea of directly controlling a human being, for example via an implant in the brain or body, has been considered an exciting possibility by those members of our species whose need for control is high.[6] More recently, methods of transcranial magnetic stimulation (TMS) have been developed, which interfere with neurons on a grand scale (temporarily) by directly applying magnetic fields to the brain. Attempts have been made at controlling simple animal behaviours, with some success, and the simpler human behaviours may also be accessible to this kind of approach, as Penfield showed. Controlling anything more complex— like individual ideas—has proved impossible. Human beings are simply too varied and unpredictable, and present-day micro-electrode and neural implant technology too imprecise, for us to have conquered—yet—the world within our skulls.

One of the largest obstacles to understanding and controlling human beings is technological. Neuroimaging has allowed scientists to look inside living human brains, but the picture remains too blurred for detailed mind manipulation. Methods like fMRI (functional magnetic resonance imaging) rely on the axiom that blood flow rises to hard-working regions of the brain, but there is a significant time lag between the neurons becoming active and the surrounding blood vessels raising their delivery rate. Many cogwebs will have shimmered and faded into silence long before then. MEG (magnetoencephalography) measures changes in the brain's electromagnetic field; this avoids the time lag problem, but MEG, unlike fMRI, cannot penetrate far into the brain. Neither technique is fine-grained enough to provide comprehensible details of anything less than massive blocks of neurons, and even at that coarse level of resolution the amount of data generated pushes the limits of current information technology and statistical analysis. These methodological problems are not, as far as we know, insoluble in principle. In practice, however, neuroimaging has much further to go before it can assist in precise mind control.[7]

Nevertheless, we may one day have enough precision and computational power to isolate distinct cogwebs within a living human brain, tracing the individual neural circuits in that particular person which respond to a given stimulus. Our statistical techniques may be so advanced that we can distinguish the signal from all the surrounding noise with a fair degree of accuracy. We may even be able to improve the technology to such an extent that brain surveillance can be done covertly. At present, scanning a brain requires the insertion of brain and owner into something resembling a gigantic washing machine. This claustrophobic experience is not easy to disguise, given that the brain involved must be awake, and held reasonably still, if useful results are to be obtained. In other words, the subject must actively co-operate, however unwillingly. Patterns of brain activity are also distorted by the subject's awareness that he or she is being scanned. Covert surveillance and analysis would require far more sophisticated compensation for movement artefacts than we have now; but that is not to say it will always be impossible.

Should such covert surveillance ever come to pass, the armoury of physics may also have supplied our finest scientific minds with methods of directly influencing the cogwebs thus identified. James Tilly Matthews' Air Loom, the first known modern conception of an influencing machine, involved powerful rays being focused on the victim's brain.[8] Future Air Looms may use electromagnetic radiation to affect, or even burn out, the neurons involved in implementing certain cogwebs. The minuscule machines promised by nanotechnology may gain entry to the body via injections, skin contact, food, or even breathing, programmed to seek and destroy their neural targets, or modify the synapses between them. Perhaps precision TMS will be available to stun an active cogweb into submission, or nanoelectrodes for exquisitely sensitive control of ion flows, or hitherto untapped techniques from the quantum world. Who knows? What does seem clear is that with a system as intricate as the human brain, human ingenuity will give future influence technicians plenty of choice.

Mechanical and organic influences

Targeting individual cogwebs may also, in the surgeries of the future, still involve hands-on interference with living brains. Whereas some of the physical techniques described above would be suitable for covert operations—where the victim is relatively unconstrained and the interference should ideally not be noticed—surgical techniques typically unleash the power of authority (doctors, backed by the State) against an individual judged sick or antisocial (these terms may come to mean much the same). Whether or not consent is required for the operation will depend heavily on how our future societies view themselves, and which ethereal ideas they hold most dear.

With or without consent, the neurosurgeon-psychiatrists of those societies will probably have much more subtle tools at their command. They too may use miniature robots, precision lasers, and immense computational power to remove the offending cogwebs, the problematic beliefs, which have led to their patients' dysfunctional behaviour. Neural implants—already technically feasible—could warn of certain behaviour before it happened, like internal weather stations, forecasting a build-up of pressure in the periaqueductal grey or storms in the temporal lobe. Or perhaps genetic screening at birth will throw up warning signals and trigger pre-emptive surgery to lower the risks of drug addiction, psychopathy, paedophilia, or whatever other conditions are deemed socially unacceptable. Implants could be inserted to adjust neurotransmitter levels or supplement existing enzymes (e.g. so that alcohol is broken down more quickly), body organs altered to produce more or less of some hormone, immune systems vaccinated against illegal drugs, or diets regulated. Given the West's current tendency to denigrate social maturity and extol technological wizardry, it seems likely that our preference for the easy over the effortful, the quick fix over the longer-term solution, will continue the medicalizing of even largely social problems, rather than attempting to change societies themselves.

Chemical influences

Another line of approach comes from our increasing understanding of disease. Once problem synapses—those involved in problematic cogwebs—can be distinguished from their peers and targeted, we may be able to affect them by making neurons ill. Viruses transported into a cell's vicinity; disrupting the cell's electrochemical balance by adding electrically charged particles; interfering with the cell's internal mechanics or even triggering cell death: all these might be used against individual neurons if identification, delivery, and controlled removal can be made effective.

On a larger scale, as we learn more about learning we may be able to identify the chemicals which play a vital role in synapse change. Perhaps chemical depatterning—the ability to erase brains functionally by resetting the synapses to a baseline level, will some day be feasible. Here again the major problem would be one of specificity, since a human being totally wiped clean in this way would probably be no use to anyone. Specificity could be increased by applying the cleaning drug only in the vicinity of neurons which are particularly active during certain thoughts and allowing it to act only on active synapses (another fearsome technical challenge, since such neurons may be distributed all over the brain). The drug's action could also be allowed to function only during a brief window of opportunity, for example by transporting it to the target neurons as an inactive, apparently innocuous precursor chemical or chemicals and then applying enzymes, first to convert it to the active form and then to deactivate it after the damage had been done. The victim could be induced to activate the offending cogwebs ('Now, Mr Jones, what is it you like about sex with small children?') while the drug took effect and removed them from the cognitive landscape. There would of course be collateral damage to other cogwebs as the victim's mind wandered during the drug's active period. But any society prepared to use such techniques on its citizens would probably find collateral damage an acceptable price to pay. After all, damage would only be inflicted on those, like paedophiles, who are already well beyond the moral pale. Indeed, some people with paedophilia might prefer such a cognitive clean-up to the current alternative: an overcrowded, hostile, and dangerous prison.

Genetic influences

I'm the ghost in the machine,
I'm the genius in the gene

The Divine Comedy, *Gin-soaked Boy*

Extending our understanding of biochemistry and cell biology, future brain scientists will no doubt consider the rich vein of influence potential provided by genetic research. Huge quantities of words have been produced on this topic; mercifully, the public debate is now moving beyond the damaging myth that 'genes are destiny' to an acknowledgement of the inextricable interconnectedness of genes and environment.[9] Of particular interest are the prospects held out for neuroscience by our increasing skill in manipulating genes. Rather than wasting time on searching for the gay gene, the crime gene, or the gene for genius, many scientists are trying to understand how genes switching on and off can grow and change and damage living brains.

Earlier we saw how techniques may become available for targeting individual neurons in living human brains, without the need for messy, convoluted surgery. However, since any given neuron is likely to be participating in multiple cogwebs, we may want to spare the neuron itself, and only adjust specific synapses. Neuroscientists are already making progress on the challenging task of understanding how synapses form and change. Some day we may be able to reorganize or disconnect our cogwebs at an extraordinary level of detail by manipulating individual synapses in individual brains.

Most scientists today would predict that in our future the dazzling searchlight of science will burn off the last fading vapours of what the philosopher Gilbert Ryle termed 'the ghost in the machine',[10] leaving souls as relics of history and wrapping minds firmly inside the nets of causality. Our ability to control genetic material will surely be an important contributor to this process. In the brain, gene manipulation may help us not only to counter common diseases, but also to increase the precision with which cogwebs can be altered or imposed. As we come to understand which genes control synaptic plasticity—a project already under way—we may be able to control which beliefs are held, and how strongly, which memories are kept and which forgotten, which actions conceived and which remain beyond imagining. Perhaps we may even work out how to trigger genes remotely, without unduly toxic side-effects and with greater accuracy in time and space.

If we can achieve the identification and manipulation of cogwebs, the implications are too far-reaching to be more than outlined here. We may be able not only to generate a certain belief, but also then to 'fix' it so that no further modification occurs, creating the ultimate impervious dogmatic. Imagine that Jane and Dan are both devout Christians, brought up in wealthy families and similar religious traditions. If some of the variation which makes Jane a fundamentalist and Dan a liberal can be traced to genetic differences, then screening programmes (at birth or even earlier) may include genetic markers for strong belief. Perhaps we will eventually be able to alter innate suggestibility using precision gene therapy, screening out—or breeding—the fanatics of the future. Conversely, we may be able to melt and reshape regions of our cognitive landscape to our preferred specification, producing designer minds for ourselves or our children. How much nicer for Dan and his new partner to show their commitment by having their opinions 'converged'. How beneficial to remove Jane's fear of heights. How alarming if such technologies become available before they become detectable, leaving people at the mercy of unscrupulous tweakers who can delete obstreperous notions without their owners realizing it.

Perhaps the medicine of the future will include brain-tidying kits which allow a patient to remove unwanted cogwebs. First: the schizophrenic's delusions; the depressive's self-excoriating thoughts; the agonizing flashbacks of post-traumatic stress disorder. Later: unruly children; social stresses; the phobic's linking of fear to innocuous target. Later still: the song heard and hated which won't stop buzzing round one's temporal lobes; the ex-wife's nastier comments; the memory of a put-down from the boss. Our minds have been losing their privacy since we learned to read faces and gestures, a Salomeic unveiling accelerated by the onset of language. That unveiling continues apace, and in the coming decades it may accelerate again as our physical subtleties—first body texts and contexts, then brain scripts—emerge into the public gaze. Perhaps the law of the future will include provision for compulsory brain adjustment, removing inappropriate thoughts to prevent inappropriate behaviours. Even before these super-specialized facilities become available, people at high risk could be monitored and controlled remotely, using implants. If, for example, scientists can reliably correlate changes in amygdala or orbitofrontal cortex activity with loss of self-control and consequent violence (even within a single individual), then those changes can be detected and appropriate counter-measures taken to prevent the violence from actually taking place. Another possibility is 'addict-engineering': using implants, for instance, as illegal drugs are already being used, to make an individual dependent on some scarce chemical, and therefore subservient to that chemical's provider.

Tweaking genes could have other applications. Why mount a long and expensive campaign against a political opponent when you can use a viral vector (a virus with extra DNA inserted into its own genetic code) to make his own brain discredit him? Let the vector carry the genetic instructions to switch on certain normally quiescent genes in your enemy's prefrontal cortex, and the resulting malignant tumour may have such catastrophic effects on his behaviour that your problem is resolved with minimal effort on your part. Alzheimer's, Parkinson's, and other neurological nightmares (perhaps including some yet to be discovered) could be used as weapons. It is even conceivable that the deliberate induction of disease could be used by the State to punish certain crimes.

Of course, using gene technology to give convicted criminals, enemies of the State, or any other outgroup an illness, be it cancer or Creutzfeldt–Jakob disease, artificial anorexia or excruciating arthritis, should count as inhuman and degrading punishment. But is the concept so different, morally speaking, from other human behaviour that if the technology were available it would never be used? Perhaps. But history reminds us of Auschwitz and Tuskegee, of atom bombs, biological and chemical warfare, drawing and quartering traitors, burning 'witches' alive—and many other equally grisly examples.[11] Sentencing people to death by induced disease, like the other speculations in this chapter, crosses no ethical line that has not already been crossed. Indeed, although genetic control will undoubtedly refine the techniques, we do not need it to implement the general method. That was done long ago.

Social influences

Many philosophers and religious thinkers have used the idea of a 'veil of perception' between our minds and 'true' reality: an impenetrable barrier which prevents us from ever knowing what the world is 'really' like. As we saw earlier, the future envisaged by Susan Greenfield is one in which virtual reality has solidified the veil of perception, providing each of us with a wraparound world of our own layered with consistent, indulgent, comforting delusions.[12] Such a world could satisfy the dream of control by granting us apparent mastery over not only the environments but also the people around us. From virtual butlers to helpful robots to cyber-friends who never complain or criticize, we would never have to compromise our cosseted egos, never have to give up the blissful childhood fantasy of being special—a prince or princess, a chosen one, in our heads at least 'the still point of the turning world'.[13] Presumably some limits on behaviour would still have to be set, at least for those limited occasions when social interactions were required, but for most of the time each of us could be the master of our own little fake world. The perfect recipe for a race of childish solipsists; but if the surrounding machines can manage us successfully who would even notice, let alone care?

As I noted in Chapter 11, objective and subjective freedom are not identical. Sometimes, like Robert Browning's painter in his poem *Andrea del Sarto*, we notice this—'So free we seem, so fettered fast we are!'—but often we are too distracted, too tired, too busy, or too lazy to notice our constricting lives.[14] Closed-circuit television everywhere; government plans to read our e-mails; supermarkets recording what we buy—but one must be secure, and if one has nothing to hide … and how else can our retailers give us the properly customized service we deserve? Besides, life is good, and we can do things our ancestors could never imagine. So we surrender objective freedoms in favour of their virtual replacements: anonymous chat on the Internet instead of talking to friends; the chance to read about celebrities instead of the freedom from peer pressure; consumer choice (thirty different kinds of toilet roll, hurrah!) instead of the freedom to be something more than just a consumer. Becoming more and more conformist, more predictable by all kinds of influence technicians, we nevertheless believe the individualist message: that each of us is free as never before.

Another concern of futurologists is that sophistication leads to atomization. This pessimistic doctrine argues, putting it crudely, that other people are such a pain in the neck that, given the choice, we would rather have virtual substitutes. Retreating into a universe populated by fake friends programmed to love us, we would lose the restraints that currently shape human personalities into interesting (and sometimes even moderately adult) forms. Chief among these restraints are those provided by having to live with other people. As with pebbles on a beach, proximity takes the rough edges off. Living in a fake world would reduce, or remove altogether, the need for us to smooth our cognitive landscapes—in other words, to be social creatures.

For many people, the idea of losing genuine social bonds is abhorrent. They reap rewards from a sense of community, from friendships and from love, and view these joys as the best of what makes life worth living. They regard their social commitments as a vital part of who they are; to replace those commitments with cyber-ties would be to render much of their existence fraudulent. For others, however, it may seem better to rule in hell than serve in a real world which may not seem much like heaven, especially if hell is padded with creature comforts (and if they have not had much luck with love and friendship). And of course, as science continues to unravel the weavings of the enchanted loom, our ability to design unreal companions will improve. If the sculptor Pygmalion could fall in love with the statue he had made, then perhaps our need for emotional attachments can be satisfied with replicas carved from information. In some cases a loving cyber-pal would be far better than the real alternative (children killed by domestic violence in Britain represent only the tip of the iceberg of child abuse perpetrated by all-too-real human 'carers'). And, after all, we dream and fantasize, read novels, go to the movies. We take steps, in other words, to insulate ourselves from reality. Moving to a fake world existence would simply be taking that final step through the looking glass.

Even today, total withdrawal into a world of one's own is possible. Yet most human beings hold back from stepping through the looking glass, pitying or despising those who do withdraw. Daydreams preserve us from stultifying jobs; with novels or movies or drugs we may escape for a while; but we eventually return to our everyday lives. Situated in a social context from which we draw sustenance, the very idea of all-encompassing fakery disturbs us. Our sympathies in Peter Weir's film *The Truman Show* are with Truman, brought up from birth on an elaborate television set, who insists on seeing through the make-believe. We are intrigued by *Nineteen Eighty-Four* and *Brave New World*, by Plato's cave and Descartes' evil demon, but we see them as visions of horror, not paradise.[15] Our sense of reactance, which warns us of a mismatch between expectation and outcome—and thus keeps us tied to truth—is outraged at the thought of such a gigantic gap between what really is and what only seems to be.

The lesson for would-be brainwashers is clear. People can be persuaded to give up objective freedoms and hand over control of their lives to others in return for apparent freedoms—in other words, as long as they are aware of the freedoms they are gaining and either contemptuous, or altogether unaware, of the freedoms which they are giving up. Our sense of freedom may be a basic emotional reaction, but its associations with particular abilities (to speak our minds, go where we please, and so on) are learned connections. The trick is to disable the brain's alarm signal by breaking the connections (or preventing them from forming in the first place) so that reactance is no longer triggered when, for example, the right to free speech is infringed. Then there will be no emotional reaction, no fire to be damped down—or stamped out by force. At present, our methods are slow and imprecise: repeatedly playing down the value of the freedom in question, emphasizing potential threats which make the freedom unsustainable, offering enjoyable distractions, and so on. In the future we may possess alternative methods giving us—or those who control us—the power to pinpoint an association's neural source and tidily remove it from our minds.

As I have emphasized throughout this book, slight variations in human DNA across our species are complemented by the variety in brains, both structural and functional. The sizes and locations of cortical folds and fissures differ from person to person; some of us process language mostly in the right hemisphere rather than the left, and as we saw in Chapter 12 brain size can vary enormously. These and other individual differences are, as individual differences always have been, a nightmare for influence technicians: the more precise the attempt at mind control, the more personalized it will have to be. Identifying a set of neurons, or neuron clusters, or brain regions which are activated in Peter's brain when he thinks about beating up his partner may enable future mindcraft to change Peter's nasty habits. But what about Paul, and Patrick, and all the other men who abuse their partners? Paul and Patrick may activate the same brain regions as Peter when they contemplate abuse; but they may not. Even if they do, the likelihood that their activity patterns will be similar enough to Peter's, at the level of neurons or groups of neurons, is so small that lessons learned from Peter may be useless when attempting to change Paul.

Of course, as the CIA was well aware, some individuals are so exceptionally influential that targeted mindcraft could be worth the effort. For mass control, however, the filter may have to be coarser: affecting entire brain regions rather than individual cogwebs, for example. Even this crude form of influence could be useful, though, particularly in the induction of artificial emotions which could then be linked to specific stimuli ('A quick jolt to the amygdala, and they're off …'). This combination of direct brain manipulation with the indirect manipulation of brain input could be a useful improvement on present-day techniques, such as those used by extreme political parties (see Chapter 9).

Facing the future

Will human beings in the future be able to resist the depredations of their more predatory peers? Will group entities (States, tribes, communities, or whatever name they take) ever gain so great an understanding of neuroscience and of social psychology that they can manipulate their members from before birth to the time appointed for a painless euthanasia? Can we escape the dystopian visions painted in twentieth-century literature (by Orwell, Huxley, J.G. Ballard, Philip K. Dick, and many others) and cinema (*Metropolis*, *The Matrix*, *Blade Runner*, *Soylent Green*, and so on)? Only time will tell.

Yet I find it hard to be as pessimistic as the dystopians. The brain sciences have plenty still to do before they can claim even to have seriously begun to solve the issues raised by individual differences in *Homo sapiens*. We are extraordinary wonders, we dirty, dysfunctional, difficult human beings, and our mysteries will defeat the best masters of mindcraft for some time yet. There is also much to celebrate in modern Western civilization, where the issues raised by technology may be faced first. The problems are huge, of course, but they are not necessarily insoluble. The question is rather how they will be solved: willingly by us, or under external compulsion.

Human systems, like human brains, tend to dislike extremes and to be self-correcting when extremes are reached. If demand drops, prices fall; if love is lost, new love is sought elsewhere; if someone is hostile to you, your impulse is to match them hate for hate. A political example is the West's overweening selfishness, which has already shaped and nurtured the counter-forces of militant Islam and the antiglobalization movement. Western emphases on economic growth and consumer capitalism, which cram people into mega-cities with little regard for older social bonds, appear to foster rather unhappy citizens. If we could come to understand why people are unhappy, we might be able to change the expectations which contribute to their unhappiness, for example by boosting the prestige of ideas of community and mutual responsibility, and downplaying the delusion that spending money will solve all our problems. On the international stage, we could reform trade tariffs, support a system of international law—with teeth—and generally stop acting like the biggest bully in the playground. Societal ideas—how people and nations view themselves and others—are a large part of the problem; they can also help us to a viable solution. We can challenge ideas such as the dream of mind control before technology gives them even more power; we can also polish our ideals, like justice and freedom, by treating others more justly, thereby removing one of their greatest incentives to loathe the West and everything it claims to stand for. Given that neuroscience is not the only source of technological advances, that loathing could soon be expressed with nuclear bombs or bioweapons. Not a pleasant prospect, and an argument for taking action now.

In the meantime, many great thinkers have come to the conclusion that eventually people will be figured out. Those thinkers have encouraged Western citizens to see themselves as in the front line against an encroaching and ever more powerful State with access to all the resources science can offer. Historically, some scientists have been happy to work with the powerful—and science, with its emphasis on the new, may not always give appropriate weight to the lessons which can already be learned from history. If new techniques for mind control are developed, will they remain out of reach of governments, or will the scientists collaborate in order to help the sick, prevent crime, build better weapons, or whatever? (Remember the fine line between sick and different, discussed in Chapter 4, and the ease with which political opposition can be labelled criminal.) If and when that happens our descendants had better look to their liberties, if they are still capable of doing so. Perhaps we should start looking on their behalf—and, given how science is gathering speed, on our behalf too.

Summary and conclusions

Those sciences whose aim is probing human minds now have direct internal access. They can look inside the living skull, that bone-box balanced on a tower of vertebrae, and map its changes in astonishing detail. Pandora's Box or John Masefield's Box of Delights—whichever it turns out to be, the lid's ajar.[16] In the future, we may come to realize the dream of mind control, at least to the extent of changing individual minds. How long it will take to refine the techniques involved, and whether they will ever be practicable, no one knows.

In a sense it doesn't matter. Technology is not the main problem; it may bring unforeseen obstacles and developments, but its full potential is already implicit in the dream of mind control. That dream may change as it converges with reality, but the change is likely to be a reduction in scope, as we learn that certain things are just not possible. Already the dream itself is of total domination, of a power capable of ensuring that no 'erroneous thought should exist anywhere in the world, however secret and powerless it may be'.[17] How could such an overwhelming concept be enhanced still further?

What matters, as always, is not the technology but what we do with it—and that depends on what ideas we have, what beliefs are commonly acceptable in our environment, and who defines what is erroneous. If we still react to difference with fear and hostility, if we give up freedom for security and accept that States control and citizens consume, then mindcraft techniques will be applied to society's outcasts. If the more secure citizens do not protest at that point, then those administering mind control will seek to spread its tendrils into wider society.

Where should we look? Are there precautions we can take to increase the chances that we and our children, in all our awkward individuality, will make it through the twenty-first century with our freedom to think intact? The next chapter will consider what defences we can raise as individuals and citizens.

Chapter 15: Taking a stand

Our remedies oft in ourselves do lie,
Which we ascribe to heaven

William Shakespeare, *All's Well That Ends Well*

Influence attempts, from the mildest persuasion to the most coercive brainwashing, are as much a part of human existence as light and decay. To live with each other we have to change each other. From socializing children to punishing criminals, humans and their cultures provide a myriad inescapable sources of influence: ideas which alter the cogwebs spun in skulls. Some are harmless, some irritating, some beneficial. Some, gloriously inspiring, have driven the creation of mesmerizing wonders, from the music of Bach to the theory of general relativity. Some, like the dream of mind control, can be lethally malign.

In this chapter we shall look at ways of drawing the fangs of this dream and others like it. We shall begin by considering how individuals can bolster their resistance to brainwashing techniques, before moving on to ask how societies can protect themselves and their citizens.

Incessant influence

Even if we wished to avoid all influence attempts, we simply do not have the cognitive resources to detect and counteract each and every one. It was estimated several years ago that 'the average American is now exposed to 254 different commercial messages in a day';[1] the figure is still rising, and that is only advertising. Add in the news, the Internet, books and magazines, friends and family, and the messages, explicit and implicit, put across in hours of television programmes, and we begin to grasp the quantities of information bombarding our brains—information directed at us with the aim of changing our minds. To reduce the bombardment to a level where we could monitor individual influence attempts, we would first have to achieve a level of social withdrawal (no human contact, no computer, TV, radio, or printed media) impossible for all but the most determined seekers of solitude.

Very few human beings choose to live entirely alone. For the majority, most influence attempts are at the lower end of the spectrum, requiring little energy to generate them; they are so mild—or so obvious—that only now and then do they seem worth challenging. More often we go with the flow, convinced that we haven't the time, energy, or motive to do otherwise. This indifference is both beneficial and problematic for influence technicians. It is useful for those who want to change minds without being seen to do so, to use the slow drip-drip of repetition to reinforce implicit assumptions ('consumerism is good', 'you are what you own', and so on). It is problematic when the aim is to distinguish one message from all the others, to trigger the target's ability to monitor and reflect so that the message is absorbed, considered, and incorporated into the target's cognitive landscape. In advertising, for instance, a single advert may combine these two approaches: the glitzy surface grabs attention (using a strong narrative, humour, distinctive music or colours, etc.), while the deeper structure strengthens societal beliefs ('woman at home' promotes traditional 'family values'; 'man at the office' emphasizes the importance of paid employment; and so on). Even if the superficial grab does not succeed, the deeper, usually conservative message(s) will be reinforced.

Indifference, ignorance, and being busy with other things protects us from many attempts to change our minds. In addition, influence technicians do not operate in a societal vacuum. The principle of the division of labour, whose importance to capitalist societies was described by Adam Smith over two hundred years ago in *The Wealth of Nations*, has led us to devolve much of our influence-monitoring to specialists. We expect journalists to flag up instances of government manipulation; we expect television news to report wrongdoing by newspaper editors (and vice versa); we have agencies tasked with regulating what we see on television; and so on. The expectations we have of our various specialists constitute the trust we place in them, and as long as we continue to trust them we feel no need to duplicate their efforts at a personal level.[2]

In many cases, however, influence attempts can dodge both the Scylla of specialists and the Charybdis of busy or indifferent brains. Some use stealth to get past our defences; others use force. In the future, as we saw in the last chapter, technology may provide an additional weapon of influence: direct interaction with a target brain. Of course, we may not wish to resist every form of mindcraft. No one is so perfect that they cannot benefit from new ideas, and not all influence technicians mean (or cause) us harm. But some do. How, then, can we protect ourselves?

Meme vaccines

Nam et ipsa scientia potestas est
[For knowledge itself is power]

Francis Bacon, *Religious Meditations*, 'Of Heresies'

One way of spiking the influence technicians' guns is to take preventative measures. If Jane, a devout Christian, believes that certain rock songs contain messages from Satan, her wish to avoid being influenced by the Prince of Darkness may lead her to switch off her radio when the songs are being played, destroy recordings of them, or even campaign for a ban on playing them in public. Alternatively, she may listen to the rock songs and analyse them closely, on the grounds that it is better to know the Enemy. She may pay more attention to her religious rituals, in the hope that devout observance will earn her God's favour and protection. She may seek out others with similar views who may have tips on how to guard against evil influences (in rock songs or anywhere else). She may even form her own Christian rock band.

In other words, Jane can take various steps to minimize what she perceives as a malevolent weapon of influence. She can avoid situations in which she may be subject to influence; this involves making an intertemporal contract (see Chapter 11) with her future selves to treat 'avoiding rock songs' as an important goal. She can seek out information to enrich the relevant areas of her cognitive landscape, turning herself into a highly motivated expert skilled in detecting such influence attempts. Or she can increase her commitment to beliefs which she knows are inconsistent with the message purveyed by the influence attempt. By changing her own behaviour, by seeking out new ideas or social support for beliefs she holds already, Jane is able to use her knowledge-based predictions about Satan's methods to prevent the Evil One from influencing her. She is fighting ideas with ideas, using certain beliefs to immunize her brain (and possibly the brains of vulnerable others) against potentially invasive memes she views as harmful.

If Jane is strongly motivated to maintain her Christian faith and ward off evil, her 'evil-related' and 'faith-related' cogwebs will be linked to powerful emotions which trigger automatic responses to certain stimuli. Her strong beliefs will control much of her behaviour, just as the thoughts and actions of someone suffering from anorexia revolve around food. New ideas, especially contradictory ones, will have difficulty taking root in this hostile landscape, where the energy they need to strengthen is continually being siphoned off by strong established cogwebs which provide a 'bigotry defence'. Despite her fears, Jane is probably safe from rock songs; her concern may well be more for other people than herself. It would take a mindcraft adept—or a really determined effort on Satan's part—to break the faith which protects her from influence attempts when they occur. As we saw in the case of Bishop Hans Barker, strong beliefs often prove a good defence against brainwashing.

Not all of us, however, are as vigorous as Jane in our beliefs. We cannot use the bigotry defence—but that does not bar us from taking other measures. Like Jane, we can predict our own and other people's behaviour. That means we can use knowledge, and/or social support, to reduce the impact of influence attempts before they happen, or to protect ourselves against them when they do. If Mary knows from bitter experience that after a few drinks her self-control evaporates, her desire to avoid the likely (disastrous) consequences may lead her to stop drinking alcohol. She predicts her behaviour in a certain situation and changes herself so as to avoid that type of situation, the converse of the 'choose to lose' behaviour discussed in Chapter 9. She has managed to link the social cues which previously triggered drinking behaviour to a new cogweb, one calling up memories of past embarrassments to implement a stop-and-think reaction. Similarly, recognizing the possibility that mindcraft exists is the first step to predicting your likely response, and changing your brain and behaviour accordingly.

Stop-and-think: the influence antidote

Many of the ways we resist influence attempts involve the triggering of stop-and-think (see Chapter 10). Critical thinking, scepticism, and humour are all examples of stop-and-think reactions. Critical thinking and scepticism analyse the message, checking the logic of its arguments, the use of emotive language, the accuracy of factual statements. They also query the authority and motive of the message's source. Humour also challenges authority, albeit by emphasizing emotion rather than argument.

Stop-and-think reactions depend on our 'situatedness', on the fact that, throughout our lives, each of us is enmeshed in the context of our memories and simultaneously immersed in ongoing experience of what George Steiner calls 'the concrete, literal, actual, daily world'.[3] How these two elements blend together over time varies. In a cinema, if the film is in any way interesting, you are likely to be absorbed in the action, with your visual cortex going full throttle and stimulation taking precedence over reflection. On a hot Friday afternoon in the office, stuck in a boring meeting, you may find the balance tipping the other way as you drift into daydream. If there is not enough input to keep your brain occupied, it will revert to its own internal resources of memory and reflection. If your memories are happy, well and good, but if you are in an uncertain and unpleasant situation, like a prison cell, reflecting on your miseries will hardly assist your morale. One solution is to boost the levels of incoming signals. Brains do this automatically, which is why busy people don't notice a clock ticking, except perhaps when they are stuck in a boring meeting. But finding something interesting in your environment can also be an explicit strategy.

In his book *Brainwashing*, Edward Hunter relates how American prisoners of war in Korea used all these methods to resist the Communist brainwashers. Some prisoners, isolated for months and deprived of any means of keeping themselves occupied, made up and memorized poems—often humorous—about their circumstances, analysing why they were being treated in this way and what their captors hoped to achieve. Some used their imagination to dream up plausible lies to tell their interrogators, making a game of this high-risk strategy of fooling the enemy without getting caught doing so, boosting their own confidence and clarity of purpose every time a falsehood was believed. Some even studied the aeronautics of passing flies in an attempt to stave off boredom.

Recognition and resistance

How likely is it that the society of the future will incorporate the science of
control into the politics of governing? The answer, we think, will depend
heavily on choices people make now
                                    Scheflin and Opton, *The Mind Manipulators*

Force, stealth, and technology are three ways in which an influence technician may try to change minds. For the target, the first challenge is to recognize that an attempt which is at least potentially harmful to the target's interests is being made; this triggers enough reactance to induce some kind of stop-and-think reaction. For techniques which use force, and for current technologies, recognition is not usually a problem. For stealthy methods, access to protective ideas—such as strongly held alternative beliefs, sceptical, critical attitudes, or past experience of similar influence attempts—can install appropriate triggers in the target's brain, as described above. However, our ability to detect deceit is far from perfect.[4] Particularly problematic are influence attempts which occur gradually over a long period, as in the example of domestic abuse discussed in Chapter 5; the influence attempt may be hard to recognize as such, especially if the victim is strongly motivated not to acknowledge it. We can, however, boost our own immunity in various ways: by publicizing and punishing instances of deceitful influence; undergoing training in critical thinking; participating in public debates; or learning from other people's experience. By making sure that we are clear about our own beliefs, we reduce the chances that they can be modified with or without our knowledge.

The lesson of Chapter 11 was that there is nothing, even in the doctrine of scientific determinism, which prevents us from going out and undertaking any or all of these preventative measures once the thought of doing so has occurred to us. We are agents, not passive recipients, and we can certainly change our brains, if we prefer that to having them changed by other people. We can also learn more about our own behaviour, thereby improving our skill at self-determination. Understanding our susceptibility to social factors, the lure of ingroup/ outgroup classifications, the stereotype-enhancing effects of stress, and so on, may make us more aware of how influence affects us.

Once recognition has been triggered, the second challenge is to resist the influence attempt. Stealthy mindcraft, which depends for its success on being covert, can not only fail but also seriously backfire if it is recognized. Jane, warily perusing a new rock album, might be told by a friend not to worry, since investigation has shown the suspect songs to be devoid of Satanic messages. Depending on her opinion of her friend, she may simply accept this. If she stops to think, however, she may decide her friend is just trying to reassure her, and ask for the source of the news, or who carried out the investigation. If the authority is legitimate (e.g. Jane's local priest), the influence attempt may still ultimately prove successful. But if the source turns out to be, say, a scientist noted for his atheistic views, Jane will not merely reject the message: her discounting of the source means she may well end up *more* convinced of the perils of rock music.

As discussed earlier, many classic brainwashing situations involve coercion or even outright torture. Force, which does not attempt to avoid being recognized, provokes reactance and resistance, which must then be overcome. A sufficiently motivated victim may be able to resist even torture, whether by psychologically withdrawing from the situation (dissociation) or by clinging to one powerful thought or image (like religious martyrs who meditate on God to withstand pain). An alternative tactic may be short-term compliance, as shown by American prisoners of war in Korea who apparently converted to Communism, only to resume their former attitudes once released. Indeed, distinguishing compliance from conversion has often been a problem for ideologues who use coercive methods.

In the previous chapter I speculated on the potential of new technology to make the dream of mind control come true. However, technology can often be used in more than one way; and not all technology's users or creators hunger to dominate others. Many advances in the human technology of conflict follow the pattern, commonly found in evolution, of an arms race in which new weapons (or defences) developed by one side are rapidly matched by new defences (or weapons) produced by the other. Mindcraft, at base a conflict between targets and aggressors, may continue this tradition. Perhaps both sides will continue to compete until resources run out, or perhaps political circumstances will change as human beings grow out of the brainwashing dream (we are, after all, laboriously outgrowing other fantasies, like the ideas of racial superiority used to justify institutions of slavery). In the meantime, the field of brain defence may produce a fine crop of wonders, from anti-indoctrination drugs to 'EM shields' to protect our brains from electromagnetic interference.

Thought warp

We now move from self-protection to the related issue of how to defuse the effects of brainwashing in others. Like viruses, ideas often come in several strains of varying potency. The most powerful strains—certain ethereal ideas—are so dangerous that they can come to dominate, or even destroy, the infected brain. Like Ebola, they can inflict tremendous suffering on their victims—both the infected themselves and the innocents they harm. Unlike most viruses, ethereal ideas may be welcomed by their targets, who may fiercely resist attempts to purge the infection. Many of the more hostile reactions to cults underestimate the degree to which they are actually fulfilling their members' needs, and thereby attracting genuine, consensual commitment.

A person infected with an ethereal idea becomes, in the extreme case, that most awe-inspiring of human deformities, the single-issue fanatic. The dominant cogweb drains energy from competing beliefs, gradually shutting down the person's horizons. The cognitive landscape warps and its scope narrows. Everything becomes interpreted relative to the dominant idea, producing a 'dark contracted Personallity'.[5] A teenage girl with anorexia, for example, believes that it's good to be thin. Many of us in the modern West hold this belief, with varying degrees of conviction. The anorexic, however, holds it so strongly that the effort to control her own body can become more important than health, or even life, leading to a focus on food and food control which, over time, becomes automatized from effortful obsession to a habit so ingrained that it becomes virtually constitutive of personality. To say that she thinks about food almost all the time is to understate the centrality of food control to the mind of someone with chronic anorexia. As with some personality disorders, it becomes increasingly hard to imagine what the person would be like without the problem.

One of the most poisonous ethereal ideas in human history is the concept of an absolute authority which overrides all other moral or legal considerations. Whether the authority cited is God or The Party, Science or Truth or The State, this particular ethereal idea has been used, and is still being used today, to justify some truly disgusting atrocities. By treating human beings as means rather than ends in their own right, it places human life, and quality of life, below some abstract goal. Whether or not it is associated with an explicitly totalitarian regime, it is a clear example of totalist thinking.

Just as someone infected with HIV may succumb to a normally non-lethal pneumonia, so ethereal ideas are particularly dangerous in combination. Authority by itself is an idea we use all the time without ill effects. Strengthen it to absolute authority, however, and put it together with some totalitarian vision of a better world, and the result can be deadly: an individual who believes he or she has a duty to make the vision real, who thinks about virtually nothing else, and whose vision-related motives outweigh even self-protective instincts. And to hell (for religious authority, literally) with anyone who gets in the way. This, at best, is the noisy, infuriating extremist who cannot be reasoned with, who says we should kill a scientist to save a puppy, kill a writer to defend our faith, or kill millions to bring about a new world order. At worst, it is the crusader, the militant, the suicide bomber, who does not dissipate his fury and frustration in noise, but uses it as fuel for terrorist violence.

How can we reduce the threat from these distorted minds? There is no sound-bite answer, because ethereal ideas vary in their lethality and draw their life-blood from a variety of sources. But that does not mean we are helpless. Ethereal ideas gain their power partly from their abstract, unchallengeable simplicity, partly because they fit with other beliefs already present, and partly by being linked to strong emotions. To defuse them (at least until technology gives us more direct methods of brain change), we can either challenge them directly, try to reduce the associated beliefs which lend them support or the emotions which give them force, or attempt to prevent them from taking hold in the first place.

Breaking the stranglehold

Let us imagine a young man, Sam, who is possessed of the notion that killing members of a neighbouring tribe is the best way to achieve freedom for his people. Sam is devoted to freedom and prepared to die for it; the struggle between the two communities has been a long and bitter one. We therefore go to Sam (or, if we are careful, send representatives) and talk to him about his ideas. We listen while he lays out his position, and then we point out some of its difficulties. What exactly does he mean by freedom? How many people does he expect to have to kill, and is this practical? Does he not realize that murder only makes the other tribe more stubborn and more oppressive, locking both sides into a cycle of violence? Does he not think that rational negotiation would be better—and may we offer ourselves as mediators? Whether Sam listens politely, and then ignores us, or expresses his opinion more directly, will probably depend on his estimation of our importance. What he is least likely to do is to say, 'Well, hey, you're right, I never thought of that; you'd better hurry along to the chaps next door with an apology on my behalf, and we'll open negotiations right away.'

Of course, we are not members of Sam's ingroup. We are certainly not the leaders who planned the campaign of violence in which Sam participates. So let us imagine that somehow we can persuade one of these leaders, Mr X, a highly influential thinker whom Sam adores, to see the error of his ways, and say so to Sam. Will Sam then repent, and turn away from violence?

Probably not. The beliefs which have made Sam a killer are ethereal ideas, grounded in totalist thinking. To put them across in the first place Mr X will have emphasized their simplicity and their absolute authority, as devolved through him. He cannot now appear to change his mind without completely undermining that authority, forcing Sam to choose between abandoning his cherished beliefs, into which he has poured so much effort and energy, and deciding that Mr X has gone soft, gone mad, or turned traitor. Sam may well have too much invested in his principles to ditch them for real-life complexity, change, and imperfection. These may even be the reasons he took up the principles; one of the joys of ethereal ideas is their apparent explanatory power, their capacity to make everything look simple. Dividing the world into clearly-marked 'us' and 'them' groups puts much less strain on one's cognitive resources than acknowledging the details of human difference.

Direct challenge, whether by outgroup or ingroup members, may not be the best way to defuse ethereal ideas. Like force, it runs straight up against the problem of reactance. More subtle work, over longer time periods, is required. One approach is to treat Sam's ethereal ideas as a network of interlocking cogwebs, in which certain core principles gain their strength in part from being supported by other beliefs. It may be possible to weaken these supports. Sam may simply not have met many members of the enemy tribe, in which case publicizing their humanity may be useful. Channelling his aggression into less damaging outlets may also help (a popular technique is known in Britain as 'football'). Educational and political initiatives may be able to open up his cognitive horizons, presenting alternatives to his current, constricted world and giving him incentives to follow a more peaceable course of action.

This slow chipping away is unlikely to succeed on its own. To work, it needs assistance from another approach: trying to reduce the emotions which give Sam's ethereal ideas their force. This is probably the most unpopular method because it is the hardest. It requires open public debate to analyse the problems (which means genuinely listening both to Sam and his enemies), followed by detailed, often long-term, and undoubtedly expensive political interventions to address the issues. People do not wake up one morning and think 'Right, today I'm going to be a bloody-minded bigot.' They adopt ethereal ideas because they feel driven to do so, because forces beyond their control provoke stresses and strong emotions which demand a simplistic response. The ideas are available, marketed, and seized on as a panacea ('if only we can gain our freedom, everything will be all right'). Sam wants a better life for himself and for his children, wants it so much that he's prepared to fight for it, precisely because his current life is so abysmal. Improving it—reining back the oppressive neighbouring tribe, insisting that Sam's rights should be respected, installing (and accepting the results of) democratic elections and independent media, reforming land rights, and generally increasing Sam's individual freedoms—is far more likely to weaken his convictions than attempting to bully or persuade him out of them.

What about prevention? One way of reducing the influence of ethereal ideas is to provide plenty of competition and widespread public debate. A common feature of brainwashing situations, from terrorist training camps to cults to domestic abuse, is not simply that they instil a (usually small) number of strongly held beliefs, but the narrowing of horizons which accompanies the process. In Chapter 8 we saw that having more cogwebs available tends to weaken the strength of any single cogweb. By encouraging the dispersal and debate of new ideas; by providing education, and access to independent media, for every citizen; by teaching history, critical thinking, and social psychology in ways which are not merely a deluge of facts; by informing ourselves about other cultures; by encouraging satire and comment and criticism; in these and many other ways we can provide a richer cognitive environment which may help to weaken the attraction of totalist schemes.

So far the discussion has been framed in terms of how individuals can resist malign ideas and those who peddle them. I have emphasized that we can do a great deal to protect ourselves. To say that some thought or behaviour is emotional does not mean that it is uncontrollable; if, as argued in Chapter 9, human cognition is suffused with emotion, the reverse is also true. We can change both our motivations and the goals we are motivated to pursue.

Large-scale resistance: from individuals to societies

Individualism has its limits. Sometimes, for example, individuals can adopt and cling to beliefs which are bad for them, but which they are unable to shake off alone. For them, the beliefs have positive value (their cogwebs are linked to positive emotions, such as a sense of fellowship or contentment). In other words, the emotion associated with a belief need not reflect its holder's long-term interests. An example already mentioned is anorexia. A teenager with anorexia may view her (less often his) belief in thinness as positive; onlookers see it as positively dangerous. Insofar as people with anorexia tend to die young, suffer severe health problems, and lead highly restricted, often unhappy lives, the onlookers are right. The anorexic, whatever she may say, is wrong; her belief is bad for her. This is part of what we say when we describe anorexia as a mental illness: people with anorexia are no longer able to pursue their own objective interests (health, freedoms, happiness, etc.) because subjective interests (thinness and food control) so dominate the cognitive landscape that these goals now hold the keys to thought and behaviour.

In other words, as we saw in Chapter 4, labelling a person as mentally ill is partly a social judgement. When it comes to the crunch, the objective majority view of what is good or bad for people dominates over the individual's subjective perception of what is good or bad for him or her. Most of the time these two judgements (of objective and subjective interests, respectively) coincide. We vote for happiness, freedom, or self-fulfilment, and expect our neighbours to do the same.

Relativism

He added that his ancestors the Scythians were the only honest people there had ever been on the earth, that admittedly they had often eaten men, but that that did not prevent their nation from being held in great respect

Voltaire, *Zadig*

But who is to say that the majority view is right? This is the relativist argument that we cannot compare cultures, that what is good for Peter may be bad for Paul, and that no society of Patricks looking on can say that Paul is right and Peter wrong. Relativism has been widely applied to morality in order to undermine the idea of absolute (often religious) moral authority. It has also been extended to make the claim of moral incommensurability. That is, if Culture A traditionally roasts unwanted babies on a Saturday night, Culture B's objections should be regarded as valid for B's members but not for A's, and in a multicultural society where Cultures A and B live side by side B-ite squeamishness must not infringe on A-ites' traditions.[6] Clearly, if relativism is correct, the anorexic's goal of thinness is just as valid as her neighbours' desire that she should stay alive, so they have no right to force their point of view upon her.

Relativism is a doctrine that at first sight seems entirely reasonable: respecting other people's opinions is an entirely laudable goal. But relativism is not the way to achieve it. Indeed, some of its consequences are so pernicious that every would-be brainwasher should embrace it wholeheartedly. Applied in the arena of international politics, it underpinned the West's insistence that it should stand by while nations like North Korea, Uganda, and the Congo trod their various paths towards perdition, abusing, torturing, and in some cases brainwashing their subjects (think of the fearsome child soldiers of the Lord's Resistance Army in Uganda, for example).

Applied to individuals with anorexia or other mental problems, relativism leads to a situation, as described above, where personal choice must be respected even when the choices made are clearly harmful. But in practice we tend to feel that this is wrong, that we have a moral obligation to intervene. We resolve this dilemma, in effect, by exempting certain individuals from the claim that relativists promote, that every point of view has its own validity. This is done by defining them as mentally ill and stripping them of all personal responsibility; if they cannot make their own decisions then it is morally acceptable for others to take control of them. As we saw in Chapter 4, this is an argument used to justify brainwashing: 'You are sick, you don't know your own mind, so we must tell you what to think.' This logic is extremely dubious: someone with mental illness may make bad choices in one area of their life, but that does not mean they are incapable of making *any* choices. It is also very dangerous, as it encourages coercive approaches to mental illness. Finally, it excludes the mentally ill from society, making them an outgroup, with all the negative consequences, not least for their mental and physical health, which that entails.

Unpleasant consequences are not the only problems with the relativist argument. As the political theorist Steven Lukes points out, there are also more theoretical objections to it. One is that it rests upon

a thoroughly misconceived and indeed inapplicable notion of culture [...]
Cultures are never (to repeat [Isaiah] Berlin's felicitous phrase) 'windowless
boxes'. They are always open systems, sites of contestation and heterogeneity,
of hybridization and cross-fertilization, whose boundaries are inevitably
indeterminate. One should never forget that the simplifying perception of the
internal coherence and distinctness of cultures from one another is invariably
perpetrated by interested parties ...

Lukes, *Liberals and Cannibals*, pp. 19–20

People who seek to differentiate cultures have their own agenda in doing so. Moreover, relativism 'cannot account for the practice of moral criticism within cultures and across them'.[7] And saying 'all cultures are equal' does not solve the problems of moral conflict between them (unless one adds 'but some are more equal than others'). We are still left with miserable B-ites forced to put up with the smell of barbecued infants.

Relativism underestimates the importance of the truism that Cultures A and B are both made up of humans. Humans can behave in an extraordinary number of ways, but that does not mean that the mind's fundamental forces differ in Texas and Tehran. Individuals, of course, may differ in how they rank basic goals, but the extent of agreement on what those goals are is likely to be considerable. John Milton's *Areopagitica* defended the freedom to publish, while Thomas Hobbes, shaken by the English Civil Wars, favoured security over liberty in *Leviathan*— but both writers held both values dearly. Human brains and bodies have a general similarity in both construction and performance, which is why we can translate languages or (to take the example used in Chapter 9) understand descriptions of fear by both Aeschylus and Poe. Humans all over the world value pleasure, happiness, and freedom, and dislike pain, misery, and control by others. They generally treat relatives better than strangers, smile at their friends, and grieve for their dead. Murder, torture, and mutilation are usually forbidden except under carefully controlled conditions (e.g. rituals), and most victims are not members of the ingroup. Like taboos, widely held societal goals such as freedom and happiness have developed over centuries of human beings living together. The ideas have adapted to the social environment—to what works for people—or they have died out. They may therefore be expected to reflect quite accurately what most people actually want.

Note my use of qualifiers: 'most people', 'usually'. Individual differences are relevant because different people will have different 'value profiles' (like Milton and Hobbes). And even if two individuals' profiles are similar there may still be a clash of values between them, for example if both esteem the rights to life and property, but one must steal from the other in order to live. At the level of individuals the ideas of values such as freedom are abstracted from particular examples: the freedom to make a living, to visit friends, to change the world in various ways. As one moves from individuals to groups, from families to neighbourhoods to nations, the ideas become more abstract, more ethereal. They lose specificity and definition, but they can still be related back to individual (sometimes strongly emotive) experiences, and it is these which give ethereal ideas their power to recruit adherents.

As discussed in Chapter 9, human beings are inherently evaluative creatures. An individual asked to value, as good or bad, a particular concept (e.g. 'living free from torture', 'being cheated') will generally find the task unproblematic. However, the process of abstracting across all the human beings in a group to generate an ethereal idea ignores so many individual differences that an unfortunate consequence arises: ethereal ideas cannot simply be assessed as good or bad. (Thought control is good when you're trying to educate a child and not so good when you've just come off worse from a sales call.) Rather than becoming entangled in the fruitless attempt to impose evaluative order on the amoeboid shapelessness of ethereal ideas, an alternative strategy is to try and minimize, not the spread of ethereal ideas themselves, but their harmful effects. How are we to achieve this? By using the methods that humans have always used—the methods of politics.

Social cohesion

No man is an island, entire of itself
        Donne, *Devotions upon Emergent Occasions*, 'XVII Meditation'

Whatever their cultural background, the overwhelming majority of human beings spend their earliest years being socialized. They learn what to expect from other people, what to do and what not to do, who can be classed as 'us' and who as 'them'. One important effect of socialization is to build up strong inhibitory cogwebs related to socially unacceptable behaviours. For example, as William Miller observes: 'Any parent knows that one- and two-year-olds show no disgust over excrement and bodily emissions and can remain blissfully immune to the disgust their parents are so eager to instill in them'.[8] Miller argues that 'To feel disgust is human and humanizing'; nevertheless, 'actual disgust needs developmental elbow room'. The same is true of other social taboos, such as murder, torture, and other serious forms of harm.

In most people, the cogwebs formed by early socialization are a powerful barrier to doing serious harm.[9] They provide a threshold which can only be overcome by extremely strong emotions. However, as we saw in Chapter 2, membership of a group, particularly a strongly cohesive group (such as the Manson Family), can weaken the inhibitory constraints and provide additional emotional energy to breach the barriers. The autonomy of individual members is reduced as they increasingly operate in what Stanley Milgram called the agentic state (see Chapter 4). To reduce the chances that this will happen, inhibitory cogwebs need to be strengthened and group cohesion weakened. One method is to reduce the costs a group member incurs by leaving the group, which can range from inconvenience through ostracism to death threats, by insisting that all groups operate within a legal framework which is supportive of individual human rights. Another is to ensure that group members are also members of other groups, for example in mainstream education or in the workplace, which expose them to alternative points of view. The worst option, as the US government discovered at Jonestown—and then learned all over again at Waco, Texas—is to insist on confronting and bullying the group; turning yourself into an obviously powerful enemy is an excellent way to boost a group's cohesion.

Another problem with attacking groups directly is the risk of throwing the baby out with the bathwater. Not all ethereal ideas are poisonous. Sometimes they can benefit society if they can gain sufficient recognition. What is required is to minimize the harmful consequences while still leaving room for beneficial ideas to flourish. The relativist argument discussed above raises an important point: all too often groups are oppressed by other groups. But the way to redress these injustices is not to give certain rights to certain groups (protecting A's right to roast babies from B's disapproval), as this leads inevitably to further injustices against both ingroup and outgroup members, as well as a proliferation of groups competing for privileges. If simply being an A-ite allows you to get away with murder or other abuses, non-members will want to form groups of their own, if only for protection. Meanwhile, as A-ites see their position of privilege eroded, they will react defensively, increasing the cohesion of their own group and viewing members of other groups in more negative and stereotypical terms. So it goes. As more groups compete for limited resources, and totalist thinking becomes more and more entrenched, the distrust between groups is likely to get worse, not better.

The political philosopher Brian Barry has cogently shown, in his critique of multiculturalism, *Culture and Equality*, that giving incentives to group membership (a move hardly likely to reduce group cohesion) is not the best way to stop the kinds of group-perpetrated abuses described in this book. Instead we should be trying to reduce the grip of totalist thinking by strengthening individuals' basic rights so that no group has special privileges.[10] We should be ensuring that groups are kept subordinate to law, so that no group doctrine can ignore an individual's free choice, whether that individual is a group member or not. We should be demanding that any such doctrine is open to free debate, that every citizen's vote counts equally, that the costs of leaving a group are not exorbitant, and that no group is allowed to impose its will on those who have not given—and maintained—informed consent. Finally, because we know that we can change ourselves and others by changing beliefs, and because we know that ideas are best fought with other ideas, we should be publicly debating, teaching, and celebrating the virtues of antitotalitarian ideologies, as well as warning against those which are demonstrably malign. We should be extolling freedom and the power of human agency, the notion that humans are ends in themselves and never just means, the value of learning to think and analyse information effectively, and the irreducible, irrepressible complexity of both human experience and the ideas we value. Freedom, Agency, Ends-not-means, Thinking, and Complexity. Let us for convenience, and in memory of the minds-as-diamonds metaphor which I used to criticize Cartesian dualism, rearrange some letters and call this the FACET approach. To see why such an approach defends against the terrors of brainwashing, we need to remember the lesson of Chapter 1, that brainwashing begins with totalist thinking.

Changing our politics

Freedom has a thousand charms to show,
That slaves, howe'er contented, never know

William Cowper, *Table Talk*

We are back, for one last time, to Robert Lifton's statement of the eight themes which characterize totalitarian ideologies: milieu control, mystical manipulation, the demand for purity, the cult of confession, sacred science, loading the language, the primacy of doctrine over person, and the dispensing of existence (see Table 1, p. 17). Let us look at each of these in turn to see how a FACET approach may be able to help us.

Milieu control

FACET emphasizes not only individual over group rights, but individual agency. By encouraging the development of critical thinking, and by viewing cultures, like other groups, as heterogeneous and porous rather than closed and cohesive, it tends to weaken rather than strengthen group cohesion, thereby reducing the likelihood that groups are able to exercise milieu control. Encouraging people to see themselves as agents with the freedom and power to change their lives also makes them more likely to challenge the kind of totalist thinking that views them not as ends, but as means to an end, and to challenge infringements of their personal freedom.

Mystical manipulation

Again, a strengthened sense of freedom is helpful here. It is hard for a brain-washer to evoke strong emotions when the potential victims quickly respond with vigorous reactance, harder still to deceive them into thinking that those emotions are spontaneous, as mystical manipulation requires. Critical thinking skills are also useful, as they allow people to understand their own beliefs and motivations better, and therefore to know which are theirs and which derived from the brainwasher. Remember the analogy of brains as gardens in Chapter 12, where well-kept gardens are harder to redesign. If a brain is clear about what it does and doesn't believe, imposing new ideas is much more difficult.

The demand for purity

FACET celebrates complexity as a virtue, not a vice, or at the very least accepts it as a fact of nature. Purity is fine if your business is diamonds, but there is no such thing as a pure human being, an ideal citizen, a perfect group member. Human beings are simply too complicated, too changeable, to fit—or stay put—in the simplifying categories that totalists devise. This makes a nonsense of the demand for purity, which thinks of categories like ingroup and outgroup as having some absolute reality. They have no such force; they are concepts, not facts. So how, as the quest for purity demands, can they possibly justify the destruction of any human life? The demand for purity hungers for simple, ethereal ideas. FACET reminds us of the dangers of oversimplifying.

The cult of confession

By acknowledging human complexity, FACET acknowledges the depths and differences of individual personalities. It also celebrates individual freedoms— including the freedom not to reveal your every thought if you so choose. By emphasizing agency and critical thinking skills, it also empowers citizens to see through, and challenge, the totalist dislike of private, independent minds which lies behind the cult of confession.

Sacred science

FACET is pragmatic, guided by trial-and-error. Like science, it tests itself against what works, using reality to shape its principles on a case-by-case basis. Totalitarian thinking, by contrast, makes reality subservient to principle, case-by-case pragmatics subservient to absolute authority, and the individual subservient to the group. Relativism, insofar as it argues that cultural differences trump basic similarities, relies on totalist ideas like the power of the group. That is, it makes the assumption, challenged by Steven Lukes, that 'cultures' are homogeneous and highly cohesive groups. They are not, as comparing them with genuinely cohesive groups like the Manson Family makes clear.

Totalitarians are extremely fond of absolutes. Authority, for example, must be absolute if it is to be valid. Finding one culture which practises infanticide is fatal to the claim that these practices are morally wrong (any time, any place), because that claim is based on some moral authority which is being held to apply across all humanity ('murder is wrong because our deity said so'—or Nature, Reason, or sometimes even Science). Without some such universal moral authority, totalist thinkers argue, we have no reason to prefer one cultural claim over another. But is this correct?

Not necessarily. If absolute authority can no longer be relied on, we may be able to replace its lawlike purity with a messier, more pragmatic statistical approach. Statistical predictions can be as—or more—useful than those derived from equations. Mathematical models are braced with the strength of logic; the truths they vouch for are true in every possible circumstance once the model's basic axioms have been accepted. In complex situations, however, they cannot adequately model all the variables. A statistical 'law' which says that chronic smoking makes people sick is true in that people who smoke for years are far more likely to fall ill than people who don't smoke. The observation that some people smoke for years and don't get ill does not imply that smoking doesn't cause illness. It just means that susceptibility to disease is lower in a few lucky individuals.

As for mathematics, so for morals. Some moral principles do appear to be held very widely in human societies. The fact that the occasional psychopath enjoys a bout of serial killing, or rapes his daughter, does not invalidate the observation that people do not usually approve of murder or incest. In other words, we need not demand absolute purity, accuracy in every single instance, for the observation to be useful. The similarity of basic human needs means that what works for most of us may well work for you (and vice versa). Beliefs can therefore be assessed (whatever their culture of origin) according to whether or not they harm either the individuals who hold them or other people; and this is in practice what we tend to do.

Loading the language

By valuing critical thinking FACET helps citizens to become more aware of how influence technicians manipulate language. By emphasizing freedom and agency, it gives them the confidence to challenge simplistic interpretations and totalist ideas, and thereby makes thought control much harder.

The primacy of doctrine over person

FACET encourages citizens to practise what they please, as long as they observe certain restrictions. It defines those restrictions as minimally as possible, aiming to shrink the sphere of State (or other group) control and maximize individual (*not* group) freedoms. FACET does not claim that we are all the same; it merely says we should be treated the same way (as citizens) irrespective of which groups we happen to belong to. It is therefore profoundly opposed to any doctrine which claims that ideas or the groups which hold them should take priority over unwilling human beings. Brainwashing, which imposes ideas, whether by force, technology, or stealth, would never be condoned by a FACET approach.

By insisting that ideals take second place to actual individual human experience, FACET makes ideas subservient to reality. It therefore mirrors the individual strategy most likely to ensure a brain's survival: accurate monitoring of, and receptivity to, the environment, balanced by well-defined but flexible cogwebs. Totalist thinking, which reverses the ranking to exalt ethereal ideas, is like a malfunctioning brain, whose increasing disregard of the external world is often fatal. Even in the cushioned West, supposedly the home of liberal democracy, we have seen entire societies become obsessed by totalitarian thinking, with catastrophic results. FACET, being complex and pragmatic, is admittedly harder to implement than totalitarian schemes. But it is far better for us, not least because it more accurately reflects the way the world is.[11]

The dispensing of existence

As I have already noted, people who think of themselves as free are less likely to submit to an authoritarian approach. If they do not accept the notion that the end justifies the means, and if they have the skills to spot the holes in totalist arguments, they are less likely to hand over power in the first place. Even the most brutal dictator needs popular support to achieve the level of control that leads to mass executions. Applying FACET would not remove that support altogether, but it would weaken it.

Why adopt a FACET approach?

So far our discussion of FACET has focused on ideas. However, as this book has shown again and again, ideas require motivations to give them power. Ethereal ideas, the most powerful of all, are fuelled by emotions so strong that they can motivate a person to kill, or die, or both. How, then, does FACET fare on motivational criteria? The answer is that here again it works. It gives individuals more freedoms, and thereby (as the economist Amartya Sen has argued) boosts their development and their quality of life, making them happier.[12] It emphasizes human agency, making citizens feel more in control of their circumstances. It accepts complexity as a natural opportunity instead of viewing it as a threat to overly simple doctrines. It treats people as ends, not just as means, thereby increasing their sense of self-worth, and along with increasing ability to stop and think come humour, tolerance, and a sense of empowerment. Finally, FACET is a better long-term solution to an increasingly crowded planet than totalitarian notions, which all too often rely on killing, brainwashing, or otherwise abusing people. Abuse may have its advantages for short-term thinkers with poorly tended brains, but in a world whose growing interconnectedness makes justice, international intervention, or (at a personal level) vengeful relatives increasingly hard to avoid, those advantages are shrinking all the time.

Making it happen: implementing a FACET approach

To implement FACET requires open debate, public trust in specialists and authorities, and mechanisms—such as a free and independent press and judiciary—for maintaining trust, enforcing openness, and limiting the drift towards absolute authority so tempting for many governments. It requires better education and the rigorous enforcement of laws supportive of individual liberties. It requires us to accept that human beings have minds of clay, not diamond, that we are embedded in existence, caught in the intricate tangles of causality, but not so tightly as to be altogether helpless. We must accept what the science of thought control teaches: that humans can be changed—and can change themselves—given the right motivation, ideas, and opportunities. Sometimes the task is almost impossibly hard, but that does not destroy the idea that we are redeemable. This applies to outgroups as well as ingroups, to psychopaths and suicide bombers, as well as to the respectable middle classes.

None of this is revolutionary, at least in the West. FACET is firmly in the traditions of liberal democracy; there is nothing new about it in that respect. But liberal democracies have been swept aside before now by totalitarian states, and they can be again. Traditions which emphasize freedom and toleration are never going to be so securely in place that we can afford to take their luxuries for granted. And even at their best, liberal democracies fall far short of what FACET demands.

Pie-in-the-sky, say the cynics. Imposing our beliefs on other people, say the relativists. Wishy-washy liberal rubbish, say the right-wingers. While I respect

Voltaire on free expression, it will be clear by now that I think all three responses are misguided.[13] FACET is anything but pie-in-the-sky. It shies away from totalist thinking, with its one-size-fits-all grand visions, to an acknowledgement of human diversity which shapes the ideas to fit the situation. Moreover, we have clear evidence that increasing human freedoms increases the quality of life (for a detailed discussion of this argument, see Amartya Sen, *Development as Freedom*, or compare the delights of 1990s living in, say, Britain with Bosnia, or Norway with North Korea). To assume that other people do not want the rights and pleasures we in the West enjoy seems both insulting and self-serving. Being a naïve optimist as well as a wishy-washy liberal, I think we either have already, or can find, a viable solution to some of the world's worst problems. Whether we have the political courage to implement those answers is another matter. I believe, however, that solutions will be tried which eventually work—not perfectly, of course, perfection is beyond us—but sufficiently well to tip the balance away from terrorism in all its forms. How many people will die by violence before we find the will to enforce those solutions is in large part up to us.

Nor need FACET mean imposing all the dross of Western consumer capital-ism on an unwilling population. Treating human beings as ends in themselves entails showing them respect—giving them more freedoms, not insisting that they do as we do. Human rights don't entail American hamburgers. FACET is also compatible with certain interpretations of the major world religions, if that's your poison. Those interpretations which are incompatible should be reinter-preted, or ditched. Being a religion, or a culture, or an ideal, is not enough by itself to justify malevolent behaviour. There are some ideals which eminently deserve to be erased from the human repertoire, and the sooner the better. Where a religion, culture, or tradition (including scientific traditions) insists on its right to do harm, to treat human beings as means to some ideological end, the onus is on it—at the very least—to come up with a more acceptable justification than faith, religious authority, or tradition.[14] Those words have often been employed as conversation stoppers, thought-terminating clichés (to use Robert Lifton's phrase); but their authority to trump all argument is only valid if we dare not query it. If ideas are bad for people, let them be dragged out into the open, publicly debated, and satirized into extinction, whatever their source. Changing the political climate to reduce the incentives for believing in bad ideas—the perks that come with a 'divine' imperative; the injustices which make believers desperate—is far from easy, but nor is it impossible.

As for being wishy-washy, FACET is anything but. A doctrine which replaces authority with pragmatics has some tough implications. For one thing, it expects maturity of its citizens, and hence requires from them a certain amount of effort. It challenges special pleading and vested interests; it also demands that cultural and religious considerations be made subservient to individual rights. Maintaining organs of accountability, for example varied and independent media, means that governments can wave goodbye to gratitude, let alone adulation. Their role is to get things wrong and be slated for it by a populace which may itself be lazy, apathetic, and more or less disorganized, but which will not let that take the edge off its criticism. If FACET is to entrench its universalist pretensions, States which adopt it must also balance domestic concerns with a consistent foreign policy, leading by example rather than by diktat.

Summary and conclusions

Certain circumstances have great power, leading many people to behave the same way. But even in the most extreme circumstances, who people are, their personalities and values (and in the case of groups, their culture), affects their reactions. Many people would not go into a burning house to save a life, but some do

Ervin Staub, *The Psychology of Good and Evil*

To a great extent human beings behave as they are expected to behave. A State which expects its citizens to be politically sophisticated, reasonably mature, and socially responsible individuals has more chance of fostering such citizens than a State which treats its people like slaves, or children. Education, economic and political freedoms, and the generous dissemination of information about other people can all help to produce citizens who take their freedoms gladly for granted and are prepared to share their benefits more widely. Liberal approaches such as FACET are not problem-free, but they are better than competitor systems at encouraging the free flow of ideas, boosting quality of life and—the problem with which this book is primarily concerned—minimizing the harmful effects of strongly held ethereal beliefs, so that abuses like brainwashing occur less frequently. Totalist thinking has failed again and again to reap the rewards it promises its followers. To try and reduce the attraction of totalist ideas means steering people away from malign visions such as the dream of mind control, and instead emphasizing individual freedoms, and challenging those who are tempted to follow the dream.

There is nothing new in any of this. We have, or we could easily acquire, the skills, the knowledge, the capabilities to solve at least some of our most pressing social problems even within our current resource limitations (especially in the developing world). With enough motivation, enough political will, we can improve—though never perfect—our own societies. Surely at least we can rid the world of horrors like the Korean prison camps, or Jonestown. One step towards that goal is understanding the beliefs we have and hold: their powers, their dangers, and how we can begin to change them.

One of my aims in this book has been to try and persuade you that brainwashing is more than just a relic of 1950s paranoia, a term of abuse to be hurled whenever we feel threatened by the beliefs of others. Intensely dedicated cults, and fanatical terrorists, continue to plague us, and thinking of them in stereotypical terms only makes the problem worse. They cannot simply be dismissed as alien, because the damage they can do, as 9/11 showed, is out of all proportion to their size. For the same reason, we need to understand that brainwashing is neither a joke nor a mystery. Previously law-abiding people can indeed be persuaded to chase the dream of mind control, even into the abyss of suicide and murder. But as I have tried to show, our increasing grasp of how brains work, and how they interact with other brains, can help us understand how brainwashing achieves these terrible results. With understanding comes power, however imperfect: the capacity to change our brains, our actions, and our politics so that ethereal ideas become less lethally attractive. We have that power. We should make the most of it.

Notes

Chapter 1: The birth of a word

[1] Hutchinson, *Order and Disorder*, p. 3.

[2] Lifton, *Thought Reform and the Psychology of Totalism*, p. 15.

[3] As brainwashing became more popular it became more academically disreputable, perhaps in part because of its highly political origins. But in the early 1950s academic psychologists and psychiatrists were still prepared to associate themselves with brainwashing research, resulting in a flurry of studies on Korean prisoners of war. One of the best known was conducted by Robert Lifton, Professor of Psychiatry at Yale University, a researcher with extensive experience of the Far East who had previously studied the psychological after-effects of the Hiroshima atomic bomb. Lifton describes in detail the historical, cultural, and psychological processes underlying the official Chinese Communist programme of thought reform.

[4] An example of loose usage comes from *The Guardian* newspaper: 'In these broccoli-enhanced days it has become fashionable in some quarters to assume the modern footballer can no longer consider himself the real thing until he has been so brainwashed with dietetics it has reached the stage where he goes to bed thinking about his greens' (Taylor, 'Ferguson has drive but not drink'). Was the footballer tortured for days and subjected to threats, vicious criticism, uncertainty, and lack of privacy, like some of the people interviewed by Lifton and Hunter? Of course not.

[5] Ultimately, of course, this fear becomes synonymous with our recognition of our own mortality; death deprives us of both freedom and identity. Terror management theory has taken this argument further, explaining many social psychological phenomena, such as self-esteem and religious faith, in terms of the human reaction to the fear of death. A detailed introduction to the theory can be found in Greenberg and colleagues, 'Terror management theory of self-esteem and cultural worldviews'.

[6] Arthur Miller's *The Crucible* is a classic exploration of 1950s US anti-Communist paranoia, seen through the lens of Salem.

[7] Pavlov's work became widely known to the West with the publication in 1941 of his *Lectures on Conditioned Reflexes*, of which the second volume, *Conditioned Reflexes and Psychiatry*, is the more relevant for his work on conditioning.

[8] Schein and colleagues, *Coercive Persuasion*. A more dramatic coinage is Joost Meerloo's 'menticide' (e.g. Meerloo, 'The crime of menticide'), but this has not been widely used.

Notes to Chapter 1

[9] The 1962 film of *The Manchurian Candidate*, starring Frank Sinatra and based on a 1959 novel by Robert Condon, became a cult classic. The story features an American soldier who is kidnapped and brainwashed by Chinese Communists, and becomes a programmed assassin for them.

[10] The modern association between 'brainwashing' and 'the machine' was anticipated in the 1790s by James Tilly Matthews, a merchant who had become caught up in the violent political events convulsing France, and terrifying England, at the time. War had broken out between the two countries following the French Revolution and the execution of the French King Louis XVI in 1793. Matthews had become convinced of the existence of a gang of terrorists whose goal was to inflame and prolong the war. Their methods were centred on the Air Loom, an influencing machine which could focus powerful rays on the victim's brain and thereby control his thoughts. Matthews—who would probably have been labelled schizophrenic if the term had existed then—was imprisoned in Bethlem Hospital, commonly known as Bedlam, following his vain attempt to warn leading politicians of the danger. During his time in Bethlem, he described the gang members, and the workings of the Air Loom itself, in astonishing detail. Jay, *The Air Loom Gang*, is a fascinating description of Matthews' ideas, his involvement in the French Revolution, and how he was treated by the psychiatry of his day.

[11] This can blur into the first, political aspect, for example when people refuse to take into account explanations that are available, but which are too complex, or don't mesh with their belief systems. An example is the current reluctance of the US and Israel to explore arguments that fear, poverty, and oppression have hugely contributed to terrorist activity in the Palestinian uprising.

[12] My description of the Patty Hearst case draws heavily on that given in Scheflin and Opton, *The Mind Manipulators*.

[13] Her sentence was commuted by President Jimmy Carter in 1979 and she was finally pardoned by Bill Clinton at the end of his presidency.

[14] I am indebted to Diarmaid MacCulloch's *Thomas Cranmer* for the description of Cranmer's last days.

[15] Hunter, *Brain-washing in Red China*, p. 192.

[16] Lobotomy is a form of psychosurgery which removes connections between the front and the rest of the brain. It was popular during the 1940s and 50s but is no longer widely used (for a history of psychosurgery, see Pressman, *Last Resort*). Sometimes the result is callousness, extreme short-term thinking, and inability to concentrate, symptoms like those displayed by Phineas Gage, a nineteenth-century engineer who miraculously survived when a metal rod was blown through his head. Phineas Gage had been a sober and hard-working man before his accident; after it he became a different person, reckless and indifferent, unable to hold down a job. The story of Phineas Gage, together with modern parallels and implications, is discussed by the neurologist Antonio Damasio throughout his book *Descartes' Error*.

[17] Lifton, *Thought Reform*, pp. 420–35.

[18] The word 'ideology', like the word 'game', tends to be easy to use but hard to define. Hannah Arendt calls ideologies 'isms which to the satisfaction of their adherents can explain everything and every occurrence by deducing it from a single premise' (Arendt, *Totalitarianism*, p. 166). Ervin Staub speaks of 'a vision about ideal social arrangements' (Staub, *The Psychology of Good and Evil*, p. 17). For an introduction to the topic of ideology, see Freeden, *Ideology*.

[19] Goldhagen, *Hitler's Willing Executioners*.

[20] See Lifton, *Thought Reform*, pp. 207–21.

[21] Orwell, *Nineteen Eighty-Four*, p. 171.

[22] Hunter, *Brain-washing in Red China*, p. 132.

Chapter 2: God or the group?

[1] Principle is one thing, practice quite another. See King, 'Secularism in France' for a discussion of French government policy, which also refers to the United States. For more on the role of religion, particularly Protestant fundamentalism, in American politics, see Lieven, 'Demon in the cellar' (in the same issue of *Prospect* as King's article); also Armstrong, *The Battle for God*.

[2] For a discussion of the concept of 'contestability', see Freeden, *Ideology*, especially pp. 52–4. Ambiguity is of course not restricted to ethereal ideas, but it 'is especially conspicuous in political language because by definition politics concerns conflicts of interest' (Edelman, *The Politics of Misinformation*, p. 80). Murray Edelman warns that 'meaning is far more volatile than is commonly supposed and so are our portrayals, beliefs, and assumptions about the worlds we inhabit' (p. 82).

[3] The term 'glittering generalities' is from a 1938 pamphlet, *Propaganda Analysis*, published by the Institute for Propaganda Analysis, which was set up in order to inform the public about propaganda techniques and how to resist them. More information can be found on the organization's website, <http://www.propagandacritic.com>.

[4] For an introduction to philosophical thinking on ends and means, see Raphael, *Moral Philosophy*, especially pp. 55–66.

[5] There is a large academic literature on cults and considerable debate over how similar cults and religions are. Using an evolutionary approach (see Stevens and Price, *Prophets, Cults and Madness*), one can think of cults as showing patterns of development similar to that of species, with population growth, stability (or stagnation), instability, decline, or catastrophic extinction, depending on circumstances. Like many species, many cults turn out to be insufficiently adaptable to their environment and disappear. Sometimes extinction is gradual, as in the space alien cult described by Leon Festinger and colleagues (see note 11 below). Sometimes, as in Jonestown, it is catastrophic. The world religions have shown sufficient adaptability to survive thus far, although the competition from alternative ideas is arguably greater today than ever before. Legal approaches to cults have tended to assume similarities with sects and religions; in Europe, for example, most countries do not accord cults a special legal status, but allow them under provisions guaranteeing freedom of conscience and religion.

[6] Female cult leaders are not unknown, but the majority are male. For a discussion of why this may be the case, see Stevens and Price, *Prophets, Cults and Madness*.

[7] The Council of Europe's Parliamentary Assembly adopted a recommendation on how European member states should deal with sects on 22 June 1999. The relevant press release can be found on <http://press.coe.int/cp/99/351a(99).htm>. The quotation is taken from the Cultic Studies Journal, *The Council of Europe's Report on Sects and New Religious Movements. 7. Case-law on sects*, available from <http://www.csj.org> (under *Publications*).

[8] For an in-depth discussion of paranoia in politics, including the politics of cults and society's responses to them, see Robins and Post, *Political Paranoia*.

[9] See, for example, Ungerleider and Wellisch, 'Coercive persuasion (brainwashing), religious cults, and deprogramming'.

[10] Naipaul, *Black and White*, pp. 226–7.

[11] *When Prophecy Fails* is the social psychologist Leon Festinger's now-legendary analysis of what happens in a cult when such a date is set and passes. After the initial shock of disappointment, cult members responded with a wave of proselytizing which contrasted with their previous secrecy and isolation. Over the longer term, however, this newfound enthusiasm petered out and the cult gradually disintegrated.

[12] For an in-depth, historical discussion of just how dangerous future-slanted thinking can be, see Weitz, *A Century of Genocide*, which argues that utopianism was an important factor in some of the most destructive ideological movements of the twentieth century, including Nazism, Stalinism, and the Khmer Rouge.

[13] Arendt, *Totalitarianism*, p. 44.

[14] For an accessible and comprehensive social psychology textbook, see Hewstone and Stroebe, *Introduction to Social Psychology*.

[15] The excerpts are taken from Wittgenstein, *Philosophical Investigations*, S. 258.

[16] Wittgenstein, *Philosophical Investigations*, S. 246 ff.

[17] The 'minimal group paradigm', in which subjects are assigned to arbitrarily defined groups about which they have no knowledge (e.g. of who else belongs), was described in a landmark paper, 'Social categorization and intergroup behaviour', by Henri Tajfel and colleagues in 1971. For more on how shallow group criteria can be, see Brown, 'Intergroup relations'; Pratkanis and Aronson, *Age of Propaganda*, pp. 216–23.

[18] Aronson and Linder, 'Gain and loss of esteem as determinants of interpersonal attractiveness'.

[19] Parks and Sanna, *Group Performance and Interaction*, pp. 11–12.

[20] Zajonc, 'Attitudinal effects of mere exposure'.

[21] Hatfield and colleagues, *Emotional Contagion*.

[22] See Cialdini, *Influence*, pp. 74–80 for more details.

[23] Descartes' highly influential musings on the self can be found in his *Selected Philosophical Writings*, particularly in the *Discourse on the Method* and the *Meditations on First Philosophy*.

[24] See, for example, Galanter, *Cults*, p. 15.

[25] See Parks and Sanna, *Group Performance and Interaction*, p. 15.

[26] The inventor of the term, Irving Janis, provides a detailed discussion of groupthink in Janis, *Groupthink*.

[27] Galanter, *Cults*, Chapter 2 describes some of the evidence for the health benefits which cults can offer.

[28] Oppenheimer's words are quoted in Giovannitti and Freed, *The Decision to Drop the Bomb*, p. 197.

[29] In Catholicism, for example, compare the brevity of the Ten Commandments (Exodus 20:3–17; 297 words in English) or the Church's doctrinal statement of AD 325, the Nicene Creed (229 words) with the massed texts of Papal Bulls such as 'Arcanum divinæ sapientiæ' (8000 words; Catholic Church, 'Arcanum'), which discusses only one small aspect of Christian life: the relationships between marriage, the Church, and the State.

[30] Dunbar, *Grooming, Gossip and the Evolution of Language*, p. 76.

[31] For an example of the 'hard atheist' attitude to religion, see Dawkins, *The Selfish Gene*, pp. 330–1; also Dawkins, *A Devil's Chaplain*.

[32] The role of Christianity in Nazi ideology remains a matter of debate. Daniel Goldhagen argues that the Holocaust, which killed approximately six million Jews, was driven by an ideology whose prophets 'were profoundly anti-Christian and would have destroyed

Christianity after the war' (Goldhagen, *Hitler's Willing Executioners*, pp. 447–8). For a contrasting view see Steigmann-Gall, *The Holy Reich*.
[33] Weitz, *A Century of Genocide* discusses the ideas behind some of these ideologies.

Chapter 3: The power of persuasion

[1] For more information about advertising history and techniques, see Stephen Fox's history of American advertising, *The Mirror Makers*, Anthony Pratkanis and Elliot Aronson's *Age of Propaganda*, or Robert Cialdini's *Influence*.
[2] Intense media coverage of certain events increases the number of copycat events in the days following the publicity. See Pratkanis and Aronson, *Age of Propaganda*, pp. 147–8, where the authors discuss sociologist David Phillips' work showing that murder rates rise immediately after nationally televised boxing matches. These appear to be 'extra' murders, and Phillips predicts that 'Within four days of the next nationally televised heavyweight championship prizefight, at least eleven innocent U.S. citizens who would not otherwise have died will be murdered in cold blood' (Pratkanis and Aronson, *Age of Propaganda*, p. 147). See also Salib, 'Effect of 11 September 2001 on suicide and homicide in England and Wales'.
[3] Jon Ronson's book *Them*, which details his observations of a variety of extremists, has a fine selection of conspiracy theories to choose from.
[4] The reference is from Juvenal's *Satire X* (line 81), probably written between AD 100 and AD 128.
[5] Milton, *Paradise Lost*, 1:263.
[6] I should point out that since some conspiracy theorists are capable of believing that the world is in fact run by seven-foot lizards, 'far-fetched' may be a reflection of my limited imagination. However, even David Icke's lizards hunt in packs, and thereby fall short of being *one* controlling mind. See Jon Ronson's *Them* for more details.
[7] Dawkins first mentioned memes in *The Selfish Gene*. A more in-depth account is Susan Blackmore's *The Meme Machine*.
[8] Aaronovitch, 'Sins of the mother'.
[9] Whether central control in education is a good or bad thing, and whether more freedom to evolve would produce a better education system, are issues beyond the scope of this book.
[10] The slogan 'creating opportunity, releasing potential, achieving excellence' was taken from the website of the Department of Education and Skills (<http://www.dfes.gov.uk/>) in January 2004.
[11] Foucault's book *Discipline and Punish* and Althusser's landmark essay 'Ideology and ideological state apparatuses' state their respective views.
[12] The phrase 'whose service is perfect freedom' is taken from the 1662 version of *The Book of Common Prayer* ('The Second Collect, for Peace', p. 80), instituted in the sixteenth century by Thomas Cranmer.
[13] Quotations are taken from the UK National Curriculum, available from <http://www.nc.uk.net/index.html>.
[14] Glover, *Humanity*, p. 363.

Chapter 4: Hoping to heal

[1] Foucault, *Discipline and Punish*, p. 228.
[2] Laing and Szasz, clinicians themselves, were hugely influential in the 'anti-psychiatry'

movement (part of the wider rebellion associated with the US in the 1960s) which argued that institutional psychiatry was less about healing and helping than about conformity and social compulsion.

³ Laing, *The Politics of Experience*, p. 95.

⁴ *Macbeth*, 5:3, lines 43–4; this is yet another metaphor of mind change: of thought as tumour, of brain-*cutting* rather than brain-*washing*. (All quotations from Shakespeare are taken from Wells and Taylor, *The Oxford Shakespeare*.)

⁵ Each camp has its own favourite examples from psychiatry's past. Supporters of the biomedical model cite cases where brain damage has led to psychiatric symptoms, as in Korsakoff's syndrome—in which deficiency of the vitamin thiamine causes detectable brain lesions, mental impairment, and severe memory problems—or delirium resulting from infections like meningitis. Social power proponents cite the vote by the APA which redefined homosexuality as no longer an illness. They also sceptically note the explosion in syndromes seen in successive editions of American psychiatry's controversial bible, the *Diagnostic and Statistical Manual* (*DSM*), from its first version in 1952 to the current version, *DSM-IV-TR* (fourth edition, text revision), in 2000. See also the more easily available *Synopsis of Psychiatry*, by Kaplan and Sadock.

⁶ The *DSM-IV-TR* classifies mental illness into sixteen major categories, excluding 'other conditions that may be a focus of clinical attention' (e.g. conditions arising from the use of medication) and 'additional codes' (jargon for 'dunno').

⁷ Hare, *Without Conscience*, p. 25.

⁸ See Bentall, *Madness Explained*.

⁹ The history of psychiatry is littered with treatments such as insulin therapy and psycho-surgery which have done considerable harm to patients. In his authoritative review of direct brain intervention techniques, the physiologist Eliot Valenstein warns against the hunger for a quick fix to social problems such as rising crime which may make it 'possible for some policymakers to be seduced into believing that surgical or biochemical interventions can make a significant contribution to the problem' (Valenstein, *Brain Control*, p. 353).

¹⁰ We may not yet have a pill for every ill, but treatment with drugs is now the regime of choice for many conditions, from schizophrenia to shyness. However, all is not perfect in the pharmaceutical Eden. Robin Dawes warns that 'We simply don't know the long-term effects of many drugs, although we do know that some can be disastrous' (Dawes, *House of Cards*, p. 292). David Healy, writing on the history of antipsychotic drugs, worries about 'a growing body of evidence that indicates a success rate and quota of therapeutic rationality per physician fifty years ago that are higher than those that characterize many current practices' (Healy, *The Creation of Psychopharmacology*, p. 4). And Thomas Szasz is typically blunt, arguing that our faith in current treatments for undesirable symptoms has been found in every generation back to and beyond the Inquisition, and may be no better founded now than it was then.

¹¹ For psychotherapy, Robin Dawes' *House of Cards* is an extensive demolition of the idea that psychotherapy based on 'clinical judgment' is worth the fees charged by its practitioners. Dawes argues against the contemporary 'tendency to "psychologize" all problems as being determined by feelings', whether feelings are viewed through the Freudian lens as unconscious drives, or seen, using what Dawes contemptuously terms 'New Age psychology', as important determinants of that be-all and end-all of modern Western existence, self-esteem. He argues that this attempt to subsume every facet of human life within the remit of mental health has not only encouraged a degree of trust in profes-

sionals which is not justified by the scientific evidence, but also 'has led to unjustifiable and pernicious obsessions: obsessions with self-esteem, with the quick attainment of desirable goals, and with an unrealistic sense of security and superiority to other people. These obsessions do not have desirable consequences for our society' (p. 228). We don't have a right to constant happiness, not everything we want is available right now, not every problem can be solved by pills or therapy, and we shouldn't try to shift our responsibilities elsewhere (abusive parents, bad school, unappreciative world) while blaming other people for their actions. We shouldn't, but we do.

[12] Adorno and colleagues summarized their research on authoritarianism in *The Authoritarian Personality*. For a brief and lucid critique questioning just what the F scale measures, see Krosnick, 'Maximizing questionnaire quality'.

[13] Rokeach, *The Open and Closed Mind*.

[14] Brown, 'Intergroup relations', p. 484.

[15] Milgram, *Obedience to Authority*, p. 48.

[16] Hobbes, *Leviathan*, p. 89.

Chapter 5: 'I suggest, you persuade, he brainwashes'

[1] Canetti, *Crowds and Power*, p. 547.

[2] Bourke, *An Intimate History of Killing*, p. 158.

[3] Buchan, *Mr Standfast*, p. 209.

[4] Baumeister, *Evil*, p. 268.

[5] The extract discussing Archimedes is from Hamilton, *Metaphysics*, Lecture xiv, quoted in James, *The Principles of Psychology*, p. 396.

[6] Wegner, *The Illusion of Conscious Will*, p. 159.

[7] Davenport-Hines, *The Pursuit of Oblivion*, p. 397.

[8] Foucault, *Discipline and Punish*, p. 227.

[9] Brehm and Brehm, *Psychological Reactance*.

[10] Mill, 'The Subjection of Women', p. 160.

[11] For an introduction to the issues surrounding domestic abuse, see the website of the National Coalition Against Domestic Violence, <http://www.ncadv.org/problem/what.htm>.

[12] I have used the appropriate pronouns for a 'traditional' case of serious adult abuse. Of course men can be victims too; research shows that both sexes can be violent abusers. Women, however, tend to come off worse in the home: the UK government's 2001/2002 British Crime Survey shows that 44% of violent incidents against women were domestic. For male victims the figure was 7%. The Survey is available from the Home Office website: <http://www.homeoffice.gov.uk/rds/pdfs2/hosb702.pdf> (see especially pp. 56–7).

[13] According to the National Society for the Prevention of Cruelty to Children, unpublished government figures for 2000/2001 show that parents were the main suspect in 78 per cent of child homicides. The number of children killed per year has not changed significantly over the past three decades, the period for which comparable statistics are available. See *Child Killings in England and Wales*, a briefing paper by the NSPCC which is available from the website <http://www.nspcc.org.uk/inform/Statistics/childkillingsenglandwales.doc>.

[14] An interdisciplinary introduction to the literature on violence can be found in Manfred Steger and Nancy Lind's edited collection *Violence and its Alternatives*. For a social psycho-

logist's take on the subject, Roy Baumeister's book *Evil* is easy to read. *Wickedness*, by the moral philosopher Mary Midgley, is also a useful introduction. A focus on political violence is provided by *Violence*, edited by Catherine Besteman, while examples of a more biological perspective on violent crime include Adrian Raine's *The Psychopathology of Crime* and Jonathan Pincus' *Base Instincts*.

[15] The full report is on the UN website: <http://193.194.138.190/pdf/report.pdf>.

[16] See <http://web.amnesty.org/web/ar2002.nsf/media/media?OpenDocument> for the Amnesty International press release.

[17] Hinkle and Wolff, 'Communist interrogation and indoctrination of "Enemies of the States"', p. 134.

[18] Conroy, *Unspeakable Acts, Ordinary People*, p. 26.

[19] Staub, 'The psychology and culture of torture and torturers', p. 51.

Chapter 6: Brainwashing and influence

[1] Frieze and Boneva, 'Power motivation and motivation to help others', p. 76. The reference cited is McClelland, *Power*.

[2] Hume, *Enquiries Concerning Human Understanding and Concerning the Principles of Morals*, p. 33.

[3] Dennett, *Freedom Evolves*, pp. 71–2.

[4] Herring, *Criminal Law*, p. 40.

Chapter 7: Our ever-changing brains

[1] This statement is a simplification. As John Horgan points out in his critique of neuroscience, *The Undiscovered Mind*, the brain had been identified as the seat of the mind by some earlier thinkers. Nor is the idea that nothing is out of bounds to science original to the Enlightenment. However, the development of both ideas was much greater after the Enlightenment.

[2] Synapses are named from the Greek συν (sun: 'with', 'together') and ἁψίς (hapsis; 'a juncture').

[3] Also like countries, cellular border controls are not perfect: sometimes undesirables can get past the phospholipid membrane. Unlike illegal immigrants, however, a virus really can take over, hijacking an entire cell to produce more virus and sometimes killing not only the cell but the entire organism.

[4] The terms 'area(s)', 'region(s)', and 'lobe(s)' are often used interchangeably with the term 'cortex'. In Chapter 10, for example, I will discuss the prefrontal cortex, the prefrontal lobes, and the prefrontal areas; these all refer to the same part of the brain.

[5] V.S. Ramachandran, who has done insightful research on phantom limbs, describes his findings in Blakeslee and Ramachandran, *Phantoms in the Brain*.

[6] Locke, *An Essay Concerning Human Understanding*, p. 148.

[7] Conway, *Principles*, pp. xvi–xvii.

[8] An example from the nineteenth century is that of Phineas Gage, discussed in Chapter 4, whose personality changed completely following an industrial accident. A more recent example is that of anorexia nervosa, usually considered a 'psychological' disorder but sometimes resulting from 'physical' brain damage (see Trummer and colleagues, 'Right hemispheric frontal lesions as a cause for anorexia nervosa').

[9] If you find oily fish completely revolting there are supplements available instead.

[10] For an academic review of the literature on phospholipids, fatty acids, brain function, and the treatment of brain disorders, see Peet, Glen, and Horrobin, *Phospholipid Spectrum Disorders in Psychiatry and Neurology*. For a less technical description, see Taylor, 'A recipe for healthy brain growth'.

[11] Koletzko and colleagues, 'Long chain polyunsaturated fatty acids (LC-PUFA) and perinatal development' reviews the benefits of unsaturated fatty acids for early development.

[12] Gesch and colleagues, 'Influence of supplementary vitamins, minerals and essential fatty acids on the antisocial behaviour of young adult prisoners. Randomised, placebo-controlled trial.' This research used the same high standards of investigation that are used to test new medical drugs: participants were randomly assigned to receive either the supplements or dummy (placebo) pills. Neither the participants or the researchers handing out the pills knew which was which, and only the participants who received the genuine supplements showed significantly less violent behaviour. Unfortunately, this powerful demonstration of how diet affects behaviour has had little impact on government policy so far. There are still too many people clinging to that vestige of Cartesian dualism, the idea that the effects of food on bodies stop at the borders of the skull.

[13] For more about TLE, see Eve LaPlante's book *Seized*.

[14] For an early statement of Persinger's hypothesis, see Persinger, 'Religious and mystical experiences as artifacts of temporal lobe function'. For work on the effects of magnetic fields, see Cook and Persinger, 'Geophysical variables and behavior: XCII'; also De Sano and Persinger, 'Geophysical variables and behavior: XXXIX'.

[15] This is an intriguing modern variation on the ancient religious doctrine of 'The Chosen People', in which a few fortunate souls are able to walk with God while the rest are marked for damnation. St Paul, writing to the Romans, talks of this doctrine in terms of the grace of God, by which individuals are elected (or not) to salvation. 'Even so then at this present time also there is a remnant according to the election of grace' (Romans 11:5). Those not so fortunately selected, Paul adds, 'were blinded (According as it is written, God hath given them the spirit of slumber, eyes that they should not see, and ears that they should not hear;) unto this day' (Romans 11:7–8). Perhaps the spirit of slumber results from an inert temporal lobe.

[16] An example of this is Joseph LeDoux's book *Synaptic Self*.

[17] The original 1991 Markus and Kitayama article is reprinted in Roy Baumeister's edited collection *The Self in Social Psychology*, from which version (p. 342) the quotations given here are taken.

[18] Baumeister, 'How the self became a problem'. Changing ideas of self from the medieval to the modern period may have been due in part to changes in knowledge technologies (e.g. the spread of printing) and reading practice (from group reading aloud to solitary, silent reading). For more detail, see Deibert, *Parchment, Printing, and Hypermedia*, especially pp. 98–101.

[19] Schacter, *The Seven Sins of Memory*, p. 4.

[20] La Rochefoucauld, *Maxims*, 89.

[21] *As You Like It*: 2:7, line 142.

[22] Schema change has been much studied by social cognition theorists, generally in relation to stereotypes. For an introduction to social cognition, see Fiedler and Bless, 'Social cognition'.

[23] Bleuler, *Dementia Praecox or The Group of Schizophrenias*, p. 26.

Chapter 8: Webs and new worlds

[1] Festinger, *A Theory Of Cognitive Dissonance*.

[2] A Gallup poll conducted in June 2003 found that 47 per cent of Americans held inconsistent positions on these topics, that is supported one but not the other.

[3] Bodenhausen, 'Stereotypes as judgmental heuristics. Evidence of circadian variations in discrimination'.

[4] For a beautifully illustrated discussion of the effects of water upon our planet, see Zevenhuizen, *Erosion and Weathering*.

[5] Pratkanis and Aronson, *Age of Propaganda*, p. 33: 'Ads that contain the words *new, quick, easy, improved, now, suddenly, amazing,* and *introducing* sell more products.'

[6] For a review of theories of interactions between the thalamus and the cortex, see Hillenbrand and van Hemmen, 'Adaptation in the corticothalamic loop'.

[7] Sacks, 'A matter of identity'.

[8] The quotation is taken from Dretske, 'Belief', p. 83.

[9] This quotation from Tertullian's *De Carne Christi* (Of the Body of Christ) is often misrendered as 'I believe [rather than 'It is certain'] because it is impossible'. For more information see Evans, *Tertullian's Treatise on the Incarnation*; the quotation itself is on pp. 18–19.

[10] Bowker, *Is God a Virus?* is a detailed critique of the claims made by Dawkins and others.

[11] Russell, *Religion and Science*, p. 7.

[12] James' notoriously ambiguous short story was first published in 1898. For an introduction to the psychology of the visual arts, see Gombrich, *Art and Illusion*.

[13] The story of Bishop Barker's experience with thought reform is told in Lifton's book *Thought Reform*, pp. 134–45. Bishop Barker showed strong faith from an early age. Despite making some concessions during his three years in prison, he held firm on the central issue of his religious principles, writing a confession but refusing to include untrue accusations about the Catholic Church.

[14] Yeats, 'The Second Coming', lines 7–8.

[15] David Aberbach discusses Winston Churchill's charismatic leadership in *Charisma in Politics, Religion and the Media*.

Chapter 9: Swept away

[1] Ekman and colleagues reported their findings in an article, 'Pan-cultural elements in facial displays of emotion', in the journal *Science* in 1969. For a more recent perspective on this research, see Scherer, 'Emotion', pp. 173–81.

[2] James, *The Principles of Psychology*, p. 1067.

[3] For further discussion of which comes first, emotions or expressions, see Damasio, *Looking for Spinoza*, especially pp. 65–73.

[4] This research is reported in Wong and Root, 'Dynamic variations in affective priming'.

[5] For more information on emotional contagion and the roles of emotions in social communication, see Hatfield and colleagues, *Emotional Contagion*; Hewstone and Stroebe, *Introduction to Social Psychology*; and Ekman, *Emotions Revealed*.

[6] Bain, *The Emotions and the Will*, p. 20.

[7] Mormède and colleagues, 'Molecular genetic approaches to investigate individual variations in behavioral and neuroendocrine stress responses'.

[8] For a review of the scientific literature on animal models of prefrontal stress responses, see Sullivan and Brake, 'What the rodent prefrontal cortex can teach us about attention-deficit/hyperactivity disorder'. For a review relating this literature to how stress sensitivity in

humans is programmed early on in life, see Matthews, 'Early programming of the hypothalamo-pituitary-adrenal axis'.

[9] See Raine and colleagues, 'Reduced prefrontal gray matter volume and reduced autonomic activity in antisocial personality disorder' for specific details of this research. For a more general introduction to related issues, see Adrian Raine's 1993 book *The Psychopathology of Crime*.

[10] The topic of representation has kept thinkers busy for centuries. I have taken the view that if a brain area is stimulated by the appearance of object X, that is, processes information about X, then that brain area can be said to contain a representation of some aspect of X.

[11] Schachter and Singer, 'Cognitive, social, and physiological determinants of emotional state'.

[12] Statistically, the supporting evidence for Schachter and Singer's hypotheses was far from overwhelming, but this did not prevent it achieving huge influence. See Scherer, 'Emotion', for a review of the experiment and its ongoing high status.

[13] For more details about Capgras syndrome, see Feinberg, *Altered Egos*, pp. 32–41; Tamam and colleagues, 'The prevalence of Capgras syndrome in a university hospital setting'.

[14] Joseph LeDoux (*The Emotional Brain*) and Antonio Damasio (*Descartes' Error*, *The Feeling of What Happens*, *Looking for Spinoza*) provide an inkling of how much more complicated the full story (as known to date) appears to be.

[15] Damasio, *Looking for Spinoza*, p. 3.

Chapter 10: The power of stop-and-think

[1] For more on the neuroscience of the prefrontal lobes, see Fuster, *Memory in the Cerebral Cortex*; Deacon, *The Symbolic Species*; or Goldberg, *The Executive Brain*.

[2] For an overview of recent research and a more detailed description of the experimental evidence supporting our current understanding of eye movement control, see Paul Glimcher's review article 'The neurobiology of visual-saccadic decision making'.

[3] The human retina, which converts light into signals the brain can process, contains a small central region, the fovea, which is capable of processing fine visual detail. The rest of the retina contains light receptors which can detect changes (e.g. motion) as well as coarse features of the visual environment. This change-detection system rapidly alerts the brain to target areas (like the flicker seen out of the corner of the eye), which can then be investigated in detail by moving the eyes so that light from the target area falls on the fovea. Even the human brain does not have enough resources to be able to process everything it sees simultaneously to the level required to identify an object. Evolution has solved this problem by providing the fovea, a spotlight frenetically leaping from point to point to weave the world we see.

[4] Not only can we choose to look at something, and then do so accurately and quickly (voluntary saccade), but we can track a moving object in three dimensions using rotation (up/down, left/right) and focus (forward/back). We can decide to look at an object later (delayed saccade), then move our eyes to the correct location even if the object has disappeared (memory-guided saccade). We can look away from an object (anti-saccade), a task which our primate relatives find extremely difficult to learn. We can move our eyes anywhere we like, when we like, whether or not there is something there to look at (internally generated saccade). And this is only how we respond to objects: people are more complicated still. Without even being aware of it, our brain adjusts our eyes to

indicate a huge range of emotions, from horror (round-eyed stare) to embarrassment (eyes down). And we can even control these subtle displays (direct, open gaze to say 'I'm honest, trust me'), faking our emotions to try and manipulate others, pulling down the shutters on the windows of the soul. All this from a pair of goo-filled balls.

[5] Temporal lobe areas do seem to respond more to features of objects (e.g. face recognition), while parietal areas focus more on information about object location. The division into 'what' and 'where', however, is an over-simplification, as visual processing actually involves many streams, operating simultaneously and heavily interconnected at every stage. I have tried to reflect something of this complexity without suffocating readers with details.

[6] For more on the PFC's role in managing contextual information, see Braver and Barch, 'A theory of cognitive control, aging cognition, and neuromodulation'.

[7] The argument that automatic routines are far more important than we often realize has been a notable feature of social psychology, which emphasizes the ways in which social factors can affect us without our knowledge. A leading proponent of this view is undoubtedly John Bargh. For a discussion of his research, see Bargh, 'The automaticity of everyday life', together with the other contributions to Wyer, *The Automaticity of Everyday Life*, in which Bargh's is the lead article.

[8] Lifton, *Thought Reform*, p. 23.

[9] See, for example, Block, 'On a confusion about a function of consciousness'.

[10] The claim that awareness is continuous ignores the changes which take place in sleep, is not essential to my argument, and is made here for simplicity. There is evidence that some environmental stimuli can be registered by the brain even in deep sleep, suggesting that wake–sleep changes may be part of an awareness continuum, rather than qualitatively different. However, the study of sleep, and other altered states of consciousness, is beyond the scope of this book. For more information, see Dement and Vaughan, *The Promise of Sleep*; also Dietrich, 'Functional neuroanatomy of altered states of consciousness'.

[11] Eliot, *Four Quartets* ('The Dry Salvages', V, lines 27–9). While this state of absorption is associated with aesthetic rapture, immersing oneself in one's activity can also be a way to avoid facing up to the consequences of that activity (see Chapter 5).

[12] For more on this argument, see Taylor, 'Applying continuous modelling to consciousness'.

[13] Mattay and colleagues, 'Catechol O-methyltransferase val[158]-met genotype and individual variation in the brain response to amphetamine'.

Chapter 11: That freedom thing

[1] van Inwagen, *An Essay on Free Will*, p. 3.

[2] Notable recent writings on freedom and determinism include *Freedom Evolves* and *The Illusion of Conscious Will*, by Daniels Dennett and Wegner, respectively; Benjamin Libet and colleagues (*The Volitional Brain*); and Robert Kane (in *Free Will*, his edition of classic philosophical essays on the subject).

[3] For more on quantum mechanics, libertarianism, and free will, see Daniel Dennett's incisive commentary in Chapter 4 of *Freedom Evolves*.

[4] Skinner, 'A third concept of liberty (the Isaiah Berlin lecture)'. My thanks to Professor Skinner for providing me with a reprint.

[5] See, for example, Milton's *Areopagitica* and *The Tenure of Kings and Magistrates*.

[6] See, for example, Hobbes' *Leviathan*.

[7] For a discussion of the role of prefrontal areas in willed behaviour, see Ingvar, 'The will of the brain'.

[8] The role of biological determinism in anti-Semitic and Nazi thinking is discussed in Daniel Goldhagen's book *Hitler's Willing Executioners*.

[9] Ainslie notes that 'What coordinates diverse interests in separate people is limitation of resources' (Ainslie, *Breakdown of Will*, p. 41). If I am antisocial and my friend is extremely friendly, no problems result as long as we live apart. If, however, we have to share a house for some reason, we will be forced to accommodate my interest in silence and solitude, as well as my friend's interest in social interaction. Ainslie argues that the same co-ordination is forced upon the interests within a human brain by the fact that that brain has only one body under direct control, and that this co-ordination gives rise to our perception of a unified self. The more our interests co-operate, the more single-minded we appear.

[10] van Inwagen, *An Essay on Free Will*, p. 3.

[11] Dennett, *Freedom Evolves*, p. 180.

[12] Attribution theory studies the ways in which people explain the causes of, and assign responsibility for, each other's behaviour. For a review of this field of social psychology, see Fincham and Hewstone, 'Attribution theory and research'.

[13] Brehm and Brehm, *Psychological Reactance*.

[14] As noted in Chapter 9, the neural basis of evaluative signals (including reactance) is not yet fully understood. Candidate areas may include the anterior cingulate cortex, the ventromedial prefrontal cortex, and the basal ganglia, a collection of subcortical nuclei thought to be important in action selection. For more on the role of the basal ganglia in signalling the values of stimuli, see Glimcher, 'The neurobiology of visual-saccadic decision making'.

[15] For a more detailed discussion of alien hand syndrome and other disorders of free will, see Spence, 'Free will in the light of neuropsychiatry'; also the commentaries, and Sean Spence's reply, in the same volume.

[16] See Blakemore and colleagues, 'Delusions of alien control in the normal brain' for more details.

[17] For a discussion of some of the conceptual issues surrounding alien control experiments, see de Vignemonta and Fourneret, 'The sense of agency'.

Chapter 12: Victims and predators

[1] Research on human skull volume (a proxy measure for brain size) suggests that human brains can vary in size by 500 cubic centimetres or more (the average volume is about 1400 cc). For more information see the talk.origins website: <http://www.talkorigins.org/faqs/homs/a_brains.html>.

[2] An example of a chemical with multiple effects is platelet-activating factor (PAF). As well as affecting blood platelets, PAF has roles in fighting infection, in reproduction, and in brain development and function. See Taylor, 'The possible role of abnormal platelet-activating factor metabolism in psychiatric disorders' for more details.

[3] Persinger, 'The neuropsychiatry of paranormal experiences' reviews work supporting this claim.

[4] For more on this theme see Ridley, *Nature via Nurture*.

[5] Hunter, *Brainwashing*, p. 118.

[6] Chapter 2 of Sekuler and Blake's *Star Trek on the Brain* explores emotions.

[7] See, for example, Hariri and Weinberger, 'Functional neuroimaging of genetic variation in serotonergic neurotransmission'; Mormède and colleagues, 'Molecular genetic approaches to investigate individual variations in behavioral and neuroendocrine stress responses'.

[8] Cialdini, *Influence*, p. 210.

[9] The dictum 'Nothing is true, everything is permitted' is doubtfully attributed to Hassan-i Sabah (1034–1124), a leader of the radical Ismaili sect of Shia Islam. See the DIS-INFO website, *Nothing is True, Everything is Permitted* (<www.disinfo.com/archive/pages/article/id1562/pg1/index.html>). Since the sentiment expressed is in keeping with nihilism (which claims that all moral restraints should be discarded) I have referred to the latter instead.

[10] Lefcourt, 'The function of the illusions of control and freedom' reviews research in a number of species which supports the link between loss of control and ill-health. For a more detailed review, see Schedlowski and Tewes, *Psychoneuroimmunology*, especially pp. 96–111.

[11] A comparison of the (translated) text of Adolf Hitler's *Mein Kampf* with a gold-standard collection of written and spoken English, the *British National Corpus* (BNC; see <www.natcorp.ox.ac.uk> for details) shows that relative frequencies of the adjective 'free' are similar in the two texts. However, *Mein Kampf* uses the verb 'free' and the adverb 'freely' more than twice as often, and the abstract noun 'freedom' more than three-and-a-half times as often, as the BNC. Hitler made effective use of ethereal ideas.

[12] See, for example, Winterer and Goldman, 'Genetics of human prefrontal function'.

[13] Those who would like to know more about this unorthodox form of poultry management may wish to consult *Three Ways To Hypnotize a Chicken*, from the Old Farmer's Almanac, available online at <www.almanac.com/preview2000/hypnotize.html>.

[14] The definition of charisma is one of two given by the *Oxford English Dictionary*; the other is 'A free gift or favour specially vouchsafed by God; a grace, a talent.'

[15] Wallace, 'Mazeway resynthesis' defines the mazeway as the totality of all 'cognitive residues of previous perceptions' (p. 170). See also Stevens and Price, *Prophets, Cults and Madness*.

[16] Schizophrenia and bipolar disorder (also called 'manic depression') tend to run in families (Potash and colleagues, 'The familial aggregation of psychotic symptoms in bipolar disorder pedigrees'), and members of such families are often extremely creative. Daniel Nettle discusses the relationship between creativity and madness in *Strong Imagination*. More specifically, Kay Redfield Jamison's *An Unquiet Mind*, Eve LaPlante's *Seized*, and Sylvia Nasar's biography of the mathematician John Nash, *A Beautiful Mind*, note the link with creativity for bipolar disorder, temporal lobe epilepsy, and schizophrenia, respectively. For more on the similarities between symptoms experienced by mentally healthy creative people and those seen in schizophrenia, see Claridge, *Schizotypy*.

[17] Polls of public opinion, for example, consistently rate crime as a major concern. Yet charities who work with offenders often have great difficulty in raising funds from public donations. If, as we tell pollsters, we are indeed greatly affected by crime and fear of crime, why doesn't our giving reflect this? Any answer must surely include ideas about crime and criminals prevalent in modern British society—ideas about freedom of action, personal responsibility, and whether criminals can be reformed.

Chapter 13: Mind factories

[1] Machiavelli's *Il Principe* (The Prince), printed in 1532, provoked particular criticism from humanists such as Innocent Gentillet, whose hugely influential book *The Anti-Machiavel*

was published in 1576. For more on this topic, see Skinner, *The Foundations of Modern Political Thought. Volume 1*, especially pp. 128–38, 180–6, 250–1. The change from medieval to (early) modern is clear when you compare the minds behind the *Malleus Maleficarum* ('Here follows the Way whereby Witches copulate with those Devils known as Incubi', p. 243) with the sophisticated political theorizing of Machiavelli less than half a century later.

[2] According to Cruden's *Concordance*, 'pestilence' is mentioned as often as 'food' in the Bible.

[3] The 2003 epidemic of Severe Acute Respiratory Syndrome (SARS) is an example.

[4] When two people meet for the first time, similarity of beliefs can have a greater influence on whether they get along than more 'obvious' factors such as racial background (Walker and Campbell, 'Similarity of values and interpersonal attraction of Whites toward Blacks'; see also Rokeach, *The Open and Closed Mind*). People in relationships will adjust their own attitudes, the better to match those of their partner (Davis and Rusbult, 'Attitude alignment in close relationships').

[5] The phrase 'faint conviction' is from the last line of Betjeman's poem 'Huxley Hall' (*John Betjeman Collected Works*, p. 160).

[6] Preston, *The Hot Zone*, p. 29.

[7] This poetic metaphor is from the physiologist Charles Sherrington. 'The brain is waking and with it the mind is returning. It is as if the Milky Way entered upon some cosmic dance. Swiftly the head-mass becomes an enchanted loom where millions of flashing shuttles weave a dissolving pattern, always a meaningful pattern though never an abiding one; a shifting harmony of subpatterns' (Sherrington, *Man on His Nature*, p. 178).

[8] Daniel Goldhagen discusses this argument further in *Hitler's Willing Executioners*.

[9] See Atran, 'Genesis of suicide terrorism'; Townshend, *Terrorism*.

[10] The Nobel prize-winning economist Amartya Sen explores the relationship between economic and political freedoms in *Development as Freedom*.

[11] The quotation is taken from Eagleton, *Literary Theory*, pp. 12–13. An excellent, if challenging, introduction to the work of Martin Heidegger is George Steiner's *Heidegger*. The reference to Wittgenstein is to his later works, notably the posthumously published *Philosophical Investigations*.

[12] Street, *Mass Media, Politics and Democracy*, pp. 36–8.

[13] Smith, *An Inquiry into the Nature and Causes of the Wealth of Nations*.

[14] Street, *Mass Media*, p. 37.

[15] Street, *Mass Media*, p. 41.

[16] Ofek, *Second Nature*, p. 120.

[17] An example: an online search of *The Guardian* newspaper (<http://www.guardian.co.uk/Archive/>), which is more left-wing and liberal than other mainstream British daily newspapers, showed that the outgroup term 'right-wing' was used almost twice as much (on average, 1999–2002) as the ingroup term 'left-wing'. That is, *The Guardian* emphasizes its rivals' politics much more than its own point of view. Incidentally, the 'right–left' description of politics, which dates back to the French Revolution, is regarded by some commentators as flawed and outdated (e.g. see Freeden, *Ideology*, p. 79). Nevertheless, to judge from this web search the terminology is still in frequent use.

[18] Street, *Mass Media*, p. 38.

[19] An example of Socratic dialogue, from the end of Plato's *Euthyphro*, gives the flavour:

Socrates: 'Surely you remember that earlier in the discussion the holy and the "divinely approved" did not appear the same to us.'

Euthyphro: 'I do.'
Socrates: 'Well, don't you realize that you're now saying that the holy is what's approved by the gods? Surely that's what's "divinely approved", isn't it?'
Euthyphro: 'Certainly.'
Socrates: 'Well, either our conclusion then was wrong, or, if it was right, our present position is not correct.'

[20] An example: 'Of course I don't think religion is *total* nonsense; it must have something going for it to have lasted since our caveman days' can easily be interpreted as meaning 'religion is rubbish and should have died out long ago'.

[21] Elias Canetti's *Crowds and Power*, to which I owe a considerable debt here, is rich with fascinating discussions of crowd (i.e. outgroup) metaphors.

Chapter 14: Science and nightmare

[1] Marks, *The Search for the 'Manchurian Candidate'*, pp. 155–6.

[2] For a 'biography' of the Manhattan Project, see Richard Rhodes, *The Making of the Atomic Bomb*.

[3] Marks, *The Search for the 'Manchurian Candidate'*, p. 228.

[4] A declassified version of the research into Communist interrogation methods was published in 1956: see Hinkle and Wolff, 'Communist interrogation' (discussed in Chapter 5).

[5] A future like that portrayed by Susan Greenfield will rely on influence techniques just as much as we do today. Even if tomorrow's people become increasingly machine-wrapped—passive, atomized recipients of ever more intricate technological cosseting—mindcraft will retain its major role; it will simply become more indirect. Downloading influence to mechanical devices (from parchment to PCs) dilutes our perception of its source, but does not dilute the influence itself—and may even strengthen it. We may be more likely to obey a computer, or a text, than another human being. Computers have the apparent authority of logic on their side, while texts, like revelations, often come with built-in belief predisposing us to think them true. We tend to forget that these devices are only silicon extensions (or paper reflections) of their creators, dictating, persuading, or moralizing to serve some human agenda. If a future computer doctor tells a future patient to change their diet or risk dropping dead of a heart attack, that is no less an influence attempt for being made through a machine.

[6] Penfield described his research in Penfield and Rasmussen, *The Cerebral Cortex of Man*.

[7] Observing neural activity at the level of individual cortical neurons has proved possible in animals using optical imaging methods. Unfortunately, optical imaging currently requires the exposure of the brain and the use of toxic dyes, so extending it to humans has not yet proved ethically feasible.

[8] Jay, *The Air Loom Gang* is a fascinating description of Matthews' ideas, his involvement in the French Revolution, and how he was treated by the psychiatry of his day. See also n.1(10).

[9] Peter Little's *Genetic Destinies* and Matt Ridley's *Nature via Nurture* are two notable examples of many.

[10] Ryle, *The Concept of Mind*, pp. 15–16.

[11] Nazi scientists, most notoriously Josef Mengele at Auschwitz, used Jewish prisoners as subjects for (often lethal) experiments, a practice condemned by the Nuremberg Code drawn up by the Allies after the Second World War. That the victors' attitude to human rights was, to say the least, somewhat flexible was clearly demonstrated in post-war

America by, among other things, the Tuskegee syphilis trials, which deliberately withheld treatment from 399 infected African-American men so that the course of the disease could be observed. For details of these and many other government experiments on non-consenting human beings, see The Tuskegee Syphilis Study Legacy Committee website (<http://hsc.virginia.edu/hs-library/historical/apology/report.html>); Cornwell, *Hitler's Scientists* (especially pp. 356–66); Blum, *Rogue State*; and Marks, *The Search for the 'Manchurian Candidate'*.

[12] Retreating from reality into delusions is of course a hallmark of psychotic syndromes such as schizophrenia, but we all use dreams as a cushion. 'Human kind cannot bear very much reality', as T.S. Eliot observed in *Four Quartets* ('Burnt Norton', I, lines 45–6). The clinical psychologist Louis Sass argues that modern Western life already has features in common with psychosis (Sass, *Madness and Modernism*), in which case the construction of virtual realities envisaged by Greenfield would be an extension of a trend rather than a radical departure.

[13] The quotation is from Eliot, *Four Quartets* ('Burnt Norton', II, line 16).

[14] The quotation is from Browning, 'Andrea del Sarto', line 51.

[15] Plato's famous simile of the cave (*The Republic*, VII, pp. 255–64) compares human existence to that of prisoners in a cave, who can only know the external world by watching shadows on the cave wall. Descartes' evil demon, who could have created a fake universe to trick the philosopher into false beliefs, is described in the second of his *Meditations on First Philosophy*; see Descartes, *Selected Philosophical Writings*, pp. 79–83.

[16] Masefield, *The Box of Delights*.

[17] Orwell, *Nineteen Eighty-Four*, p. 205.

Chapter 15: Taking a stand

[1] Gladwell, *The Tipping Point*, p. 98.

[2] The issues surrounding public trust in specialists warrant further exploration, but this would take me too far from the theme of this book. For an incisive introduction to the topic of trust and its difficulties, see O'Neill, *A Question of Trust*.

[3] I have previously described the Cartesian model of mind, which views minds as distinct substances set apart by God from the matter which makes up the rest of the world. Early in the twentieth century, Descartes' dualistic approach was notably challenged by Martin Heidegger, whose core term *Dasein* George Steiner is glossing in the quotation given here (Steiner, *Heidegger*, p. 83). Heidegger is notoriously difficult to translate, but, roughly, *Dasein* (literally, 'to be there') expresses his sense that human beings are, as Steiner puts it, encapsulated in reality. To be human at all is necessarily to be in the world. According to Heidegger, human beings can have no existence whatsoever separate from their being-in-the-world. Bang goes the immortal soul, at least as traditionally conceived. It is this sense of being inescapably grounded in real life that the term 'situatedness' is attempting to capture.

[4] Two books which bring home human limitations in detecting deceit are Paul Ekman's *Telling Lies* and Robert Hare's *Without Conscience*.

[5] Philips, 'On Controversies in Religion', p. 131.

[6] The example of roasting babies may seem extreme, but it is worth bearing in mind that human cultures have been observed to practise—and in some cases are still practising—ritual sacrifice, death by burning, and female infanticide.

[7] Lukes, *Liberals and Cannibals*, p. 8.

[8] Miller, *The Anatomy of Disgust*, p. 12.

[9] When the processes of socialization go wrong the results can be severely damaging to a child's ability to interact with its peers. Some researchers have suggested that child-hood neglect/abuse may be a major risk factor for later psychopathic behaviour (see, for example, Jonathan Pincus' *Base Instincts*).

[10] The thoughts on liberalism outlined here are heavily influenced by Barry's approach, and I cannot do better than recommend *Culture and Equality* as further reading. For a critical commentary on Barry's ideas, see Kelly, *Multiculturalism Reconsidered*.

[11] It is worth making the obvious point that I do not equate liberal thinking with Western culture—and I certainly do not link totalist thinking exclusively to other cultures. In *The Origins of Totalitarian Democracy* Jacob Talmon traces the roots of modern totalitarianism to eighteenth-century Western sources such as Rousseau. Although totalist thinking long predates Rousseau, it is not unique to any particular culture, and the totalitarian plague has flourished in cultures as disparate as Europe and China. Nor is liberalism unique to the modern West. Islam, for example, is often seen by Westerners as a predominantly illiberal religion; yet Islam has a distinguished tradition of tolerance, scholarship, free-thinking, and respect for other cultures. Medieval Islamic Spain, for instance, gave sanctuary to Jews fleeing persecution in other European countries, a generosity not often matched by Europe's Christians. When Ferdinand and Isabella, the married rulers of Aragon and Castile, conquered Granada in 1492 and united Spain under Catholicism, Spanish Jews were expelled or forced to convert to Christianity. See Armstrong, *The Battle for God*, pp. 3–8 for more details.

[12] See Sen, *Development as Freedom*. Increasing freedoms includes the economic domain: providing the basic security of property ownership and reducing the transaction costs associated with economic (and other social) exchanges. In *The Mystery of Capital* the economist Hernando de Soto discusses the importance of such measures for economic growth.

[13] 'I disapprove of what you say, but I will defend to the death your right to say it.' Whether Voltaire ever actually said the French equivalent is doubtful, but the phrase is an apt summary of his attitude as expressed, for example, in his *Treatise on Tolerance*.

[14] See, for example, Dawkins, 'Good and bad reasons for believing'.

References

Movies and music

Adams, J. (1988), 'News has a kind of mystery'. In *Nixon in China: highlights*. Recording number: 7559-79436-9. Nonesuch.

Blade Runner (1982), dir. R. Scott. Columbia TriStar Pictures.

A Clockwork Orange (1971), dir. S. Kubrick. Warner Brothers.

Groundhog Day (1993), dir. H. Ramis. Columbia.

Lehrer, T. (1965), 'The Folk Song Army'. In *That Was The Year That Was*. Recording number: R/RS 6179. Reprise Records.

Lehrer, T. (1965), 'Wernher von Braun'. In *That Was The Year That Was*. Recording number: R/RS 6179. Reprise Records.

The Manchurian Candidate (1962), dir. J. Frankenheimer. United Artists.

The Matrix (1999), dir. A. Wachowski and L. Wachowski. Warner Brothers.

Memento (2001), dir. C. Nolan. Newmarket Films.

Metropolis (1927), dir. F. Lang. Paramount Pictures.

Pink Floyd—The Wall (1982), dir. A. Parker. Sony/Columbia.

Soylent Green (1973), dir. R. Fleischer. MGM.

The Truman Show (1998), dir. P. Weir. Paramount Pictures.

Books, journals, pamphlets, and websites

'Belarus leader orders teachers of "ideology"'. *Irish Times*. 14 August 2003.

The Holy Bible: Authorized King James version (1611/1957). Glasgow: Collins World.

Diagnostic and Statistical Manual of Mental Disorders 4th Edition Text Revision: DSM-IV-TR (2000). Washington, DC: American Psychiatric Association.

International Statistical Classification of Diseases and Related Health Problems. Tenth Revision: ICD-10 (1992). Geneva: World Health Organisation.

Malleus Maleficarum: the classic study of witchcraft (c.1486/1986), trans. M. Summers. London: Arrow.

'The Nicene Creed'. In *The Book of Common Prayer* (1662/1999). London: David Campbell, pp. 470–1.

Oxford English Dictionary (2002), CD-ROM v. 3.0; 2nd edition. Oxford: Oxford University Press.

The Qur'an: text, translation and commentary (c.632/2001), trans. A. Yusuf Ali, US edition. Elmhurst, NY: Tahrike Tarsile Qur'an.

References

'The Second Collect, for Peace'. In *The Book of Common Prayer* (1662/1999). London: David Campbell, p. 80.

Aaronovitch, D., 'Sins of the mother'. *The Observer*. 21 September 2003.

Aberbach, D. (1996), *Charisma in Politics, Religion and the Media: private trauma, public ideals*. Houndmills, Basingstoke: Macmillan.

Adorno, T.W., Frenkel-Brunswik, E., Levinson, D.J., et al. (1950), *The Authoritarian Personality*. New York: Harper and Brothers.

Aeschylus (*c.*458 BC/1999), *The Oresteia: a new version by Ted Hughes*, trans. T. Hughes. London: Faber and Faber.

Ainslie, G. (2001), *Breakdown of Will*. New York: Cambridge University Press.

Althusser, L. (1971), 'Ideology and ideological state apparatuses'. In *Lenin and Philosophy and Other Essays*, trans. B. Brewster. London: New Left Books, pp. 121–73.

Amnesty International, *Amnesty International Report 2002: no trade off between human rights and security*. <http://web.amnesty.org/web/ar2002.nsf/media/media?OpenDocument>.

Arendt, H. (1951), *Totalitarianism*. New York: Harcourt, Brace and World.

Armstrong, K. (2001), *The Battle for God: fundamentalism in Judaism, Christianity and Islam*. London: HarperCollins.

Arnold, M. (1853/1950), 'The Scholar-Gypsy'. In *The Poetical Works of Matthew Arnold*, eds. C.B. Tinker and H.F. Lowry. London: Oxford University Press, pp. 255–62.

Aronson, E. and Linder, D. (1965), 'Gain and loss of esteem as determinants of interpersonal attractiveness', *Journal of Experimental Social Psychology*, 1, pp. 156–71.

Atran, S. (2003), 'Genesis of suicide terrorism', *Science*, 299, pp. 1534–9.

Bain, A. (1899), *The Emotions and the Will*, 4th edition. London: Longmans, Green, and Co.

Bargh, J.A. (1997), 'The automaticity of everyday life'. In *The Automaticity of Everyday Life. Advances in Social Cognition. Volume X*, ed. R.S. Wyer. Mahwah, NJ: Lawrence Erlbaum, pp. 1–61.

Barker, E. (1984), *The Making of a Moonie: choice or brainwashing?* Oxford: Basil Blackwell.

Barry, B. (2001), *Culture and Equality: an egalitarian critique of multiculturalism*. Cambridge: Polity.

Baumeister, R.F. (1987), 'How the self became a problem: a psychological review of historical research', *Journal of Personality and Social Psychology*, 52, pp. 163–76.

Baumeister, R.F., ed. (1999), *The Self in Social Psychology*. Philadelphia, PA: Psychology Press.

Baumeister, R.F. (2001), *Evil: inside human violence and cruelty*. New York: Owl Books.

Bentall, R.P. (2003), *Madness Explained: psychosis and human nature*. London: Allen Lane.

Berlin, I. (1958/1969), 'Two concepts of liberty'. In *Four Essays on Liberty*. New York: Oxford University Press, pp. 118–72.

Besteman, C., ed. (2002), *Violence: a reader*. Houndmills, Basingstoke: Palgrave Macmillan.

Betjeman, J. (1954/2001), 'Huxley Hall'. In *John Betjeman Collected Works (New Edition)*. London: John Murray, p. 160.

Blackmore, S. (2000), *The Meme Machine*. New York: Oxford University Press.

Blakemore, S.-J., Oakley, D.A., and Frith, C.D. (2003), 'Delusions of alien control in the normal brain', *Neuropsychologia*, 41, pp. 1058–67.

Blakeslee, S. and Ramachandran, V.S. (1998), *Phantoms in the Brain: human nature and the architecture of the mind*. London: Fourth Estate.

Bleuler, E. (1950), *Dementia Praecox or The Group of Schizophrenias*, trans. J. Zinkin. New York: International Universities Press.

Block, N. (1995), 'On a confusion about a function of consciousness', *Behavioral and Brain Sciences*, 18, pp. 227–87.

Blum, W. (2003), *Rogue State: a guide to the world's only superpower*, 2nd edition. London: Zed Books.

Bodenhausen, G.V. (1990), 'Stereotypes as judgmental heuristics: evidence of circadian variations in discrimination', *Psychological Science*, 1, pp. 319–22.

Bourke, J. (2000), *An Intimate History of Killing: face-to-face killing in twentieth-century warfare*. London: Granta.

Bowker, J. (1995), *Is God a Virus? Genes, culture and religion*. London: SPCK.

Braver, T.S. and Barch, D.M. (2002), 'A theory of cognitive control, aging cognition, and neuromodulation', *Neuroscience and Biobehavioral Reviews*, 26, pp. 809–17.

Brehm, S.S. and Brehm, J.W. (1981), *Psychological Reactance: a theory of freedom and control*. New York: Academic Press.

British National Corpus, *British National Corpus (BNC)*. <www.natcorp.ox.ac.uk>.

British National Party, *Manifesto for the UK Council Elections, May 2003*. <www.bnp.org.uk>.

Brown, R. (2001), 'Intergroup relations'. In *Introduction to Social Psychology*, eds. M. Hewstone and W. Stroebe, 3rd edition. Oxford: Blackwell, pp. 479–515.

Browning, R. (1855/1983), 'Andrea del Sarto'. In *The Norton Anthology of Poetry*, eds. A.W. Allison, H. Barrows, C.R. Blake, *et al.*, 3rd edition. New York: W.W. Norton, pp. 737–42.

Browning, R. (1855/1983), '"Childe Roland to the Dark Tower Came"'. In *The Norton Anthology of Poetry*, eds. A.W. Allison, H. Barrows, C.R. Blake, *et al.*, 3rd edition. New York: W.W. Norton, pp. 732–6.

Buchan, J. (1919/1956), *Mr Standfast*. London: Penguin.

Burgess, A. (1962/1972), *A Clockwork Orange*. London: Penguin.

Cacioppo, J.T., Berntson, G.G., Adolphs, R., *et al.*, eds. (2002), *Foundations in Social Neuroscience*. Cambridge, MA: MIT Press.

Canetti, E. (1960/1973), *Crowds and Power*. London: Penguin.

Carter, R. (2000), *Mapping the Mind*. London: Phoenix.

Catholic Church (1880/1981), 'Arcanum: Encyclical of Pope Leo XIII on Christian marriage, February 10, 1880'. In *The Papal Encyclicals. Volume 2: 1878–1903*, ed. C. Carlen. Wilmington, NC: McGrath, pp. 29–40.

Cialdini, R.B. (2002), *Influence: science and practice*, 4th edition. Needham Heights, MA: Allyn and Bacon.

Claridge, G. (1997), *Schizotypy: implications for illness and health*. Oxford: Oxford University Press.

Condon, R. (1959/1973), *The Manchurian Candidate*. Harmondsworth: Penguin.

Conroy, J. (2001), *Unspeakable Acts, Ordinary People: the dynamics of torture*. London: Vision.

Conway, A. (1690/1996), *The Principles of the Most Ancient and Modern Philosophy*, eds. A.P. Coudert and T. Corse. Cambridge: Cambridge University Press.

Cook, C.M. and Persinger, M.A. (2001), 'Geophysical variables and behavior: XCII. Experimental elicitation of the experience of a sentient being by right hemispheric, weak magnetic fields: interaction with temporal lobe sensitivity', *Perceptual and Motor Skills*, 92, pp. 447–8.

Cornwell, J. (2003), *Hitler's Scientists: science, war and the Devil's pact*. London: Viking.

Council of Europe Committee on Legal Affairs and Human Rights, *Report: illegal activities of sects* (Doc. 8373: 13 April 1999). <http://press.coe.int/cp/99/351a(99).htm>.

References

Cruden, A. (1977), *Cruden's Complete Concordance to the Bible*, revised edition. Cambridge: Lutterworth Press.

Cultic Studies Journal, *The Council of Europe's Report on Sects and New Religious Movements*. 7. Case-law on sects. <http://www.csj.org/>.

Damasio, A. (1996), *Descartes' Error: emotion, reason and the human brain*. London: Papermac.

Damasio, A. (2000), *The Feeling of What Happens: body, emotion and the making of consciousness*. London: Heinemann.

Damasio, A. (2003), *Looking for Spinoza: joy, sorrow and the feeling brain*. London: Heinemann.

Darwin, C. (1872/1999), *The Expression of the Emotions in Man and Animals*, ed. P. Ekman, 3rd edition. London: HarperCollins.

Davenport-Hines, R. (2001), *The Pursuit of Oblivion: a global history of narcotics 1500–2000*. London: Weidenfeld and Nicolson.

Davis, J.L. and Rusbult, C.E. (2001), 'Attitude alignment in close relationships', *Journal of Personality and Social Psychology*, 81, pp. 65–84.

Dawes, R.M. (1996), *House of Cards: psychology and psychotherapy built on myth*. New York: Free Press.

Dawkins, R. (1976/1989), *The Selfish Gene*, new edition. Oxford: Oxford University Press.

Dawkins, R. (2003), *A Devil's Chaplain*. London: Weidenfeld and Nicolson.

Dawkins, R. (2003), 'Good and bad reasons for believing'. In *A Devil's Chaplain*. London: Weidenfeld and Nicolson, pp. 242–8.

De Sano, C.F. and Persinger, M.A. (1987), 'Geophysical variables and behavior: XXXIX. Alterations in imaginings and suggestibility during brief magnetic field exposures', *Perceptual and Motor Skills*, 64, pp. 968–70.

de Soto, H. (2001), *The Mystery of Capital: why capitalism triumphs in the West and fails everywhere else*. London: Black Swan.

de Vignemonta, F. and Fourneret, P. (2004), 'The sense of agency: a philosophical and empirical review of the "Who" system', *Consciousness and Cognition*, 13, pp. 1–19.

Deacon, T.W. (1997), *The Symbolic Species: the co-evolution of language and the human brain*. London: Allen Lane.

Deibert, R.J. (1997), *Parchment, Printing, and Hypermedia: communication in world order transformation*. New York: Columbia University Press.

Dement, W.C. and Vaughan, C. (2001), *The Promise of Sleep: the scientific connection between health, happiness, and a good night's sleep*. London: Pan.

Dennett, D.C. (2003), *Freedom Evolves*. London: Allen Lane.

Department of Education and Skills, *Department of Education and Skills: creating opportunity, releasing potential, achieving excellence*. <http://www.dfes.gov.uk/>.

Descartes, R. (1988), *Selected Philosophical Writings*, trans. J. Cottingham, R. Stoothoff and D. Murdoch. Cambridge: Cambridge University Press.

Dietrich, A. (2003), 'Functional neuroanatomy of altered states of consciousness: the transient hypofrontality hypothesis', *Consciousness and Cognition*, 12, pp. 231–56.

DISINFO, *Nothing is True, Everything is Permitted: a deconstruction of the last words of Hassan-i Sabbah*, by Brian D. Hodges. <www.disinfo.com/archive/pages/article/id1562/pg1/index.html>.

Dretske, F. (1995), 'Belief'. In *The Oxford Companion to Philosophy*, ed. T. Honderich. New York: Oxford University Press, pp. 82–3.

Dunbar, R. (1997), *Grooming, Gossip and the Evolution of Language*. London: Faber and Faber.

Eagleton, T. (1983), *Literary Theory: an introduction*. Oxford: Basil Blackwell.

Edelman, M. (2001), *The Politics of Misinformation*. New York: Cambridge University Press.

Ekman, P. (1985), *Telling Lies: clues to deceit in the marketplace, politics, and marriage*. New York: W.W. Norton.

Ekman, P. (2003), *Emotions Revealed: understanding faces and feelings*. London: Weidenfeld and Nicolson.

Ekman, P., Sorenson, E.R., and Friesen, W.V. (1969), 'Pan-cultural elements in facial displays of emotion', *Science*, 164, pp. 86–8.

Eliot, T.S. (1935/1974), 'Burnt Norton'. In *Collected Poems 1909–1962*. London: Faber and Faber, pp. 189–95.

Eliot, T.S. (1941/1974), 'The Dry Salvages'. In *Collected Poems 1909–1962*. London: Faber and Faber, pp. 205–13.

Evans, E. (1956), *Tertullian's Treatise on the Incarnation*. London: SPCK.

Feinberg, T.E. (2002), *Altered Egos: how the brain creates the self*. New York: Oxford University Press.

Festinger, L. (1957), *A Theory of Cognitive Dissonance*. New York: Row, Peterson and Co.

Festinger, L., Riecken, H.W., and Schacter, S. (1964), *When Prophecy Fails: a social and psychological study of a modern group that predicted the destruction of the world*. New York: Harper and Row.

Fiedler, K. and Bless, H. (2001), 'Social cognition'. In *Introduction to Social Psychology*, eds. M. Hewstone and W. Stroebe, 3rd edition. Oxford: Blackwell, pp. 115–49.

Fincham, F. and Hewstone, M. (2001), 'Attribution theory and research: from basic to applied'. In *Introduction to Social Psychology*, eds. M. Hewstone and W. Stroebe, 3rd edition. Oxford: Blackwell, pp. 197–238.

Foucault, M. (1977/1991), *Discipline and Punish: the birth of the prison*. London: Penguin.

Fox, S. (1984), *The Mirror Makers: a history of American advertising*. New York: Morrow.

Freeden, M. (2003), *Ideology: a very short introduction*. Oxford: Oxford University Press.

Frieze, I.H. and Boneva, B.S. (2001), 'Power motivation and motivation to help others'. In *The Use and Abuse of Power*, eds. A.Y. Lee-Chai and J.A. Bargh. Philadelphia, PA: Psychology Press, pp. 75–89.

Fromm, E. (1941/2001), *The Fear of Freedom*. London: Routledge.

Fuster, J.M. (1995), *Memory in the Cerebral Cortex: an empirical approach to neural networks in the human and nonhuman primate*. Cambridge, MA: MIT Press.

Galanter, M. (1999), *Cults: faith, healing, and coercion*, 2nd edition. New York: Oxford University Press.

The Guardian, *Archive*. <http://www.guardian.co.uk/Archive/>.

Gesch, C.B., Hammond, S.M., Hampson, S.E., *et al.* (2002), 'Influence of supplementary vitamins, minerals and essential fatty acids on the antisocial behaviour of young adult prisoners. Randomised, placebo-controlled trial.' *British Journal of Psychiatry*, 181, pp. 22–8.

Giovannitti, L. and Freed, F. (1967), *The Decision to Drop the Bomb*. London: Methuen.

Gladwell, M. (2000), *The Tipping Point: how little things can make a big difference*. London: Little, Brown and Company.

Glimcher, P.W. (2003), 'The neurobiology of visual-saccadic decision making', *Annual Reviews of Neuroscience*, 26, pp. 133–79.

Glover, J. (2001), *Humanity: a moral history of the twentieth century*. London: Pimlico.

References

Goldberg, E. (2001), *The Executive Brain: frontal lobes and the civilized mind.* Oxford: Oxford University Press.

Goldhagen, D.J. (1997), *Hitler's Willing Executioners: ordinary Germans and the Holocaust.* London: Abacus.

Golding, W. (1958), *Lord of the Flies.* London: Faber and Faber.

Gombrich, E.H. (1977), *Art and Illusion: a study in the psychology of pictorial representation,* 5th edition. London: Phaidon.

Greenberg, J., Solomon, S., and Pyszczynski, T. (1997), 'Terror management theory of self-esteem and cultural worldviews: empirical assessments and conceptual refinements'. In *Advances in Experimental Social Psychology.* Volume 29, ed. M.P. Zanna. New York: Academic Press, pp. 61–139.

Greenfield, S. (2000), *Brain Story: unlocking our inner world of emotions, memories, ideas and desires.* London: BBC Worldwide.

Greenfield, S. (2003), *Tomorrow's People: how 21st century technology is changing the way we think and feel.* London: Allen Lane.

Hamilton, W. (1870–74), *Lectures on Metaphysics and Logic,* 5th edition. Edinburgh: Blackwood.

Hare, R.D. (1999), *Without Conscience: the disturbing world of the psychopaths among us.* London: Guilford Press.

Hariri, A.R. and Weinberger, D.R. (2003), 'Functional neuroimaging of genetic variation in serotonergic neurotransmission', *Genes, Brain and Behavior,* 2, pp. 341–9.

Hatfield, E., Cacioppo, J.T., and Rapson, R.L. (1994), *Emotional Contagion.* Cambridge: Cambridge University Press.

Healy, D. (2002), *The Creation of Psychopharmacology.* Cambridge, MA: Harvard University Press.

Heinlein, R. (1961), *Stranger in a Strange Land.* New York: G. P. Putnam's Sons.

Henley, W.E. (1875/1982), 'Invictus'. In *The Rattle Bag,* eds. S. Heaney and T. Hughes. London: Faber and Faber, pp. 215–16.

Herring, J. (2002), *Criminal Law,* 3rd edition. Houndmills, Basingstoke: Palgrave Macmillan.

Hewstone, M. and Stroebe, W. (2001), *Introduction to Social Psychology,* 3rd edition. Oxford: Blackwell.

Hillenbrand, U. and van Hemmen, J.L. (2002), 'Adaptation in the corticothalamic loop: computational prospects of tuning the senses', *Philosophical Transactions of the Royal Society: Biological Sciences,* 357, pp. 1859–67.

Hinkle, L.E. and Wolff, H.G. (1956), 'Communist interrogation and indoctrination of "Enemies of the States"', *American Medical Association Archives of Neurology and Psychiatry,* 76, pp. 115–74.

Hitler, A. (1939), *Mein Kampf,* trans. J. Murphy, unexpurgated edition. London: Hutchinson and Co. in association with Hurst and Blackett.

HMSO, *National Curriculum.* <http://www.nc.uk.net/index.html>.

Hobbes, T. (1651/1996), *Leviathan,* ed. R. Tuck, revised student edition. Cambridge: Cambridge University Press.

Home Office, *British Crime Survey (BCS) for 2001/2002.* <http://www.homeoffice. gov.uk/rds/pdfs2/hosb702.pdf>.

Horgan, J. (2000), *The Undiscovered Mind: how the brain defies explanation.* London: Phoenix.

Hume, D. (1777/1975), *Enquiries Concerning Human Understanding and Concerning the Principles of Morals,* eds. L.A. Selby-Bigge and P.H. Nidditch, 3rd edition. Oxford: Oxford University Press.

Hunter, E. (1951), *Brain-washing in Red China: the calculated destruction of men's minds*. New York: Vanguard Press.

Hunter, E. (1956/1959), *Brainwashing: the story of men who defied it*. London: World Distributors (Manchester).

Hutchinson, L. (1679/2001), *Order and Disorder*, ed. D. Norbrook. Oxford: Blackwell.

Huxley, A. (1932/1994), *Brave New World*. London: Flamingo.

Ingvar, D.H. (1994), 'The will of the brain: cerebral correlates of willful acts', *Journal of Theoretical Biology*, 171, pp. 7–12.

Institute for Propaganda Analysis (1938), *Propaganda Analysis*. New York: Columbia University Press. See <http://www.propagandacritic.com>.

James, H. (1898/1992), 'The Turn of the Screw'. In *The Turn of the Screw and Other Stories*. Oxford: Oxford University Press.

James, W. (1890/1983), *The Principles of Psychology*. Cambridge, MA: Harvard University Press.

Janis, I.L. (1982), *Groupthink: psychological studies of policy decisions and fiascos*, 2nd edition. Boston: Houghton Mifflin.

Jay, M. (2003), *The Air Loom Gang: the strange and true story of James Tilly Matthews and his visionary madness*. London: Bantam Press.

Juvenal (c.100–128/1940), 'Satire X'. In *Juvenal and Persius*, trans. G.G. Ramsay, Loeb Classical Library edition. London: Heinemann, pp. 192–221.

Kandel, E.R., Schwartz, J.H., and Jessell, T.M., eds. (2000), *Principles of Neural Science*, 4th edition. London: McGraw-Hill.

Kane, R., ed. (2002), *Free Will*. Oxford: Blackwell.

Kaplan, H.I. and Sadock, B.J. (1998), *Kaplan and Sadock's Synopsis of Psychiatry: behavioral sciences/clinical psychiatry*, 8th edition. Baltimore, MD: Williams and Wilkins.

Kelly, P., ed. (2002), *Multiculturalism Reconsidered: 'Culture and Equality' and its critics*. Cambridge: Polity.

King, T. (2004), 'Secularism in France', *Prospect*, 96, pp. 64–8.

Koestler, A. (1940/1994), *Darkness at Noon*. London: Vintage.

Koletzko, B., Agostoni, C., Carlson, S.E., *et al.* (2001), 'Long chain polyunsaturated fatty acids (LC-PUFA) and perinatal development', *Acta Paediatrica*, 90, pp. 460–4.

Krosnick, J.A. (1999), 'Maximizing questionnaire quality'. In *Measures of Political Attitudes*, eds. J.P. Robinson, P.R. Shaver, and L.S. Wrightsman. San Diego: Academic Press, pp. 37–57.

La Rochefoucauld, F. (1665/1959), *Maxims*, trans. L.W. Tancock. Harmondsworth: Penguin.

Laing, R.D. (1967), *The Politics of Experience; and, The Bird of Paradise*. Harmondsworth: Penguin.

LaPlante, E. (2000), *Seized: temporal lobe epilepsy as a medical, historical, and artistic phenomenon*. Lincoln, NE: iUniverse.com.

LeDoux, J. (1998), *The Emotional Brain: the mysterious underpinnings of emotional life*. London: Weidenfeld and Nicolson.

LeDoux, J. (2002), *Synaptic Self: how our brains become who we are*. London: Macmillan.

Lefcourt, H.M. (1973), 'The function of the illusions of control and freedom', *American Psychologist*, 28, pp. 417–25.

Libet, B., Freeman, A., and Sutherland, K., eds. (1999), *The Volitional Brain: towards a neuroscience of free will*. Thorverton: Imprint Academic.

Lieven, A. (2004), 'Demon in the cellar', *Prospect*, 96, pp. 28–33.

References

Lifton, R.J. (1961), *Thought Reform and the Psychology of Totalism: a study of 'brainwashing' in China*. London: Victor Gollancz.

Little, P. (2002), *Genetic Destinies*. Oxford: Oxford University Press.

Locke, J. (1689/1997), *An Essay Concerning Human Understanding*, ed. R. Woolhouse. London: Penguin.

Lukes, S. (2003), *Liberals and Cannibals: the implications of diversity*. London: Verso.

MacCulloch, D. (1996), *Thomas Cranmer: a life*. London: Yale University Press.

Marks, J. (1977/1991), *The Search for the 'Manchurian Candidate'*. New York: W.W. Norton.

Markus, H.R. and Kitayama, S. (1991/1999), 'Culture and the self: implications for cognition, emotion, and motivation'. In *The Self in Social Psychology*, ed. R.F. Baumeister. Philadelphia, PA: Psychology Press, pp. 339–67.

Masefield, J. (1935/1984), *The Box of Delights*. London: Fontana Lions.

Mattay, V.S., Goldberg, T.E., Fera, F., *et al.* (2003), 'Catechol *O*-methyltransferase val^{158}-*met* genotype and individual variation in the brain response to amphetamine', *Proceedings of the National Academy of Sciences USA*, 100, pp. 6186–91.

Matthews, S.G. (2002), 'Early programming of the hypothalamo-pituitary-adrenal axis', *Trends in Endocrinology and Metabolism*, 13, pp. 373–80.

McClelland, D. (1975), *Power: the inner experience*. New York: Wiley.

Meerloo, J.A.M. (1951), 'The crime of menticide', *American Journal of Psychiatry*, 107, pp. 594–8.

Merriam-Webster, *Merriam Webster Online Dictionary*. 2002. <http://www.merriam-webster.com>.

Midgley, M. (1984/2001), *Wickedness*. London: Routledge.

Milgram, S. (1974/1997), *Obedience to Authority*. London: Pinter and Martin.

Mill, J.S. (1869/1989), 'The Subjection of Women'. In *On Liberty and Other Writings*, ed. S. Collini. Cambridge: Cambridge University Press, pp. 119–217.

Miller, A. (1953/1968), *The Crucible*. London: Penguin.

Miller, W.I. (1997), *The Anatomy of Disgust*. Cambridge, MA: Harvard University Press.

Milton, J. (1644/1991), 'Areopagitica'. In *John Milton: a critical edition of the major works*, eds. S. Orgel and J. Goldberg. Oxford: Oxford University Press, pp. 236–73.

Milton, J. (1649/1991), 'The Tenure of Kings and Magistrates'. In *John Milton: a critical edition of the major works*, eds. S. Orgel and J. Goldberg. Oxford: Oxford University Press, pp. 273–307.

Milton, J. (1674/1991), 'Paradise Lost'. In *John Milton: a critical edition of the major works*, eds. S. Orgel and J. Goldberg. Oxford: Oxford University Press, pp. 355–618.

Mormède, P., Courvoisier, H., Ramos, A., *et al.* (2002), 'Molecular genetic approaches to investigate individual variations in behavioral and neuroendocrine stress responses', *Psychoneuroendocrinology*, 27, pp. 563–83.

Nabokov, V. (1955/1997), *Lolita*. London: Weidenfeld and Nicolson.

Naipaul, S. (1981), *Black and White*. London: Sphere Books.

Nasar, S. (2001), *A Beautiful Mind*. London: Faber and Faber.

National Coalition Against Domestic Violence, *The Problem*. <http://www.ncadv.org/problem/what.htm>.

National Society for the Prevention of Cruelty to Children, *Child Killings in England and Wales*. <http://www.nspcc.org.uk/inform/Statistics/childkillingsenglandwales.doc>.

Nettle, D. (2002), *Strong Imagination: madness, creativity, and human nature*. New York: Oxford University Press.

Nietzsche, F.W. (1883–92/1958), *Thus Spake Zarathustra*, trans. A. Tille, eds. M.M. Bozman and R. Pascal. London: Dent; Dutton.

Ofek, H. (2001), *Second Nature: economic origins of human evolution*. Cambridge: Cambridge University Press.

Old Farmer's Almanac, *Three Ways To Hypnotize a Chicken*. <www.almanac.com/preview2000/hypnotize.html>.

O'Neill, O. (2002), *A Question of Trust: the BBC Reith Lectures 2002*. Cambridge: Cambridge University Press.

Orwell, G. (1945/1951), *Animal Farm: a fairy story*. Harmondsworth: Penguin.

Orwell, G. (1949/1954), *Nineteen Eighty-Four: a novel*. Harmondsworth: Penguin.

Parks, C.D. and Sanna, L.J. (1999), *Group Performance and Interaction*. Boulder, CO: Westview Press.

Pavlov, I.P. (1941), *Lectures on Conditioned Reflexes. Volume Two. Conditioned Reflexes and Psychiatry*, trans. W.H. Gantt. London: Lawrence and Wishart.

Peet, M., Glen, I., and Horrobin, D.F., eds. (2003), *Phospholipid Spectrum Disorders in Psychiatry and Neurology*, 2nd edition. Carnforth: Marius Press.

Penfield, W. and Rasmussen, T. (1950), *The Cerebral Cortex of Man: a clinical study of localization of function*. New York: Macmillan.

Persinger, M.A. (1983), 'Religious and mystical experiences as artifacts of temporal lobe function: a general hypothesis', *Perceptual and Motor Skills*, 57, pp. 1255–62.

Persinger, M.A. (2001), 'The neuropsychiatry of paranormal experiences', *Journal of Neuropsychiatry and Clinical Neurosciences*, 13, pp. 515–23.

Philips, K. (1664/1990), 'On Controversies in Religion'. In *The Collected Works of Katherine Philips: the matchless Orinda. Volume I: The Poems*, ed. P. Thomas. Stump Cross, Essex: Stump Cross Books, pp. 130–2.

Pincus, J.H. (2001), *Base Instincts: what makes killers kill?* New York: W.W. Norton.

Plato (*c*.360 BC/1987), *The Republic*, trans. D. Lee, 2nd (revised) edition. London: Penguin.

Plato (*c*.380 BC/1993). 'Euthyphro'. In *The Last Days of Socrates*, trans. H. Tredinnick and H. Tarrant, revised edition. London: Penguin, pp. 1–27.

Poe, E.A. (1835/1982), 'Berenice'. In *The Complete Tales and Poems of Edgar Allan Poe*, Modern Library edition. London: Penguin, pp. 642–8.

Poe, E.A. (1839/1982), 'The Fall of the House of Usher'. In *The Complete Tales and Poems of Edgar Allan Poe*, Modern Library edition. London: Penguin, pp. 231–45.

Poe, E.A. (1842/1982), 'The Pit and the Pendulum'. In *The Complete Tales and Poems of Edgar Allan Poe*, Modern Library edition. London: Penguin, pp. 246–57.

Poe, E.A. (1844/1982), 'The Premature Burial'. In *The Complete Tales and Poems of Edgar Allan Poe*, Modern Library edition. London: Penguin, pp. 258–68.

Potash, J.B., Willour, V.L., Chiu, Y., *et al.* (2001), 'The familial aggregation of psychotic symptoms in bipolar disorder pedigrees', *American Journal of Psychiatry*, 158, pp. 1258–64.

Pratkanis, A.R. and Aronson, E. (2001), *Age of Propaganda: the everyday use and abuse of persuasion*, revised edition. New York: W.H. Freeman.

Pressman, J.D. (1998), *Last Resort: psychosurgery and the limits of medicine*. New York: Cambridge University Press.

Preston, R. (1994), *The Hot Zone*. London: Doubleday.

Pullman, P. (1995), *Northern Lights*. London: Scholastic.

Pullman, P. (1997), *The Subtle Knife*. London: Scholastic.

Pullman, P. (2000), *The Amber Spyglass*. London: Scholastic.

References

Raine, A. (1993), *The Psychopathology of Crime: criminal behavior as a clinical disorder*. San Diego: Academic Press.

Raine, A., Lencz, T., Bihrle, S., *et al.* (2002), 'Reduced prefrontal gray matter volume and reduced autonomic activity in antisocial personality disorder'. In *Foundations in Social Neuroscience*, eds. J.T. Cacioppo, G.G. Berntson, R. Adolphs, *et al.* Cambridge, MA: MIT Press, pp. 1023–36.

Raphael, D.D. (1994), *Moral Philosophy*, 2nd edition. Oxford: Oxford University Press.

Raven, B.H. (2001), 'Power/interaction and interpersonal influence: experimental investigations and case studies'. In *The Use and Abuse of Power*, eds. A.Y. Lee-Chai and J.A. Bargh. Philadelphia, PA: Psychology Press, pp. 217–40.

Redfield Jamison, K. (1996), *An Unquiet Mind: a memoir of moods and madness*. London: Picador.

Rhodes, R. (1988), *The Making of the Atomic Bomb*. London: Penguin.

Ridley, M. (2003), *Nature via Nurture: genes, experience and what makes us human*. London: Fourth Estate.

Robins, R.S. and Post, J.M. (1997), *Political Paranoia: the psychopolitics of hatred*. New Haven, CT: Yale University Press.

Rokeach, M. (1960), *The Open and Closed Mind: investigations into the nature of belief systems and personality systems*. New York: Basic Books.

Ronson, J. (2002), *Them: adventures with extremists*. London: Picador.

Rushdie, S. (1996), *The Moor's Last Sigh*. London: Vintage.

Russell, B. (1935), *Religion and Science*. London: Thornton Butterworth.

Ryle, G. (1949), *The Concept of Mind*. London: Hutchinson's University Library.

Sacks, O. (1986), 'A matter of identity'. In *The Man who Mistook his Wife for a Hat*. London: Picador, pp. 103–10.

Salib, E. (2003), 'Effect of 11 September 2001 on suicide and homicide in England and Wales', *British Journal of Psychiatry*, 183, pp. 207–12.

Sargant, W. (1957), *Battle for the Mind: a physiology of conversion and brain-washing*. London: Heinemann.

Sass, L.A. (1994), *Madness and Modernism: insanity in the light of modern art, literature, and thought*. London: Harvard University Press.

Schachter, S. and Singer, J.E. (1962), 'Cognitive, social, and physiological determinants of emotional state', *Psychological Review*, 69, pp. 379–99.

Schacter, D.L. (2001), *The Seven Sins of Memory: how the mind forgets and remembers*. New York: Houghton Mifflin.

Schedlowski, M. and Tewes, U. (1999), *Psychoneuroimmunology: an interdisciplinary introduction*. New York: Kluwer Academic/Plenum.

Scheflin, A.W. and Opton, E.M. (1978), *The Mind Manipulators: a non-fiction account*. New York: Paddington Press.

Schein, E.H., Schneier, I., and Barker, C.H. (1961), *Coercive Persuasion: a socio-psychological analysis of the 'brainwashing' of American civilian prisoners by the Chinese Communists*. New York: W.W. Norton.

Scherer, K.R. (2001), 'Emotion'. In *Introduction to Social Psychology*, eds. M. Hewstone and W. Stroebe, 3rd edition. Oxford: Blackwell, pp. 151–95.

Sekuler, R. and Blake, R. (1999), *Star Trek on the Brain: alien minds, human minds*. New York: W.H. Freeman.

Sen, A. (1999), *Development as Freedom*. Oxford: Oxford University Press.

Sherrington, C. (1940/1963), *Man on His Nature*. London: Cambridge University Press.

Skinner, Q. (1978), *The Foundations of Modern Political Thought. Volume One: the Renaissance.* Cambridge: Cambridge University Press.

Skinner, Q. (2002), 'A third concept of liberty (the Isaiah Berlin lecture)', *Proceedings of the British Academy*, 117, pp. 237–68.

Smith, A. (1776/1998), *An Inquiry into the Nature and Causes of the Wealth of Nations: a selected edition*, ed. K. Sutherland. Oxford: Oxford University Press.

Spence, S.A. (1996), 'Free will in the light of neuropsychiatry', *Philosophy, Psychiatry, and Psychology*, 3, pp. 75–90.

Staub, E. (1990), 'The psychology and culture of torture and torturers'. In *Psychology and Torture*, ed. P. Suedfeld. Washington, DC: Hemisphere Publishing, pp. 49–76.

Staub, E. (2003), *The Psychology of Good and Evil: why children, adults, and groups help and harm others.* New York: Cambridge University Press.

Steger, M.B. and Lind, N., eds. (1999), *Violence and its Alternatives: an interdisciplinary reader.* Houndmills, Basingstoke: Macmillan.

Steigmann-Gall, R. (2003), *The Holy Reich: Nazi conceptions of Christianity, 1919–1945.* Cambridge: Cambridge University Press.

Steiner, G. (1992), *Heidegger*, 2nd edition. London: Fontana Press.

Stevens, A. and Price, J. (2000), *Prophets, Cults and Madness.* London: Duckworth.

Street, J. (2001), *Mass Media, Politics and Democracy.* Houndmills, Basingstoke: Palgrave.

Suedfeld, P. (1990), 'Torture: a brief overview'. In *Psychology and Torture*, ed. P. Suedfeld. Washington, DC: Hemisphere Publishing, pp. 1–11.

Sullivan, R.M. and Brake, W.G. (2003), 'What the rodent prefrontal cortex can teach us about attention-deficit/hyperactivity disorder: the critical role of early developmental events on prefrontal function', *Behavioural Brain Research*, 146, pp. 43–55.

Szasz, T.S. (1970/1997), *The Manufacture of Madness: a comparative study of the Inquisition and the mental health movement.* Syracuse, NY: Syracuse University Press.

Tajfel, H., Flament, C., Billig, M.G., *et al.* (1971), 'Social categorization and intergroup behaviour', *European Journal of Social Psychology*, 1, pp. 149–78.

talk.origins, *Creationist Arguments: brain sizes.* <http://www.talkorigins.org/faqs/homs/a_brains.html>.

Talmon, J.L. (1961), *The Origins of Totalitarian Democracy.* London: Mercury Books.

Tamam, L., Karatas, G., Zeren, T., *et al.* (2003), 'The prevalence of Capgras syndrome in a university hospital setting', *Acta Neuropsychiatrica*, 15, pp. 290–5.

Taylor, D., 'Ferguson has drive but not drink'. *The Guardian*, 22 January 2001.

Taylor, K. (2001), 'Applying continuous modelling to consciousness', *Journal of Consciousness Studies*, 8, pp. 45–60.

Taylor, K., 'A recipe for healthy brain growth: start with fish oil'. *Times Higher Education Supplement*, 29 March 2002.

Taylor, K. (2003), 'The possible role of abnormal platelet-activating factor metabolism in psychiatric disorders'. In *Phospholipid Spectrum Disorders in Psychiatry and Neurology*, eds. M. Peet, I. Glen and D.F. Horrobin, 2nd edition. Carnforth: Marius Press, pp. 93–110.

Townshend, C. (2002), *Terrorism: a very short introduction.* New York: Oxford University Press.

The Tuskegee Syphilis Study Legacy Committee, *A Request for Redress of the Wrongs of Tuskegee.* <http://hsc.virginia.edu/hs-library/historical/apology/report.html>.

Trummer, M., Eustacchio, S., Unger, F., *et al.* (2002), 'Right hemispheric frontal lesions as a cause for anorexia nervosa: report of three cases', *Acta Neurochirurgica*, 144, pp. 797–801.

References

Ungerleider, J.T. and Wellisch, D.K. (1979), 'Coercive persuasion (brainwashing), religious cults, and deprogramming', *American Journal of Psychiatry*, 136, pp. 279–82.

United Nations, *Status of Ratifications of the Principal International Human Rights Treaties, as of 09 December 2002*. <http://193.194.138.190/pdf/report.pdf>.

Valenstein, E.S. (1973), *Brain Control: a critical examination of brain stimulation and psychosurgery*. New York: John Wiley and Sons.

van Inwagen, P. (1983), *An Essay on Free Will*. Oxford: Clarendon Press.

Voltaire (1763/2000), *Treatise on Tolerance and Other Writings*, trans. B. Masters and S. Harvey, ed. S. Harvey. Cambridge: Cambridge University Press.

Walker, W.V. and Campbell, J.B. (1982), 'Similarity of values and interpersonal attraction of Whites toward Blacks', *Psychological Reports*, 50, pp. 1199–1205.

Wallace, A.F.C. (1956/2003), 'Mazeway resynthesis: a biocultural theory of religious inspiration'. In *Revitalizations and Mazeways: essays on culture change, volume 1*, ed. R.S. Grumet. Lincoln, NE: University of Nebraska Press, pp. 164–77.

Wegner, D.M. (2002), *The Illusion of Conscious Will*. London: MIT Press.

Weitz, E.D. (2003), *A Century of Genocide: utopias of race and nation*. Princeton, NJ: Princeton University Press.

Wells, H.G. (1895/1946), *The Time Machine and Other Stories*. Harmondsworth: Penguin.

Wells, S. and Taylor, G., eds. (1986), *The Oxford Shakespeare*. Oxford: Oxford University Press.

Whitman, W. (1855/1975), 'Song of Myself'. In *Walt Whitman: the complete poems*, ed. F. Murphy. Harmondsworth: Penguin, pp. 63–124.

Winterer, G. and Goldman, D. (2003), 'Genetics of human prefrontal function', *Brain Research Reviews*, 43, pp. 134–63.

Wittgenstein, L. (1953/1974), *Philosophical Investigations*, trans. G.E.M. Anscombe, 3rd edition. Oxford: Blackwell.

Wong, P.S. and Root, J.C. (2003), 'Dynamic variations in affective priming', *Consciousness and Cognition*, 12, pp. 147–68.

Wyer, R.S., ed. (1997), *The Automaticity of Everyday Life: advances in social cognition*. Volume X. Mahwah, NJ: Lawrence Erlbaum.

Yeats, W.B. (1921/1983), 'The Second Coming'. In *The Norton Anthology of Poetry*, eds. A.W. Allison, H. Barrows, C.R. Blake, *et al.*, 3rd edition. New York: W.W. Norton, p. 883.

Zajonc, R.B. (1968), 'Attitudinal effects of mere exposure', *Journal of Personality and Social Psychology Monograph Supplement*, 9, pp. 1–29.

Zevenhuizen, A. (1998), *Erosion and Weathering*, trans. K.M.M. Hudson-Brazenall. London: New Holland.

Further reading

Brainwashing

Three seminal early works on brainwashing are Edward Hunter's journalistic *Brain-washing* and *Brain-washing in Red China*, and Robert Lifton's more scholarly *Thought Reform and the Psychology of Totalism*. Hunter's books convey the paranoid atmosphere of 1950s anti-Communist America. Lifton's book, despite its offputting title, is a fascinating account of the Chinese Communists' programmes of thought reform. More recently, John Marks' *The Search for the 'Manchurian Candidate'* describes CIA research into mind control.

Cults and social psychology

Cults, by Marc Galanter, is a psychological analysis of cult behaviour, while John Ronson's *Them* is a lighter look at extremists of various kinds. For a detailed history of fundamentalist thinking, see Karen Armstrong's *The Battle for God*.

For more on influence techniques, *Influence*, by Robert Cialdini, and *Age of Propaganda*, by Pratkanis and Aronson, are both immensely readable. For a psychologist's investigation of group behaviour, see Ervin Staub, *The Psychology of Good and Evil*. For social psychology in general, Hewstone and Stroebe's *Introduction to Social Psychology* is a good place to start.

Neuroscience

Susan Greenfield's *Brain Story* and Rita Carter's *Mapping the Mind* are introductions to the field. For the academic detail, see Cacioppo and colleagues' *Foundations in Social Neuroscience* or Kandel and colleagues' *Principles of Neural Science*.

Free will

Daniel Dennett's *Freedom Evolves* is a good, if at times fairly technical, introduction to recent philosophical thinking on free will. A useful selection of classic essays on the subject is *Free Will*, edited by Robert Kane. The analysis of psychological function in economic terms is exemplified by George Ainslie's *Breakdown of Will*, which is also technical in parts, but well worth the effort. *The Volitional Brain*, by Benjamin Libet and colleagues, looks at the neuroscience of free will.

Further reading

The media and politics
Murray Edelman's *The Politics of Misinformation* and John Street's *Mass Media, Politics and Democracy* are good sources for more information about the distorting effects of mass communications. Isaiah Berlin's 'Two concepts of liberty' is a seminal essay on liberalism, a theme elaborated on by Brian Barry in *Culture and Equality*. For the other end of the political spectrum, Hannah Arendt's *Totalitarianism* is a classic of the field.

Glossary

Amygdala   a small subcortical nucleus (cluster of cells) buried deep in the brain's **temporal lobe** (i.e. there is one amygdala on either side of the brain). Named from the Greek for almond, whose shape it is said to resemble, it is crucially involved in the processing of emotions. See also **subcortex**.

Anterior cingulate   the forward part of the cingulate cortex. See also **cingulate**.

Anti-psychiatrists   a small group of (predominantly American) psychiatrists who argue that institutional psychiatry is a mechanism of State control and social compulsion. At its extreme, the anti-psychiatry movement claims that mental illnesses such as schizophrenia are conditions arising entirely from social pressures.

APD (antisocial personality disorder)   has been described as 'modern psychiatric jargon for a really unpleasant person'. Characteristics include aggression, callousness, deceit, and persistently anti-social or criminal behaviour. See also **psychopathy**.

Automatization   the process whereby the brain becomes more adept at an activity or more familiar with a thought.

Awareness   a form of consciousness which is continuous and which does not involve a specific sense of self. It is experienced whenever a person is absorbed in thought, meditation, or action but is not specifically paying attention to or explicitly memorizing what is being thought or done. When you emerge from a good book or riveting movie of which you remember only highlights and the overall 'atmosphere', and looking back wonder 'where was my "self" in all of that?', you are looking back on a state of awareness. See also **monitoring**.

Bipolar disorder (manic depression)   a form of depression, often associated with extreme creativity, which may include psychotic symptoms such as hallucinations. Periods of severe depression, which may render the sufferer suicidal, guilt-ridden, or so inert as to be unable to function, alternate with high-energy 'manic' periods in which anything seems possible and in which ideas, plans, and activities occur at an astonishing rate.

Brainwashing   a term coined by the journalist and CIA operative Edward Hunter in 1950 to describe the mechanism(s) by which Chinese Communists had apparently produced fundamental changes in the beliefs of American prisoners, and commonly used since to describe a range of situations involving deliberate attempts to change people's minds without their consent. I have divided these into two categories (though they are really aspects of an underlying unity, and any given situation will probably contain elements of both). The first category, brainwashing by force, is faster, more intensive, and may use coercion or even torture to overwhelm the victim's **reactance**. The second, brainwashing by stealth, is slower, less intensive, and relies on its efforts going largely unnoticed, so that reactance is not triggered in the first place.

Capgras syndrome a rare condition possibly arising when connections between the **amygdala** and the **cortex** are damaged. Sufferers have normal vision and can recognize other people's faces, but the feelings which normally accompany the sight of a familiar person seem to be missing, leading the patient to insist that the familiar person has in fact been replaced by a robot or other impostor.

Cingulate (cingulate cortex, cingulate gyrus) an area of **cortex** curled around the inner side of each brain hemisphere, which takes its name from the Latin word for a girdle. Its functions are numerous and poorly understood, but it is thought to play a crucial role in linking subcortical and cortical areas and in integrating information about the world with stored knowledge and awareness of the current state of the body. See also **anterior cingulate**.

Cognitive dissonance a term from social psychology which refers to stress resulting from the awareness of conflict. Dissonance may arise when inconsistency between two beliefs becomes apparent to the believer or when negative emotions such as guilt are aroused by an **influence technician**: the sense of stress motivates efforts to resolve the conflict.

Cognitive landscape the mental environment, containing all information stored in a person's brain (see **history inputs**) as well as ongoing mental activity. For anthropologists, this term covers much the same territory as Anthony F.C. Wallace's **mazeway**, albeit incorporating current cognitions as well as neural history.

Cogweb (cognitive web) a generic term for mental objects incorporating cognitive networks and schemas, thoughts, concepts, beliefs, hopes, desires, action plans, and so on. Cogwebs can be active or inactive.

Compatibilism the claim that free will and causation can live together; that is, that a meaningful, coherent concept of human free will is not ruled out by the doctrine of **determinism**.

Consequentialism the claim that actions are judged to be right or wrong by their results, better known as 'the end justifies the means'.

Cortex (grey matter) the outermost layer of the brain, mostly comprised of densely packed nerve cells (neurons) and supporting cells (glia). The brain is made up of two halves (hemispheres), the left and right. The left and the right cortices are in turn each divided into four lobes. See also **frontal lobe, occipital lobe, parietal lobe, temporal lobe**.

Cotard syndrome a rare neurological syndrome in which the sufferer believes himself or herself to be dead.

CSF (cerebrospinal fluid) the fluid in which living brains continually soak (dead ones soak in formaldehyde). The CSF provides the medium through which neurons transmit their messages to one another.

Determinism the idea that future events are determined by past events (i.e. cannot be otherwise). This is often taken to imply that human free will cannot exist, a position known as 'hard determinism'.

DNA (deoxyribonucleic acid) the molecule of which genes are made.

Ethereal ideas concepts such as God, beauty, justice, and freedom which are value-laden and can arouse extremely strong emotions. They are highly abstract and so ambiguous that they can have different, even contradictory meanings for different people. The emphasis given to different ethereal ideas varies to some extent across cultures, but the ideas themselves are widely expressed, valued, and debated in human societies.

FACET (**Freedom, Agency, Complexity, Ends-not-means, Thinking**) the acronym summarizing the major ideas whose adoption and propagation may best protect individuals and societies against totalitarian thinking.

FEF (**frontal eye fields**) an area of **cortex** towards the front of the brain which is involved in generating **saccades** and other eye movements.

fMRI (**functional magnetic resonance imaging**) a form of **neuroimaging** which measures changes in the blood supply to brain areas.

Frontal lobe one of the four major divisions of each of the two brain hemispheres (left and right). The frontal lobe in humans occupies most of the front half of the **cortex** and is involved in, among other things, movement planning and control, decision making, and short-term memory.

Glucocorticoid hormones in general, hormones, such as testosterone and adrenaline, are molecules made by body organs which act at some distance from their site of origin. The glucocorticoid hormones, of which cortisol is the most important, are produced by the adrenal glands and regulate the body's stress response to perceived threats.

Habituation a phenomenon in which neurons tire out when subjected to ongoing stimulation, responding less and less to successive incoming signals.

History inputs a brain's uniquely personalized stored knowledge, used by the prefrontal cortex (**PFC**) and other brain areas to filter and modulate incoming information, ongoing thought, and planned activity. See also **mazeway**.

Influence technician a person who deliberately employs methods of manipulating other people's beliefs.

Ingroup a term from social psychology, referring to the universal human tendency to group other people into us (*my* tribe, nation, or other collective entity) and them (outsiders, members of other groups, enemies). The ingroup is us. Ingroup members receive privileged treatment relative to others. See also **outgroup**.

Intertemporal contract a person's attempt at a certain time (time A) to ensure that at some future time (time B) that person will act according to his or her wishes *as they were at time A*. An example is resolving to go on a diet.

ITC (**inferotemporal cortex**) see **temporal lobe**.

Just-world thinking making the (often unconscious) assumption that the world is essentially a fair and decent place whose inhabitants (particularly those in positions of authority) operate rationally and only do harm for good reason. This can lead to the dangerous conclusion that if a person is visibly suffering or being hurt, he or she must have done something to deserve it.

Lability a neuroscientific term describing how easily activated **neurons** are. Some neurons require considerable stimulation before they will respond with any enthusiasm; other, more labile cells will fire off a signal much more readily. High lability in the temporal lobes is associated with spirituality, **schizotypy**, and creativity. See also **TLE**.

Lesion damage to an area of the brain, which may be caused by disease (e.g. a stroke or tumour), accidentally (e.g. the industrial accident which blew an iron rod through the front of Phineas Gage's skull), or deliberately (e.g. **lobotomy**).

Libertarianism the doctrine that human free will is independent of normal laws of cause and effect; that is, that at least some human actions are free in the sense of not being caused by anything other than the human in question.

Glossary

Lobotomy   a form of **psychosurgery** which cuts connections between the **frontal lobe** and the rest of the brain. It was used to treat a variety of psychiatric conditions, but fell out of favour after ethical concerns were raised.

Mazeway   a term coined by the anthropologist Anthony F.C. Wallace to refer to the sum of all 'cognitive residues of previous perceptions' (Wallace, 'Mazeway resynthesis', p. 170). The mazeway incorporates an individual's conceptions of his or her culture. When an environment changes, as for example following a natural disaster, the old mazeway may no longer fit with new perceptions, leading to immense internal stress which may result in the collapse of the mazeway and either its repair or the formation of a new mazeway. See also **history inputs**.

MEG (magnetoencephalography)   a form of **neuroimaging** which measures small changes in a brain's magnetic field.

Memetics   an analogy between genes and ideas which postulates that the latter are memes, entities able to replicate (spread from brain to brain), mutate, and compete for resources (audiences) just as genes do.

Mindcraft   a collective noun for processes by which people change other people's minds.

Monitoring   a specialized, intermittent form of consciousness associated with the sense of having a self. Monitoring samples the most active areas of the brain's activity (i.e. 'dips into' **awareness**) when triggered to do so by a novel or challenging situation. This allows the samples to be stored as specific memories. See also **awareness**.

mPFC (medial prefrontal cortex)   an area of **cortex** towards the middle of the front of the brain, thought to be involved in sophisticated emotional and evaluative processing.

Neuroimaging   the collective name for modern scientific techniques that look inside living human brains by monitoring, analysing, and displaying the levels of phenomena which vary with brain activity, such as local electrical or magnetic fields (which are affected by the electrical signals emitted by active neurons). See also **MEG, fMRI**.

Neuron (nerve cell)   a brain cell, the basic unit of all brains.

Neurotransmitters   the molecules used by **neurons** to send signals to each other.

Occipital lobe   one of the four major divisions of each of the two brain hemispheres (left and right), located at the back of the brain. The occipital lobe is primarily concerned with visual processing.

OFC (orbitofrontal cortex, orbital frontal cortex)   an area of the brain located above the eye sockets which is involved in emotion processing and the interpretation and application of moral rules.

Outgroup   a term from social psychology, referring to the universal human tendency to group other people into us (*my* tribe, nation, or other collective entity) and them (outsiders, members of other groups, enemies). The outgroup is them. Outgroup members tend to be seen as having second-class status. In extreme cases (e.g. Nazi treatment of Jews) they can be demonized as subhuman and therefore excluded from the domain of normal moral rules.

PAG (periaqueductal grey)   an area of **subcortex** which is involved in generating emotional sensations.

Parietal lobe   one of the four major divisions of each of the two brain hemispheres (left and right), located at the top of the brain. The parietal lobe is thought to play an important role co-ordinating movements to their targets, as well as in self-perception and the brain's representations of body position, and in integrating these with information from external senses such as vision, hearing, and touch.

PFC (prefrontal cortex)   the foremost part of the human brain's **frontal lobe**. Prefrontal areas are thought to monitor the activity of other brain areas and to be involved in higher functions such as decision making and self-consciousness.

Pharmacotherapy   treatment using chemicals (drugs).

Phospholipids   the basic building blocks of cell membranes, a cell's equivalent of skin. Each phospholipid molecule contains a molecule of fat. The type of fat (unsaturated or saturated) determines the shape of the phospholipid molecules (crinkly or straight) and hence how closely they can be packed together. Tighter packing leads to less flexible cell membranes, which reduces the efficiency with which **neurons** can signal to each other.

PPC (posterior parietal cortex)   an area of **cortex** towards the top of the brain which is involved in linking perceptions to eye movements.

Psychopathy   a syndrome characterized by extreme self-centredness and remorseless exploitation of other human beings, often coexisting with charm and high intelligence. Many of the West's most violent and destructive criminals in recent years have been diagnosed as psychopathic. Where **APD** is normally diagnosed on the basis of behaviour, a diagnosis of psychopathy will refer to character traits as well. Some research suggests that psychopathic individuals may process emotional information abnormally, but the causes of the condition are not well understood.

Psychopharmacology   the study of the effects of chemicals on psychological phenomena such as anxiety and psychosis.

Psychosurgery   the collective name for medical techniques which attempt to change psychological features (such as personality or mental illness) using brain surgery. Cutting connections between brain areas and cutting or burning out selected parts of the brain are common methods. See also **lobotomy**.

Reactance   a negative emotional state triggered by a perceived threat to personal freedom which can motivate extremely vigorous defensive action.

Receptors   specialized molecules located on or in neurons which change their shape when activated by a **neurotransmitter** molecule, telling the neuron that another cell is signalling to it.

Saccade   a rapid, jumping movement of the eyes.

SC (superior colliculus)   a small nucleus buried deep in the brain, named after the Latin word for 'little hill', which is critically involved in eye movement control.

Schizotypy   a personality trait characterized by creativity and unusual patterns of thought and experience. Brief hallucinations, such as hearing a voice when no other person is present, are common. High schizotypy is often associated with belief in paranormal and/or spiritual phenomena. See also **lability**.

Stimulus-driven   the state of being unable to stop and think before reacting to a stimulus (impulsivity).

Subcortex   the core of the brain, made up of white matter (the connecting fibres that link **neurons** together) in which nuclei (clusters of neurons) such as the **amygdala** are embedded.

Temporal lobe   one of the four major divisions of each of the two brain hemispheres (left and right), located to the side of each hemisphere. The temporal lobe is involved in, among other things, recognizing and remembering objects, places, and people, and in language processing. The lower part of the temporal lobe, which appears to be particularly concerned with object recognition, is also called the inferotemporal cortex (**ITC**).

Glossary

Thalamus a large collection of nuclei (cell clusters) in the centre of the brain, which transmits information between the **cortex** and the body.

Thought reform a translation of the term used by Chinese Communists to describe their methods of 're-educating' (changing the behaviour and/or beliefs of) people who disagreed with them.

TLE (temporal lobe epilepsy) a form of epilepsy which affects the temporal lobe. Epilepsy is a condition in which some **neurons** (the epileptic 'focus') start to fire much more than usual, triggering a wave of firing that can sweep across the entire brain, seriously interfering with normal function. Temporal lobe epilepsy can be associated with extreme creativity, intense religious or other hallucinations, and **schizotypy**. See also **lability**.

TMS (transcranial magnetic stimulation) a technique for changing the activity of large numbers of **neurons** at a time by applying a magnetic field to an area of the brain.

Totalism the tendency to think in black and white and to dislike and denigrate those who prefer shades of grey. While extreme totalist thinking is a characteristic vice of totalitarian regimes, it would be hard to find a human being who has not succumbed at some time to the lure of prejudice and thinking in stereotypes. Highly totalist thinkers extol values such as simplicity, purity, loyalty, and authority over more liberal ideals like freedom and diversity.

Weapons of influence another name for influence techniques, particularly associated with the social psychologist Robert Cialdini, whose book *Influence* describes six weapons of influence: reciprocation, commitment and consistency, social proof, liking, authority, and scarcity.

Index

When using this index, please bear in mind that:

- notes are referenced by chapter (e.g. n.7(11) is Chapter 7, note 11) and are given after text entries but before figures
- a listing in the glossary is given by *[g]* immediately after the main entry word or phrase
- figures are referred to by chapter (e.g. Fig. 7.1) and are listed at the end of the entry
- notes which only give a reference are not listed separately from the page number on which they appear

Index

Index

Index

Index

PAG *[g], see* periaqueductal grey
Palestinians, *see* Middle East
parietal lobe *[g]* 113, 137, 203, Fig. 7.4; *see also* posterior parietal cortex
Pavlov, Ivan 7, n.1(7)
Penfield, Wilder 235–6
People's Temple, *see* Jones
periaqueductal grey (PAG) *[g]* 160, 168, 237, Fig. 9.2–9.3
Persinger, Michael 119
personality disorders 71, 253; *see also* antisocial personality disorder
PFC *[g], see* prefrontal cortex
phantom limb syndrome 115–6
pharmacotherapy *[g], see* drugs therapy
phospholipids *[g], see* fatty acids and phospholipids
Pink Floyd 61, 64, 76
pituitary gland 156, 160, Fig. 9.2–9.3
platelet-activating factor (PAF) 136, n.12(2)
Plato
   cave metaphor 243, n.14(15)
   Euthyphro n.13(19)
   Socrates and 231, n.13(19)
Poe, Edgar Allan 118, 148, 149, 258
possession, demonic 6–7
posterior parietal cortex (PPC) *[g]* Fig. 10.2
   prediction and 193
   'where' pathway and 175–7, 182
post-traumatic stress disorder 4, 240
PPC *[g], see* posterior parietal cortex
Pratkanis, Anthony 50, 53, 54, 134, 154, n.8(5)
predestination 17, 85–6, 188
prediction
   control and 85
   Daniel Dennett on freedom and 192–3, 195, 199, 203–4
   determinism and, *see* determinism
   freedom and 189, 193–9, 201, 249; *see also* intertemporal contracts
   hypothesis testing and 137–9, 141, 176, 201
   memory and 137, 193, 196–8
prefrontal cortex (PFC) *[g]* n.7(4), Fig. 7.4, Fig. 10.1–10.2, Fig. 10.5
   automatization and 133–4, 183, 210, 253
   consciousness and 182, 183–5
   damage to 178; *see also* Gage
   as defence against brainwashing 154, 185; *see also* resistance to brainwashing; stop-and-think
   drugs and 99–100 185, 215

gender differences in development of 185
history inputs 158, 178–82, 195, 201, 211
as implementing brain's ideology 169, 185
individual differences in 154, 185, 215–16
management metaphor 134, 167–9, 177, 182, 221
medial prefrontal cortex 162, 164, Fig. 9.2–9.3
neuroscience of 167–86
orbitofrontal cortex 162, 164, 169, 240, Fig. 9.2–9.3
self-limiting nature of 183
self-control and 165, 191; *see also* stop-and-think
effects of stress on 154, 215, 231
prejudice, *see* stereotyping and prejudice
primacy of doctrine over person, *see* totalism, Robert Lifton's eight themes of
privacy
   cult of confession and 16, 88, 262
   lack of 14, 20–1, 61, 88, 191
   as a liberal value 191
   loss of over evolutionary history 240
   opposition to in thought reform 15, 22
private sphere 191, 225
propaganda
   anti-Semitism 65, 122, 164, 192, 221–2
   British National Party 136, 151, 225
   Communist 23; see also *The Question of Thought*
   in definition of brainwashing 51
   Edward Hunter's books as 4
   'glittering generalities' 27, n.2(3)
   linguistic origins 7
proteins 109, 111, 208
Protestantism 13, 14, 28
psychiatry, *see* mental health professions
psychism 143
psychopathy *[g]*
   analogy with totalitarianism 15–16
   and antisocial personality disorder 71, 154
   relativist critiques of morality and 263
   risk factors for n.15(9)
   statistics of 89
   threatened self-esteem and 89, 91, 212
psychopharmacology *[g]* n.4(10)
psychosurgery *[g]* 34, 76, 160, 234, 237, n.1(16), n.4(9)
psychotherapy 68, 70, 71, 76, n.4(11); *see also* Dawes

Index

Index

Index